M000286493

JUDICIAL
POLICYMAKING

Readings on Law, Politics, and Public Policy

SECOND EDITION

Edited By JEB BARNES

University of Southern California

 cognella® | ACADEMIC PUBLISHING

Bassim Hamadeh, CEO and Publisher
Kassie Graves, Director of Acquisitions
Jamie Giganti, Senior Managing Editor
Jess Estrella, Senior Graphic Designer
Carrie Montoya, Manager, Revisions and Author Care
Kaela Martin, Associate Editor
Natalie Lakosil, Licensing Manager
Abbey Hastings, Associate Production Editor

Copyright © 2017 by Cognella, Inc. All rights reserved. No part of this publication may be reprinted, reproduced, transmitted, or utilized in any form or by any electronic, mechanical, or other means, now known or hereafter invented, including photocopying, microfilming, and recording, or in any information retrieval system without the written permission of Cognella, Inc.

Trademark Notice: Product or corporate names may be trademarks or registered trademarks, and are used only for identification and explanation without intent to infringe.

Cover image Copyright © Depositphotos/Kuzmafoto.

Printed in the United States of America

ISBN: 978-1-5165-1282-9 (pbk) / 978-1-5165-1283-6 (br)

Contents

Introduction

Studying judicial policymaking and the relationship between law, politics, and public policy is daunting. It requires students to combine nuanced understandings of arcane legal jargon, procedures and norms of reasoning with equally subtle conceptions of the political ins-and-outs of specific issue areas. American federalism makes this difficult task even harder, because it creates a multi-tiered set of federal and state legal and court systems, so that issues not only involve dense layers of federal policy-making dynamics but also entail complex interactions within and across federal, state, and local levels of government. Moreover, the fault line between law, politics, and policy is a moving target, as it significantly shifts across issue areas and over time.

Faced with this complexity, it is tempting to isolate the study of law and courts and seek to master the details of judicial processes and decision-making. Indeed, specialization is the dominant approach of textbooks on the courts and American politics. The problem is that American policymaking is not neatly assembled in stages. It is deeply interactive. These interactions emerge in part from a constitutional design that features overlapping policy-making forums designed to respond to different constituencies and political resources; in part from a political culture that distrusts centralized authority and thus encourages actors to challenge to any momentary concentration of influence in a policy area; and in part from the emergence of interest groups on the right and the left which combine litigation and lobbying strategies and use outcomes—either victories or losses—in one branch or level of government as leverage in others. As a result, a narrow, specialized approach to the study of law and the courts—or any other branch or level of American government—may lead to incomplete and even misleading accounts.

This volume takes a different and more holistic approach. Instead of compartmentalizing the study of law and courts, it seeks to embed the analysis of law and courts in fundamental questions about their role in ongoing political and policymaking processes. Along the way, these readings will explore a wide range of fundamental questions: What is the promise of law and courts in society? What are their limits? How is the American legal system organized? How does our system compare with those in other industrialized democracies? What are relative advantages and disadvantages of our system? To what extent (and under what conditions) does our system fulfill its promise of providing orderly dispute resolution, sound policy, and social justice? And, finally, what are the political consequences of all of this litigation?

Organization of the Book

The readings are organized into four parts. Part I is the most general. It explores the basic promises of and limits on the courts. Part II examines the American legal system and how it differs from its counterparts abroad. Part III takes a closer look at role of law and courts in several policy areas, including environmental regulation and discrimination. Part IV explores the political consequences of all of this litigation.

Each major part of the book will be introduced by an overview and further divided into sub-sections. Each sub-section will begin with a brief thematic overview, a list of readings, and study questions. In some cases, further materials will be recommended and additional study tools will be provided.

PART I
Law and Society

A lmost every society features some form of law and courts, ranging from tribal laws and councils in rural villages to detailed regulations and tribunals in urban, modernized societies. This suggests that law and courts—broadly defined—serve core social functions. What are those functions? What are the alternatives to formal dispute resolution? What are the advantages and limits of "self-help"?

These readings explore these questions. They begin with materials on the promise of law and courts, which examine their basic social logic, provide examples of these functions, and illustrate what happens when the courts fail to serve these functions.

The readings then turn to the limits on law and courts in fulfilling these promises, including doctrinal, institutional, and cultural constraints on judicial power and policy-making.

In reviewing these materials, pay close attention to the selection from Gerald Rosenberg's widely cited book on law and social change, *The Hollow Hope* (1991), which outlines a broader debate on whether American courts are "dynamic" or "constrained." As seen in the study materials at the end of the section, this debate can be used to pull together these readings into a series of competing claims about whether American legal doctrine, institutional arrangements, and cultural dispositions empower or limit the role of courts in American politics and policy-making.

A. The Promises of Law and Courts
Orderly Dispute Resolution

I n exploring the role of law and courts in American politics and public policy, it is useful to take a step back and consider their basic societal functions. The following readings aim to illustrate two core functions: (1) orderly dispute resolution and (2) judicial policy-making. Note that these promises are not always consistent. Indeed, they can be in tension, reflecting fundamentally different social logics and bases of legitimacy, as orderly dispute resolution requires courts to appear as neutral referees who apply the law as written whereas judicial policy-making often requires courts to reinterpret the law in light of new social mores and changing circumstances and thus move beyond existing rules and precedents.

Executive Summary

E ffective rule of law reduces corruption, combats poverty and disease, and protects people from injustices large and small. It is the foundation for communities of peace, opportunity, and equity—underpinning development, accountable government, and respect for fundamental rights.

The World Justice Project (WJP) joins efforts to produce reliable data on rule if law through the *WJP Rule of Law Index* 2015, the fifth report in an annual series, which measures rule of law based on the experiences and perceptions of the general public and in-country experts worldwide. We hope this annual publication, anchored in actual experiences, will help identify strengths and weaknesses in each country under review and encourage policy choices that strengthen the rule of law.

The *WJP Rule of Low Index* 2015 presents a portrait of the rule of law in each country by providing scores and rankings organized around eight factors: constraints on government powers, absence of corruption, open government, fundamental rights, order and security, regulatory enforcement, civil justice, and criminal justice (A ninth factor, informal justice, is measured but not included in aggregated scores and rankings). These factors are intended to reflect how people experience rule of law in everyday life.

The country scores and rankings for the *WJP Rule of Law Index* 2015 are derived from more than 100,000 household and expert surveys in 102 countries and jurisdictions. The Index is the world's most comprehensive data set of its kind and the only to rely solely on primary data, measuring a nation's adherence to the rule of law from the perspective of how ordinary people experience it. These features make the Index a powerful tool that can help identify strengths and weaknesses in each country, and help to inform policy debates, both within and across countries, that advance the rule of law.

"Executive Summary," World Justice Report: Rule of Law Index 2015, pp. 5-7. Copyright © 2015 by World Justice Project. Reprinted with permission.

RULE OF LAW AROUND THE WORLD:
SCORES AND RANKINGS

The table below presents the scores and rankings of the *WJP Rule of Law Index 2015*. Scores range from 0 to 1 (with 1 indicating strongest adherence to the rule of law). Scoring is based on answers drawn from a representative sample of 1,000 respondents in the three largest cities per country and a set of in-country legal practitioners and academics. Tables organized by region and income group, along with disaggregated data for each factor, can be found in the "Scores and Rankings" section of this report. The methodology used to compute the scores and determine the mapping of survey questions to the conceptual framework is available in the methodology section of the WJP Rule of Law Index website (worldjusticeproject. org/methodology).

COUNTRY	SCORE	GLOBAL RANKING	COUNTRY	SCORE	GLOBAL RANKING	COUNTRY	SCORE	GLOBAL RANKING
Denmark	0.87	1	Croatia	0.60	35	Moldova	0.48	69
Norway	0.87	2	South Africa	0.58	36	Ukraine	0.48	70
Sweden	0.85	3	Hungary	0.58	37	China	0.48	71
Finland	0.85	4	Senegal	0.57	38	Tanzania	0.47	72
Netherlands	0.83	5	Malaysia	0.57	39	Zambia	0.47	73
New Zealand	0.83	6	Bosnia and Herzegovina	0.57	40	kyrgyzstan	0.47	74
Austria	0.82	7	Jordan	0.56	41	Russia	0.47	75
Germany	0.81	8	Jamaica	0.56	42	Cote d'Ivoire	0.47	76
Singapore	0.81	9	Tunisia	0.56	43	Ecuador	0.47	77
Australia	0.80	10	Macedonia, FYR	0.55	44	Burkina Faso	0.47	78
Republic of Korea	0.79	11	Bulgaria	0.55	45	Mexico	0.47	79
United Kingdom	0.78	12	Brazil	0.54	46	Turkey	0.46	80
Japan	0.78	13	Mongolia	0.53	47	Uzbekistan	0.46	81
Canada	0.78	14	Nepal	0.53	48	Madagascar	0.45	82
Estonia	0.77	15	Panama	0.53	49	Liberia	0.45	83
Belgium	0.77	16	Belarus	0.53	50	Kenya	0.45	84
Hong Kong SAR China	0.76	17	Philippines	0.53	51	Guatemala	0.44	85
France	0.74	18	Indonesia	0.52	52	Egypt	0.44	86
United States	0.73	19	Albania	0.52	53	Sierra Leone	0.44	87

Country	Score	Rank	Country	Score	Rank	Country	Score	Rank
Czech Republic	0.72	20	Argentina	0.52	54	Iran	0.43	88
Poland	0.71	21	Morocco	0.52	55	Nicaragua	0.43	69
Uruguay	0.71	22	Thailand	0.52	56	Honduras	0.42	90
Portugal	0.70	23	El Salvador	0.51	57	Ethiopia	0.42	91
Spain	0.68	24	Sri Lanka	0.51	58	Myanmar	042	92
Costa Rica	0.68	25	India	0.51	59	Bangladesh	0.42	93
Chile	0.68	26	Serbia	0.50	60	Bolivia	0.41	94
United Arab Emirates	0.67	27	Malawi	0.50	61	Uganda	0.41	95
Slovenia	0.66	28	Colombia	0.50	62	Nigeria	0.41	96
Georgia	0.65	29	Peru	0.50	63	Cameroon	0.40	97
Italy	0.64	30	Vietnam	0.50	64	Pakistan	0.38	98
Botswana	0.64	31	Kazakhstan	0.50	65	Cambodia	0.37	99
Romania	0.62	32	Belize	0.49	66	Zimbabwe	0.37	100
Greece	0.60	33	Dominican Republic	0.48	67	Afghanistan	0.35	101
Ghana	0.60	34	Lebanon	0.48	68	Venezuela	0.12	102

THE WJP RULE OF LAW INDEX®

The World Justice Project (WJP) is an independent, multi-disciplinary organization working to advance the rule of law around the world. The rule of law provides the foundation for communities of peace, opportunity, and equity - underpinning development, accountable government, and respect for fundamental rights.

Where the rule of law is weak, medicines fail to reach health facilities, criminal violence goes unchecked, laws are applied unequally across societies, and foreign investments are held back. Effective rule of law helps reduce corruption, improve public health, enhance education, alleviate poverty, and protect people from injustices and dangers large and small.

Strengthening the rule of law is a major goal of governments, donors, businesses, and civil society organizations around the world. To be effective, however, rule of law development requires clarity about the fundamental features of the rule of law, as well as an adequate basis for its evaluation and measurement. In response to this need, the World Justice Project has developed the WJP Rule of Law Index, a quantitative measurement tool that offers a comprehensive picture of the rule of law in practice.

The WJP Rule of Law Index presents a portrait of the rule of law in each country by providing scores and rankings organized around nine themes: constraints on government powers, absence of corruption, open government, fundamental rights, order and security, regulatory enforcement, civil justice, criminal justice, and informal justice. These country scores and rankings are based on answers drawn from more than 100.000 household and expert surveys in 102 countries and jurisdictions.

The *WJP Rule of Law Index* 2015 is the fifth report in an annual series, and is the product of years of development, intensive consultation, and vetting with academics, practitioners, and community leaders from over 100 countries and 17 professional disciplines. The Index is intended for a broad audience of policy makers, civil society practitioners, academics, and others, The rule of law is not the rule of lawyers and judges: all elements of society are stakeholders. It is our hope that, over time, this diagnostic tool will help identify strengths and weaknesses in each country under review and encourage pokey choices that strengthen the rule of law.

1. Vigilantism and "Self-Help"

Dispute Resolution Without the Courts

Disputes inevitably arise in any society, especially socially, economically, and politically diverse societies like the United States. One of the central functions of government is to provide mechanisms for orderly dispute resolution. These readings examine this function by first considering the potential costs and benefits of allowing individuals to take matters in their own hands and engage in "self-help." They next explore the social logic of having courts and the importance of the appearance of neutrality under the law. They end with a few contemporary examples of major disputes over political succession, some in the United States, others abroad.

On Self-Help in Modern Society

Donald J. Black with M. P. Baumgartner

In a modern society, conflict between people is often defined as crime and is handled by officials of the state such as police, prosecutors, and judges. It is taken for granted that ordinary citizens are unable to solve many of their problems with others, but must turn to law for help.[1] This mode of social control has several distinctive consequences: It dramatizes the deviant character of an offense, for example (see Tannenbaum, 1938:19-21), and it may escalate hostility between the parties involved (see, e.g., Gibbs, 1963). Its patterns of detection and other procedures also affect the nature and distribution of crime itself, making some kinds of conduct in some places more vulnerable to observation and intervention, leaving other kinds in other places relatively immune. Finally, for the offender, law tends to be more stigmatizing and disabling than other social control and so may even render future conformity less likely.[2] If, however, people were to engage in more self-help rather than relying so heavily upon law, that is, if they were to exercise more social control on their own, a different kind of public order would prevail. In the nature of the case, many incidents would effectively be decriminalized, since they would no longer be formally defined and handled as criminal, and beyond this, many patterns of conduct themselves would surely change in response to new risks and opportunities. In this chapter we specify several conditions under which self-help flourishes, and suggest a number of techniques by which it might be stimulated.

Self-help is by no means a new phenomenon. Rather, it is a social practice that has been commonplace in many settings, and which is present to some degree nearly everywhere. It is

---

1 For these purposes, we define law as governmental social control (Black, 1972:1096), in other words, any process by which the state defines or responds to deviant behavior.

2 Social control as a cause of deviant behavior has been a major theme of labeling theory in sociology (for an overview, see Schur, 1971). The conduct so produced has come to be known as "secondary deviation" (Lemert, 1967).

Donald Black & M. P. Baumgartner, "On Self-Help in Modern Society," The Manners and Customs of the Police, pp. 193-194, 205-207. Copyright © 1980 by Donald Black. Reprinted with permission.

a quantitative variable, which may be greater in one place and weaker in another. Historically, for instance, the amount of self-help has been highest in the simplest societies, in bands and tribes, and has declined progressively with social evolution and the growth of law (see Hobhouse, 1951: Chapter 3). Within modern societies as well, some groups of people engage in much self-help—even to a point of organized vigilantism—while others are more dependent upon legal control. The same individuals may have recourse to self-help upon some occasions and turn to law upon others. It might also be noted that, like law, self-help has both preventive and remedial aspects, and these vary quantitatively and to some degree independently across social locations. The problem is to isolate the conditions that permit us to predict and explain variation of this kind.

SOCIAL CONTROL THROUGH SELF-HELP

Self-help is a mode of social control with a logic and an organization of its own. Not merely a substitute for other modes such as law, it is rather an alternative with distinctive patterns of mobilization, agent recruitment, procedures, outcomes, and other features. Hence, if self-help were to grow to a new prominence in modern society, it would have a number of implications for the normative life of the communities involved.

Perhaps the most significant differences between self-help and law lie in the actual settlements produced by each. In matters of public order, the style of social control[3] found in legal settlements tends toward the penal, with expiation through punishment a standard outcome. It is routine that only one side of any conflict is the object of this sanction, while the other is vindicated and supported. This penal style has a severity rarely seen in other idioms of social control. Another response of law to problems of public order is therapeutic in style, with people processed as "sick" and in need of corrective treatment, coercively applied if necessary. Self-help, by contrast is more frequently conciliatory. Its settlements are more commonly negotiated between the two or more opposing factions involved in a dispute, both or all of whom make some concessions in pursuit of a resolution (see Gulliver, 1969:67-68). If one of the parties is defined as the greater transgressor, this occurs through mutual agreement, and it is usual for him or her to supply the offended person or group with compensation of some kind, whether in the form of reparation or simply an apology. It might be added that, since it is generally a compromise reached through give and take rather than a decision imposed upon one party who is defined as a loser, a resolution of this kind differs from civil as well as criminal law. Finally, although civil settlements are as a rule less severe than penal settlements, self-help is likely to be less severe than either.

---

3   There are at least four basic styles of social control, or strategies by which people define and respond to deviant behavior. These are the penal, therapeutic, compensatory, and conciliatory styles. For an elaboration, see Black (1976:4-5).

Several characteristics of self-help explain these differences. In the first place, self-help is a radically decentralized mode of social control (see Sennett, 1970:164). In many cases, this means that the people immediately involved in a dispute participate in its resolution, and no one else. In other instances, one or both parties may draw upon a network of family, friends, or even situational acquaintances or bystanders for assistance, but this remains much different from the formal organization of law with its headquarters, chains of command, and courts. In criminal cases, moreover, it is the state itself—a centralized group par excellence—that brings the complaint. These features arc highly consequential in themselves since, all else constant, social control is most penal and most severe where its organization is most centralized, and least where the most decentralization prevails (see Black, 1976:86-91, 98, 101-103). There is even evidence that individuals are less punitive than small groups (see Wolosin, Sherman, and Mynatt, 1975). Accordingly, the relative leniency of self-help, and its conciliatory character, reconditioned by its decentralization as well as the role of individuals in the settlements reached.

Another feature of self-help also explains its patterns to some degree. When parties to a conflict do not invoke legal agents of social control, but draw upon others in solving their problems by self-help, they typically seek the participation of people who are closest to and most like themselves. Those with whom the disputants are intimate and with whom they share tastes and experiences thus come to perform a normative role in their lives. Even situationally, people with whom the parties have had some contact—rather than complete strangers—are most likely to be solicited for a role of this kind. People relatively intimate with the disputants are also more likely to intervene on their own initiative. For that matter, many disputes are settled by the participants alone, and often they themselves have priorities of some kind. Theory suggests that social control is least severe and most conciliatory precisely when social-control agents are relationally and culturally closest to the parties with whom they are involved (see Black, 1976:40–47, 55–57, 73–80, 82–83). It is therefore understandable that social control through self-help is quite unlike that exercised by police and other legal authorities, who are usually socially unknown and often culturally alien to the people whose problems they handle.

In addition to differences in severity and style, still another difference between self-help and law pertains to the variability in settlements arising from each. While there is substantial variability in outcomes at every stage of the legal process, cases handled by self-help vary considerably more.[4] This is a result of the greater diversity of participation across cases handled by people on their own. Legal agents are relatively homogeneous in background and

---

4 A similar point is made by Philip Gulliver. Contrasting the Arusha of Tanzania, a stateless people, with groups who have law, Gulliver distinguishes two modes of dispute settlement: a "judicial process," where a superordinate official hands down decisions in accordance with established norms, and a "political process," where decisions are negotiated between the parties in dispute without the intervention of an external authority of any kind, and where variability in outcomes is relatively extensive (1963:297-301).

other social characteristics, whereas agents of self-help are not. At different times, virtually all citizens—those of all sexes, ages, ethnicities, occupations, and other categories—serve as mediators for others and undertake social control on their own behalf. They emerge from throughout the population, make their contribution to social order, and fade back again. And since there is more variability in participation, there is more variability in result.

Yet other differences between law and self-help could be detailed, such as the lesser emphasis upon issues of procedural fairness in a self-help system, the greater importance of personal networks and alliances (see Gulliver, 1963:297–301), its lesser orientation toward rules or principles (see Northrop, 1958:349-351: Henderson, 1965: Volume 2, 241), and its more immediate resolution of disputes (Gulliver, 1963:233). Nevertheless, it is impossible at this point to be exhaustive or definitive about the changes that would accompany any new growth of self-help. The opportunity for an assessment of this kind depends upon the evolution of social control.

Securing the Borders Just Got Personal

Michael Sandler

California Assembly member Ray Haynes says it's bad enough that illegal immigrants cost his state's taxpayers billions of dollars, but what really irks him is watching as Washington, run by fellow Republicans, does nothing.

Tired of standing on the sidelines, Haynes wants to offer his own solution to California voters: patrol our own border and enforce federal immigration laws ourselves.

Haynes heard all the arguments: It's unconstitutional, borders are a federal responsibility and the state cannot afford it. But when considering the alternative, he concludes that it would be wrong to wait for Congress and President Bush to act.

"The federal government is not doing its job," said Haynes, who has begun gathering signatures to get his California Border Patrol initiative on the state's 2006 ballot. "I'm tired of people whining about whether the federal government is doing its job or not. I decided the best way to do this was to take control of the circumstances myself."

Haynes is not alone. Creating a state agency to enforce immigration laws has attracted support from at least one member of California's delegation to Congress, a slew of state legislators and the political team that led the 2003 election recall of Gov. Gray Davis. Andy Ramirez of Chino has established a group called Friends of the Border Patrol that he says has already attracted 400 volunteers and will begin monitoring the California-Mexico border Aug. 1.

The grass-roots effort to crack down on illegal immigration has gone beyond California. In Arizona, a volunteer civilian patrol of "minutemen" spent weeks this spring guarding 40 miles of the state's border with Mexico. They were criticized by the White House and praised by California Gov. Arnold Schwarzenegger. In New Hampshire, police chiefs are using trespassing charges to detain illegal immigrants and try to get them deported.

These disparate local efforts aren't linked, but their participants share common concerns about the costs of illegal immigration and a deep dissatisfaction with federal enforcement efforts. So they are turning away from Washington and testing the boundaries of the

Michael Sandler, "Securing the Border Just Got Personal," CQ Weekly. Copyright © 2005 by CQ Roll Call, Inc. Reprinted with permission.

Constitution with their own solutions. They are getting sympathy, if not sustenance, from some in Washington.

"Unfortunately, we see the states frustrated with a lack of federal security trying to fill that gap," said Sen. John Cornyn, R-Texas. "Both of those speak volumes of the federal government's failure to live up to its responsibility." Cornyn nevertheless says that protecting the border is Washington's task, not Sacramento's or Austin's.

Cornyn is backed by Western lawmakers of both parties. "This is a federal responsibility, and the federal government should carry it out," said Sen. Dianne Feinstein, D-Calif., a sentiment echoed by her home-state Democratic colleague, Barbara Boxer, and by John McCain, R-Ariz.

Cornyn's admission of the federal government's failure is not an everyday occurrence for a lawmaker. But it is difficult to find anyone in Washington boasting about the record on illegal immigration.

Topping the list of congressional supporters for the California Border Patrol is Republican Ed Royce, who serves as chairman of the House International Relations Subcommittee on International Terrorism and Nonproliferation.

Tom Tancredo, R-Colo., a vigorous opponent of illegal immigration and leader of the House Immigration Reform Caucus, said he was not familiar with the initiative, but heartily endorsed the idea: "I like it!" he said. "I think that is the kind of thing that is going to happen around the country."

GIVE AND TAKE

At the root of the debate is a fundamental paradox regarding those entering the United States illegally.

On one hand, most illegal immigrants work, often filling jobs that citizens pass up. Many U.S. employers are willing to hire illegals, who work for lower wages and few benefits.

But illegal immigrants use public resources paid for with taxpayer money. Without health insurance, they show up at emergency rooms in need of medical care. They often send their children to public schools. And the beds in state prisons and county jails are filled with illegals caught committing crimes beyond their illegal jump across the border.

An estimated 10 million illegal immigrants reside in the United States, according to the latest research by the Pew Hispanic Center; more than half are from Mexico. Pew estimates that one in 11 Mexican citizens lives in the United States, counting both legal and illegal residents. About 2.5 million illegals, or 24 percent of the total, are from South and Central America. More than half of all illegal immigrants—6.7 million—arrived in the last 10 years.

"I think the frustration is understandable," said Marshall Fitz, associate director for the American Immigration Lawyers Association. But while he is sympathetic to those feeling the crunch, he is troubled by Haynes' proposed solution, calling it "misguided." Turning border enforcement over to local authorities would "turn the Constitution on its head" and create a scenario in which 50 states have their own immigration enforcement policies, Fitz said.

Fitz envisions poorly trained officers, without a clearly defined plan and plenty of money, detaining legal residents simply because they speak poor English.

He has an ally in the Homeland Security Department, home of the U.S. Customs and Border Protection agency. Jarrod Agen, a spokesman for the department, said enforcing the nation's borders is dangerous work that should be left to federal officers.

"Our agents are the professionals," he said.

Facing criticism back home and pressure from business groups, lawmakers are doing their best to straddle concerns and come up with a solution that would please everyone.

Cornyn, chairman of the Senate Judiciary Subcommittee on Immigration, Border Security and Citizenship, is drafting legislation with Jon Kyl, R-Ariz., that would add 10,000 border patrol agents and 1,000 immigration inspectors at ports over the next five years, plus add 10,000 detention beds.

"In order for the American people to accept temporary worker permits, it has to be coupled with increased security," Cornyn said. "We have to address the frustration many people feel with illegal immigration."

McCain has been working on a bill with Edward M. Kennedy, D-Mass., that would offer limited guest worker visas. He said Arlen Specter, R-Pa., chairman of the Senate Judiciary Committee, is ready to hold hearings on both proposals. Only one player is missing; the president. "We need more involvement on the part of the White House," McCain said.

Last year, Bush proposed creating a temporary-worker program that matches foreign workers with U.S. companies, provided no U.S. citizens could fill the jobs. Bush wants to include undocumented immigrants now employed in the United States, a proposal critics liken to amnesty for the millions of illegal immigrants now living in legal shadows.

Though he repeated the call during his State of the Union address in February, Bush has paid scant attention to the subject since. Cornyn said he expects a package from the White House in the next few weeks.

BORDER CONTROL IS A 'BARGAIN'

Haynes said he isn't holding his breath, and enlisted political consultant David Gilliard to begin gathering signatures to get the California Border Patrol initiative on the June 2006 ballot. They'll need nearly 600,000 valid signatures.

Gilliard may be little known in Washington, but in California he is famous as the man who led the effort to recall Democratic Gov. Davis. His firm, Gilliard, Blanning, Wysocki and Associates, also managed campaigns for several GOP members of the state's House delegation.

He estimates that California could start a border patrol with 3,500 officers for $300 million, based on the cost of running the state's highway patrols. He calls the border patrol a bargain compared with the hundreds of millions of dollars that Los Angeles County alone spends on health care for illegal immigrants.

As for the constitutional issues, Gilliard and Haynes point to Florida. The Sunshine State started a pilot program in 2002 that trained 35 law enforcement officers to enforce immigration laws. The Florida program was launched shortly after the Sept. 11 terrorist attacks. Of the 19 hijackers, 15 had Florida connections, and three held expired visas.

Florida's program was authorized by a 1996 federal law that permits deputizing local authorities to enforce immigration laws.

James Edwards, an adjunct fellow at the conservative Hudson Institute in Washington, said California has the legal right to create any kind of police force it chooses, and says state and local authorities should play a larger role in arresting suspected illegal immigrants.

But Edwards said states are limited in their ability to enforce federal laws. Local authorities can detain suspected illegal immigrants for short periods of time, check their immigration status and even fingerprint them for a local charge—such as the trespassing violations used in New Hampshire. But deportation decisions must be made by a federal immigration judge.

California has been down a similar road before. Hans Johnson, a research fellow with the Public Policy Institute of California, a private research group, recalled voters' support in 1994 of Proposition 187, designed to keep children of illegal immigrants from attending public schools. It was later ruled unconstitutional by a federal judge, who said only the federal government can regulate public benefits.

"The campaign in favor of that proposition was largely one of, 'We need to send a message to Washington,'" Johnson recalled. "While I think a lot of people who voted for it didn't want to prevent children from going to school, they didn't think Washington was being responsive. It will be interesting to see whether times have changed."

2. The Social Logic of Courts

"The Logic of the Triad"

S ociolegal scholars argue that courts rest on a nearly universal social logic: the logic of the triad. These reading explore this social logic and how it applies to our public discourse about judicial decisions and the confirmation process.

In addition to the readings that follow, I recommend two additional pieces by Martin Shapiro that provide more information on this topic:

- Martin Shapiro, *Courts: A Comparative and Political Analysis (1988)*
- *Martin Shapiro and Alec Stone Sweet, On Law, Politics and Judicialization (2002)*

Martin Shapiro and the Logic of the Triad

Jeb Barnes

I n his classic study, *Courts: A Comparative and Political Analysis* (1981), Martin Shapiro argues that courts (and their legitimacy) reflect a nearly universal social logic, which he calls "the logic of the triad." The gist is that members of any society inevitably get into disputes that they cannot resolve themselves (i.e., where "self-help" is not available). When this happens, they naturally turn to a third party for help. The result is a "triad," or triangular relationship, among the competing disputants and the court (see the figure below). Put differently, every society needs referees and courts serve that function.

The Logic of the Triad (Shapiro 1981)

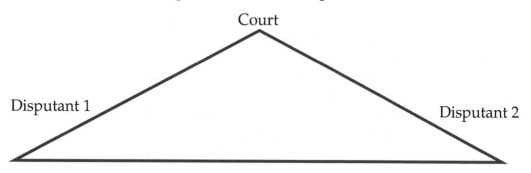

If courts serve as society's referees, what about the law? What is the role of the law in this triadic relationship? Why can't judges just decide cases based on their professional judgment and dispense with the formality of applying pre-existing rules and procedures?

Answering these questions requires us to think more carefully about the logic of the triad and its relationship to the dispute resolution process. By definition, third party dispute resolution requires the court to render a decision. The act of rendering a decision, however, threatens to undermine the logic of the triad. Why? As soon as the court decides a case in favor of one disputant, the triad devolves into a two-against-one relationship from the perspective of the loser.

According to Shapiro, legal systems employ all sorts of mechanisms to ameliorate this problem by seeking to preserve the appearance of courts' neutrality, although no mechanism can eliminate the triad's inherent instability. One of the simplest mechanisms is consent. In some legal systems, disputants must agree (or "consent") to the rules and procedures governing their case prior to adjudication. Consent helps to maintain the logic of the triad because it is harder to complain that judges were acting unfairly when they applied the parties' own rules to the resolve the dispute. Legal ceremony is another. It is no coincidence that judges wear robes, like clergy, and that courtrooms are often solemn places, where the judge sits behind a magnificent bench that towers over the disputants. In terms of the triad, this signals that judges are not ordinary people, who are apt to play favorites. They are special, set apart from the rest of us.

In modern democracies, laws are passed by elected representatives and apply to citizens whether they formally consent to them or not. Under these circumstances, the rule of law—the expectation that judges will decide cases based on pre-existing rules and procedures without regard to the status of the disputants—provides a crucial device for preserving the logic of the triad. The idea is that if judges apply pre-existing laws when deciding them, then they are not playing personal favorites when deciding cases; they are merely applying the law as written.

Of course, there will be instances where the law is unclear (and its application contested) and there will always be some people who think that judges are being unfair when ruling against their interests, no matter how carefully judges explain their legal reasoning. Indeed, as we will see in the following readings, concerns about judicial bias (and thus the courts' legitimacy from the vantage of the logic of the triad) are a common refrain in public discourse about the courts, as judges themselves are judged based on the extent to which they can credibly maintain the appearance of neutrality.

Sotomayor and Identity Politics

Nate Beeler

Nate Beeler, "Sotomayor and Identity Politics," The Washington Examiner. Copyright © 2009 by Nate Beeler. Reprinted with permission.

Blame It On My Reagan Youth

By R.J. Matson

"BLAME IT ON MY REAGAN YOUTH!"

RJ Matson, "Blame It on My Reagan Youth," The St. Louis Dispatch. Copyright © 2005 by RJ Matson. Reprinted with permission.

A Judge Too Far

Nominating Sotomayor Reveals the President's True Colors

With his nomination of Judge Sonia Sotomayor for the U.S. Supreme Court, President Obama has abandoned all pretense of being a post-partisan president. While he may like to think of himself as a thoughtful moderate soaring above the issues that divide America, his actions reveal what hides under that hopeful lining.

Presidents usually nominate judges that espouse their philosophy. So what does this nomination tell us about Mr. Obama's true colors?

Even the liberal establishment worries that Judge Sotomayor tilts too far to the left. New Republic essayist Jeffrey Rosen reports that fellow liberals who have watched or worked with her closely "expressed questions about her temperament, her judicial craftsmanship, and ... [they have said] she is 'not that smart and kind of a bully on the bench'"

A suspiciously high number of her decisions have been overruled by higher courts. Wendy Long of the Judicial Confirmation Network said that record shows "she is far more of a liberal activist than even the current liberal activist Supreme Court."

There will be much to say in days to come about Judge Sotomayor's manifest lack of appropriate judicial restraint and about other problems in her record. For now, though, three red flags beg for attention.

"Where policy is made" : Speaking at Duke University Law School in 2005, Judge Sotomayor said the "Court of Appeals is where policy is made." On its face, the assertion runs counter to more than 200 years of American legal tradition holding that courts are merely meant to interpret existing law, not actively make policy choices.

Immediately realizing she was on thin ice, the judge continued: "... and I know this is on tape and I should never say that, because we don't 'make' law." To much laughter, and with facial and hand gestures to indicate that her next line was to be taken with humor as a useful fiction, she added: "I'm not promoting it and I'm not advocating it."

"A Judge Too Far: Nominating Sotomayor Reveals President's True Colors," The Washington Times. Copyright © 2009 by Washington Times. Reprinted with permission.

But judicial activism is no joke. It undermines the Constitution and substitutes judicial whim for democratic decision-making. Unelected judges, answerable to no one but themselves and serving for life, can all too easily become dangerous oligarchs.

White judges know less: Judge Sotomayor seems to think that inherent racial and sexual differences are not simply quirks of genetics, but make some better than others. Consider her 2002 speech at the University of California-Berkeley School of Law.

"I would hope that a wise Latina woman with the richness of her experiences would more often than not reach a better conclusion than a white male who hasn't lived that life," she said. "I simply do not know exactly what that difference will be in my judging. But I accept there will be some based on my gender and my Latina heritage."

She also accepted as potentially valid the idea that the "different perspectives" of "men and women of color" are due to "basic differences in logic in reasoning" due to "inherent physiological or cultural differences."

If a white male had said these openly racialist words in a prepared speech, his chances of reaching the U.S. Supreme Court would be gone in an instant. Instead, it seems that these outlandish remarks are what qualified Judge Sotomayor in Mr. Obama's eyes.

Rewarding discrimination: Judge Sotomayor seems to favor racial discrimination. Consider the case of *Ricci v. DeStefano*. In that controversial case, 19 white firemen were denied promotion because no blacks scored high enough on a race-neutral test to also be promoted. Judge Sotomayor ruled against the white firefighters.

If Mr. Obama wanted a judge with the right "empathy," he struck out with Judge Sotomayor. One of the white firefighters denied promotion, Frank Ricci, is dyslexic. In order to ace the promotion exam, he quit a second job, spent $1,000 for instruction materials, and spent many hours reading those books into an audio tape to help him study. For his extraordinary efforts, he finished sixth out of 77 applicants for promotion—but then was denied, simply because he is white.

Second Circuit Court of Appeals Judge Jose Cabranes, appointed by a Democratic president, complained that the ruling written by Judge Sotomayor and two other judges "contains no reference whatsoever to the constitutional claims at the core of this case."

The Supreme Court is expected to rule on Ricci v. DeStefano before the Senate votes on Judge Sotomayor's nomination. It would be an extraordinary rebuke were a current nominee to be overruled on such a controversial case by the very justices she is slated to join.

Judge Sotomayor seems to be the most radical person ever nominated for the high court. To continue to command public respect, the Senate will have to ask her some hard questions. The simplest one to ask will be the hardest one for her to answer: Given her statements against whites and males, can she be fair to all Americans?

Pot, Meet Kettle

Charles M. Blow

Fringe Republican race-baiting on Sonia Sotomayor, the Supreme Court nominee, has fallen flat. According to polls, most Americans want to see her confirmed.

Furthermore, the picture that those Republicans painted of Sotomayor doesn't seem to be supported by her actions. The Scotusblog examined her court of appeals decisions in race-related cases and found that she rejected claims of discrimination 80 percent of the time.

Even so, she apologized, in a sense, for the "wise Latina woman" line that got many on the right so bent out of shape. Senator Dianne Feinstein said that Sotomayor told her that it was a "poor choice of words."

What about those Republicans? Did they apologize? Only Newt Gingrich, in a sense, but his sights may be set on the White House in 2012.

What about Tom Tancredo, the former congressman who not only called Sotomayor a racist but compared her to members of the Ku Klux Klan?

Not a peep, even as the appearance of his hypocrisy on Sotomayor soared to new heights as details were revealed of a racial attack two years ago by a man who is now the executive director of a political action committee co-founded by Tancredo.

The offender's name is Marcus Epstein. He is half-Jewish, half-Korean and apparently cavorts with white supremacists. (This sounds like a "Chappelle's Show" skit.)

As The Washington Independent reported, on the evening of July 7, 2007, Epstein "bumped into a black woman" on the street in the Georgetown section of Washington after consuming "too much to drink." He "called her a 'nigger,' and struck her in the head with an open hand." The Independent called it a "karate chop."

Surely Tancredo, the vociferous voice of racial justice, was champing at the bit to denounce Epstein in the same terms and tenor as Sotomayor. Or maybe, just maybe, he might want to apologize to her. Yeah, right.

Charles Blow, "Pot, Meet Kettle," The New York Times. Copyright © 2009 by The New York Times Company. Reprinted with permission provided by PARS International Corp. All rights reserved.

Reached by phone, Tancredo conceded that the Georgetown incident was "ugly" and "racist" but didn't apply the word personally to Epstein. Quite the contrary, he seemed to want to shield Epstein. As for an apology: no dice.

Is such a stubborn stance good for the Republican Party?

No. Racial wounds are deeply felt and slowly healed. Having Hispanics feel racially slighted by the Republicans is suicidal. Hispanics are 15 percent of the nation's population, and, unlike blacks, they're not so monolithically democratic, at least not yet.

Even so, Rush Limbaugh, who also had called the judge a racist and compared her to a member of the K.K.K., made clear this week that anyone waiting for a retraction from him shouldn't hold their breath: "If the word means something—words mean something—and if it fits, I use it."

Really? Well in that case, let me use two words: shameful and defeatist.

Court Says Judges Must Avoid Appearance of Bias with Donors

By Joan Biskupic

The Supreme Court enhanced the ability of litigants to challenge judges as potentially biased because of campaign contributions as it ruled 5-4 that a West Virginia judge who won election with big-money support from a coal company executive should have sat out the company's case.

The high court for the first time set down a rule for disqualifications arising from money judges receive as they campaign for election to the bench. The court said judges must pull out of a dispute when "a serious risk of actual bias" arises because "a person with a personal stake in a particular case had a significant and disproportionate influence" in getting the judge on the bench to hear the case.

Numerous questions remain about how the majority's new rule may affect the millions of dollars spent on state judicial elections nationwide or requests in specific cases for judges to sit out. Thirty-nine states elect at least some of their judges.

Writing for the majority, Justice Anthony Kennedy emphasized the importance of public confidence in the courts and objective criteria to avoid the appearance of bias, as well as actual bias. Dissenting justices complained that the majority's standard was too vague. Chief Justice John Roberts, writing for dissenters, offered 40 questions raised by the majority opinion, including "How do we determine whether a given (campaign) expenditure is 'disproportionate'? Disproportionate to what?"

Monday's groundbreaking decision comes amid increasing debate over potential corruption in state judicial elections by wealthy contributors.

The Kennedy majority acknowledged that its standard would have to be worked out in lower courts in future cases. In the West Virginia case, however, Kennedy said it was clear that constitutional due process of law was violated when state Supreme Court Justice Brent Benjamin cast the deciding vote to overturn a $50 million jury verdict against a company whose chief executive had heavily backed Benjamin in an election.

Joan Biskupic, "Court Says Judges Must Avoid Appearance of Bias With Donors," USA Today. Copyright © 2009 by Gannett Company, Inc. Reprinted with permission.

CEO Don Blankenship had contributed $3 million to unseat incumbent Democratic Judge Warren McGraw in his 2004 race against Benjamin, a Republican. Two years earlier, Blankenship's A.T. Massey Coal had lost a fraud lawsuit to Hugh Caperton and his Harman Mining Co.

Justice Kennedy noted that the amount Blankenship spent in the race far exceeded the total spent by all other Benjamin supporters and by Benjamin himself.

He also noted that Benjamin had said he did not feel beholden to Blankenship and could be fair in the appeal by Blankenship's Massey Coal. Even so, Kennedy said that more is required than a judge's subjective assessment of the situation.

Kennedy termed the Blankenship-Benjamin situation "extreme," largely because of the $3 million amount and the timing of the contribution as the case was on appeal. "Not every campaign contribution by a litigant or attorney creates a probability of bias that requires a judge's recusal," Kennedy said, "but this is an exceptional case."

There "is a serious risk of actual bias—based on objective and reasonable perceptions—when a person with a personal stake in a particular case had a significant and disproportionate influence in placing the judge on the case" as it was pending, Kennedy said.

Caperton's effort to restore the $50 million verdict of a Boone County jury now returns to West Virginia courts.

The larger question is how Monday's ruling will affect state court rules on disqualifications. Many states, like West Virginia, had left a decision regarding disqualification up to the individual judge. Kennedy's decision would require a more objective test.

"It is a narrow decision, but it breaks new constitutional ground," said James Sample, a lawyer with the Brennan Center for Justice, which tracks money in state judicial elections and had sided with Caperton.

Sample said states would now determine how the specifics of the new rule are implemented, for example, through setting up separate panels to review a judge's decision on whether to disqualify, or by establishing a percentage of campaign money that would trigger scrutiny.

Joining Kennedy were liberal justices John Paul Stevens, David Souter, Ruth Bader Ginsburg and Stephen Breyer. Dissenting with Roberts were fellow conservative justices Antonin Scalia Clarence Thomas, and Samuel Alito.

Rejection of Iowa Judges Over Gay Marriage Raises Fears of Political Influence

Maura Dolan

CALIFORNIA SUPREME COURT CHIEF JUSTICE VOICES CONCERNS ABOUT PARTISAN PRESSURES ON JURISTS AND BACKS A SINGLE, 15-YEAR TERM WITHOUT BEING PUT TO A VOTE.

Iowa's rejection of three state supreme court justices who ruled in favor of same-sex marriage underscored the growing electoral vulnerability of state judges as more and more are targeted by special interest groups, legal scholars and jurists said Thursday.

"It just illustrated something that has been troubling many of us for many, many years," California Chief Justice Ronald M. George said. "The election of judges is not necessarily the best way to select them."

The three Iowa high court justices were ousted in the kind of retention election California uses for appeals court judges: They face no opposing candidates and list no party affiliation, and voters can select "yes" or "no." Legal scholars have generally said that system is among the most effective ways of avoiding a politicized judiciary.

But a report by the Brennan Center for Justice this year found a "transformation" in state judicial elections during the last decade throughout the country. Big money and a campaign emphasis on how a judge votes on the bench has become "the new normal," the report said.

"For more than a decade, partisans and special interests of all stripes have been growing more organized in their efforts to use elections to tilt the scales of justice their way," said the report, which examined 10 years of judicial elections. "Many Americans have come to fear that justice is for sale."

Although Iowa's vote will have no immediate effect on marriage rights there, it sends a signal to other judges that voters are watching.

"It will pressure judges, or some judges anyway, perhaps even subconsciously, in their decision-making by what would be popular or what might meet the political preferences of

Maura Dolan, "Rejection of Iowa Judges Over Gay Marriage Raises Fears of Political Influence," Los Angeles Times. Copyright © 2010 by Los Angeles Times Syndicate. Reprinted with permission.

the moment," George said. "And the judge's loyalty has to be first and foremost to the rule of law, and not to the political or social or economic pressures or personal preferences."

Several jurists cited recent U.S. Supreme Court decisions that they believe will further politicize the bench. One ruling permitted judges to take political positions during judicial races, and another overturned campaign contribution limits.

Anti-abortion forces targeted George and California Supreme Court Justice Ming W. Chin for removal in 1998 after they voted to overturn a state parental consent law. Both raised money and mounted campaigns to save their seats.

More dramatically, voters ousted the late California Chief Justice Rose Bird and two colleagues in 1986 after a campaign that charged the court was failing to uphold death sentences.

"The Rose Bird situation is now being replicated throughout the United States," said Justice J. Anthony Kline of the 1st District Court of Appeal in San Francisco. What happened in Iowa is likely to happen in other states, including California, where the Bird election generally has been seen as an aberration, he said.

"The independence of California courts has never been seriously challenged," Kline said. "But those days may be numbered."

Most states elect judges, whereas federal judges receive lifetime tenure. Judges for Superior Court in California can be challenged.

A group opposed to gay marriage targeted the Iowa justices, who were on the ballot for their regular retention election, after last year's unanimous Iowa Supreme Court decision to lift a ban on same-sex marriage. Even though a new governor will now appoint their replacements, the recall is not expected to affect same-sex marriage rights in Iowa.

"It was an attempt to intimidate judges," said Dean Allan W. Vestal of Drake University Law School in Des Moines. "It had no immediate practical effect."

The justices who were ejected from the bench blamed "an unprecedented attack by out-of-state special interest groups." They included the Mississippi-based American Family Assn., the Washington-based Family Research Council and the New Jersey-based National Organization for Marriage.

Liberty Counsel, one of the groups that has been fighting gay marriage, praised the results.

"The justices crossed the line when they played the role of a legislator and abandoned judicial restraint," said Mathew Staver, founder of the group.

George said pressure has come from both the left and the right in California judicial retention elections.

Rep. Maxine Waters (D-Los Angeles) sent out a slate mailer urging her constituents to vote against Republican appointees to the bench, including Court of Appeal Justice Tani Cantil-Sakauye, who will become chief justice when George retires in January, according to the Metropolitan News-Enterprise, a legal newspaper. A spokesman for Waters could not immediately confirm the report.

In liberal San Francisco, Superior Court jurists went to bat for Republican appointee Judge Richard Ulmer, a registered independent, after he was challenged by a gay Latino

Democrat. The San Francisco Democratic County Central Committee, whose slate cards can be influential, endorsed Ulmer's Democratic challenger.

Kline, a Democratic appointee, helped organize support for Ulmer. Kline said Ulmer had to raise about $300,000 to fend off the challenge on Tuesday.

"That is the problem," Kline said. "We don't realize it in California because we don't have a history of courts being for sale. But look at Texas, Mississippi, New Mexico and an increasing number of states where trial judges can be challenged."

In Texas, lawyers check the financial disclosure records of judges hearing their cases and bring in other lawyers who contributed heavily to the judges' campaigns, Kline said.

In Ohio, candidates for the state Supreme Court have run either as the Chamber of Commerce candidate or the labor candidate, George said.

"One year there were competing candidates for the Texas Supreme Court backed by competing oil companies," he added.

George favors a system in which a Supreme Court judge would be appointed to a single 15-year term without ever appearing on the ballot. Justices now serve 12-year terms, subject to retention by voters.

"That would be your one shot," he said. "There would be no influence, conscious or unconscious, in terms of having to face a possibly political elective process."

Jon W. Davidson, legal director of Lambda Legal, said he was distressed by the judges' defeat in Iowa but added that it would not deter gay rights lawyers from bringing cases in state court.

"In my mind, it is an attack on our country, an attack on our form of government, which has three branches, one of which is supposed to be making decisions without giving in to the majority will," Davidson said.

Supreme Court Of The United States

Nos. 14-556, 14-562, 14-571 and 14-574

Scalia, J., dissenting

JAMES OBERGEFELL, ET AL., PETITIONERS 14-556

v.

RICHARD HODGES, DIRECTOR, OHIO DEPARTMENT OF
HEALTH, ET AL.;
VALERIA TANCO, ET AL., PETITIONERS 14-562

v.

BILL HASLAM, GOVERNOR OF TENNESSEE, ET AL.;
APRIL DEBOER, ET AL. PETITIONERS 14-571

v.

RICK SNYDER, GOVERNOR OF MICHIGAN,
ET AL.; AND
GREGORY BOURKE, ET AL., PETITIONERS 14-574

v.

STEVE BESHEAR, GOVERNOR OF KENTUCKY ON WRITS
OF CERTIORARI TO THE UNITED STATES COURT OF
APPEALS FOR THE SIXTH CIRCUIT
[June 26, 2015]

JUSTICE SCALIA, with whom JUSTICE THOMAS joins, dissenting.

I join THE CHIEF Justice's opinion in full. I write separately to call attention to this Court's threat to American democracy.

The substance of today's decree is not of immense personal importance to me. The law can recognize as marriage whatever sexual attachments and living arrangements it wishes, and can accord them favorable civil consequences, from tax treatment to rights of inheritance.

Copyright in the Public Domain.

Those civil consequences—and the public approval that conferring the name of marriage evidences—can perhaps have adverse social effects, but no more adverse than the effects of many other controversial laws. So it is not of special importance to me what the law says about marriage. It is of overwhelming importance, however, who it is that rules me. Today's decree says that my Ruler, and the Ruler of 320 million Americans coast-to-coast, is a majority of the nine lawyers on the Supreme Court. The opinion in these cases is the furthest extension in fact— and the furthest extension one can even imagine—of the Court's claimed power to create "liberties" that the Constitution and its Amendments neglect to mention. This practice of constitutional revision by an unelected committee of nine, always accompanied (as it is today) by extravagant praise of liberty, robs the People of the most important liberty they asserted in the Declaration of Independence and won in the Revolution of 1776: the freedom to govern themselves.

I

Until the courts put a stop to it, public debate over same-sex marriage displayed American democracy at its best. Individuals on both sides of the issue passionately, but respectfully, attempted to persuade their fellow citizens to accept their views. Americans considered the arguments and put the question to a vote. The electorates of 11 States, either directly or through their representatives, chose to expand the traditional definition of marriage. Many more decided not to.[1] Win or lose, advocates for both sides continued pressing their cases, secure in the knowledge that an electoral loss can be negated by a later electoral win. That is exactly how our system of government is supposed to work.[2]

The Constitution places some constraints on self-rule—constraints adopted *by the People themselves* when they ratified the Constitution and its Amendments. Forbidden are laws "impairing the Obligation of Contracts,"[3] denying "Full Faith and Credit" to the "public Acts" of other States,[4] prohibiting the free exercise of religion,[5] abridging the freedom of speech,[6] infringing the right to keep and bear arms,[7] authorizing unreasonable searches and seizures,[8] and so forth. Aside from these limitations, those powers "reserved to the States respectively, or to the people"[9] can be exercised as the States or the People desire. These cases ask us to decide whether the Fourteenth Amendment contains a limitation that requires the States

---

1   Brief for Respondents in No. 14–571, p. 14.
2   Accord, *Schuette* v. *BAMN*, 572 U. S._, _-_(2014) (plurality opinion) (slip op., at 15–17).
3   U. S. Const., Art. I, §10.
4   Art. IV, §1.
5   Amdt. 1.
6   *Ibid.*
7   Amdt. 2.
8   Amdt. 4.
9   Amdt. 10.

to license and recognize marriages between two people of the same sex. Does it remove *that* issue from the political process?

Of course not. It would be surprising to find a prescription regarding marriage in the Federal Constitution since, as the author of today's opinion reminded us only two years ago (in an opinion joined by the same Justices who join him today):

> "[Regulation of domestic relations is an area that has long been regarded as a virtually exclusive province of the States."[10]
>
> "[T]he Federal Government, through our history, has deferred to state-law policy decisions with respect to domestic relations."[11]

But we need not speculate. When the Fourteenth Amendment was ratified in 1868, every State limited marriage to one man and one woman, and no one doubted the constitutionality of doing so. That resolves these cases. When it comes to determining the meaning of a vague constitutional provision—such as "due process of law" or "equal protection of the laws"—it is unquestionable that the People who ratified that provision did not understand it to prohibit a practice that remained both universal and uncontroversial in the years after ratification.[12] We have no basis for striking down a practice that is not expressly prohibited by the Fourteenth Amendment's text, and that bears the endorsement of a long tradition of open, widespread, and unchallenged use dating back to the Amendment's ratification. Since there is no doubt whatever that the People never decided to prohibit the limitation of marriage to opposite-sex couples, the public debate over same-sex marriage must be allowed to continue.

But the Court ends this debate, in an opinion lacking even a thin veneer of law. Buried beneath the mummeries and straining-to-be-memorable passages of the opinion is a candid and startling assertion: No matter *what* it was the People ratified, the Fourteenth Amendment protects those rights that the Judiciary, in its "reasoned judgment," thinks the Fourteenth Amendment ought to protect.[13] That is so because "[t]he generations that wrote and ratified the Bill of Rights and the Fourteenth Amendment did not presume to know the extent of freedom in all of its dimensions. ... "[14] One would think that sentence would continue: "... and therefore they provided for a means by which the People could amend the Constitution," or perhaps "... and therefore they left the creation of additional liberties, such as the freedom to marry someone of the same sex, to the People, through the never-ending process of legislation." But no. What logically follows, in the majority's judge-empowering estimation, is: "and

---

10   *United States* v. *Windsor*, 570 U. S. _, _, (2013) (slip op., at 16) (internal quotation marks and citation omitted).

11   *Id.*, at _ (slip op., at 17).

12   See *Town of Greece* v. *Galloway*, 572 U. S. _, _-_(2014) (slip op., at 7-8).

13   *Ante*, at 10.

14   *Ante*, at 11.

so they entrusted to future generations a charter protecting the right of all persons to enjoy liberty as we learn its meaning."[15] The "we," needless to say, is the nine of us. "History and tradition guide and discipline [our] inquiry but do not set its outer boundaries."[16] Thus, rather than focusing on *the People's* understanding of "liberty"—at the time of ratification or even today—the majority focuses on four "principles and traditions" that, *in the majority's view*, prohibit States from defining marriage as an institution consisting of one man and one woman.[17]

This is a naked judicial claim to legislative—indeed, *super*-legislative—power; a claim fundamentally at odds with our system of government. Except as limited by a constitutional prohibition agreed to by the People, the States are free to adopt whatever laws they like, even those that offend the esteemed Justices' "reasoned judgment." A system of government that makes the People subordinate to a committee of nine unelected lawyers does not deserve to be called a democracy.

Judges are selected precisely for their skill as lawyers; whether they reflect the policy views of a particular constituency is not (or should not be) relevant. Not surprisingly then, the Federal Judiciary is hardly a cross-section of America. Take, for example, this Court, which consists of only nine men and women, all of them successful lawyers[18] who studied at Harvard or Yale Law School. Four of the nine are natives of New York City. Eight of them grew up in east- and west-coast States. Only one hails from the vast expanse in-between. Not a single South-westerner or even, to tell the truth, a genuine Westerner (California does not count). Not a single evangelical Christian (a group that comprises about one quarter of Americans[19]), or even a Protestant of any denomination. The strikingly unrepresentative character of the body voting on today's social upheaval would be irrelevant if they were functioning as *judges*, answering the legal question whether the American people had ever ratified a constitutional provision that was understood to proscribe the traditional definition of marriage. But of course the Justices in today's majority are not voting on that basis; *they say they are not.* And to allow the policy question of same-sex marriage to be considered and resolved by a select, patrician, highly unrepresentative panel of nine is to violate a principle even more fundamental than no taxation without representation: no social transformation without representation.

---

15 *Ibid.*

16 *Ante*, at 10–11.

17 *Ante*, at 12–18.

18 The predominant attitude of tail-building lawyers with respect to the questions presented m these cases is suggested by the fact that the American Bar Association deemed it in accord with the wishes of its members to file a brief in support of the petitioners. See Brief for American Bar Association as *Amicus Curiae* in Nos. 14–571 and 14–574, pp. 1–5.

19 See Pew Research Center, America's Changing Religious Land-scape 4 (May 12, 2015).

But what really astounds is the hubris reflected in today's judicial Putsch. The five Justices who compose today's majority are entirely comfortable concluding that every State violated the Constitution for all of the 135 years between the Fourteenth Amendment's ratification and Massachusetts' permitting of same-sex marriages in 2003.[20] They have discovered in the Fourteenth Amendment a "fundamental right" overlooked by every person alive at the time of ratification, and almost everyone else in the time since. They see what lesser legal minds— minds like Thomas Cooley, John Marshall Harlan, Oliver Wendell Holmes, Jr., Learned Hand, Louis Brandeis, William Howard Taft, Benjamin Cardozo, Hugo Black, Felix Frankfurter, Robert Jackson, and Henry Friendly—could not. They are certain that the People ratified the Fourteenth Amendment to bestow on them the power to remove questions from the democratic process when that is called for by their "reasoned judgment." These Justices *know* that limiting marriage to one man and one woman is contrary to reason; they *know* that an institution as old as government itself, and accepted by every nation in history until 15 years ago,[21] cannot possibly be supported by anything other than ignorance or bigotry. And they are willing to say that any citizen who does not agree with that, who adheres to what was, until 15 years ago, the unanimous judgment of all generations and all societies, stands against the Constitution.

The opinion is couched in a style that is as pretentious as its content is egotistic. It is one thing for separate concurring or dissenting opinions to contain extravagances, even silly extravagances, of thought and expression; it is something else for the official opinion of the Court to do so.[22] Of course the opinion's showy profundities are often profoundly incoherent. "The nature of marriage is that, through its enduring bond, two persons together can find other freedoms, such as expression, intimacy, and spirituality."[23] (Really? Who ever thought that intimacy and spirituality [whatever that means] were freedoms? And if intimacy is, one would think Freedom of Intimacy is abridged rather than expanded by marriage. Ask the nearest hippie. Expression, sure enough, *is* a freedom, but anyone in a long-lasting marriage will attest that that happy state constricts, rather than expands, what one can prudently say.) Rights, we are told, can "rise ... from a better informed understanding of how constitutional imperatives define a liberty that remains urgent in our own era."[24] (Huh? How can a better

---

20 *Goodridge* v. *Department of Public Health*, 440 Mass. 309, 798 N. E. 2d 941 (2003).

21 *Windsor*, 570 U. S., at _ (ALITO, J., dissenting) (slip op., at 7).

22 If, even as the price to be paid for a fifth vote, I ever joined an opinion for the Court that began: "The Constitution promises liberty to all within its reach, a liberty that includes certain specific rights that allow persons, within a lawful realm, to define and express their identity," I would hide my head in a bag. The Supreme Court of the United States hag descended from the disciplined legal reasoning of John Marshall and Joseph Story to the mystical aphorisms of the fortune cookie.

23 *Ante*, at 13.

24 *Ante*, at 19.

informed understanding of how constitutional imperatives [whatever that means] define [whatever that means] an urgent liberty [never mind], give birth to a right?) And we are told that, "[i]n any particular case," either the Equal Protection or Due Process Clause "may be thought to capture the essence of [a] right in a more accurate and comprehensive way," than the other, "even as the two Clauses may converge in the identification and definition of the right."[25] (What say? What possible "essence" does substantive due process "capture" in an "accurate and comprehensive way"? It stands for nothing whatever, except those freedoms and entitlements that this Court *really* likes. And the Equal Protection Clause, as employed today, identifies nothing except a difference in treatment that this Court *really* dislikes. Hardly a distillation of essence. If the opinion is correct that the two clauses "converge in the identification and definition of [a] right," that is only because the majority's likes and dislikes are predictably compatible.) I could go on. The world does not expect logic and precision in poetry or inspirational pop- philosophy; it demands them in the law. The stuff contained in today's opinion has to diminish this Court's reputation for clear thinking and sober analysis.

* * *

Hubris is sometimes defined as o'erweening pride; and pride, we know, goeth before a fall. The Judiciary is the "least dangerous" of the federal branches because it has "neither Force nor Will, but merely judgment; and must ultimately depend upon the aid of the executive arm" and the States, "even for the efficacy of its judgments."[26] With each decision of ours that takes from the People a question properly left to them—with each decision that is unabashedly based not on law, but on the "reasoned judgment" of a bare majority of this Court—we move one step closer to being reminded of our impotence.

---

25   *Ibid.*
26   The Federalist No. 78, pp. 522, 523 (J. Cooke ed. 1961) (A. Hamilton).

3. Dispute Resolution in Action
Cases of Contested Political Succession Here and Abroad

ADDITIONAL RECOMMENDED MATERIAL:

Frontline: Law and Disorder (2010) (a documentary on police shootings in the chaotic aftermath of Hurricane Katrina)

The Votes That Counted. Howard Gillman (University of Chicago Press 2001)

Decision '04

John Trever

John Trever, "Decision '04," The Albuquerque Journal. Copyright © 2004 by John Trever. Reprinted with permission.

United States v. Nixon
(No. 73-1766)

BURGER, C.J., Opinion of the Court
SUPREME COURT OF THE UNITED STATES

418 U.S. 683 United States v. Nixon
CERTIORARI BEFORE JUDGMENT TO THE UNITED STATES COURT OF
APPEALS FOR THE DISTRICT OF COLUMBIA CIRCUIT

No. 73–1766 Argued: July 8, 1974—Decided: July 24, 1974 [*]

Mr. Chief Justice Burger delivered the opinion of the Court.

This litigation presents for review the denial of a motion, filed in the District Court on behalf of the President of the United States, in the case of United States v. Mitchell (D.C.Crim. No. 7110), to quash a third-party subpoena *duces tecum* issued by the United States District Court for the District of Columbia, pursuant to Fed.Rule Crim.Proc. 17(c). The subpoena directed the President to produce certain tape recordings and documents relating to his conversations with aides and advisers. The court rejected the President's claims of absolute executive privilege, of lack of jurisdiction, and of failure to satisfy the requirements of Rule 17(c). The President appealed to the Court of Appeals. We granted both the United States' petition for certiorari before judgment (No. 7 1766),1 and also the President's cross-petition for certiorari [p687] before judgment (No. 73-1834),2 because of the public importance of the issues presented and the need for their prompt resolution. 417 U.S. 927 and 960 (1974).

On March 1, 1974, a grand jury of the United States District Court for the District of Columbia returned an indictment charging seven named individuals with various offenses, including conspiracy to defraud the United States and to obstruct justice. Although he was

Copyright in the Public Domain.

not designated as such in the indictment, the grand jury named the President, among others, as an unindicted coconspirator.[4] On April 18, 1974, upon motion of the Special [p688] Prosecutor, see n. 8, *infra*, a subpoena *duces tecum* was issued pursuant to Rule 17(c) to the President by the United States District Court and made returnable on May 2, 1974. This subpoena required the production, in advance of the September 9 trial date, of certain tapes, memoranda, papers, transcripts, or other writings relating to certain precisely identified meetings between the President and others.[5] The Special Prosecutor was able to fix the time, place, and persons present at these discussions because the White House daily logs and appointment records had been delivered to him. On April 30, the President publicly released edited transcripts of 43 conversations; portions of 20 conversations subject to subpoena in the present case were included. On May 1, 1974, the President's counsel filed a "special appearance" and a motion to quash the subpoena under Rule 17(c). This motion was accompanied by a formal claim of privilege. At a subsequent hearing,[6] further motions to expunge the grand jury's action naming the President as an unindicted coconspirator and for protective orders against the disclosure of that information were filed or raised orally by counsel for the President.

On May 20, 1974, the District Court denied the motion to quash and the motions to expunge and for protective orders. 377 F.Supp. 1326. It further ordered "the President or any subordinate officer, official, or employee with custody or control of the documents or [p689] objects subpoenaed," *id.* at 1331, to deliver to the District Court, on or before May 31, 1974, the originals of all subpoenaed items, as well as an index and analysis of those items, together with tape copies of those portions of the subpoenaed recordings for which transcripts had been released to the public by the President on April 30. The District Court rejected jurisdictional challenges based on a contention that the dispute was nonjusticiable because it was between the Special Prosecutor and the Chief Executive and hence "intra-executive" in character; it also rejected the contention that the Judiciary was without authority to review an assertion of executive privilege by the President. The court's rejection of the first challenge was based on the authority and powers vested in the Special Prosecutor by the regulation promulgated by the Attorney General; the court concluded that a justiciable controversy was presented. The second challenge was held to be foreclosed by the decision in *Nixon v. Sirica*, 159 U.S.App.D.C. 58, 487 F.2d 700 (1973).

The District Court held that the judiciary, not the President, was the final arbiter of a claim of executive privilege. The court concluded that, under the circumstances of this case, the presumptive privilege was overcome by the Special Prosecutor's *prima facie* "demonstration of need sufficiently compelling to warrant judicial examination in chambers. ... " 377 F.Supp. at 1330. The court held, finally, that the Special Prosecutor had satisfied the requirements of Rule 17(c). The District Court stayed its order pending appellate review on condition that review was sought before 4 p.m., May 24. The court further provided that matters filed under seal remain under seal when transmitted as part of the record.

On May 24, 1974, the President filed a timely notice of appeal from the District Court order, and the certified record from the District Court was docketed in the United [p690]

States Court of Appeals for the District of Columbia Circuit. On the same day, the President also filed a petition for writ of mandamus in the Court of Appeals seeking review of the District Court order.

Later on May 24, the Special Prosecutor also filed, in this Court, a petition for a writ of certiorari before judgment. On May 31, the petition was granted with an expedited briefing schedule. 417 U.S. 927. On June 6, the President filed, under seal, a cross-petition for writ of certiorari before judgment. This cross-petition was granted June 1, 1974, 417 U.S. 960, and the case was set for argument on July 8, 1974.

JURISDICTION

The threshold question presented is whether the May 20, 1974, order of the District Court was an appealable order and whether this case was properly "in" the Court of Appeals when the petition for certiorari was filed in this Cort. 28 U.S.C. § 1254. The Court of Appeals' jurisdiction under 28 U.S.C. § 1291 encompasses only "final decisions of the district courts." Since the appeal as timely filed and all other procedural requirements were met, the petition is properly before this Court for consideration if the District Court order was final. 28 U.S.C. §§ 1254(1), 2101(e).

The finality requirement of 28 U.S.C. § 1291 embodies a strong congressional policy against piecemeal reviews, and against obstructing or impeding an ongoing judicial proceeding by interlocutory appeals. *See,* e.g., *Cobbledick v. United States,* 309 U.S. 323, 324-326 (1940). This requirement ordinarily promotes judicial efficiency and hastens the ultimate termination of litigation. In applying this principle to an order denying a motion to quash and requiring the production of evidence pursuant [p691] to a subpoena *duces tecum,* it has been repeatedly held that the order is not final, and hence not appealable. *United States v. Ryan,* 402 U.S. 530, 532 (1971); *Cobbledick v. United States, supra; Alexander v. United States,* 201 U.S. 117 (1906). This Court has

> consistently held that the necessity for expedition in the administration of the criminal law justifies putting one who seeks to resist the production of desired information to a choice between compliance with a trial court's order to produce prior to any review of that order, and resistance to that order with the concomitant possibility of an adjudication of contempt if his claims are rejected on appeal.

United States v. Ryan, supra, at 533.

The requirement of submitting to contempt, however, is not without exception, and in some instances the purposes underlying the finality rule require a different result. For example, in *Perlman v. United States,* 247 U.S. 7 (1918), a subpoena had been directed to a third party requesting certain exhibits; the appellant, who owned the exhibits, sought to raise a claim of privilege. The Court held an order compelling production was appealable because it was unlikely that the third party would risk a contempt citation in order to allow immediate review of the appellant's claim of privilege. *Id.* at 12-13. That case fell within the "limited class of cases where denial of immediate review would render impossible any review whatsoever of an individual's claims." *United States v. Ryan, supra*, at 533.

Here too, the traditional contempt avenue to immediate appeal is peculiarly inappropriate due to the unique setting in which the question arises. To require a President of the United States to place himself in the posture of disobeying an order of a court merely to trigger the procedural mechanism for review of the ruling would be [p692] unseemly, and would present an unnecessary occasion for constitutional confrontation between two branches of the Government. Similarly, a federal judge should not be placed in the posture of issuing a citation to a President simply in order to invoke review. The issue whether a President can be cited for contempt could itself engender protracted litigation, and would further delay both review on the merits of his claim of privilege and the ultimate termination of the underlying criminal action for which his evidence is sought. These considerations lead us to conclude that the order of the District Court was an appealable order. The appeal from that order was therefore properly "in" the Court of Appeals, and the case is now properly before this Court on the writ of certiorari before judgment. 28 U.S.C. § 1254; 28 U.S.C. § 2101(e). *Gay v. Ruff*, 292 U.S. 25, 30 (1934).[7]

JUSTICIABILITY

In the District Court, the President's counsel argued that the court lacked jurisdiction to issue the subpoena because the matter was an intra-branch dispute between a subordinate and superior officer of the Executive Branch, and hence not subject to judicial resolution. That argument has been renewed in this Court with emphasis on the contention that the dispute does not present a "case" or "controversy" which can be adjudicated in the federal courts. The President's counsel argues that the federal courts should not intrude into areas committed to the other branches of Government. [p693] He views the present dispute as essentially a "jurisdictional" dispute within the Executive Branch which he analogizes to a dispute between two congressional committees. Since the Executive Branch has exclusive authority and absolute discretion to decide whether to prosecute a case, *Confiscation Cases, 1* Wall. 454 (1869); *United States* v. *Cox*, 342 F.2d 167, 171 (CAS), *cert denied sub nom. Cox v. Hauber*, 381 U.S. 935 (1965), it is contended that a President's decision is final in determining what evidence is to be used in a given criminal case. Although his counsel concedes that the President ha delegated certain specific powers to the Special Prosecutor, he has not

> waived nor delegated to the Special Prosecutor the President's duty to claim privilege as to all materials ... which fall within the President's inherent authority to refuse to disclose to any executive officer.

Brief for the President 42. The Special Prosecutor's demand for the items therefore presents, in the view of the President's counsel, a political question under *Baker v. Carr*, 369 U.S. 186 (1962), since it involves a "textually demonstrable" grant of power under Art. II.

The mere assertion of a claim of an "intra-branch dispute," without more, has never operated to defeat federal jurisdiction; justiciability does not depend on such a surface inquiry. In *United States v. ICC*, 337 U.S. 426 (1949), the Court observed, "courts must look behind names that symbolize the parties to determine whether a justiciable case or controversy is presented." Id. at 430. *See also Powell v. McCormack*, 395 U.S. 486 (1969); *ICC v. Jersey City*, 322 U.S. 503 (1944); *United States ex rel. Chapman v. FPC*, 345 U.S. 153 (1953); *Secretary of Agriculture v. United States*, 347 U.S. 645 (1954); *FMB v. Isbrandtsen Co.*, 356 U.S. 481, 483 n. 2 (1958); *United States v. Marine Bancorporation, ante*, p. 602; and *United States v. Connecticut National Bank, ante*, p. 656. [p694]

Our starting point is the nature of the proceeding for which the evidence is sought - here, a pending criminal prosecution. It is a judicial proceeding in a federal court alleging violation of federal laws, and is brought in the name of the United States as sovereign. *Berger v. United States*, 295 U.S. 78, 88 (1935). Under the authority of Art. II, § 2, Congress has vested in the Attorney General the power to conduct the criminal litigation of the United States Government. 28 U.S.C. § 516. It has also vested in him the power to appoint subordinate officers to assist him in the discharge of his duties. 28 U.S.C. §§ 509 510, 515, 533. Acting pursuant to those statutes, the Attorney General has delegated the authority to represent the United States in these particular matters to a Special Prosecutor with unique authority and tenure.[8] The regulation gives the [p695] Special Prosecutor explicit power to contest the invocation of executive privilege in the process of seeking evidence deemed relevant to the performance of these specially delegated duties.[9] 38 Fed.Reg. 30739, as amended by 38 Fed.Reg. 32805.

So long as this regulation is extant, it has the force of law. In *United States ex rel. Accardi v. Shaughnessy*, 347 U.S. 260 (1954), regulations of the Attorney General delegated certain of his discretionary powers to the Board [p696] of Immigration Appeals and required that Board to exercise its own discretion on appeals in deportation cases. The Court held that, so long as the Attorney General's regulations remained operative, he denied himself the authority to exercise the discretion delegated to the Board even though the original authority was his and he could reassert it by amending the regulations. *Service v. Dulles*, 354 U.S. 363, 388 (1957), and *Vitarelli v. Seaton*, 359 U.S. 535 (1959), reaffirmed the basic holding of *Accardi*.

Here, as in *Accardi*, it is theoretically possible for the Attorney General to amend or revoke the regulation defining the Special Prosecutor's authority. But he has not done so.[10] So long as this regulation remains in force, the Executive Branch is bound by it, and indeed the United States, as the sovereign composed of the three branches, is bound to respect and to enforce it. Moreover, the delegation of authority to the Special Prosecutor in this case is not an ordinary delegation by the Attorney General to a subordinate officer: with the authorization of the President, the Acting Attorney General provided in the regulation that the Special

Prosecutor was not to be removed without the "consensus" of eight designated leaders of Congress. N. 8, *supra*.

The demands of and the resistance to the subpoena present an obvious controversy in the ordinary sense, but that alone is not sufficient to meet constitutional standards. In the constitutional sense, controversy means more than disagreement and conflict; rather it means the kind of controversy courts traditionally resolve. Here [p697] at issue is the production or nonproduction of specified evidence deemed by the Special Prosecutor to be relevant and admissible in a pending criminal case. It is sought by one official of the Executive Branch within the scope of his express authority; it is resisted by the Chief

Executive on the ground of his duty to preserve the confidentiality of the communications of the President. Whatever the correct answer on the merits, these issues are "of a type which are traditionally justiciable." *United States v. ICC*, 337 U.S. at 430. The independent Special Prosecutor, with his asserted need for the subpoenaed material in the underlying criminal prosecution, is opposed by the President, with his steadfast assertion of privilege against disclosure of the material. This setting assures there is

> that concrete adverseness which sharpens the presentation of issues upon which
> the court so largely depends for illumination of difficult constitutional questions.

Baker v. Carr, 369 U.S. at 204. Moreover, since the matter is one arising in the regular course of a federal criminal prosecution, it is within the traditional scope of Art. III power. *Id.* at 198.

In light of the uniqueness of the setting in which the conflict arises, the fact that both parties are officer of the Executive Branch cannot be viewed as a barrier to justiciability. It would be inconsistent with the applicable law and regulation, and the unique facts of this case, to conclude other than that the Special Prosecutor has standing to bring this action, and that a justiciable controversy is presented for decision.

RULE 17(C)

The subpoena *duces tecum* is challenged on the ground that the Special Prosecutor failed to satisfy the requirements of Fed.Rule Crim.Proc. 17(c), which governs [p698] the issuance of subpoenas *duces tecum* in federal criminal proceedings. If we sustained this challenge, there would be no occasion to reach the claim of privilege asserted with respect to the subpoenaed material. Thus, we turn to the question whether the requirements of Rule 17(c) have been satisfied. *See Arkansas Louisiana Gas Co. v. Dept. of Public Utilities*, 304 U.S. 61, 64 (1938); *Ashwander v. TVA*, 297 U.S. 288, 346-347 (1936) (Brandeis, J., concurring).

Rule 17(c) provides:

A subpoena may also command the person to whom it is directed to produce the books, papers, documents or other objects designated therein. The court on motion made promptly may quash or modify the subpoena if compliance would be unreasonable or oppressive. The court may direct that books, papers, documents or objects designated in the subpoena be produced before the court at a time prior to the trial or prior to the time when they are to be offered in evidence and may upon their production permit the books, papers, documents or objects or portions thereof to be inspected by the parties and their attorneys.

A subpoena for documents may be quashed if their production would be "unreasonable or oppressive," but not otherwise. The leading case in this Court interpreting this standard is *Bowman Dairy Co. v. United States*, <u>341 U.S. 214</u> (1951). This case recognized certain fundamental characteristics of the subpoena *duces tecum* in criminal cases: (1) it was not intended to provide a means of discovery for criminal cases, id. at 220; (2) its chief innovation was to expedite the trial by providing a time and place before trial for the inspection of [p699] subpoenaed materials,[11] *ibid*. As both parties agree, cases decided in the wake of *Bowman* have generally followed Judge Weinfeld's formulation in *United States v. Iozia*, 13 F.R.D. 335, 338 (SDNY 1952), as to the required showing. Under this test, in order to require production prior to trial, the moving party must show: (1) that the documents are evidentiary[12] and relevant; (2) that they are not otherwise procurable reasonably in advance of trial by exercise of due diligence; (3) that the party cannot properly prepare for trial without such production and inspection in advance of trial, and that the failure to obtain such inspection may tend unreasonably to delay the trial; and (4) that [p700] the application is made in good faith and is not intended as a general "fishing expedition."

Against this background, the Special Prosecutor, in order to carry his burden, must clear three hurdles: (1) relevancy; (2) admissibility; (3) specificity. Our own review of the record necessarily affords a less comprehensive view of the total situation than was available to the trial judge, and we are unwilling to conclude that the District Court erred in the evaluation of the Special Prosecutor's showing under Rule 17(c). Our conclusion is based on the record before us, much of which is under seal. Of course, the contents of the subpoenaed tapes could not at that stage be described fully by the Special Prosecutor, but there was a sufficient likelihood that each of the tapes contains conversations relevant to the offenses charged in the indictment. *United States v. Gross*, 24 F.R.D. 138 (SDNY 1959). With respect to many of the tapes, the Special Prosecutor offered the sworn testimony or statements of one or more of the participants in the conversations as to what was said at the time. As for the remainder of the tapes, the identity of the participants and the time and place of the conversations, taken in their total context, permit a rational inference that at least part of the conversations relate to the offenses charged in the indictment.

We also conclude there was a sufficient preliminary showing that each of the subpoenaed tapes contains evidence admissible with respect to the offenses charged in the indictment. The most cogent objection to the admissibility of the taped conversations here at issue is that they are a collection of out-of-court statements by declarants who will not be subject to cross-examination, and that the statements are therefore inadmissible hearsay. Here, however, most of the tapes apparently contain conversations [p701] to which one or more of the defendant named in the indictment were party. The hearsay rule does not automatically bar all out-of-court statements by a defendant in a criminal case.[13] Declarations by one defendant may also be admissible against other defendant upon a sufficient showing, by independent evidence,14 of a conspiracy among one or more other defendants and the declarant and if the declarations at issue were in furtherance of that conspiracy. The same is true of declarations of coconspirators who are not defendants in the case on trial. *Button v. Evans*, 400 U.S. 74, 81 (1970). Recorded conversations may also be admissible for the limited purpose of impeaching the credibility of any defendant who testifies or any other coconspirator who testifies. Generally, the need for evidence to impeach witnesses is insufficient to require its production in advance of trial. *See, e.g., United States v. Carter*, 15 F.R.D. 367, [p702] 371 (DC 1954). Here, however, there are other valid potential evidentiary uses for the same material, and the analysis and possible transcription of the tapes may take a significant period of time. Accordingly, we cannot conclude that the District Court erred in authorizing the issuance of the subpoena *duces tecum*.

Enforcement of a pretrial subpoena *duces tecum* must necessarily be committed to the sound discretion of the trial court, since the necessity for the subpoena most often turns upon a determination of factual issues. Without a determination of arbitrariness or that the trial court finding was without record support, an appellate court will not ordinarily disturb a finding that the applicant for a subpoena complied with Rule 17(c). *See, e.g., Sue v. Chicago Transit Authority*, 279 F.2d 416, 419 (CA7 1960); *Shotkin v. Nelson*, 146 F.2d 402 (CA10 1944).

In a case such as this, however, where a subpoena is directed to a President of the United States, appellate review, in deference to a coordinate branch of Government, should be particularly meticulous to ensure that the standards of Rule 17(c) have been correctly applied. *United States v. Burr*, 25 F.Cas. 30, 34 (No. 14,692d) (CC Va. 1807). From our examination of the materials submitted by the Special Prosecutor to the District Court in support of his motion for the subpoena, we are persuaded that the District Court's denial of the President's motion to quash the subpoena was consistent with Rule 17(c). We also conclude that the Special Prosecutor has made a sufficient showing to justify a subpoena for production before trial. The subpoenaed materials are not available from any other source, and their examination and processing should not await trial in the circumstances shown. *Bowman Dairy Co. v. United States*, 341 U.S. 214 (1951); *United States v. Iozia*, 13 F.R.D. 335 (SDNY 1952). [p703]

THE CLAIM OF PRIVILEGE

A

Having determined that the requirements of Rule 17(c) were satisfied, we turn to the claim that the subpoena should be quashed because it demands "confidential conversations between a President and his close advisors that it would be inconsistent with the public interest to produce." App. 48a. The first contention is a broad claim that the separation of powers doctrine precludes judicial review of a President's claim of privilege. The second contention is that, if he does not prevail on the claim of absolute privilege, the court should hold as a matter of constitutional law that the privilege prevails over the subpoena *duces tecum.*

In the performance of assigned constitutional duties, each branch of the Government must initially interpret the Constitution, and the interpretation of its powers by any branch is due great respect from the others. The President's counsel, as we have noted, reads the Constitution as providing an absolute privilege of confidentiality for all Presidential communications. Many decisions of this Court, however, have unequivocally reaffirmed the holding of *Marbury v. Madison*, 1 Cranch 137 (1803), that "[i]t is emphatically the province and duty of the judicial department to say what the law is." Id. at 177. No holding of the Court has defined the scope of judicial power specifically relating to the enforcement of a subpoena for confidential Presidential communications for use in a criminal prosecution, but other exercises of power by the Executive Branch and the Legislative Branch have been found invalid as in conflict with the Constitution. *Powell v. McCormack*, 395 U.S. 486 (1969); *Youngstown Sheet & Tube Co. v. Sawyer*, 343 U.S. 579 (1952). In a [p704] series of cases, the Court interpreted the explicit immunity conferred by express provisions of the Constitution on Members of the House and Senate by the Speech or Debate Clause, U.S.Const. Art. I, § 6. *Doe v. McMillan*, 412 U.S. 306 (1973); *Gravel v. United States*, 408 U.S. 606 (1972); *United States v. Brewster*, 408 U.S. 501 (1972); *United States v. Johnson* 383 U.S. 169 (1966). Since this Court has consistently exercised the power to construe and delineate claims arising under express powers, it must follow that the Court has authority to interpret claims with respect to powers alleged to derive from enumerated powers.

Our system of government

> requires that federal courts on occasion interpret the Constitution in a manner at variance with the construction given the document by another branch.

Powell v. McCormack, supra, at 549. And in *Baker v. Carr*, 369 U.S. at 211, the Court stated:

> Deciding whether a matter has in any measure been committed by the Constitution to another branch of government, or whether the action of that branch exceeds

whatever authority has been committed, is itself a delicate exercise in constitutional interpretation, and is a responsibility of this Court as ultimate interpreter of the Constitution.

Notwithstanding the deference each branch must accord the others, the "judicial Power of the United States" vested in the federal courts by Art. III, § 1, of the Constitution can no more be shared with the Executive Branch than the Chief Executive, for example, can share with the Judiciary the veto power, or the Congress share with the Judiciary the power to override a Presidential veto. Any other conclusion would be contrary to the basic concept of separation of powers and the checks and balances that flow from the scheme of a tripartite government. The Federalist, No. 47, p. 313 (S. Mittell ed. [p705] 1938). We therefore reaffirm that it is the province and duty of this Court "to say what the law is" with respect to the claim of privilege presented in this case. *Marbury v. Madison, supra* at 177.

B

In support of his claim of absolute privilege, the President's counsel urges two grounds, one of which is common to all governments and one of which is peculiar to our system of separation of powers. The first ground is the valid need for protection of communications between high Government officials and those who advise and assist them in the performance of their manifold duties; the importance of this confidentiality is too plain to require further discussion. Human experience teaches that those who expect public dissemination of their remarks may well temper candor with a concern for appearances and for their own interests to the detriment of the decision-making process.[15] Whatever the nature of the privilege of confidentiality of Presidential communications in the exercise of Art. II powers, the privilege can be said to derive from the supremacy of each branch within its own assigned area of constitutional duties. Certain powers and privileges flow from the nature of enumerated powers;[16] the protection of the confidentiality of [p706] Presidential communications has similar constitutional underpinnings.

The second ground asserted by the President's counsel in support of the claim of absolute privilege rests on the doctrine of separation of powers. Here it is argued that the independence of the Executive Branch within its own sphere, *Humphrey's Executor v. United States*, 295 U.S. 602, 629-630 (1935); *Kilbourn v. Thompson*, 103 U.S. 168, 190-191 (1881), insulates a President from a judicial subpoena in an ongoing criminal prosecution, and thereby protects confidential Presidential communications.

However, neither the doctrine of separation of powers nor the need for confidentiality of high-level communications, without more, can sustain an absolute, unqualified Presidential privilege of immunity from judicial process under all circumstances. The President's need for complete candor and objectivity from advisers calls for great deference from the courts. However, when the privilege depends solely on the broad, undifferentiated claim of public interest in the confidentiality of such conversations, a confrontation with other values arises.

Absent a claim of need to protect military, diplomatic, or sensitive national security secrets, we find it difficult to accept the argument that even the very important interest in confidentiality of Presidential communications is significantly diminished by production of such material for *in camera* inspection with all the protection that a district court will be obliged to provide. [p707]

The impediment that an absolute, unqualified privilege would place in the way of the primary constitutional duty of the Judicial Branch to do justice in criminal prosecutions would plainly conflict with the function of the courts under Art. III. In designing the structure of our Government and dividing and allocating the sovereign power among three co-equal branches, the Framers of the Constitution sought to provide a comprehensive system, but the separate powers were not intended to operate with absolute independence.

> While the Constitution diffuses power the better to secure liberty, it also contemplate that practice will integrate the dispersed powers into a workable government. It enjoins upon its branches separateness but interdependence, autonomy but reciprocity.

Youngstown Sheet & Tube Co. v. Sawyer, 343 U.S. at 635 (Jackson, J., concurring). To read the Art. II powers of the President as providing an absolute privilege as against a subpoena essential to enforcement of criminal statutes on no more than a generalized claim of the public interest in confidentiality of nonmilitary and nondiplomatic discussions would upset the constitutional balance of "a workable government" and gravely impair the role of the courts under Art. III.

C

Since we conclude that the legitimate needs of the judicial process may outweigh Presidential privilege, it is necessary to resolve those competing interests in a manner that preserves the essential functions of each branch. The right and indeed the duty to resolve that question does not free the Judiciary from according high respect to the representations made on behalf of the President. *United States v. Burr,* 25 F.Cas. 187, 190, 191-192 (No. 14,694) (CC Va. 1807). [p708]

The expectation of a President to the confidentiality of his conversations and correspondence, like the claim of confidentiality of judicial deliberations, for example, has all the values to which we accord deference for the privacy of all citizens and, added to those values, is the necessity for protection of the public interest in candid, objective, and even blunt or harsh opinions in Presidential decision-making. A President and those who assist him must be free to explore alternatives in the process of shaping policies and making decisions, and to do so in a way many would be unwilling to express except privately. These are the considerations justifying a presumptive privilege for Presidential communications.

The privilege is fundamental to the operation of Government, and inextricably rooted in the separation of powers under the Constitution.[17] In *Nixon v. Sirica*, 159 U.S.App.D.C. 58, 487 F.2d 700 (1973), the Court of Appeals held that such Presidential communications are "presumptively privileged," *id.* at 75, 487 F.2d at 717, and this position is accepted by both parties in the present litigation. We agree with Mr. Chief Justice Marshall's observation, therefore, that "[i]n no case of his kind would a court be required to proceed against the president as against an ordinary individual." *United States v. Burr*, 25 F.Cas. at 192.

But this presumptive privilege must be considered in light of our historic commitment to the rule of law. This [p709] is nowhere more profoundly manifest than, in our view, that "the twofold aim [of criminal justice] is that guilt shall not escape or innocence suffer." *Berger v. United States*, 295 U.S. at 88. We have elected to employ an adversary system of criminal justice in which the parties contest all issues before a court of law. The need to develop all relevant facts in the adversary system is both fundamental and comprehensive. The ends of criminal justice would be defeated if judgments were to be founded on a partial or speculative presentation of the facts. The very integrity of the judicial system and public confidence in the system depend on full disclosure of all the facts, within the framework of the rules of evidence. To ensure that justice is done, it is imperative to the function of courts that compulsory process be available for the production of evidence needed either by the prosecution or by the defense.

Only recently the Court restated the ancient proposition of law, albeit in the context of a grand jury inquiry, rather than a trial,

> that "the public ... has a right to every man's evidence," except for those persons protected by a constitutional, common law, or statutory privilege, *United States v. Bryan*, 339 U.S. [323, 331 (1950)]; *Blackmer v. United States*, 284 U.S. 421, 438 (1932). ...

Branzburg v. Hayes, 408 U.S. 665, 688 (1972). The privileges referred to by the Court are designed to protect weighty and legitimate competing interests. Thus, the Fifth Amendment to the Constitution provides that no man "shall be compelled in any criminal case to be a witness against himself." And, generally, an attorney or a priest may not be required to disclose what has been revealed in professional confidence. These and other interests are recognized in law by privileges [p710] against forced disclosure, established in the Constitution, by statute, or at common law. Whatever their origins, these exceptions to the demand for every man's evidence are not lightly created nor expansively construed, for they are in derogation of the search for truth.[18]

In this case, the President challenges a subpoena served on him as a third party requiring the production of materials for use in a criminal prosecution; he does so on the claim that he has a privilege against disclosure of confidential communications. He does not place his claim of privilege on the ground they are military or diplomatic secrets. As to these areas of Art. II duties, the courts have traditionally shown the utmost deference to Presidential responsibilities. In C. & S. *Air Lines v. Waterman S.S. Corp.*, <u>333 U.S. 103</u>, 111 (1948), dealing with Presidential authority involving foreign policy considerations, the Court said:

> The President, both as Commander-in-Chief and as the Nation's organ for foreign affairs, has available intelligence services whose reports are not and ought not to be published to the world. It would be intolerable that courts, without the relevant information, should review and perhaps nullify actions of the Executive taken on information properly held secret.

In *United States v. Reynolds*, <u>345 U.S. 1</u> (1953), dealing [p711] with a claimant's demand for evidence in a Tort Claims Act case against the Government, the Court said:

> It may be possible to satisfy the court, from all the circumstances of the case, that there is a reasonable danger that compulsion of the evidence will expose military matters which, in the interest of national security, should not be divulged. When this is the case, the occasion for the privilege is appropriate, and the court should not jeopardize the security which the privilege is meant to protect by insisting upon an examination of the evidence, even by the judge alone, in chambers.

Id. at 10. No case of the Court, however, has extended this high degree of deference to a President's generalized interest in confidentiality. Nowhere in the Constitution, as we have noted earlier, is there any explicit reference to a privilege of confidentiality, yet to the extent this interest relates to the effective discharge of a President's powers, it is constitutionally based.

The right to the production of all evidence at a criminal trial similarly has constitutional dimensions. The <u>Sixth Amendment</u> explicitly confers upon every defendant in a criminal trial the right "to be confronted with the witnesses against him" and "to have compulsory process for obtaining witnesses in his favor." Moreover, the Fifth Amendment also guarantees that no person shall be deprived of liberty without due process of law. It is the manifest duty of the courts to vindicate those guarantees, and to accomplish that it is essential that all relevant and admissible evidence be produced.

In this case, we must weigh the importance of the general privilege of confidentiality of Presidential communications in performance of the President's responsibilities against the inroads of such a privilege on the fair [p712] administration of criminal justice.[19] The interest in preserving confidentiality is weighty indeed, and entitled to great respect. However, we cannot conclude that advisers will be moved to temper the candor of their remarks by the infrequent occasions of disclosure because of the possibility that such conversations will be called for in the context of a criminal prosecution.[20]

On the other hand, the allowance of the privilege to withhold evidence that is demonstrably relevant in a criminal trial would cut deeply into the guarantee of due process of law and gravely impair the basic function of the court. A President's acknowledged need for confidentiality [p713] in the communications of his office is general in nature, whereas the constitutional need for production of relevant evidence in a criminal proceeding is specific and central to the fair adjudication of a particular criminal case in the administration of justice. Without access to specific facts, a criminal prosecution may be totally frustrated. The President's broad interest in confidentiality of communications will not be vitiated by disclosure of a limited number of conversations preliminarily shown to have some bearing on the pending criminal cases.

We conclude that, when the ground for asserting privilege as to subpoenaed materials sought for use in a criminal trial is based only on the generalized interest in confidentiality, it cannot prevail over the fundamental demands of due process of law in the fair administration of criminal justice. The generalized assertion of privilege must yield to the demonstrated, specific need for evidence in a pending criminal trial.

D

We have earlier determined that the District Court did not err in authorizing the issuance of the subpoena. If a President concludes that compliance with a subpoena would be injurious to the public interest, he may properly, as was done here, invoke a claim of privilege on the return of the subpoena. Upon receiving a claim of privilege from the Chief Executive, it became the further duty of the District Court to treat the subpoenaed material as presumptively privileged and to require the Special Prosecutor to demonstrate that the Presidential material was "essential to the justice of the [pending criminal] case." *United States v. Burr*, 25 FXas. at 192. Here, the District Court treated the material as presumptively privileged, proceeded to find that the Special [p714] Prosecutor had made a sufficient showing to rebut the presumption, and ordered an *in camera* examination of the subpoenaed material. On the basis of our examination of the record, we are unable to conclude that the District Court erred in ordering the inspection. Accordingly, we affirm the order of the District Court that subpoenaed materials be transmitted to that court. We now turn to the important question of the District Court's responsibilities in conducting the *in camera* examination of Presidential materials or communications delivered under the compulsion of the subpoena *duces tecum*.

E

Enforcement of the subpoena *duces tecum* was stayed pending this Court's resolution of the issues raised by the petitions for certiorari. Those issues now having been disposed of, the matter of implementation will rest with the District Court.

> [T]he guard, furnished to [the President] to protect him from being harassed by vexatious and unnecessary subpoenas, is to be looked for in the conduct of a [district] court after those subpoenas have issued; not in any circumstance which is to precede their being issued.

United States v. Burr, 25 F.Cas. at 34. Statements that meet the test of admissibility and relevance must be isolated; all other material must be excised. At this stage, the District Court is not limited to representations of the Special Prosecutor as to the evidence sought by the subpoena; the material will be available to the District Court. It is elementary that *in camera* inspection of evidence is always a procedure calling for scrupulous protection against any release or publication of material not found by the court, at that stage, probably admissible in evidence and relevant to the issues of the trial for which it is sought. That being true of an ordinary situation, it is obvious that the District Court has [p715] a very heavy responsibility to see to it that Presidential conversations, which are either not relevant or not admissible, are accorded that high degree of respect due the President of the United States. Mr. Chief Justice Marshall, sitting as a trial judge in the *Burr* case, *supra*, was extraordinarily careful to point out that

> [i]n no case of this kind would a court be required to proceed against the president as against an ordinary individual.

25 F.Cas. at 192. Marshall's statement cannot be read to mean in any sense that a President is above the law, but relates to the singularly unique role under Art. II of a President's communications and activities, related to the performance of duties under that Article. Moreover, a President's communications and activities encompass a vastly wider range of sensitive material than would be true of any "ordinary individual." It is therefore necessary[21] in the public interest to afford Presidential confidentiality the greatest protection consistent with the fair administration of justice. The need for confidentiality even as to idle conversations with associates in which casual reference might be made concerning political leaders within the country or foreign statesmen is too obvious to call for further treatment. We have no doubt that the District Judge will at all times accord to Presidential records that high degree of deference suggested in *United States v. Burr, supra*, and will discharge his responsibility to see to [p716] it that, until released to the Special Prosecutor, no *in camera* material is revealed to anyone. This burden applies with even greater force to excised material; once the decision is made to excise, the material is restored to its privileged status, and should be returned under seal to its lawful custodian.

Since this matter came before the Court during the pendency of a criminal prosecution, and on representations that time is of the essence, the mandate shall issue forthwith.

Affirmed.

MR. JUSTICE REHNQUIST took no part in the consideration or decision of these cases.

Together with No. 73-1834, Nixon, President of the United States v. United States, also on certiorari before judgment to the same court.

NOTES

1. See 28 U.S.C. §§ 1254(1) and 2101(e) and our Rule 20. See, e.g., *Youngstown Sheet & Tube Co. v. Sawyer*, 343 U.S. 579 (1952); *United States v. United Mine Workers*, 330 U.S. 258 (1947); *Carter v. Carter Coal Co*, 298 U.S. 238 (1936); *Rickert Rice Mills v. Fontenot*, 297 U.S. 110 (1936); *Railroad Retirement Board v. Alton R. Co.*, 295 U.S. 330 (1935); *Norman v. Baltimore & Ohio R. Co*, 294 U.S. 240 (1935)

2. The cross-petition in No. 73-1824 raised the issue whether the grand jury acted within its authority in naming the President as an unindicted coconspirator. Since we find resolution of this issue unnecessary to resolution of the question whether the claim of privilege is to prevail, the cross-petition for certiorari is dismissed as improvidently granted and the remainder of this opinion is concerned with the issues raised in No. 73-1766. On June 19, 1974, the President's counsel moved for disclosure and transmittal to this Court of all evidence presented to the grand jury relating to its action in naming the President as an unindicted coconspirator. Action on this motion was deferred pending oral argument of the case, and is now denied.

3. The seven defendants were John N. Mitchell, H. R. Haldeman, John D. Ehrlichman, Charles W. Colson, Robert C. Mardian, Kenneth W. Parkinson, and Gordon Strachan. Each has occupied either a position of responsibility on the White House Staff or a position with the Committee for the Re-election of the President. Colson entered a guilty plea on another charge, and is no longer a defendant.

4. The President entered a special appearance in the District Court on June 6 and requested that court to lift its protective order regarding the naming of certain individuals as coconspirators and to any additional extent deemed appropriate by the Court. This motion of the President was based on the ground that the disclosures to the news media made the reasons for continuance of the protective order no longer meaningful. On June 7, the District Court removed its protective order and, on June 10, counsel for both parties jointly moved this Court to unseal those parts of the record which related to the action of the grand jury regarding the President. After receiving a statement in opposition from the defendants, this Court denied that motion on June 15, 1974, except for the grand jury's immediate finding relating to the status of the President as an unindicted coconspirator. 417 U.S. 960.

5. The specific meetings and conversations are enumerated in a schedule attached to the subpoena. App. 42a-46a.

6. At the joint suggestion of the Special Prosecutor and counsel for the President, and with the approval of counsel for the defendants, further proceedings in the District Court were held in camera.

7. The parties have suggested that this Court has jurisdiction on other grounds. In view of our conclusion that there is jurisdiction under 28 U.S.C. § 1254(1) because the District Court's order was appealable, we need not decide whether other jurisdictional vehicles are available.

8. The regulation issued by the Attorney General pursuant to his statutory authority vests in the Special Prosecutor plenary authority to control the course of investigations and litigation related to

> all offenses arising out of the 1972 Presidential Election for which the Special Prosecutor deems it necessary and appropriate to assume responsibility,

allegations involving the President, members of the White House staff, or Presidential appointees, and any other matters which he consents to have assigned to him by the Attorney General.

38 Fed.Reg. 30739, as amended by 38 Fed.Reg. 32805. In particular, the Special Prosecutor was given full authority, *inter alia*, "to contest the assertion of 'Executive Privilege'... and handl[e] all aspects of any cases within his jurisdiction." *Id.* at 30739. The regulation then goes on to provide:

> In exercising this authority, the Special Prosecutor will have the greatest degree of independence that is consistent with the Attorney General's statutory accountability for all matters falling within the jurisdiction of the Department of Justice. The Attorney General will not countermand or interfere with the Special Prosecutor's decisions or actions. The Special Prosecutor will determine whether and to what extent he will inform or consult with the Attorney General about the conduct of his duties and responsibilities. In accordance with assurances given by the President to the Attorney General that the President will not exercise his Constitutional powers to effect the discharge of the Special Prosecutor or to limit the independence that he is hereby given, the Special Prosecutor will not be removed from his duties except for extraordinary improprieties on his part and without the President's first consulting the Majority and the Minority Leaders and Chairmen and ranking Minority Members of the Judiciary Committees of the Senate and House of Representatives and ascertaining that their consensus is in accord with his proposed action.

9. That this was the understanding of Acting Attorney General Robert Bork, the author of the regulation establishing the independence of the Special Prosecutor, is shown by his testimony before the Senate Judiciary Committee:

> Although it is anticipated that Mr. Jaworski will receive cooperation from the White House in getting any evidence he feels he needs to conduct investigations and prosecutions, it is clear and understood on all sides that he has the power to use judicial processes to pursue evidence if disagreement should develop.

Hearings on the Special Prosecutor before the Senate Committee on the Judiciary, 93d Cong., 1st Sess., pt. 2, p. 450 (1973). Acting Attorney General Bork gave similar assurances to the House Subcommittee on Criminal Justice. Hearings on H. J Res. 784 and H.R. 10937 before the Subcommittee on Criminal Justice of the House Committee on the Judiciary, 93d Cong., 1st Sess., 266 (1973). At his confirmation hearings, Attorney General William Saxbe testified that he shared Acting Attorney General Bork's views concerning the Special Prosecutor's authority to test any claim of executive privilege in the courts. Hearings on the Nomination of William B. Saxbe to be Attorney General before the Senate Committee on the Judiciary, 93d Cong., 1st Sess., 9 (1973).

10. At his confirmation hearings, Attorney General William Saxbe testified that he agreed with the regulation adopted by Acting Attorney General Bork, and would not remove the Special Prosecutor except for "gross impropriety." Id. at 5-6, 8-10. There is no contention here that the Special Prosecutor is guilty of any such impropriety.

11. The Court quoted a statement of a member of the advisory committee that the purpose of the Rule was to bring documents into court

> in advance of the time that they are offered in evidence, so that they may then be inspected in advance, for the purpose ... of enabling the party to see whether he can use [them] or whether he wants to use [them].

341 U.S. at 220 n. 5. The Manual for Complex and Multidistrict Litigation published by the Federal Judicial Center recommends that use of Rule 17(c) be encouraged in complex criminal cases in order that each party may be compelled to produce its documentary evidence well in advance of trial and in advance of the time it is to be offered. P. 150.

12. The District Court found here that it was faced with

> the more unusual situation ... where the subpoena, rather than being directed to the government by defendants, issues to what, as a practical matter, is a third party.

United States v. Mitchell, 377 F.Supp. 1326, 1330 (DC 1974). The Special Prosecutor suggests that the evidentiary requirement of *Bowman Dairy Co.* and *Iozia* does not apply in its full vigor when the subpoena *duces tecum* is issued to third parties, rather than to government prosecutors. Brief for United States 128-129. We need not decide whether a lower standard exists, because we are satisfied that the relevance and evidentiary nature of the subpoenaed tapes were sufficiently shown as a preliminary matter to warrant the District Court's refusal to quash the subpoena.

13. Such statements are declarations by a party defendant that "would surmount all objections based on the hearsay rule ..." and, at least as to the declarant himself, "would be admissible for whatever inferences" might be reasonably drawn. *United States v. Matlock*, 415 U.S. 164, 172 (1974). On *Lee v. United States*, 343 U.S. 747, 757 (1952). See also C. McCormick, Evidence § 270, pp. 651-652 (2d ed.1972).

14. As a preliminary matter, there must be substantial, independent evidence of the conspiracy, at least enough to take the question to the jury. *United States v. Vaught*, 485 F.2d 320, 323 (CA4 1973); *United States v. Hoffa*, 349 F.2d 20, 412 (CA6 1965), affd on other grounds, 385 U.S. 293 (1966); *United States v. Santos*, 385 F.2d 43, 45 (CA7 1967), cert, denied, 390 U.S. 954 (1968); *United States v. Morton*, 483 F.2d 573, 576 (CA8 1973); United States v. Spanos, 462 F.2d 1012, 1014 (CA9 1972); *Carbo v. United States*, 314 F.2d 718, 737 (CA9 1963), cert, denied, 377 U.S. 953 (1964). Whether the standard has been satisfied is a question of admissibility of evidence to be decided by the trial judge.

15. There is nothing novel about governmental confidentiality. The meetings of the Constitutional Convention in 1787 were conducted in complete privacy. 1 M. Farrand, The Records of the Federal Convention of 1787, pp. xi-xxv (1911). Moreover, all records of those meetings were sealed for more than 30 years after the Convention. See 3 Stat. 475, 15th Cong., 1st Sess., Res. 8 (1818). Most of the Framers acknowledged that,

without secrecy, no constitution of the kind that was developed could have been written. C. Warren, The Making of the Constitution 134-139 (1937).

16. The Special Prosecutor argues that there is no provision in the Constitution for a Presidential privilege as to the President's communications corresponding to the privilege of Members of Congress under the Speech or Debate Clause. But the silence of the Constitution on this score is not dispositive.

> The rule of constitutional interpretation announced in *McCulloch v. Maryland*, 4 Wheat. 316, that that which was reasonably appropriate and relevant to the exercise of a granted power was to be considered as accompanying the grant, has been so universally applied that it suffices merely to state it.

Marshall v. Gordon, 243 U.S. 521, 537 (1917).

17. Freedom of communication vital to fulfillment of the aims of wholesome relationships is obtained only by removing the specter of compelled disclosure ... [Government ... needs open but protected channels for the kind of plain talk that is essential to the quality of its functioning.
Carl Zeiss Stiftung v. v. E. B. Carl Zeis, Jena, 4 F.R.D. 318, 325 (DC 1966). *See Nixon v. Sirica*, 159 U.S.App.D.C. 58, 71, 487 F.2d 700, 713 (1973); *Kaiser Aluminum & Chem. Corp. v. United States*, 141 Ct.Cl. 38, 157 F.Supp. 939 (1958) (Reed, J.); The Federalist, No. 64 (S. Mittell ed.1938).

18. Because of the key role of the testimony of witnesses in the judicial process, courts have historically been cautious about privileges. Mr. Justice Frankfurter, dissenting in *Elkins v. United States*, 364 U.S. 206, 234 (1960), said of this:

> Limitations are properly placed upon the operation of this general principle only to the very limited extent that permitting a refusal to testify or excluding relevant evidence has a public good transcending the normally predominant principle of utilizing all rational means for ascertaining truth.

19. We are not here concerned with the balance between the President's generalized interest in confidentiality and the need for relevant evidence in civil litigation, nor with that between the confidentiality interest and congressional demands for information, nor with the President's interest in preserving state secrets. We address only the conflict between the President's assertion of a generalized privilege of confidentiality and the constitutional need for relevant evidence in criminal trials.

20. Mr. Justice Cardozo made this point in an analogous context. Speaking for a unanimous Court in *Clark v. United States*, 289 U.S. 1 (1933), he emphasized the importance of maintaining the secrecy of the deliberations of a petit jury in a criminal case.

> Freedom of debate might be stifled and independence of thought checked if jurors were made to feel that their arguments and ballots were to be freely published to the world.

Id. at 13. Nonetheless, the Court also recognized that isolated inroads on confidentiality designed to serve the paramount need of the criminal law would not vitiate the interests served by secrecy:

> A juror of integrity and reasonable firmness will not fear to speak his mind if the confidences of debate are barred to the ears of mere impertinence or malice. He will not expect to be shielded against the disclosure of his conduct in the event that there is evidence reflecting upon his honor. The chance that now and then there may be found some timid soul who will take counsel of his fears and give way to their repressive power is too remote and shadowy to shape the course of justice.

Id. at 16.

21. When the subpoenaed material is delivered to the District Judge in camera, questions may arise as to the excising of parts, and it lies within the discretion of that court to seek the aid of the Special Prosecutor and the President's counsel for in camera consideration of the validity of particular excision, whether the basis of excision is relevancy or admissibility or under such cases as United States v. Reynolds, 345 U.S. 1 (1953), or C. & S. Air Line v. Waterman S.S. Corp., 333 U.S. 103 (1948).

Finally, It's President Bush

Gore Concedes Defeat in Wake of U.S. Supreme Court's Recount Ruling

Chris Starrs

GEORGE W. Bush, the Republican governor of Texas, was last night packing his bags for the White House.

The way was cleared for him to become the 43rd president of the United States when Al Gore, his Democratic rival, conceded defeat, having abandoned his recount battle in the courts, and phoned the president-elect to offer his congratulations.

In a televised address, Mr. Gore later told the American people he had surrendered his battle for the White House.

"I accept the finality of this outcome," the vice president said. He vowed to work with his former rival to "heal the divisions" of their long and bitter election battle.

"I offered to meet with him as soon as possible so that we can start to heal the divisions of the campaign and the contest through which we've just passed," Mr. Gore said in a valedictory from the ceremonial office at the White House he will vacate.

However, Mr. Gore signaled some of the reluctance to concede defeat that propelled his 36-day legal battle for Florida ballot recounts. "Now the US supreme court has spoken, let there be no doubt," Mr. Gore said. "While I strongly disagree with the court's position, I accept it."

He called for his supporters to unite behind his Mr. Bush.

"We close ranks when the contest is done," he said.

"While we yet hold, and do not yield, our opposing beliefs, there is a higher duty than the one we owe to political party. This is America and we put country before party. We will stand together behind our new president."

Addressing members of the international community, he said: "Let no one see this contest as a sign of American weakness. The strength of American democracy is seen most clearly through the difficulties it can overcome."

Standing behind Mr. Gore in the ornate White House office were his wife, Tipper, their four children, running mate Senator Joseph Lieberman and his family.

Chris Starrs, "Finally, It's President Bush. Gore Concedes Defeat in Wake of US Supreme Court Recount Ruling," The Herald. Copyright © 2000 by Herald & Times Group. Reprinted with permission.

A similar address by Mr. Bush, the son of the 41st president, George Bush, was planned for one hour later. He was expected finally to lay claim to the title of president-elect. He is expected to be sworn in on January 20.

Earlier yesterday, Mr. Gore told the committee he had appointed to fight for a manual recount of thousands of disputed ballots in Florida to close down. One of his senior advisers said: "The race is over. We're done."

In the early hours of yesterday morning the US supreme court voted by 5-4 to stop the recounts, which had been ordered by the Florida supreme court and which could have enabled Mr. Gore to overtake Mr. Bush.

The US supreme court ruling came exactly five weeks after election day on November 7. The nine justices in the nation's highest court sent the case back to the Florida court for further consideration, but hedged its ruling with so many limitations that it seemed there was no way for the vice-president to prevail.

It came as the final crushing blow to Mr. Gore after a long roller-coaster ride in which he struggled to erase Mr. Bush's narrow lead of just a few hundred votes in Florida.

The US supreme court ruling stopped any further recounts, saying there was no time to complete them before the electoral college meets on Monday to pick the next president. Florida's 25 electoral votes would have given either candidate the 270 votes needed to become president.

The ruling essentially gave the state's electoral votes, along with the White House, to the Texas governor.

Mr. Gore has argued that he probably won the most votes in Florida, which officially went to Mr. Bush by a margin of 537 out of nearly six million votes cast, but he was unable to get a hand count to try to prove it.

Nationally, the vice president outpolled the Texas governor by about 300,000 votes—50,158,094 to 49,820,518.

Some Democrats openly expressed anger about the US supreme court ruling. One, Senator Patrick Leahy said he accepted the recount ruling but talked of "actions many Americans will consider to be political rather than judicial".

Jesse Jackson, the civil rights leader who made his own bid twice for the presidency, claimed that blacks, who traditionally vote Democrat, had their votes "taken away" from them due to a range of alleged voter irregularities in Florida and elsewhere.

He said civil rights leaders would continue their quest to get votes counted in Florida and there would be mass protests across America to coincide with either Martin Luther King Day on January 15 or January 20, when the new president will take office.

Mr. Gore conferred with aides and lawyers as well as Mr. Lieberman before deciding early yesterday to end his run for the presidency rather than fight on.

Bill Clinton, the outgoing president, on a visit to Northern Ireland, spoke on the phone to Mr. Gore for about five minutes. No details were available about the conversation.

Dan Bartlett, the Bush campaign spokesman, said Mr. Bush would speak from the chambers of the Texas House of Representatives where, in a sign of the bipartisanship he hopes to bring to Washington, he would be introduced by Pete Laney, the Democratic speaker.

Richard Cheney, the Republican vice presidential candidate, visited congressional Republicans to discuss transition issues but declined to speak in public until Mr. Gore's address.

Mr. Bush's biggest initial task will be to try to unite the country after a bitter period of partisan strife and legal wrangling following the closest elections in US history. He has a tough task, taking office after the election was essentially decided by a court's 5-4 vote and those few hundred votes in Florida.

John Paul Stevens, one of the four US supreme court justices who voted in favour of Mr. Gore, said in his dissent: "Although we may never know with complete certainty the identity of the winner of this year's presidential election, the identity of the loser is perfectly clear.

"It is the nation's confidence in the judge as an impartial guardian of the rule of law."Ordinary Americans appeared ready to put the crisis behind them. "I'm glad that we finally have a president-elect," said Melissa Glasgow, a bartender in Nashville in Mr. Gore's home state of Tennessee.

Defiance Grows as Iran's Leader Sets Vote Review

Robert F. Worth and Nazila Pathi

T EHRAN—Hundreds of thousands of people marched in silence through central Tehran on Monday to protest Iran's disputed presidential election in an extraordinary show of defiance from a broad cross section of society, even as the nation's supreme leader called for a formal review of results he had endorsed two days earlier.

Having mustered the largest antigovernment demonstrations since the 1979 revolution, and defying an official ban, protesters began to sense the prospect—however slight at the moment—that the leadership's firm backing of President Mahmoud Ahmadinejad had wavered.

The massive outpouring was mostly peaceful. But violence erupted after dark when protesters surrounded and attempted to set fire to the headquarters of the Basij volunteer militia, which is associated with the Revolutionary Guards, according to news agency reports. At least one man was killed, and several others were injured in that confrontation.

On Tuesday, Radio Payam, a state-owned station, reported that seven people were killed and others were wounded Monday night when "several thugs" tried to attack a military post and vandalize public property in the same area as the demonstration earlier in the day, according to Agence France-Presse.

In his first public comment on the situation in Iran, President Obama said Monday that he was deeply troubled by the postelection violence and he called on Iranian leaders to respect free speech and the democratic process. He told reporters he would continue pursuing a direct dialogue with Tehran, but he urged that any Iranian investigation of election irregularities be conducted without bloodshed.

The protests showed how the government's assertion that Mr. Ahmadinejad had won reelection by a ratio of almost two to one further cleaved Iranian society into rival camps.

On one side are the most powerful arms of the Islamic system of government: the supreme leader, Ayatollah Ali Khamenei; the military; the paramilitary; and the Guardian Council. On the other is a diverse coalition that has grown emboldened by the day, with some clerics joining two former presidents and Mir Hussein Moussavi, the former prime minister and main

Robert Worth & Nazila Fathi, "Defiance Grows as Iran's Leader Sets Vote Review," The New York Times. Copyright © 2009 by The New York Times Company. Reprinted with permission provided by PARS International Corp.

opposition candidate, who addressed the crowd from the roof of a car near Freedom Square in downtown Tehran.

Protesters were especially enraged that Mr. Ahmadinejad on Sunday dismissed them as nothing more than soccer fans who had just lost a game and as "dust." One demonstrator fired off a Twitter message, one of thousands of brief electronic dispatches that kept the outside world up-to-the-minute on the protests, proclaiming, "Ahmadinejad called us Dust, we showed him a sandstorm."

Earlier Monday, Ayatollah Khamenei stepped in to try to calm a growing backlash, forcing him into a public role he generally seeks to avoid as the country's top religious authority. Under Iran's dual system of government, with civil and religious institutions, the supreme leader can usually operate in the shadows while elected officials serve as the public face of governance and policy.

He called for the Guardian Council to conduct an inquiry into the opposition's claims that the election was rigged and then had that announcement repeated every 15 minutes on Iranian state radio throughout the day. It was a rare reversal.

Ayatollah Khamenei announced Saturday that the election results showing a landslide victory for Mr. Ahmadinejad were fair. But on Sunday he met with Mr. Moussavi, a moderate, to listen to his concerns. And on Monday, he promised the inquiry into the results.

Nevertheless, his announcement could not calm the anger of the people. There was so much distrust that some people said they believed the leader was just trying to buy time and to calm the crowds, rather than attempting to really investigate the outcome.

Hours later, a broad river of people in Tehran—young and old, dressed in traditional Islamic gowns and the latest Western fashions—marched slowly from Revolution Square to Freedom Square for more than three hours, many of them wearing the signature bright green ribbons of Mr. Moussavi's campaign and holding up their hands in victory signs.

The silent march was a deliberate and striking contrast to the chaos of the past few days, when riot police officers sprayed tear gas and wielded clubs to disperse scattered bands of angry and frightened young people. When the occasional shout or chant went up, the crowd quickly hushed it, and some held up signs with the word silence.

"These people are not seeking a revolution," said Ali Reza, a young actor in a brown T-shirt who stood for a moment watching on the rally's sidelines. "We don't want this regime to fall. We want our votes to be counted, because we want reforms, we want kindness, we want friendship with the world."

Mr. Moussavi, who had called for the rally on Sunday but never received official permission for it, joined the crowd, as did Mohammad Khatami, the reformist former president. But the crowd was so vast, and communications had been so sporadic—the authorities have cut off phone and text-messaging services repeatedly in recent days—that many marchers seemed unaware they were there.

"We don't really have a leader," said Mahdiye, a 20-year-old student, who like many protesters declined to give a last name because of fears of repercussions. "Moussavi wants to do something, but they won't let him. It is dangerous for him, and we don't want to lose him. We don't know how far this will go."

The protesters said they would continue, with another major rally planned for Tuesday. But it was too soon to tell whether Ayatollah Khamenei's decision to launch an inquiry, or the government's decision to let the silent rally proceed, would change the election results. Many in the crowd said they believed that officials expected the protests to dissipate, as smaller protest movements did in 1999 and 2003.

Later on Monday, Mr. Moussavi said on his Web site that he was not optimistic that the authorities would overturn the election results. Demonstrators, though, expressed hopes that the tide had turned in their favor.

"Anything is possible," said Hamid, a 50-year-old financial adviser. "If the people insist on this movement, if it continues here and in other parts of Iran, the pressure will build and maybe Ahmadinejad will be forced to resign."

The police mostly stood on the sidelines on Monday. But after sunset, violence erupted after members of the Basij militia opened fire, leaving one dead and several others injured.

In Isfahan, south of Tehran, more violence broke out on Monday, with the police attacking a crowd of several thousand opposition protesters and rioters setting fires in parts of the city.

In Washington, a State Department spokesman, Ian C. Kelly, said that the United States was "deeply troubled" by the unrest in Iran and was concerned about allegations of ballot fraud. But he stopped short of condemning Iran's security forces for cracking down on demonstrators and said that Washington did not know whether the allegations of fraud were, in fact, true.

In Moscow, meanwhile, an official at the Iranian Embassy said that Mr. Ahmadinejad had delayed a visit to Russia that was to have started Monday. The meeting, in Yekaterinburg, is of the Shanghai Cooperation Organization, which includes Russia, China and four Central Asian countries. Reuters reported that he arrived on Tuesday.

As concern about the vote spread among Western governments, the European Union's 27 member states planned to issue a joint call on Iran to clarify the election outcome, Reuters reported. The French government summoned the Iranian ambassador to register concern about the fairness of the vote, and Germany planned to follow suit.

The Guardian Council, which will have 10 days to review the results, is closely aligned with the supreme leader and with Mr. Ahmadinejad. It also has the full support of the Revolutionary Guards and the Basij militia. Until now, there have been no signs of that unity fraying. Political analysts said that the coalition of hard-line thinkers had hoped to finish off the reform movement and its leaders with this election.

However, at least for the moment, they have inadvertently empowered them.

"People feel really insulted, and nothing is worse than that," said Azi, a 48-year-old woman in a yellow headscarf who participated in the massive rally on Monday. "We won't let the regime buy time, we will hold another march tomorrow."

At nightfall, large numbers of people in Tehran took to their roofs for a second night, chanting "God is great!" and "Death to the dictator!" in neighborhoods across the city. The Associated Press, quoting residents, also reported that shooting was also heard in three districts of wealthy northern Tehran.

Khamenei's Coup

Mehdi Khalaji

Large-scale manipulation of Friday's presidential election in Iran was to be expected, but few could have predicted that Iran's supreme leader, Ayatoilah Ali Khamenei, had a military coup in mind. By declaring incumbent Mahmoud Ahmadinejad the winner, Khamenei conveyed a clear message to the West: Iran is digging in on its nuclear program, its support to Lebanese Hezbollah and Palestinian Hamas, and its defiant regional policies.

In the streets of Tehran and other major cities, riot police, members of the Islamic Revolutionary Guard Corps and Basij militias are battling reformist demonstrators who are protesting the results. The government has cut Internet connections and cellphone service and jammed foreign satellite TV and radio broadcasts. Most foreign journalists in Iran to cover the election were expelled after the voting ended. More than 100 leaders of the reform movement have been detained so far, and others are under what amounts to house arrest.

Even though Khamenei asked the candidates not to dispute the results, a reformist group called the Council of Militant Clerics, led by former president Mohammad Khatami, apologized to the people for not being able to protect their votes and asked the government to overturn this result and hold new elections. In statements Sunday, two of the presidential candidates, Mir Hossein Mousavi and Mehdi Karroubi, asked people to continue their "nonviolent demonstration" throughout the country and criticized the government for using violence against demonstrators.

More than 80 percent of Iranian voters turned out primarily because Ahmadinejad's three challengers succeeded in mobilizing Iran's silent majority, especially in the two weeks before the election. All three warned explicitly about the risks of Ahmadinejad's domestic and foreign policies. Although Ahmadinejad enjoys the support of Iran's powerful supreme leader, in the final two weeks before the election—all reputable polls inside and outside of Iran showed that Ahmadinejad's popularity had decreased significantly—particularly following televised campaign debates—even in rural areas and among the urban working class.

Mehdi Khalaji, "Khamenei's Coup," The Washington Post. Copyright © 2009 by The Washington Post. Reprinted with permission.

Ahmadinejad took office four years ago through an engineered election. This time Khamenei announced—before the official Interior Ministry count had been issued—that Ahmadinejad had won more than 24 million votes, surpassing even the record set by Khatami 12 years ago.

Mousavi and Karroubi have called the announced results "ridiculous." Mousavi said Sunday that invalidating the election is now the only way to restore the people's trust. The Iranian supreme leader's post-election statement, in which he described a "people's epic" through a "completely fair and free election," did not prevent shocked followers of reformist candidates from rioting over the weekend to chants of "down with the dictator."

The challengers also asked people to go to the roof of their homes and shout "Allah is great," a slogan that reminds people of the 1979 revolution. Mousavi has invited protesters to gather this afternoon on Enghelab Square in Tehran; gatherings are expected in more than 20 other cities.

The current social solidarity and political unity in Iran is unprecedented since the revolution. Banners, headbands and signs in green, the color of the anti-Ahmadinejad movement, were prominent before the election and are still on display. No one can predict where this situation will lead and whether Khamenei's nightmare of a "velvet revolution" will come true.

Earlier this year, in his message on the occasion of the Iranian New Year (Nowruz), Barack Obama became the first U.S. president since the hostage crisis to address "Iranian leaders" and the "Islamic Republic" rather than the Iranian "regime." The Obama administration had been careful not to take any position that could be seen as supporting a particular candidate in the Iranian election. Obama's Iran team was surely watching the decreasing support for Ahmadinejad and waiting to see what would happen. While Venezuela's Hugo Chavez and leaders of the Palestinian Hamas and Egyptian Muslim Brotherhood movements were among the first to congratulate Ahmadinejad, people everywhere, certainly including in Iran, expect the United States to speak out.

This military coup is a turning point in Iran's domestic and foreign policies that the West cannot ignore. The U.S. reaction in particular is meaningful not only for Iran's democratic movement but for all democrats in Islamic countries who suffer under autocratic governments. In coordination with European and other nations, the United States should respond to the message being sent by Iran's supreme leader by condemning the election and backing the Iranian people's demand for a free and fair revote under the supervision of international observers.

Iran's people have a living memory of U.S. involvement in the 1950s coup against the government of Mohammed Mossadegh. They expect the Obama administration not to make the same mistake at this crucial time in U.S.-Iranian relations by recognizing the coup carried out under the cover of this election.

It will be easier to bring an end to Iran's controversial nuclear program and defiant foreign policy working with a democratic Iran rather than the military government that is in power. Iranian society will not forget this historic moment and is watching to see how the free world reacts.

And Then There Were Four

A SEAT on Malaysia's Supreme Court seems to confer no job security. The prime minister, Dr. Mahathir Mohamad, has long made it clear that he finds independent judges irksome. He has hit on the happy solution of arranging for the suspension of six of the ten judges on the country's top court.

In May his willing ally King Mahmood Iskandar suspended Mr. Salleh Abas, who was lord president of the Supreme Court. Mr. Salleh was accused of having shown a bias against the government. The king struck again on July 6th by suspending five more Supreme Court judges. Malaysians now expect Dr. Mahathir to get parliament to abolish the court and replace it with a body friendlier to the prime minister.

The suspension of the five followed their order that the government-named tribunal which was hearing the case for Mr. Salleh's dismissal should not disclose its findings. He had refused to appear before this body and had asked a High Court judge to suspend it. When that judge dragged his feet, the five Supreme Court judges intervened. They too must now face a tribunal, which may recommend their dismissal.

Mr. Salleh contends that the crackdown is the direct result of some rulings made by him against the prime minister's wishes. Ten days before his suspension, he had ruled that the full Supreme Court should hear an appeal against an important High Court decision that had gone in Dr. Mahathir's favour. Dissident members of the prime minister's party, the United Malays National Organisation, had claimed that his appointment last year as leader of UMNO was invalid because of improprieties in the conduct of the party election. The High Court skirted around this issue; instead, it ruled that UMNO itself was no longer a lawful organisation. Dr. Mahathir was not looking forward to an appeal that might go against him.

Another decision by Mr. Salleh that upset the government was his appointment of a five-member Supreme Court panel to hear a petition by Mr. Karpal Singh, a lawyer who is being detained under Malaysia's Internal Security Act. Mr. Singh is a political opponent of Dr. Mahathir.

"And Then There Were Four," The Economist. Copyright © 1988 by Economist Newspaper Group. Reprinted with permission.

Dr. Mahathir commands an overwhelming majority in parliament, where his coalition holds 151 seats out of 177. The 151 include some wobblers, but they are unlikely to be in a position to block the prime minister if he asks parliament to remove the present Supreme Court and replace it with a more pliant body.

However, his friend the king may face difficulties. The nine hereditary princes of Malaysia's component states take turns acting as king (and head of state) of the whole federation. The present king's fellow-royals are unhappy about his enthusiastic support for Dr. Mahathir's campaign against the judiciary. Two weeks ago they told the king he should wind up the tribunal that was hearing Mr. Salleh's case. He refused. Some people think the other sultans are so angry that they may try to remove the king from office.

Discussion Questions

1. What is "self-help"?

2. What are the advantages and disadvantages of it?

3. Should citizens take the initiative and patrol their borders if they feel the government has failed to act? What are their options?

4. What is the "logic of the triad"? Why is it inherently unstable? What is the role of the law and the rule of law in preserving it?

5. No one would object if members of Congress were influenced by their constituents or made decisions based on their political beliefs. Why do we care if judges are influenced by political actors or public opinion?

6. Political scandals and contested elections arise in every society and often create crises over who rules. How did the controversies described in the readings differ in the United States than other countries? How do these stories relate to the broader themes in this section on the importance of orderly dispute resolution as a governmental function? Should appointed judges decide elections?

7. Given the logic of the triad, should federal judges be elected? Why or why not? If not, what would be preferable? The current confirmation process? A civil service examination process?

B. The Promises of Law and Courts

Judicial Policymaking

C ourts do more than resolve disputes. They also make policy. These readings introduce the concept of courts as a policymaking forum and provide some examples of judicial policymaking on behalf of historically under-represented or unpopular groups.

1. Courts as a Policy-making Forum

We often distinguish litigation and legislation. Yet both are forms of policy-making. The problem is that judicial policymaking functions are often buried under a dense fog of legal jargon. These readings seek to define judicial policy-making, explain why judicial policy-making is likely to be prevalent in the United States, and clarify how judicial policy-making differs from legislative policymaking.

Supreme Court Policy Making

Jeffrey A. Segal and Harold J. Spaeth

We live in a democracy, but within that democracy we give the nine unelected, virtually unremovable members of the Supreme Court broad discretion to determine, for instance, whether abortions should be allowed, death penalties inflicted, and homosexuality criminally punished. Although the justices might claim for public consumption that they do not make public policy, that they merely interpret the law, the truth is closer to Chief Justice (then Governor) Charles Evans Hughes's declaration: "We are under a Constitution, but the Constitution is what the judges say it is."[1]

This chapter focuses on why the Supreme Court, along with other American courts, makes policy. We initially present a set of reasons for judicial policy making. Though these reasons are crucial to our understanding of the institution's importance, they do not tell us anything about the considerations that cause the justices to make the choices that produce the Court's policies. In Chapter 2, we describe and critique the legal model of decision making, which purportedly identifies the criteria that cause the justices to decide their cases the way they do, and the school of interpretivist thought that takes its cue from one of the variants of the legal model. As we demonstrate, the legal model serves only to cloak—to conceal—the motivations that cause the justices to decide as they do. As an alternative, we present an attitudinal model, based on the political attitudes and values of the justices, that does explain why the justices vote as they do.

---

1   Quoted in Craig Ducat and Harold Chase, *Constitutional Interpretation*, 4th ed. (New York: West, 1988), p. 3.

Jeffrey Segal & Harold Speath, "Supreme Court Policy Making," The Supreme Court and the Attitudinal Model, pp. 1-14. Copyright © 1993 by Cambridge University Press. Reprinted with permission.

WHAT COURTS DO

In order to explain why justices vote as they do, we begin with a specification of what courts themselves do. From the most general and non-technical standpoint, they resolve disputes. Not all disputes, of course. Only those that possess certain characteristics. The party initiating legal action must be a "proper plaintiff," and the court in which the dispute is brought must be a "proper forum." That is, it must have the authority—the jurisdiction—to resolve the dispute. For example, courts generally, and the federal courts in particular, may only resolve a "case" or "controversy."[2] In Chapter 5 we detail the specific characteristics that enable a litigant to be a proper plaintiff and those pertaining to the proper forum.

The Supreme Court has described the judiciary's function as follows:

> Perhaps no characteristic of an organized and cohesive society is more fundamental than its creation and enforcement of a system of rules defining the various rights and duties of its members, enabling them to govern their affairs and definitively settle their differences in an orderly, predictable manner. Without such a "legal system," social organization and cohesion are virtually impossible; with the ability to seek regularized resolution of conflict individuals are capable of interdependent action that enables them to strive for achievements without the anxieties that would beset them in a disorganized society. Put more succinctly, it is this injection of the rule of law that allows society to reap the benefits of what political theorists call the "state of nature."[3]

The Court also noted that courts are not the only available means for resolving disputes. Indeed, "private structuring of individual relationships and repair of their breach is largely encouraged in American life, subject only to the caveat that the formal judicial process, if resorted to, is paramount."[4]

The process whereby courts resolve disputes produces a decision. This decision, unless overruled by a higher court, is binding on the parties to the dispute. If a higher court does

---

2   For all practical purposes, the two terms are synonymous. A "case" includes all judicial proceedings, whereas a "controversy" is a civil matter. As Justice Iredell pointed out in the lead opinion in *Chishom* v. Georgia, 2 Dallas 419 (1792), at 432: "It cannot be presumed that the general word, 'controversies[,]' was intended to include any proceedings that relate to criminal cases ..." Although the Eleventh Amendment nullified the Court's decision in *Chishom* v. *Georgia*, Iredell's distinction survives.

3   *Boddie v. Connecticut*, 401 U.S. 371 (1971), at 374.

4   Id. at 375. Also see Christine Harrington, *Shadow Justice* (Westport, CT: Greenwood Press, 1985).

overrule the trial or a lower appellate court, then its decision replaces the earlier one. A court's decision, binding the litigants, is authoritative in the sense that non-judicial decision makers, such as legislators or executive officials, cannot alter or nullify it.5 Judicial authority is not subverted by the possibility that the legislature may at some point in the future alter the law that the court applied to the case it decided,[6] or that a constitutional amendment may undo the Court's decision, as the Eleventh Amendment undid Chisholm v. Georgia, which permitted a nonresident to sue a state in federal court.[7]

Not only does a constitutional amendment not subvert judicial authority, courts themselves—ultimately the Supreme Court—authoritatively determine the sanctioning amendment's meaning. Although the Court's interpretation of an amendment that overturns one of its decision may give the amendment the effect its words or purpose conveys, this need not be the case. Thus, the Twenty-Sixth Amendment, ratified in 1971, did indeed enable eighteen-year-olds to vote in state and federal elections, which was indisputably its purpose.[8] But the Fourteenth and Sixteenth Amendments are a different matter. The former clearly overturned the Court's decision in Scott v. Sandford[9] and was meant to give blacks legal equality with whites. Scholars disagree about what other objectives the Amendment had, but it does appear that the prohibition of sex discrimination was not among them.[10] Nonetheless, in 1971 the Court held that the equal protection clause of the Fourteenth Amendment encompassed women.[11] As for the Sixteenth Amendment, it substantially, but not completely,

---

5   This assumes, of course, that the court in question had authority to resolve the dispute in the first place. If, for example, a court were to decide a matter for which a legislative or executive agency has ultimate responsibility, its decision lacks authority.

6   A recent example of Congressional override involves the Court's decision in *Ohio* v. *Betts*, 106 L Ed 2d 134 (1989), which held that the Age Discrimination in Employment Act did not require an employer to justify differential benefits for older workers on the basis of cost. Lower benefits are valid unless imposed for a discriminatory purpose. A county's speech pathologist was diagnosed as having Alzheimer's disease at age fifty-eight. She continued working until sixty-one. The state retirement system prohibits workers over sixty from receiving disability benefits. She lost her case.

If concurred in by the House of Representatives and approved by the President, Senate action protecting workers' insurance, severance, and disability benefits will overturn the Court's decision. See Richard L. Berke, "Senate, 94-1, Votes to Protect Benefits of Older Workers," *New York Times*, September 25, 1990, p. C16.

7   2 Dallas 419 (1793). Although it has virtually never happened, Congress can grant relief to a losing litigant by way of a private bill, assuming no constitutional violation occurs in doing so.

8   Thereby overruling *Oregon v. Mitchell*, 400 U.S. 112 (1970), which voided an act of Congress that authorized eighteen-year-olds to vote in state elections.

9   19 Howard 393 (1857).

10   See *Bradwell v. Illinois*, 16 Wallace 130 (1873).

11   *Reed v. Reed*, 404 U.S. 71 (1971).

reversed the Court's decisions in Pollock v. Farmers' Loan and Trust Co., which declared unconstitutional the income tax that Congress had enacted in 1894.[12] In 1913, the requisite number of states ratified an amendment that authorized Congress to levy a tax on income "from whatever source derived." The language is unequivocal. Yet for the next twenty-six years the Supreme Court ruled that this language excluded the salaries of federal judges. Why the exclusion? Because Article III, Section 1, of the original Constitution orders that judges' salaries "not be diminished during their continuance in office." Though it is an elementary legal principle that later language erases incompatible earlier language, the justices ruled that any taxation of their salaries, and those of their lower court colleagues, would obviously diminish them.[13] Finally, in 1939, the justices overruled their predecessors and unselfishly allowed themselves to be taxed.[14]

Judges as Policy Makers

The authoritative character of judicial decisions results because judges make policy. Policy making involves choosing among alternative courses of action, where the choice binds the behavior of those subject to the policy-maker's action. Phrased more succinctly, a policy maker authoritatively allocates resources.

Although the typical judicial decision will only authoritatively allocate the limited resources at issue between the parties to a lawsuit, the resources allocated at appellate court levels commonly affect persons other than the litigants. Appellate courts support their decisions with opinions precisely because of their broader impact, so that persons who find themselves in similar situations may be apprised of the fate that may befall them if they engage in actions akin to those of the relevant litigant.

Note, however, that trial court decisions may also have wide-ranging policy effects. Few cases are appealed; as a result, unappealed decisions become as authoritative as those of a supreme court. Multiparty litigation is becoming increasingly common. A class of thousands of human or legal persons may institute a single lawsuit, the decision in which binds all participants—for example, all taxpayers in the State of California, or all stockholders of General Motors. Organizations frequently sue or are sued as surrogates for their members—for example, the Sierra Club or the Teamsters Union. A lawsuit brought by or against the United States or a state or local government may have very broad and pervasive effects.

Courts make policy only on matters that they have authority to decide—that is, within their jurisdiction. The subjects of the jurisdiction of American courts range from the purely trivial to matters of utmost societal importance. As an eminent Canadian jurist phrases it:

---

12 157 U.S. 429 (1895) and 158 U.S. 601 (1895).
13 See *Evans v. Gore*, 253 U.S. 245 (1920), and *Miles v. Graham*, 268 U.S. 501 (1925).
14 Id. at 282.

Reading through an American constitutional law text is like walking through modern human existence in an afternoon. From a woman's control of her own body to the Vietnam war and from desegregation of schools to drunken drivers, it is hard to imagine a facet of American existence that has not been subjected to constitutional scrutiny.[15]

American courts derive their jurisdiction from the constitution that established them and/or from legislative enactments. Because judges' decisions adjudicate the legality of contested matters, judges of necessity make law. Only those who believe in fairy tales deny this statement. Even so, Americans find it unsettling to admit to judicial policy making because we have surrounded judicial decisions with a panoply of myth, the essence of which avers that judges and their decisions are objective, impartial, and dispassionate. In the language of Chief Justice John Marshall:

> Judicial power, as contradistinguished from the power of the laws, has no existence. Courts are the mere instruments of the law and can will nothing. When they are said to exercise a discretion, it is a mere legal discretion, a discretion to be exercised in discerning the course prescribed by law; and, when that is discerned, it is the duty of the court to follow it. Judicial power is never exercised for the purpose of giving effect to the will of the judge; always for the purpose of giving effect to the will of the legislature ...[16]

More than Marshall's words, myth makers favor the language of Justice Owen Roberts in *United States v. Butler*, to which five of his colleagues subscribed:

> It is sometimes said that the court assumes a power to overrule or control the action of the people's representatives. This is a misconception. The Constitution is the supreme law of the land ordained and established by the people. All legislation must conform to the principles it lays down. When an act of Congress is appropriately challenged in the courts as not conforming to the constitutional mandate, the judicial branch of the Government has only one duty—to lay the article of the Constitution which is invoked beside the statute which is challenged and to decide whether the latter squares with the former.[17]

One might wish that such statements only harked back to an earlier time and that today everyone admits that "judges make law."[18] Unfortunately, this is not the case. The assertion

---

15   Bertha Wilson, "The making of a constitution," 71 *Judicature* 334 (1988).
16   *Osborn v. Bank of the United States*, 9 Wheaton 738 (1824), at 866.
17   297 U.S. 1 (1936), at 62.
18   Wilson, op.cit. fn. 15 supra, p. 334.

that judges merely "find" or "discover" the law, and do not ever make it, continues to be propounded with the same vigor as of yore, even though, as one authority documents, "Seventeenth-century Americans viewed lawmaking and judging as synonymous activities."[19] Three cases illustrate this.

The very framing of the issue that we purport to decide today—whether our decision ... shall "apply" retroactively—presupposes a view of our decisions as *creating* the law, as opposed to *declaring* what the law already is. Such a view is contrary to that understanding of "the judicial Power," US Const, Art III, Sec. 1, cl 1, which is not only the common and traditional one, but which is the only one that can justify courts in denying force and effect to the unconstitutional enactments of duly elected legislatures ... To hold a governmental act to be unconstitutional is not to announce that we forbid it, but that the *Constitution* forbids it...[20]

These words were written by Justice Scalia, a justice whom many view as the Court's brightest member. Apparently, intelligence does not preclude self-deception. Alternatively, perhaps he believes it appropriate to apply a bit of "spin" to his opinions. At least Scalia spoke only for himself here, unlike Justice Roberts in the quotation from *United States v. Butler,* the first illustrative case. Even so, Scalia's remarks are puzzling. If it is he and his colleagues through whom the Constitution speaks, and not vice-versa, how can he consistently assert a few paragraphs later that he might not adhere to what "the *Constitution* forbids"? Thus:

> Stare decisis—that is to say, a respect for the needs of stability in our legal system—would normally cause me to adhere to a decision of this Court [sic] already rendered as to the unconstitutionality of a particular type of state law.[21]

Note the use of the phrase, "a decision of this Court." Scalia presumably distinguishes between "what the Constitution forbids" or commands, and the Court's decisions. Some of the latter must only contain matters that a majority of lawmaking justices forbid or command. Scalia has provided no objective criteria for determining in which decisions the Constitution speaks and which merely voice the willful utterances of a biased majority. Perhaps those from which he dissents?

Notwithstanding the justices' denials, Congress commonly authorizes the Court to make law. Consider, for example, federal subsidization of allegedly obscene arts projects. A heated 1989 controversy over support for the exhibition of the work of a deceased gay photographer, Robert Mapplethorpe, ended with the repeal of explicit anti-obscenity curbs that Congress

---

19 Kermit L. Hall, *The Magic Mirror: Law in American History* (New York: Oxford University Press, 1989), p. 17.

20 *American Trucking Assns.* v. *Smith,* 110 L Ed 2d 148 (1990), at 174. The emphasis is in the original.

21 Id. at 176.

had imposed on the National Endowment for the Arts. In October 1990, by a vote of 382-42, the House of Representatives authorized the federal courts, rather than Congress, to make such determinations.[22]

The second of the three illustrative cases required the Court to directly answer the question whether judges make policy. The Age Discrimination in Employment Act exempts appointed state court judges from its ban on mandatory retirement, and the Court construed the relevant language—"appointees ... 'on a policymaking level'"—to encompass judges. But not without considerable waffling. The majority noted that exemption only requires judges to function on a policymaking level, not that they "actually make policy." And though "It is at least ambiguous whether a state judge is an 'appointee' on the policymaking level," nonetheless "we conclude that the petitioning judges fall presumptively under the policymaking exception."[23] Justices White and Stevens, concurring in the result, had no hesitation in calling a spade a spade. Using Webster's definition of policy, they concluded by quoting the lower court whose decision the Supreme Court reviewed: "Each judge, as a separate and independent judicial officer, is at the very top of his particular 'policymaking' chain, responding ... only to a higher appellate court."[24]

Unfortunately, the justices further muddied matters in the last of three illustrative cases, one that was decided on the same day as *Gregory v. Ashcroft*. The issue was the retroactive application of a decision that declared unconstitutional a state statute that discriminatorily taxed liquor produced out of state.[25] The six-member majority required four opinions to state their varied positions, none of which commanded more than three votes.[26] Justice White continued the realistic thrust of his *Ashcroft* opinion by acerbically criticizing the opinion of Justice Scalia, who, it will be recalled, wrote the opinion quoted in the first illustrative case. This time, Blackmun and Marshall, the two *Ashcroft* dissenters, joined Scalia's opinion, which read:

---

22   Robert M. Andrews, "House says let courts decide what's obscene," Associated Press wire story, October 12, 1990.

23   *Gregory v. Ashcroft,* 115 L Ed 2d 410 (1991), at 427, 428.

24   Id. at 440. Justice Blackmun, whom Marshall joined, dissented, refusing to accept Webster's definition as authoritative: "I hesitate to classify judges as policymakers ... Although some part of a judge's task may be to fill in the interstices of legislative enactments, the *primary* task of a judicial officer is to apply rules reflecting the policy choices made by, or on behalf of, those elected to legislative and executive positions." At 441, note 1. The dissent relied on the opinion of Judge Amalya Kearse of the Second Circuit who flatly asserted that "the performance of traditional judicial functions is not policy making." Linda Greenhouse, "Justices to Hear Retirement Age Case," *New York Times,* November 27, 1990, p. A12. Judge Kearse's opinion, and one from the Eastern District of Virginia, are the only ones that held judges not to be policymakers. The majority of judges, holding to the contrary, are listed at 438, note 2.

25   Bacchus Imports, Ltd *v.* Dias, *468 U.S. 263 (1984).*

26   *James B. Beam Distilling Co. v. Georgia, 115 L Ed 2d 481 (1991).*

I am not so naive (nor do I think our forebears were) as to be unaware that judges in a real sense "make" law. But they make it *as judges make it,* which is to say *as though* they were "finding" it—discerning what the law *is,* rather than decreeing what it is today *changed to,* or what it will *tomorrow* be. Of course, this mode of action poses "difficulties of a ... practical sort ... when courts decide to overrule prior precedent. (Italics in original.)[27]

White replied:

... even though the Justice is not naive enough (nor does he think the Framers were naive enough) to be unaware that judges in a real sense "make" law, he suggests that judges (in an unreal sense, I suppose) should never concede that they do and must claim that they do no more than discover it, hence suggesting that there are citizens who are naive enough to believe them.[28]

The foregoing evidence, such as it is, suggests that the fairy tale of a discretionless judiciary survives, even though its mouthpieces carry their tongues in their cheeks.

REASONS FOR JUDICIAL POLICY MAKING

No other nation empowers its courts to resolve so broad a range of disputes as does the United States. Neither does any other nation concede to its courts such authoritative decision making. Furthermore, in making their decisions, the courts do so with a minimum of interference from other governmental bodies or officials.

Why do American judges have such virtually untrammeled policy-making authority? Five interrelated factors provide an answer: fundamental law, distrust of governmental power, federalism, separation of powers, and judicial review. Because they are so closely interconnected, we cannot empirically judge their relative importance.

Fundamental Law

The original English colonizers of New England brought with them the concept of a fundamental law: the idea that all human and governmental action should accord with the word of God or the strictures of nature as the leadership of the decreed.[29] These individuals had left Europe because they were unwilling or unable to conform to the teachings of England's established church. Their arrival in America did not produce religious harmony. Much of the

---

27 Id. at 497.

28 Id. at 495

29 Hall, Op. Cit. fn. 19 Supra, pp. 12-17, 24-27.

settlement of Rhode Island and Connecticut, for example, resulted from the expulsion of dissenters from Plymouth and Massachusetts Bay.

The overtly religious motivations that inspired the founding of new settlements was reflected in the charters and constitutions that their inhabitants devised. Although the theocratic parochialism of the early colonies, if not of specific towns and villages within each of them, had largely vanished by the beginning of the Revolutionary War, the notion of a fundamental law retained its vitality.[30]

The environment in which the colonists found themselves did not lend itself to the stabilizing influences of the Old World. Religious diversity flourished. Dissenters—with or without a theomanic preacher—merely had to move a few miles west to establish their own kindred community. The process of westward settlement produced marked social and economic turbulence, which continued throughout the nineteenth century and into the twentieth century, and persists still. The industrial and technological revolutions transformed a society of yeoman farmers and artisans into one of urban employees. Culturally, well before the Revolution, the original English settlers had been supplemented by substantial numbers from the Netherlands, Germany, Scotland, and Ireland, to say nothing of the forcible importation of African slaves. The cultural diversity that resulted became vastly more eclectic with the mass immigration of the latter half of the nineteenth century and the early years of the twentieth century.

The changes in lifestyle and status that these and associated forces have wrought preclude the establishment of a fixed and stable religious, social, economic, or cultural system. Indeed, Americans generally view change in these areas of human activity to be desirable, considering them synonymous with progress and freedom. Only in the political realm do we view drastic change as undesirable.

This schizoid orientation reflects the reality of American life. No one can function well in an unduly dynamic environment. To a substantial extent, human beings are creatures of habit. Economic misfortune, the unexpected breakup of personal relationships, and the demolition of cherished beliefs produces trauma, to those who find events in the saddle riding herd on them. But the political sphere appears to be an arena amenable to stability. This was the goal the Framers set for themselves when they gathered in Philadelphia in the summer of 1787: to transpose the religious notion of a fundamental law into a secular context, to enshrine the Constitution that they intended to create as a secular substitute for Holy Writ.

The fact that the Constitution has lasted longer than that of any other nation is evidence of the Framers' success. Its long life has added political stability to the distinguishing features of American life. Although a resurrected Framer might be appalled at the size of the governmental system he helped create, he most assuredly would recognize the workings of what he had wrought. Other societies may achieve stability through an established church, to which the citizenry pays at least pro forma obeisance, or through the hierarchical social

---

30 See Edward S. Corwin, *The "Higher Law" Background of American Constitutional Law* (Ithaca: Cornell University Press, 1955).

control that a hereditary caste or group exercises. Alternatively, the economic system may prove unchanging, as in a non-industrialized society where subsistence farming occupies all but a privileged elite. Or national boundaries may coincide with ethnic or tribal lines, insuring cultural homogeneity. In these environments, the political sphere provides the vehicle for change. Radical regime changes, bloody or otherwise, become commonplace. Not so in the United States. The Constitution and its system of government furnish us with our link to the unchanging.

Distrust of governmental power

Judicial policy making also inheres in our historic distrust of governmental power, especially that exercised from a central level. Like the concept of fundamental law, this factor also dates from the colonial era. Americans viewed British insistence that they defray the costs of the French and Indian War, which ended in 1763, as inimical to their rights and liberties. Opposition to these policies led to the onset of the Revolution, which coincided with an internal struggle for control of the newly formed governments that the patriots (i.e., the non-Loyalists) established in each of the colonies. This internal struggle roughly pitted the socioeconomic elite, such as it was, against the rural yeomanry and urban artisans. It was continuing apace when the Framers convened in Philadelphia in 1787.

Unsettled economic conditions that persisted beyond the end of the Revolution severely strained the governmental capabilities of both the Continental Congress and the individual states. The Articles of Confederation, which took effect in 1781, made no provision for a chief executive or a federal judiciary; the Continental Congress had no power to levy taxes; nor could it exercise any of its limited powers over individuals; amendment of the Articles required unanimous approval of the thirteen state legislatures. A number of states yielded to debtor demands and printed large quantities of paper money that they issued as legal tender, while others enacted stay laws that lengthened the period of time during which debtors could legally pay their creditors. To protect their own interests, some states imposed tariffs and other trade barriers that inhibited the free flow of interstate commerce. Of the money that Congress requested to defray the costs of the Confederation and the Revolutionary War, the states paid so little that Congress could not meet the interest payments on the national debt.

Support for strengthening the governmental system came from a number of sources: leaders who believed that the power of a single state to prevent change endangered them all; merchants and shipowners concerned about commercial restrictions; frontiersmen threatened by Indian attacks; and veterans and members of the Continental Congress who had developed national loyalties. Of the fifty-five delegates to the Constitutional Convention, thirty-nine had served in Congress, at least thirty were veterans, eight had signed the Declaration of Independence, and all were experienced in the politics of their respective states.

They clearly recognized that any effort to replace the Articles of Confederation with a more capable government required the creation of a system that no single interest or "faction" (to use the word then in vogue) could control or dominate; one that—from the broadest standpoint—neither the "haves" nor the "have nots" could dominate. The governmental capability of the federal level had to be strengthened while that of the states required diminution. The hoped for result was a system in which neither level· would do much governing. The federal government would be empowered to defend the Union, coin money, operate a postal system, regulate interstate commerce, and—needless to say—levy taxes. The states would be saddled with restrictions to prevent them from interfering with the responsibilities given to the federal level, as Article I, Section 10, illustrates:

> 1. No State shall enter into any treaty, alliance, or confederation; ... coin money; emit bills of credit; make anything but gold and silver coin a tender in payment of debts; pass any bill of attainder, ex post facto law, or law impairing the obligation of contracts ...
>
> 2. No State shall, without the consent of the Congress, lay any imposts or duties on imports or exports; ... the net produce of all duties and imposts ... shall be for the use of the treasury of the United States; and all such laws shall be subject to the revision and control of the Congress.
>
> 3. No State shall, without the consent of the Congress, lay any duty of tonnage, keep troops, or ships of war in time of peace, enter into any agreement or compact with another State, or with a foreign power, or engage in war, unless actually invaded, or in such imminent danger as will not admit of delay.

The federal government did not escape similar strictures. Section 9 of Article I, for example, contains eight clauses of "thou shalt nots" that specify things that Congress may not do.

In short, the Framers limited the powers of government in two different ways. First, they severely limited what government could do. Second, they specified in considerable derail the *way* in which government could exercise the powers that it did possess. Thus, Article III stipulates that persons accused of committing a federal crime, other than impeachment, be tried by a jury , and Article I, Section 7, details the procedure whereby a bill becomes a law. The sum total of these substantive and procedural limitations on the exercise of power is clear evidence of the "constitutionalism" of the Constitution.[31]

The resulting system gained the support of the major elements of American society, though not without a sharp and hard fought struggle. The lower socioeconomic echelons stood to benefit from limited government because they lacked experience in the affairs of state. Some had been deprived of the right to vote or hold public office because of property qualifications. Others, though entitled to vote and hold office, lacked the political seasoning of their more experienced neighbors. Their preference for states' rights and local self-government made them suspicious of what might become a strong and efficient centralized government. If

---

31   For a classic treatment of constitutionalism, see Charles H. McIlwain, *Constitutionalism: Ancient and Modern,* rev. ed. (Ithaca: Cornell University Press, 1947).

not in their own experience, then in that of their ancestors, government had been a vehicle of oppression and tyranny. For the many who lived along the frontier, the utility of a federal government was limited to an occasional band of cavalry to pacify unruly natives.

Nor were the landed gentry and mercantile interests necessarily opposed to a government invulnerable to any group's effective control. They chiefly feared loss of position on the socioeconomic ladder. As long as governmental power was not used against them, they sensibly assumed that they could perpetuate their position in society, given their education and wealth and the status that accompanied it.

Consequently, for self-interested reasons that varied from one group and segment to another, the Jeffersonian ideal that that government is best that governs least quickly became an article of faith for Americans generally. Subsequent developments insured its retention: The lure of the frontier and the opportunities it provided individuals to begin again, the immigrating refugees of the nineteenth and twentieth centuries for whom government was synonymous with tyranny and oppression, the Darwinian thesis of the survival of the fittest, the gospel of wealth, and rugged individualism all paid homage to the concept of limited government.

Federalism

In addition to rigorously circumscribing the powers of government, the Framers divided those that were provided between the national government and the states. For the most part, certain powers are delegated to the federal government, whereas others are reserved to the states. Some, however, are shared, such as the power to tax.

The constitutional language that pertains to this geographical division of power lacks precision. As a result, the Supreme Court has confronted a constant stream of litigation that has required the justices to determine the relative power of the federal government vis-a-vis the states. The Court's first major case, *Chisholm v. Georgia*32 concerned federal-state relations. Resolution of these conflicts tilts in favor of the federal government in part because of the language of the supremacy clause (Article VI, Section 2):

> This Constitution, and the laws of the United States which shall be made in pursuance thereof; and all treaties made, or which shall be made, under the authority of the United States, shall be the supreme Jaw of the land; and the Judges in every State shall be bound thereby, anything in the Constitution or laws of any State to the contrary notwithstanding.

The resolution of federal-state conflicts also tilts in favor of the federal government because the Supreme Court has arrogated to itself the authority to ultimately decide these

---

32   2 Dallas 419 (1793).

disputes. It did so early in the nineteenth century, in a pair of landmark decisions, *Martin v. Hunter's Lessee* and *Cohens v. Virginia*.[33]

But even though the constitutional language favors federal supremacy, and the ultimate decision maker is an arm of the federal government, centralization of power has not characterized American politics, as Chapter 3 on the political history of the Court shows. The Court's decisions have caused the degree of centralization/decentralization to vary from one period to another. Indeed, during the late nineteenth and early twentieth centuries when the Court was writing the doctrines of laissez-faire economics into the Constitution, the justices evenhandedly struck down anti-business regulations regardless of the governmental level from which they emanated.

Apart from the operation of the justices' personal policy preferences, the limited jurisdiction of the federal courts and the separate constitutional existence of the state judicial systems have enabled the states to resist a variety of centralizing tendencies rather successfully. We address these matters in the next major section of this chapter, The Federal and State Judicial Systems.

Separation of powers

Separation of powers compartmentalizes government into three separate branches, in the sense that each exercises powers distinct from the others and does so with its own personnel. The effect of this arrangement precludes any branch from compelling action by the other two. Instead, separation of powers institutionalizes conflict, particularly between the Congress and the President. To prevent one branch from overpowering another, each is provided with certain powers that functionally belong to one of the other branches. These are the so-called checks and balances. Thus, the President constitutionally possesses the legislative power to veto Congress' actions, while the Senate participates in the selection of executive officials through the constitutional requirement of advice and consent. Both check the courts—the President by nominating judges, and Congress by consenting to their selection (Senate only) and determining their number and jurisdiction. The courts in turn check the President and Congress through the power of judicial review, which we discuss next.

The Framers were most concerned about the exercise of legislative power. To lessen their fears, they divided Congress into two separate chambers, the Senate and the House of Representatives, with the membership chosen from distinct constituencies (except for those states that have only a single representative) and with a different term of office. They required that a bill pass both houses with identical provisions, down to the last comma, before it could be sent to the President for signature or veto. The judiciary, by contrast, escaped relatively unscathed. The Framers did not view the courts as a threat to the constitutionalism they so carefully crafted. They were more concerned lest the judges become subservient to either of the other branches. To insure the judiciary's independence, the Framers provided them

---

33   I Wheaton 304 (1816) and 6 Wheaton 264 (1821).

with lifetime tenure, no reduction in salary, and created a selection process that neither the President nor Congress could control.

Separation of powers enables the Supreme Court to resolve authoritatively justiciable disputes that pit Congress and the President against one another.[34] A politically charged example concerned the Gramm-Rudman Balanced Budget and Deficit Reduction Act of 1985. Congress assigned one of its own employees, the Comptroller General, responsibility for determining the cuts needed to reduce the budget deficit. By a 7-to-2 vote, the Supreme Court declared the provision unconstitutional because a person removable by Congress was given the executive power to estimate, allocate, and order the spending cuts required to satisfy the deficit targeted by the law. The Court ruled that because Congress could remove the Comptroller General from office, he was "subservient" to it.[35] The fact that Congress had never done so during the sixty-five years of the office's existence did not sway the majority.

Notwithstanding the publicity that attended this decision, the dispute turned on a trivial technicality. The Court did not void the fallback provision that allows the regular legislative process to effectuate the cuts; neither does the decision preclude Congress from merely repealing the provision that allows it to remove the Comptroller, or from bestowing the Comptroller's power on an official whom Congress can remove only through impeachment. Either of these options would make the official "executive" rather than "legislative." This arguably is a distinction without a difference. The creation of the judiciary as an independent coordinate branch of the government has appreciably promoted the policy-making capabilities of federal judges in general, and that of the Supreme Court in particular. Absent functional independence, the judges would likely be viewed—along with other government officials—as mere politicians and bureaucrats. Their efforts to distinguish themselves and their activities as principled, even-handed, and nonpartisan would likely be unsuccessful, with the result that the public would view them as on a level with the persons of minimal competence and dubious ethics who engage in the dirty business of politics.

---

34   Many such disputes are "political questions." The plaintiff lacks standing to sue because the Court believes the matter—though within the courts' subject matter jurisdiction—should be resolved by the "political" branches of government themselves.

35   *Bowsher v. Synar*, 478 U.S. 714 (1986), at 727. The dissenters were White and Blackmun.

U.S. District Courts, Litigation, and the Policy-Making Process

Jeb Barnes

Trial courts, including the U.S. District Courts, have generally received less attention from scholars than have appellate courts. Because trial courts deal with the facts of the specific cases before them, some have argued that the trial courts don't really have a policy-making role in our society. Others argue that collectively the trial courts are very important policy makers. This chapter examines the federal trial courts and their collective policy-making abilities. The chapter begins by presenting a general model of policy making. During each stage of the model, the chapter compares policy making in the courts with policy making in Congress. The chapter concludes by examining the role of the U.S. District Courts in the policy -making process, using the asbestos issue to illustrate the collective policy making found in the federal trial courts. Clearly these federal trial judges are making decisions with important political and legal ramifications.

INTRODUCTION

When we think of the federal judiciary, we tend to think of the U.S. Supreme Court. However, the U.S. District Courts, which are primarily responsible for conducting trials and managing the enormous federal caseload on a daily basis, do most of the work. In 2004, the Supreme Court disposed of 7,542 cases. Of that total, 87 cases were decided after oral argument, an average of 7.25 decisions a month. The district courts, by contrast, terminated 241,864 cases, which is almost one case every two minutes of every day. Meanwhile, 60,505 district court cases were appealed to the U.S. Courts of Appeals, which in turn, terminated 56,243 cases (see Martinek this volume, chapter 9). Using these numbers, over 180,000 cases were resolved in the district courts in 2004, more than three

Jeb Barnes, "U.S. District Courts, Litigation, and the Policy-Making Process," Exploring Judicial Politics, ed. Mark Miller, pp. 97-104. Copyright © 2009 by Oxford University Press. Reprinted with permission.

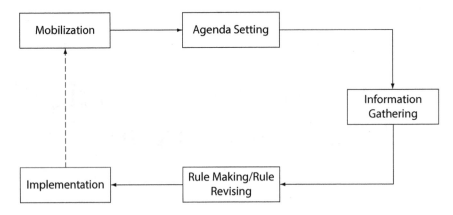

Figure 1: A Working Definition of the Policy-Making Process

times the total in the U.S. Courts of Appeal, and over 23 times the number in the Supreme Court (Administrative Office of the U.S. Courts 2005b, Tables A-I, C, B).

Given their relative output, one might expect scholars to focus on district courts first, U.S. Courts of Appeal next, and the Supreme Court last. However, scholars have tended to do just the opposite. They have concentrated on the Supreme Court and have asked whether the law or "nonlegal" factors, such as political ideology, primarily motivate justices' decisions. Over time, this approach has yielded an elegant model of judicial behavior, known as the attitudinal model, which holds, "judges decide disputes in light of the facts of the case vis-a-vis their sincere ideological attitudes and values" (Segal 1997, 28; see also Pritchett 1948; Schubert 1960,1965; Segal and Cover 1989; Segal and Spaeth 1993, 2002).

Although understanding what motivates Supreme Court decision making is clearly important, this narrow focus has at least two disadvantages. First, it draws our attention away from the front lines of the federal judiciary. Second, focusing on the determinants of judicial behavior and the internal workings of the Supreme Court obscures how courts serve broader policy-making processes (Shapiro 1993; Barnes 2007a). This is particularly problematic in the context of the United States, where lower federal courts have shaped issues ranging from contested constitutional matters, such as the right to abortion, to the interpretation of far-reaching statutes, such as the tax code, the Clean Air and Water Acts, the Americans with Disabilities Act, and others.

Instead of concentrating on judicial behavior and the Supreme Court, this chapter explores how litigation at the district court level constitutes a distinct mode of policy making. To examine this issue on a preliminary basis—a comprehensive account would require whole volumes—this chapter begins by offering a working definition of the policy-making process. It next describes civil litigation in terms of this definition, contrasting judicial policy making with its more familiar congressional counterpart. With this conceptual framework in place, it then discusses some of the policy trade-offs associated with judicial policy making and briefly considers the normative debate over its proper role in American democracy. Along the way, it is hoped that students will gain a better understanding of the litigation process and how seemingly arcane legal proceedings relate to the everyday practice of policy making.

A WORKING DEFINITION OF THE
POLICY-MAKING PROCESS

For purposes of this chapter, we can divide the generic policy-making process into five analytic stages: *mobilization, agenda setting, information gathering, rulemaking,* and *implementation* (see generally Kingdon 1995; Feeley and Rubin 1998). Each stage, in turn, represents a discrete process. Mobilization involves organizing claimants for making demands on official decision makers. Agenda setting entails placing demands on the list of issues governmental decision makers are taking seriously at any given moment. Information gathering assembles facts and expert opinions about the underlying issues, including their scope, underlying causes, and alternative solutions. Rulemaking produces authoritative choices about the official response—or lack of response—to the issues. Implementation applies general rules to specific cases. During implementation, concerns may arise that trigger the entire process anew, resulting in the revision of policies.

This framework is admittedly a gross oversimplification. Any attempt to impose a single definition on the "barroom brawl" of American policy making (Wilson 1989, 299-300) will inevitably fail to capture its interactive, contingent, and ad hoc nature and its variability across issue areas and over time (see Lindblom 1959, 1979; Lowi 1972; Barnes 2004b; Barnes and Miller 2004a; 2004b). In addition, policy making does not always proceed from agenda setting to implementation in linear fashion. In some cases, policy makers have solutions ready-made and seek to find problems and political opportunities to implement them (March and Olson 1989). Nevertheless, even an imperfect working definition can be analytically useful. It can provide temporary scaffolding to organize thoughts about a very complicated subject and offer a touchstone for comparing core policy-making functions across institutional settings.

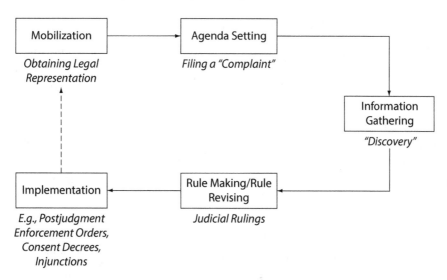

Figure 2: An Overview of Litigation as a Policy-Making Process

AN OVERVIEW OF LITIGATION AS A POLICY-MAKING PROCESS

This simplified framework represents a useful first step, but understanding litigation as a policy-making process remains daunting because litigation in the trial courts unfolds according to detailed, technical rules and specialized professional norms. So, when lawyers talk about litigation, they are likely to use an array of unfamiliar terms, such as *contingency fees,* the *rules of justiciability, interrogatories,* and so on (see also Mather this volume, chapter 4). This is not a criticism—every profession has its own language that serves as convenient and necessary shorthand for practitioners. However, this jargon creates a barrier to recognizing how litigation constitutes a policymaking process that involves the same analytic stages that unfold in Congress or elsewhere.

The implication is *not* that judicial policy making is the same as policy making in other institutional settings. To the contrary, the civil litigation process structures each stage of policy making differently than other institutions. The point is that viewing civil litigation in terms of general policy-making stages reveals functions that are routinely missed when courts and litigation are examined through the narrow prisms of law and judicial behavior. Thus, as discussed later, a policy-making perspective envisages the legal claiming process as a form of mobilization; the filing of a lawsuit as a type of agenda setting; "discovery" as a method of information gathering; judicial decision making as a mode of rulemaking; and postjudgment enforcement orders, consent decrees, and injunctions as tools of implementation.

A CLOSER LOOK

Litigation and Mobilization

Public policy does not just happen. Some one or some group must organize for action. In the context of congressional action, individual citizens, interest groups, lobbyists, elected officials, and their staffs all can play a role in mobilization. In the classic formulation, citizens with common interests band together in response to a problem and organize at the grassroots level (Madison 1788; Truman 1951; Dahl 1961). Others stress how well-established interests use their organizational advantages, extensive networks, and resources to mobilize for action through insider channels (Mills 1956; Olsen 1971; Easterbrook 1983, 1984). In addition, policy entrepreneurs, such as Ralph Nader, can use sophisticated media campaigns to drum up public interest and pressure elected officials (Wilson 1980). Inside government, elected officials can mobilize interests from the top down by "going public" (Kernell 1993) or from the bottom up by sponsoring the formation of groups (Walker 1991; Knott and Miller 1989).

With respect to litigation, mobilization typically involves finding a lawyer who can translate an injury into a legal claim. Structurally, the American legal system facilitates mobilization in a number of ways. In contrast to other countries, the United States permits lawyers to work on contingency fees, which allow them to represent clients in exchange for a percentage of any eventual verdict or settlement. Fueled by the prospect of recovering 30 to 40 percent of large verdicts and aided by the easing of restrictions on the advertising of legal services *(Bates v. State Bar* 1977), a highly competitive litigation industry has emerged (Kagan 2001, 133-34). As a result, entrepreneurial lawyers now routinely hold press conferences at the sites of accidents, deploy representatives to screen potential clients, and market themselves on television, radio, bus stops, and billboards. The American Trial Lawyers Association (ATLA), the Center for Automotive Safety, Public Citizen Health Research Group, and others have created litigation databases, standing lists of experts, and strategy kits to help lawyers find new clients and sue for injuries allegedly caused by specific automobiles, medical products, lead paint, silicone breast implants, and the list goes on (Rabin 1993; Stipp 1993; Kolata 1995; see also Seager 1991).

At first blush, these legal practices may seem far removed from policy making, but they have significant policy and political implications. Through the lens of mobilization, contingency fees not only fund litigation, they create a class of policy entrepreneurs. Legal advertising and media strategies not only offer lawyers a method to sign up new clients but also provide lawyers-as-policy-entrepreneurs a means of going public, educating the public of their rights, and energizing interests.

This is not an exhaustive list. Consider another example: *class-action lawsuits.* From a narrow legal viewpoint, class actions are a procedural mechanism for combining similar individual claims into a single lawsuit (Federal Rules of Civil Procedure [hereinafter "FRCP"], Rule 23). From the vantage of mobilization, however, they offer lawyers-as-policy-entrepreneurs a tool for organizing diffuse individual interests into a potent group of claimants and thus overcome a potential collective action problem—the inherent difficulty of mobilizing diffuse interests, especially when the expected individual rewards for taking action on behalf of the group are relatively small (Olsen 1971). Pushing this logic further, recent federal legislation aimed at reining in the filing of class actions in state courts is not merely a technical adjustment of legal procedures. It is an attempt to limit access to a key policy-making forum—the courts—by curtailing a potentially potent method for mobilizing diffuse interests (Barnes 2007a).

The argument is not that legal mobilization is easy in the United States or that Americans are litigation crazy. Contrary to popular perception, most injuries do not produce litigation (see generally Tarr 2006, 219-22). Studies show that only ten of every one hundred Americans hurt in accidents file any type of claim, and only two of one hundred file lawsuits (Hensler et al. 1991, 121). Only five of every one hundred Americans who believe that another's illegal conduct cost them over $1,000 file lawsuits (Trubek et al. 1983, summary 19, Figure 2). Even in the area of medical malpractice—a supposed hotbed of litigation—a leading study shows that only one of every eight patients seriously injured by doctors' negligence file lawsuits (Weiler et al. 1993). Thus, like any form of mobilization, legal mobilization is not automatic and may be better suited for some types of claims than others (Rosenberg 1991).

At the same time, litigation undoubtedly represents a significant channel for mobilization in the United States, one that is supported by an active network of entrepreneurial lawyers.

Given this network, there is no shortage of legal activity or lawsuits in the district court in absolute terms. According to the U.S. Statistical Abstract, Americans spent $149.7 billion on legal services in 2003 alone. By comparison, Americans spent $27.9 billion on agricultural services, $34.6 billion on the making of movies and sound recordings, and $30.6 billion on the manufacture of furniture and related products. And although many injuries never produce a lawsuit, Americans still managed to file an average of 261,763 civil lawsuits *per year* in the district courts from 1995 to 2005 (Administrative Office of the U.S. Courts 2005a, Table S-7; 2003a, Table S-7; 1997, Table S-7).

Litigation and Agenda Setting

Once mobilized, advocates must place their demands on the "to do" list of governmental decision makers. In Congress, agenda setting is highly politicized and subject to many factors outside of the control of claimants (Kingdon 1995; Hacker 1997). An unexpected crisis or sudden shift in media attention can push items off Congress' radar screen. Budgetary constraints or a negative cost assessment from the Congressional Budgeting Office can derail a proposal. A popular issue can be joined with less popular ones and be robbed of momentum.

By contrast, an individual claimant or "plaintiff" has greater control over agenda setting in the district courts. Specifically, a plaintiff places an issue on a district court's agenda or "docket" by filing a *complaint* (the first step in a lawsuit), which must satisfy a number of substantive and procedure requirements (FRCP, Rules 3–6). Substantively, it must (a) allege at least one valid *cause of action* that asserts that the target of the lawsuit, the "defendant," has violated the law and caused the plaintiff harm; and (b) set forth a "demand for judgment" that seeks a *remedy* for the alleged harm. This remedy might be money damages, an injunction, clarification of legal rights, or other such judicial actions. Procedurally, civil complaints must establish *jurisdiction* and *venue,* meaning that the district court is authorized to address the issues in the complaint and that the case is filed in the proper location (see 28 U.S.C. § 1331–1355, 1391). They must also satisfy the *rules of justiciability.* These rules include the doctrine of standing, which lays out when a claimant has a sufficient stake in a controversy to sue; the doctrines of ripeness and mootness, which determine whether the underlying controversy is either too premature or settled for adjudication; and the political question doctrine, which holds that some controversies are better left to the other branches. There are other requirements as well, such as rules governing the notification of interested parties and "statutes of limitation" that set time limits for bringing specific types of claims.

These requirements may seem onerous in the abstract but typically are not in practice. The rules of jurisdiction and venue are reasonably flexible, allowing some plaintiffs to engage in "forum shopping"—choosing a court that is most likely to be sympathetic to their claims. Similarly, the rules of justiciability are relatively open, allowing a wide range of claimants to bring a broad spectrum of controversies. In addition, the federal rules of civil procedure allow plaintiffs in most cases to make broad allegations that can be amended as the case proceeds (FRCP, Rule 8(a)). This is called *notice pleading,* which means that the complaint will be allowed as long as it gives the defendant fair warning of the underlying grievance and relief sought.

Again, it is easy to become lost in the technical ins- and-outs of these rules and lose sight of the fact that these rules related to core policy-making functions. They govern a distinctive mode of agenda setting, one that sharply differs from congressional agenda setting and has been central to groups fighting for civil rights, woman's equality, environmental protection, states' rights, abortion rights, and many others.

Litigation and Information Gathering

Once on the agenda, the next step is information gathering. Members of Congress have an elaborate tool kit for collecting background material and expert opinions on policy issues (Fisher 2002). They have staffs on Capitol Hill and their home districts. The Congressional Research Service, Government Accounting Office, Congressional Budget Office, and many others are available to answer congressional inquiries and provide analysis of legislation and governmental programs. Members of Congress also serve on committees, which have their own staffs and hold hearings. As part of the hearing process, members and their staffs can subpoena witnesses and documents. And members of Congress can—and do—turn to an army of lobbyists, pollsters, interest groups, and think tanks, which are more than willing to lend their expertise to a policy debate.

Civil litigation also features tools for information gathering. Once a complaint is filed (and the defendant answers), litigation moves to a new stage called *discovery* (see FRCP, Rules 26-37). During discovery, lawyers on each side independently investigate the facts of the case by, among other things, (a) filing *interrogatories*, which are written questions (FRCP, Rule 33); (b) taking *depositions,* which are interviews recorded by a court stenographer (FRCP, Rules 30,31); and (c) *subpoenaing documents* (FRCP, Rule 34). As a general matter, each side enjoys considerable latitude in deciding what information to pursue and have the right to investigate broadly.

During discovery, district court judges mainly serve as referees, determining whether each side is entitled to certain types of information, ruling on whether information can be used at trial, and facilitating negotiations through a variety of mechanisms, such as pretrial conferences. It should be added that, although lawyers dominate discovery, district judges have their own staffs, including law clerks from top law schools, which can help gather information, especially about the relevant law.

Perhaps not surprisingly, discovery can be very costly, as each side engages in parallel and often redundant investigations and seeks to leave no stone unturned prior to "all-at-once" trials (Kagan 2001; Langbein 1985).[3] In high profile cases, such as the battle over the fortune of Seward Johnson, the heir to the Johnson & Johnson fortune, discovery can cost millions of dollars (Langbein 1994). Even in routine cases, the costs of litigation are striking. In auto accident cases, lawyers' fees consume more than 40 percent of insurance settlements (Hensler et al. 1985, 27-28). A systematic study of 1,649 federal and state lawsuits similarly found that, in cases where plaintiffs recovered less than $10,000, the median plaintiff's legal costs totaled 35 percent when lawyers worked on contingency fees and 46 percent when the lawyers were paid on an hourly basis (Trubeck et al. 1983, 111). Defendants' legal costs were similar, suggesting legal fees accounted for more than half of the total recovery in relatively small stakes cases.

Studies of specific types of lawsuits reinforce these findings. A 1993 survey found that corporations paid law firms an average of $967,000 per case in defending their officers and directors in stockholders' securities fraud claims, which includes the 'less expensive" cases where the responding company won without paying a settlement (Lambert 1995, B16). The American Intellectual Property Law Association (AIPLA) found that the median cost per party of a patent case with $1 to $25 million at risk was almost $1.5 million in 2001 and $2 million in 2003. As the stakes increased, so did the costs. In cases with more than $25 million at stake, these costs were $3 million in 2001 and $4 million in 2003 (AIPLA 2001, 84-85, 2003, 93).

When viewed from the perspective of the legal system, the costliness of litigation can distort the process (Kagan 2001). Sometimes plaintiffs use the threat of litigation to coerce defendants to settle questionable claims—called *strike suits*—because it is cheaper for defendants to pay a few thousand dollars and settle a claim quickly than spend thousands on protracted litigation. In other cases, defendants use the cost of litigation to their advantage, burying plaintiffs under an avalanche of requests and depositions. Faced with such an on-slaught, plaintiffs may agree to settle cheaply or even walk away from a small but meritorious claim.

Yet discovery can advance the pubic interest. In the case of asbestos litigation, discussed later, it uncovered sometimes egregious corporate conduct that concealed significant health risks (Brodeur 1986). This information, in turn, has become part of the public record. The central point is that discovery is a powerful—albeit often costly—means for gathering information that not only shapes the resolution of specific lawsuits but also can shape broader public discourse on policy issues.

Litigation and Rulemaking

Once information is gathered, officials can make rules designed to address the underlying issues. Congress makes rules by passing legislation. The legislative process begins when an individual member of Congress or a group of members sponsor a bill. Before becoming a law, a bill must run a gauntlet of subcommittee and committee hearings and mark-up sessions, floor debates, and majority votes in both chambers of Congress. If differences exist between the House and Senate versions of a bill, a final compromise must be hammered out in confer-ence committees and a majority in both chambers must approve it. Once it passes Congress, the bill goes to the president, who can veto the bill and send it back to Congress, which can override a veto with a two-thirds vote (see, e.g., Davidson and Oleszek 2004).

Under these circumstances, congressional rulemaking power can be seen as collective and broad. It is collective in that, although individual members can initiate a bill, only a majority may pass a law. It is broad in that, if individual members can build stable majority coalitions that withstand the multiple-veto points in the rulemaking process, Congress passes statutes that are nationally binding, provided that the laws are constitutional.

In a sense, the district court's formal rulemaking power is the mirror opposite; it is individual and limited. Throughout the litigation process, individual district court judges can make authoritative decisions. Prior to trial, judges may rule on the admissibility of evidence; the validity of claims; and the proper jurisdiction, venue, and justiciability of a claim. During trial, judges make decisions on the proper scope of testimony, the appropriateness of evidence, and, if there is a jury, the wording of the jury instructions. After trial, district courts issue decisions with findings of fact and rulings of law and may become involved in enforcing their orders.

At the same time, when compared to Congress' lawmaking power, the scope of district court judges' rulemaking power is formally limited. As a legal matter, the doctrine of *stare decisis* provides that district court judges' decisions only formally bind the parties to the specific litigation and not other courts. In addition, district court judges must adhere to the decisions of higher courts within their circuit. From a policymaking perspective, *stare decisis* is not only a formal limitation on judicial power but also a distinct norm of judicial rulemaking, which requires judges to use specialized modes of legal reasoning to convince other judges to adopt their decisions and arguably promotes incrementalism (Feeley and Rubin 1998, 242).

Despite these limitations, district court decisions can pack significant policy-making punch. Although not binding, district court decisions are often cited as persuasive precedents. Moreover, federal legislation and legal precedents are often vague or distinguishable on the facts, which leave district court judges considerable room to maneuver in shaping the law. Indeed, district court judges often must engage in "interstitial legislation," filling gaps that inevitably appear when general legal rules are applied to particular cases (Cardozo 1921). Filling gaps in the law can require leaps in policy. The Americans with Disabilities Act, for example, was vague with respect to whether a disability for purposes of the statute should be assessed in its treated or untreated state. Resolving this ambiguity in the statute literally affected millions of Americans and tens of thousands of businesses (Barnes 2004a).

Litigation and Implementation

Making rules is one thing; implementing them is quite another. *Implementation* means actually putting the specific policy into practice. In general, Congress delegates the difficult and often contentious task of implementation to agencies, which have the power to promulgate specific regulations for enforcing general federal laws. Congress then can engage in "fire alarm" oversight (McCubbins and Schwartz 1984), addressing issues raised by disgruntled groups who appeal to Congress for assistance in dealing with agencies.

Unlike Congress, district courts are often directly engaged in enforcing their own decisions. For instance, if the defendant refuses to pay a judgment for damages, the plaintiff can return to court and seek an order that places a lien on the defendant's assets or garnish the defendant's wages. In law school, these orders fall under the broad headings of *remedy law* and *postenforcement judgments.* From a policy-making vantage, these actions represent a form of judicial implementation.

District court judges also implement decisions using their injunctive powers, which enable them to order specific conduct, and shaping consent decrees, which are agreements among the litigants enforced by the courts. For example, courts have-with mixed results-used these powers to reform schools, public housing, mental health institutions, police practices, and prisons (Sabel and Simon 1999; Feeley and Rubin 1998; Sandler and Schoenbrod 2004; see also Chayes 1976; Fuller 1978). These cases, in turn, have produced diverse styles of judicial implementation, which underscore the flexibility of the courts' implementation powers.

Compare efforts to reform mental health institutions in Alabama and the District of Columbia. In Alabama, the court adopted a top-down, fixed rule approach to reforming mental health institutions (*Wyatt v. Stickney* 1972), mandating at least ten square feet of space per patient in the dining room, an air temperature between 68°P and 83°F, hot water at 110°, one toilet for every eight patients, no more than six patients per room, and specific patient-staff ratios for thirty-five job categories. In the District of Columbia, the court rejected the command and control model of *Wyatt* and fostered an "experimentalist" approach, which set forth broad goals, such as "appropriate individualized" treatment in the "least restrictive, most integrated, and least restrictive setting" and required the individualized service plans for treatment to be updated at least annually (Sabel and Simon 1999, 18).

Of course, judicial implementation of court decisions and consent decrees barely scratches the surface of the district courts' role in implementing federal policy (Melnick 2004; Kagan 2001; Shapiro 1988). Shifts in the structure of legislative programs have greatly extended the district courts' influence over administrative procedures and rulemaking. To elaborate briefly, beginning in the late 1960's, Congress passed laws that sought to address widespread social problems, such as discrimination, consumer safety, and environment degradation. To implement this ambitious agenda, Congress created an alphabet soup of new, often overlapping federal agencies. At the same time, Congress feared that industries would eventually dominate the very agencies designed to regulate their conduct. To inoculate agencies from industry capture, Congress created a host of procedural mechanisms, such as "private attorneys general" provisions, which allow public interest groups to participate in administrative rulemaking and haul agencies into court for failure to meet their obligations.

During the same period, federal judges created new legal doctrines that extended their role in reviewing agency decisions. For example, the landmark Supreme Court decision of *Goldberg v. Kelly* (1970) required hearings for those facing the loss of welfare benefits and triggered the creation of myriad administrative hearings subject to district court review. Meanwhile, federal judges relaxed the rules of justiciability, such as the standing doctrine, which facilitated public interest group litigation against agencies (Stewart and Sunstein 1982).

This pincer movement by Congress and the courts has had a predictable and profound effect judicial power in the United States. Today, district court judges not only serve their traditional role of resolving politically important legal cases and enforcing their decisions, but also play a significant role in overseeing federal agencies and deciding regulatory disputes under the "hard look" doctrine, which can serve as a doctrine of judicial second guessing (Melnick 2004).[5] In this dual role, district court judges have shaped polices far beyond the reach of judges in other industrialized democracies, including coal mine safety, nursing home care, corporate insolvency, educational opportunity, labor relations, the introduction of new drugs, air pollution, the use of polyvinyl chlorides, and others (Kagan 2001, Table 8, collecting authority).

The D.C. Circuit: Small Load, Big Clout

John Gramlich

Within hours of President Barack Obama's June 4 nomination of three candidates to the Court of Appeals for the District of Columbia Circuit, Senate Republicans sharply questioned whether the court needs the additional judges. A cursory look at the 12 regular federal appellate courts shows, indeed, that the D.C. Circuit is at or near the bottom in most measures of judicial caseload

But there are plenty of reasons, from the political to the practical for Obama to push to fill all the vacancies on the D.C. Circuit.

OBAMA'S PICKS: Judicial nominees, from left: Robert L. Wilkins, Cornelia T.L. "Nina" Pillard and Patricia Ann Millet. *Copyright in the Public Domain.*

The court's unique jurisdiction provides an obvious explanation. Two landmark environmental laws, the Clean Air Act and the Safe Drinking Water Act, stipulate that legal actions taken in response to government actions under those statutes "may be filed only in the United States Court of Appeals for the District of Columbia Circuit." Appeals filed on behalf of the detainees at Guantanamo Bay, Cuba, also go directly to the D.C. Circuit for review.

John Gramlich, "The D.C. Circuit: Small Load, Big Clout," CQ Weekly, pp. 974-975. Copyright © 2013 by CQ Roll Call, Inc. Reprinted with permission.

When it comes to elections, federal law grants the D.C. Circuit a prominent role in approving changes to state and local voting practices. By law, one member of the court must participate in all court reviews of electoral changes that are proposed in states and localities with a history of racial discrimination.

"The nature of the D.C. Circuit's caseload is what sets it apart from other courts," Patricia M. Wald, a former chief judge of the 11-seat court, wrote in a Washington Post op-ed in February.

If the D.C. Circuit's jurisdiction is heavy on cases of national importance, it is light on the kinds of routine criminal appeals that occupy other appeals courts, notes Amanda Frost, an Amencan University law professor who clerked at the court Frost says the reason is simple: The court's physical jurisdiction covers the District of Columbia, white other circuits, particularly the San Francisco-based 9th Circuit, cover huge geographical areas with many more potential criminal appellants

Wald, therefore, argues that caseload is an inadequate measure of the court's importance.

The court's exclusive jurisdiction over key legal areas also presents a more practical concern for the Obama administration: Because it is the only court that hears certain kinds of cases, its decisions are often final.

The Supreme Court is really unlikely to take a case when there's not a circuit split," notes Sean Helte, legislative counsel for the environmental legal advocacy group Earthjustice. "When the D.C. Circuit is the only court that can consider an issue, you're never going to have a circuit court split."

That is where politics may enter the debate. The D.C. Circuit is currently divided between four Democratic and four Republican appointees, and the addition of three more of Obama's judges would certainly shift the balance—a point that Senate Republicans are not shy about making.

The D.C. Circuit has issued some stinging rebukes to Obama in recent months—led by its January ruling that the president's appointments to the National Labor Relations Board violated the Constitution. Adding three judges might improve the administration's chances of finding a sympathetic audience.

Iowa Republican Charles E. Grassley, the top Republican on the Senate Judiciary Committee, is building GOP support for a bill that would prevent Obama's appointments by stripping the D.C. Circuit of the three seats he hopes to fill.

Some observers see the legislation as a kind of statement of approval for the court's recent rulings

"I don't think Grassley and the Republicans would be fighting so hard to keep more judges off the court if they didn't Jike the way it's going now," says Russell Wheeler, a Brookings Institution scholar who studies the federal courts.

Court Upholds Health Care Law

Emily Ethridge

T he Supreme Court's historic June 28 ruling that President Obama's signature health care law (PL 111-148, PL 11M52) can go forward as written gave Democrats a reason to cheer and Republicans a compelling issue to take with them on the campaign trail this fall.

In a 5-4 opinion written by Chief Justice John G. Roberts Jr., the court decided that the central part of the 2010 health care overhaul—the individual mandate that most Americans buy health insurance or pay a penalty—could be enforced as a tax under Congress' constitutional powers and did not need to be struck down.

While agreeing with plaintiffs that the mandate would be unconstitutional under the Commerce Clause, the court essentially chose to uphold the entire law with the mandate penalty treated as a tax.

Republicans, saying the decision was disappointing but not a surprise, immediately shot back with a two-pronged agenda vote on legislation to repeal the law—an effort that will go no further than the House, given the Democratic majority in the Senate—and make the case to the people that the only way to overturn what they call Obamacare will be to put the GOP in charge in both chambers of Congress as well as in the White House via this November's election.

"I think the real outcome of today's decision is to strengthen our resolve to make sure that this law is in fact repealed," House Speaker John A. Boehner, R-Ohio, said immediately after the court issued Its ruling. "We're going to work every single day between now and Election Day, and the American people then will get an opportunity to make their decision on Election Day, because elections have consequences:

The Republicans' first move was to schedule a July 11 House floor vote on a bill to repeal the entire law—just after lawmakers return from the July Fourth recess. In January 2011, in one of their first major votes after taking the majority, Republicans in the House passed a repeal bill (HR 2).

Emily Ethridge, "Court Upholds Health Care Law," CQ Weekly, pp. 1380-1382. Copyright © 2012 by CQ Roll Call, Inc. Reprinted with permission.

But just as they did 18 months ago, Senate Democrats, who hold a tenuous majority that could vanish after the fall election, can for now block any such measure. Senate Majority Leader Harry Reid, O-Nev., dismissed the House plan as "just a show Vote."

END OF A LONG WAIT

The court's decision ended months of waiting in Washington and in state capitals, where legislatures and governors' offices had placed on hold plans to implement their part of the law until they knew whether it would continue to exist. Throngs of people, including many activists on both sides of the issue as well as lawmakers, parked in front of the Supreme Court the morning the decision was to be announced, ready to cheer or protest the outcome, or just to witness history.

In writing the majority opinion, Roberts sided with the liberals on the bench, shutting out the other conservatives. He wrote that the law's requirement that most individuals obtain health Insurance falls within Congress' constitutional power to levy taxes.

"The federal government does not have the power to order people to buy health Insurance; Roberts wrote. "Section 5000A would therefore be unconstitutional if read as a command. The federal government does have the power to impose a tax on those without health insurance. Section 5000A is therefore constitutional because it can reasonably be read as a tax."

Many court observers had expected that Justice Anthony M. Kennedy, who wrote the dissent, would be the swing vote. Instead, it was Roberts, who is generally more conservative than Kennedy and was appointed to the court in 2005 by President George W. Bush. Obama voted against Roberts' confirmation when he was an Illinois senator.

ROOM FOR IMPROVEMENT

The decision did include some bad news for the law's supporters. The court ruled that states can opt out of a provision in the law that significantly expands the Medicaid health care program for the poor without losing all of their federal Medicaid funds. The law had included such a punishment for failure to participate. (Medcaid opt-out fallout, p. 1366)

But overall, Democrats were pleased with the outcome of the case and called on Republicans to work with them to improve the law rather than continue to try to repeal it.

"We know that when we come back here after the elections, there may be some things we need to do to improve the law, and we'll do that working together," Reid said. An aide said the maiority leader did not have any specific changes in mind.

Obama also suggested that there could be some targeted revisions

"The highest court in the land has now spoken. We will conlinue to implement this law. And we'll work together to improve on it where we can," Obama said shortly after the court's ruling. "But what we won't do, what the country can't afford to do, is refight the political battles of two years ago or go back lo the way things were."

But with nearly all GOP lawmakers opposed to the entire law, Republicans are unlikely to be interested in merely fine-tuning legislation they have opposed from the beginning of the debate and have pledged to overturn whenever they can do so

In addition to the July vote in the House, Republicans may continue to offer bills that go after individual provisions or the law—even though those bills probably will not get past Senate Democrats.

One likely target is the board created by the health care law to restrict Medicare spending growth, which some opponents say is a vehicle for rationing care and have called a "death panel."

Republicans might also try to change how the law addresses health insurance coverage of contraceptive services. Among many other targets is the proposed repeal of a 2.3 percent tax on medical devices set to go into effect next year. (Repeal and replace bills, p. 1382)

Meanwhile, Senate Republicans signaled that they will target the scope of subsidies provided under the overhaul.

"One of the things that is so offensive to me is families earning upwards of $90,000 a year are going to get subsidies. . . My God, where does it end?" asked Orrin G. Hatch of Utah, the top-ranking Republican on the Senate Finance Committee.

The GOP could also go after the law's funding through the appropriations process Republicans have tried to cut money for various parts of the law in previous spending bills, and they have advanced measures to change some mandatory funding to discretionary spending subject to the appropriations process.

REPEAL BY RECONCILIATION

Some Republicans are looking for ways to bring down the law after the November election. Senate Minority Whip Jon Kyl of Arizona said a Republican-led Senate in the next Congress could seek to repeal much of the health care law with a simple majority vote using the budget reconciliation process.

The expedited process bars filibusters In the Senate and would allow Republicans to avoid the 60 -vote minimum required to limit debate. But the rules governing reconciliation pose considerable challenges, even if the GOP is in the majority

Using reconciliation would only be filling, given that Democrats used reconciliation in 2010 to enact a portion of the overhaul law.

"I think with a 50-vote majority in the Senate, Republicans could do the same things that Democrats did," said Kyl, who is retiring this year. The GOP can use reconciliation to reverse the more onerous provisions of Obamacare and replace them with what Republicans have been talking about," he said.

Rep. Cathy McMorris Rodgers, R-Wash, alluded to such a strategy in responding to the Supreme Court's ruling that the health care law's requirement that individuals obtain insurance or pay a penalty amounts to a tax and thus is constitutionally permissible.

"They upheld the law as a tax, and therefore this is the largest tax increase in America's history," McMorris Rodgers said. "But it also will change the course as we move forward, in that if it's the tax that made it constitutional, then that gives us some options through the budget to repeal this tax."

But budget observers say a full repeal would be impossible using the special procedures of reconciliation.

Sarah Binder, a Senate expert al George Washington University and the Brookings Institution, was quick to point out the pitfalls. An effort to repeal the health care law might run afoul of a Senate rule named for Robert C. Byrd, the late West Virginia Democrat.

"The Byrd rule prevents provisions that are 'extraneous' to budget targets from being included in reconciliation—unless proponents can muster 60 votes to waive a Byrd rule challenge or to reject a point of order under the rule," Binder wrote at the Monkey Cage blog on June 28.

Further, budget rules generally do not allow provisions in reconciliation bills that would increase the budget deficit. And repealing the health care law would cost money, since it has been scored by the Congressional Budget Office as saving billions of dollars.

Rep. Michele Bachman, R-Minn., in an interview on CNN, also suggested using reconciliation to repeal the health care law but she added that Republicans will still need a two-thirds majority to override a presidential veto—unless the GOP can also win the White House this fall.

"So, if there is a majority in the Senate, and a majority In the House, and if we have Mitt Romney as the next president of the United Slates, we can and we will repeal Obamacare," Bachmann said.

REPLACEMENT PARTS

Any GOP effort to replace aspects of the health care law might also await the election results. While Republicans have insisted that repeal of the current law must happen first, many also say they want to offer solutions for problems in the health care system.

McMorris Rodgers said no decision has been made on whether to act on Republican replacement bills before the elections.

"We support reforms like allowing the individual and families to choose whether that is the best health insurance for them, whether it's outside of state boundaries or allowing small groups to pool," said McMorris Rodgers. She also mentioned Republicans' desire to change the medical liability system,

Democrats also acknowledged that the political battle over the health care overhaul is not finished. Although many provisions of the law are popular on their own, the law as a whole does not have broad public support. Democrats said their party needs to continue to highlight its benefits.

"The court's validation of the law may cause many Americans to reconsider their opinion of it as well," said Sen. Charles E. Schumer, D-N.Y.

"I think the American people now will begin to pay attention, now that it's settled", said Iowa Democrat Tom Harkin, chairman of the Senate Health, Education, Labor and Pensions Committee. "I think people are going to say, 'Yes, that's the health care we want.'"

Melissa Attias, Jane Norman, Niels Lesniewski and Alan K. Ota contributed to this story

Illinois' $105-billion public pension fix struck down by state Supreme Court

Michael Muskal

A ruling striking down Illinois' pension law means Republican Gov. Bruce Rauner and the state Legislature will have to find another way to handle a massive budget deficit.

Court says public employee pensions are protected even if Illinois faces acute financial problems.

Taxpayers are facing a $ I-trillion public pension headache across the nation—and that remains untouched after an Illinois Supreme Court ruling on Friday.

The top court in Illinois unanimously threw out a legislative fix designed to erase a $105-billion pension liability the state is facing. In its 38-page written opinion, the court said that the state constitution bars public employee pension benefits from being diminished or impaired.

The ruling has a profound impact in Illinois, on its political system and on the city of Chicago, which also faces pension problems. But while many states face similar issues, the Illinois court decision had been expected, said Jean-Pierre Aubry, assistant director for state and local research at the Center for Retirement Research at Boston College.

"If the court decision had gone against the expectation then it would have had a greater impact," Aubry said. "That would have been more meaningful and might have been more broad."

The Illinois court did not mince words in making it clear that the constitution protected employees even if the state was facing acute problems.

"The financial challenges facing state and local government in Illinois are well known and significant. In ruling as we have today, we do not mean to minimize the gravity of the state's problems or the magnitude of the difficulty facing our elected representatives," Justice Lloyd Karmeier said, writing for the court.

"It is our obligation, however, just as it is theirs, to ensure that the law is followed," he wrote. "That is true at all times. It is especially important in times of crisis when, as this case

Michael Muskal, "Illinois $105 Billion Public Pension Fix Struck Down by State Supreme Court," Los Angeles Times. Copyright © 2015 by Los Angeles Times Syndicate. Reprinted with permission.

demonstrates, even clear principles and long-standing precedent are threatened. Crisis is not an excuse to abandon the rule of law."

The public pension problem has been well-documented and touches municipalities across the country. Local governments negotiated contracts including what conservatives say are overly generous benefits. As the economy contracted in recent years because of the recession, meeting state obligations became more difficult. Payments to the pension systems took up a larger and larger share of municipal budgets, cutting the funds available for other government needs like roads and police.

Nationwide, state pension plans are about 72% funded with about 6% of the municipal budgets going to pension systems, Aubry estimated. The total shortfall is believed to be about $1 trillion.

Illinois is in especially dire straits, facing a hole of more than $100 billion. To solve the problem, lawmakers pushed through a deal near the end of 2013 designed to save an estimated $160 billion over 30 years by changing the rules for current employees. The new pension plan included a lower future cost-of-living adjustment, an increase in the age when employees could retire and a cap on pension payments for those at the high end of the scale.

The deal was politically contentious in a state with strong unions that tend to support the ruling Democrats. Still, state officials argued that they had no choice.

"Our economy is and has always been subject to fluctuations, sometimes very extreme fluctuations," said Karmeier, a Republican.

But, he noted, "the law was clear that the promised benefits would therefore have to be paid and that the responsibility for providing the state's share of the necessary funding fell squarely on the Legislature's shoulders."

According to Aubry, about 15 states that face pension problems have some form of constitutional language protecting existing pension rules. Those states include California, Georgia, Kansas, Nebraska, Oregon and Pennsylvania.

Though many of the states have altered how benefits are calculated for existing employees, the biggest changes, like those in California, involve major revisions for new hires.

That is important because it allows the changes to affect the new workforce over the long term instead of trying to impose the shock on workers who are approaching retirement age.

"If the system can tread water," Aubry said, "eventually the cost of the system starts shrinking."

Rick Pearson and Kim Geiger of the Chicago Tribune contributed to this report.

2. Judicial Policy Making as A Means to "Correct" Political Failures

A s will be explored later in the reader, judicial policy-making can be a disaster and undermine democratic values. Nevertheless, many scholars insist that one of the promises of the courts, especially in the American system of fragmented power, is its ability to act on behalf of unpopular groups when the elected branches of government are either unwilling or unable to do so. These readings provide several potential examples of courts "correcting"—or trying to correct—political failures by standing up for unpopular or disadvantaged groups.

ADDITIONAL RECOMMENDED MATERIALS:

Malcolm Feeley and Edward Rubin, *Judicial Policy Making and the Modern State* (1998)

Lee Epstein, Jack Knight, and Andrew D. Martin, "The Supreme Court as a Strategic National Policy Maker," *Emory Law Journal* 50 (2001): 583-611

Paul Frymer, "Acting When Elected Officials Won't: Federal Courts and Civil Rights Enforcement in U.S. Labor Unions, 1935-85," *APSR* 97(3):483-499

Michael McCann, "How the Supreme Court Matters in American Politics: New Institutionalists Perspectives." In *The Supreme Court in American Politics*. Edited by Howard Gillman and Cornell Clayton (1999).

Brown v. Board
of Education of Topeka
(no. 1.)

WARREN, C.J., Opinion of the Court
SUPREME COURT OF THE UNITED STATES
347 U.S. 483
Brown v. Board of Education of Topeka
APPEAL FROM THE UNITED STATES DISTRICT COURT FOR THE DISTRICT OF
KANSAS

No. 1. Argued: Argued December 9, 1952, Reargued December 8, 1953 — Decided: Decided May 17, 1954

[p*486] MR. CHIEF JUSTICE WARREN delivered the opinion of the Court.

These cases come to us from the States of Kansas, South Carolina, Virginia, and Delaware. They are premised on different facts and different local conditions, but a common legal question justifies their consideration together in this consolidated opinion.[1][p487]

In each of the cases, minors of the Negro race, through their legal representatives, seek the aid of the courts in obtaining admission to the public schools of their community on a nonsegregated basis. In each instance,[p488] they had been denied admission to schools attended by white children under laws requiring or permitting segregation according to race. This segregation was alleged to deprive the plaintiffs of the equal protection of the laws under the Fourteenth Amendment. In each of the cases other than the Delaware case, a three-judge federal district court denied relief to the plaintiffs on the so-called "separate but equal" doctrine announced by this Court in Plessy v. Fergson, 163 U.S. 537. Under that doctrine, equality of treatment is accorded when the races are provided substantially equal facilities, even though these facilities be separate. In the Delaware case, the Supreme Court

Copyright in the Public Domain.

of Delaware adhered to that doctrine, but ordered that the plaintiffs be admitted to the white schools because of their superiority to the Negro schools.

The plaintiffs contend that segregated public schools are not "equal" and cannot be made "equal," and that hence they are deprived of the equal protection of the laws. Because of the obvious importance of the question presented, the Court took jurisdiction.[2] Argument was heard in the 1952 Term, and reargument was heard this Term on certain questions propounded by the Court.[3][p489]

Reargument was largely devoted to the circumstances surrounding the adoption of the Fourteenth Amendment in 1868. It covered exhaustively consideration of the Amendment in Congress, ratification by the states, then-existing practices in racial segregation, and the views of proponents and opponents of the Amendment. This discussion and our own investigation convince us that, although these sources cast some light, it is not enough to resolve the problem with which we are faced. At best, they are inconclusive. The most avid proponents of the post-War Amendments undoubtedly intended them to remove all legal distinctions among "all persons born or naturalized in the United States." Their opponents, just as certainly, were antagonistic to both the letter and the spirit of the Amendments and wished them to have the most limited effect. What others in Congress and the state legislatures had in mind cannot be determined with any degree of certainty.

An additional reason for the inconclusive nature of the Amendment's history with respect to segregated schools is the status of public education at that time.[4] In the South, the movement toward free common schools, supported [p490] by general taxation, had not yet taken hold. Education of white children was largely in the hands of private groups. Education of Negroes was almost nonexistent, and practically all of the race were illiterate. In fact, any education of Negroes was forbidden by law in some states. Today, in contrast, many Negroes have achieved outstanding success in the arts and sciences, as well as in the business and professional world. It is true that public school education at the time of the Amendment had advanced further in the North, but the effect of the Amendment on Northern States was generally ignored in the congressional debates. Even in the North, the conditions of public education did not approximate those existing today. The curriculum was usually rudimentary; ungraded schools were common in rural areas; the school term was but three months a year in many states, and compulsory school attendance was virtually unknown. As a consequence, it is not surprising that there should be so little in the history of the Fourteenth Amendment relating to its intended effect on public education.

In the first cases in this Court construing the Fourteenth Amendment, decided shortly after its adoption, the Court interpreted it as proscribing all state-imposed discriminations against the Negro race.[5] The doctrine of[p491] "separate but equal" did not make its appearance in this Court until 1896 in the case of Plessy v. Ferguson, supra, involving not education but transportation.[6] American courts have since labored with the doctrine for over half a century. In this Court, there have been six cases involving the "separate but equal" doctrine in the field of public education.[7] In Gumming v. County Board of Education, 175 U.S. 528, and Gong Lum v. Rice, 275 U.S. 78, the validity of the doctrine itself was not challenged.[8] In more recent cases, all on the graduate school[p492] level, inequality was found in that specific benefits enjoyed by white students were denied to Negro students of the same educational qualifications. Missouri ex rel. Gaines v. Canada, 305 U.S. 337; Sipuel v. Oklahoma, 332 U.S. 631; Sweatt v. Painter, 339 U.S. 629; McLaurin v. Oklahoma State Regents, 339 U.S. 637. In none of these cases was it necessary to reexamine the doctrine to grant relief to the Negro plaintiff. And in Sweatt v. Painter, supra, the Court expressly reserved decision on the question whether Plessy v. Ferguson should be held inapplicable to public education.

In the instant cases, that question is directly presented. Here, unlike Sweatt v. Painter, there are findings below that the Negro and white schools involved have been equalized, or are being equalized, with respect to buildings, curricula, qualifications and salaries of teachers, and other "tangible" factors.[9] Our decision, therefore, cannot turn on merely a comparison of these tangible factors in the Negro and white schools involved in each of the cases. We must look instead to the effect of segregation itself on public education.

In approaching this problem, we cannot turn the clock back to 1868, when the Amendment was adopted, or even to 1896, when Plessy v. Ferguson was written. We must consider public education in the light of its full development and its present place in American life throughout[p493] the Nation. Only in this way can it be determined if segregation in public schools deprives these plaintiffs of the equal protection of the laws.

Today, education is perhaps the most important function of state and local governments. Compulsory school attendance laws and the great expenditures for education both demonstrate our recognition of the importance of education to our democratic society. It is required in the performance of our most basic public responsibilities, even service in the armed forces. It is the very foundation of good citizenship. Today it is a principal instrument in awakening the child to cultural values, in preparing him for later professional training, and in helping him to adjust normally to his environment. In these days, it is doubtful that any child may reasonably be expected to succeed in life if he is denied the opportunity of an education. Such an opportunity, where the state has undertaken to provide it, is a right which must be made available to all on equal terms.

We come then to the question presented: Does segregation of children in public schools solely on the basis of race, even though the physical facilities and other "tangible" factors may be equal, deprive the children of the minority group of equal educational opportunities? We believe that it does.

In Sweatt v. Painter, supra, in finding that a segregated law school for Negroes could not provide them equal educational opportunities, this Court relied in large part on "those qualities which are incapable of objective measurement but which make for greatness in a law school." In McLaurin v. Oklahoma State Regents, supra, the Court, in requiring that a Negro admitted to a white graduate school be treated like all other students, again resorted to intangible considerations: "... his ability to study, to engage in discussions and exchange views with other students, and, in general, to learn his profession." [p*494] Such considerations apply with added force to children in grade and high schools. To separate them from others of similar age and qualifications solely because of their race generates a feeling of inferiority as to their status in the community that may affect their hearts and minds in a way unlikely ever to be undone. The effect of this separation on their educational opportunities was well stated by a finding in the Kansas case by a court which nevertheless felt compelled to rule against the Negro plaintiffs: Segregation of white and colored children in public schools has a detrimental effect upon the colored children. The impact is greater when it has the sanction of the law, for the policy of separating the races is usually interpreted as denoting the inferiority of the negro group. A sense of inferiority affects the motivation of a child to learn. Segregation with the sanction of law, therefore, has a tendency to [retard] the educational and mental development of negro children and to deprive them of some of the benefits they would receive in a racial[ly] integrated school system.[10] Whatever may have been the extent of psychological knowledge at the time of Plessy v. Ferguson, this finding is amply supported by modern authority.[11] Any language[p495] in Plessy v. Ferguson contrary to this finding is rejected.

We conclude that, in the field of public education, the doctrine of "separate but equal" has no place. Separate educational facilities are inherently unequal. Therefore, we hold that the plaintiffs and others similarly situated for whom the actions have been brought are, by reason of the segregation complained of, deprived of the equal protection of the laws guaranteed by the Fourteenth Amendment. This disposition makes unnecessary any discussion whether such segregation also violates the Due Process Clause of the Fourteenth Amendment.[12]

Because these are class actions, because of the wide applicability of this decision, and because of the great variety of local conditions, the formulation of decrees in these cases presents problems of considerable complexity. On reargument, the consideration of appropriate relief was necessarily subordinated to the primary question—the constitutionality of segregation in public education. We have now announced that such segregation is a denial of the equal protection of the laws. In order that we may have the full assistance of the parties in formulating decrees, the cases will be restored to the docket, and the parties are requested to present further argument on Questions 4 and 5 previously propounded by the Court for the reargument this Term.[13] The Attorney General[p496] of the United States is again invited to participate. The Attorneys General of the states requiring or permitting segregation in public education will also be permitted to appear as amici curiae upon request to do so by September 15, 1954, and submission of briefs by October 1, 1954.[14]

It is so ordered.

NOTES

* Together with No. 2, *Briggs et al. v. Elliott et al*, on appeal from the United States District Court for the Eastern District of South Carolina, argued December 9-10, 1952, reargued December 7-8, 1953; No. 4, *Davis et al. v. County School Board of Prince Edward County*, Virginia, et al., on appeal from the United States District Court for the Eastern District of Virginia, argued December 10, 1952, reargued December 7-8, 1953, and No. 10, *Gebhart et al. v. Belton et al.*, on certiorari to the Supreme Court of Delaware, argued December 11, 1952, reargued December 9, 1953.

1. In the Kansas case, *Brown v. Board of Education*, the plaintiffs are Negro children of elementary school age residing in Topeka. They brought this action in the United States District Court for the District of Kansas to enjoin enforcement of a Kansas statute which permits, but does not require, cities of more than 15,000 population to maintain separate school facilities for Negro and white students. Kan.Gen.Stat. § 72-1724 (1949). Pursuant to that authority, the Topeka Board of Education elected to establish segregated elementary schools. Other public schools in the community, however, are operated on a nonsegregated basis. The three-judge District Court, convened under 28 U.S.C. §§ 2281 and 2284, found that segregation in public education has a detrimental effect upon Negro children, but denied relief on the ground that the Negro and white schools were substantially equal with respect to buildings, transportation, curricula, and educational qualifications of teachers. 98 F.Supp. 797. The case is here on direct appeal under 28 U.S.C. § 1253.

In the South Carolina case, *Briggs v. Elliott,* the plaintiffs are Negro children of both elementary and high school age residing in Clarendon County. They brought this action in the United States District Court for the Eastern District of South Carolina to enjoin enforcement of provisions in the state constitution and statutory code which require the segregation of Negroes and whites in public schools. S.C.Const., Art. XI, § 7; S.C.Code § 5377 (1942). The three-judge District Court, convened under 28 U.S.C. §§ 2281 and 2284, denied the requested relief. The court found that the Negro schools were inferior to the white schools, and ordered the defendants to begin immediately to equalize the facilities. But the court sustained the validity of the contested provisions and denied the plaintiffs admission to the white schools during the equalization program. 98 F.Supp. 529. This Court vacated the District Court's judgment and remanded the case for the purpose of obtaining the court's views on a report filed by the defendants concerning the progress made in the equalization program. 342 U.S. 350. On remand, the District Court found that substantial equality had been achieved except for buildings and that the defendants were proceeding to rectify this inequality as well. 103 F.Supp. 920. The case is again here on direct appeal under 28 U.S.C. § 1253.

In the Virginia case, *Davis v. County School Board,* the plaintiffs are Negro children of high school age residing in Prince Edward County. They brought this action in the United States District Court for the Eastern District of Virginia to enjoin enforcement of provisions in the state constitution and statutory code which require the segregation of Negroes and whites in public schools. Va.Const., § 140; Va.Code § 22-221 (1950). The three-judge District Court, convened under 28 U.S.C. §§ 2281 and 2284, denied the requested relief. The court found the Negro school inferior in physical plant, curricula, and transportation, and ordered the defendants forthwith to provide substantially equal curricula and transportation and to "proceed with all reasonable diligence and dispatch to remove" the inequality in physical plant. But, as in the South Carolina case, the court sustained the validity of the contested provisions and denied the plaintiffs admission to the white schools during the equalization program. 103 F.Supp. 337. The case is here on direct appeal under 28 U.S.C. § 1253.

In the Delaware case, *Gebhart v. Belton,* the plaintiffs are Negro children of both elementary and high school age residing in New Castle County. They brought this action in the Delaware Court of Chancery to enjoin enforcement of provisions in the state constitution and statutory code which require the segregation of Negroes and whites in public schools. Del.Const., Art. X, § 2; Del.Rev.Code § 2631 (1935). The Chancellor gave judgment for the plaintiffs and ordered their immediate admission to schools previously attended only by white children, on the ground that the Negro schools were inferior with respect to teacher training, pupil-teacher ratio, extracurricular activities, physical plant, and time and distance involved in travel. 87 A.2d 862. The Chancellor also found that segregation itself results in an inferior education for Negro children *(see* note 10, *infra),* but did not rest his decision on that ground. *Id.* at 865. The Chancellor's decree was affirmed by the Supreme Court of Delaware, which intimated, however, that the defendants might be able to obtain a modification of the decree after equalization of the Negro and white schools had been accomplished. 91 A.2d 137, 152. The defendants, contending only that the Delaware courts had erred in ordering the immediate admission of the Negro plaintiffs to the white schools, applied to this Court for certiorari. The writ was granted, 344 U.S. 891. The plaintiffs, who were successful below, did not submit a cross-petition.

2. 344 U.S. 1, 141, 891.
3. 345 U.S. 972. The Attorney General of the United States participated both Terms as amicus curiae.
4. For a general study of the development of public education prior to the Amendment, see Butts and Cremin, A History of Education in American Culture (1953), Pts. I, II; Cubberley, Public Education in the United States (1934 ed.), cc. II-XII. School practices current at the time of the adoption of the Fourteenth Amendment are described in Butts and Cremin, supra, at 269-275; Cubberley, supra, at 288-339, 408-431; Knight, Public Education in the South (1922), cc. VIII, IX. See also H. Ex.Doc. No. 315, 41st Cong., 2d Sess. (1871). Although the demand for free public schools followed substantially the same pattern in both the North and the South, the development in the South did not begin to gain momentum until about 1850, some twenty years after that in the North. The reasons for the somewhat slower development in the South (e.g., the rural character of the South and the different regional attitudes toward state assistance) are well explained in Cubberley, supra, at 408-423. In the country as a whole, but particularly in the South, the War virtually stopped all progress in public education. Id. at 427-428. The low status of Negro education in all sections of the country, both before and immediately after the War, is described in Beale, A History of Freedom of Teaching in American Schools (1941), 112-132, 175-195. Compulsory school attendance laws were not generally adopted until after the ratification of the Fourteenth Amendment, and it was not until 1918 that such laws were in force in all the states. Cubberley, supra, at 563-565.
5. Slaughter-House Cases, 16 Wall. 36, 67-72 (1873); Strauderv. West Virginia, 100 U.S. 303, 307-308 (1880): It ordains that no State shall deprive any person of life, liberty,

or property, without due process of law, or deny to any person within its jurisdiction the equal protection of the laws. What is this but declaring that the law in the States shall be the same for the black as for the white; that all persons, whether colored or white, shall stand equal before the laws of the States, and, in regard to the colored race, for whose protection the amendment was primarily designed, that no discrimination shall be made against them by law because of their color? The words of the amendment, it is true, are prohibitory, but they contain a necessary implication of a positive immunity, or right, most valuable to the colored race—the right to exemption from unfriendly legislation against them distinctively as colored—exemption from legal discriminations, implying inferiority in civil society, lessening the security of their enjoyment of the rights which others enjoy, and discriminations which are steps towards reducing them to the condition of a subject race. See also Virginia v. Rives, 100 U.S. 313, 318 (1880); Ex parte Virginia, 100 U.S. 339, 344-345 (1880).

6. The doctrine apparently originated in *Roberts v. City of Boston*, 59 Mass. 198, 206 (1850), upholding school segregation against attack as being violative of a state constitutional guarantee of equality. Segregation in Boston public schools was eliminated in 1855. Mass. Acts 1855, c. 256. But elsewhere in the North, segregation in public education has persisted in some communities until recent years. It is apparent that such segregation has long been a nationwide problem, not merely one of sectional concern.

7. See also *Berea College v. Kentucky*, 211 U.S. 45 (1908).

8. In the Cummin case, Negro taxpayers sought an injunction requiring the defendant school board to discontinue the operation of a high school for white children until the board resumed operation of a high school for Negro children. Similarly, in the Gong Lum case, the plaintiff, a child of Chinese descent, contended only that state authorities had misapplied the doctrine by classifying him with Negro children and requiring him to attend a Negro school.

9. In the Kansas case, the court below found substantial equality as to all such factors. 98 F.Supp. 797, 798. In the South Carolina case, the court below found that the defendants were proceeding "promptly and in good faith to comply with the court's decree." 103 F.Supp. 920, 921. In the Virginia case, the court below noted that the equalization program was already "afoot and progressing" (103 F.Supp. 337, 341); since then, we have been advised, in the Virginia Attorney General's brief on reargument, that the program has now been completed. In the Delaware case, the court below similarly noted that the state's equalization program was well underway. 91 A.2d 137, 149.

10. A similar finding was made in the Delaware case: I conclude from the testimony that, in our Delaware society, State-imposed segregation in education itself results in the Negro children, as a class, receiving educational opportunities which are substantially inferior to those available to white children otherwise similarly situated. 87 A.2d 862, 865.

11. K.B. Clark, Effect of Prejudice and Discrimination on Personality Development (Mid-century White House Conference on Children and Youth, 1950); Witmer and Kotinsky, Personality in the Making (1952), c. VI; Deutscher and Chein, The Psychological Effects of Enforced Segregation A Survey of Social Science Opinion, 26 J.Psychol. 259 (1948); Chein, What are the Psychological Effects of Segregation Under Conditions of Equal Facilities?, 3 Int J.Opinion and Attitude Res. 229 (1949); Brameld, Educational Costs, in Discrimination and National Welfare (Maclver, ed., 1949), 44-48; Frazier, The Negro in the United States (1949), 674-681. And see generally Myrdal, An American Dilemma (1944).

12. See *Boiling v. Sharpe*, post, p. 497, concerning the Due Process Clause of the Fifth Amendment.

13. 4. Assuming it is decided that segregation in public schools violates the Fourteenth Amendment(a) would a decree necessarily follow providing that, within the limits set by normal geographic school districting, Negro children should forthwith be admitted to schools of their choice, or(b) may this Court, in the exercise of its equity powers, permit an effective gradual adjustment to be brought about from existing segregated systems to a system not based on color distinctions? 5. On the assumption on which questions 4(a) and (b) are based, and assuming further that this Court will exercise its equity powers to the end described in question 4(b),(a) should this Court formulate detailed decrees in these cases;(b) if so, what specific issues should the decrees reach;(c) should this Court appoint a special master to hear evidence with a view to recommending specific terms for such decrees;(d) should this Court remand to the courts of first instance with directions to frame decrees in these cases and, if so, what general directions should the decrees of this Court include and what procedures should the courts of first instance follow in arriving at the specific terms of more detailed decrees?

14. See Rule 42, Revised Rules of this Court (effective July 1, 1954).

Bay of Pigs II

John Cole

John Cole, "[Image]: Bay of Pigs II," The Scranton-Times Tribune. Copyright © 2005 by John Cole. Reprinted with permission.

Detainee Case Hits on Limits of Presidency

Linda Greenhouse

When the Supreme Court agreed two months ago to hear an appeal from a Yemeni detainee at Guantanamo Bay, Cuba, named Salim Ahmed Hamdaiir it was evident that an important test of the limits of presidential authority to conduct the war on terror was under way. Now that the final briefs have begun to arrive at the court, in advance of a late March argument, the dimensions of that test appear greater than ever.

Several of the two dozen briefs filed on Mr. Harndart's behalf late Friday address an issue that was not even part of the case when the justices granted review on Nov. 7: whether the court has jurisdiction to proceed or whether Congress, in a measure that President Bush supported and signed into law on Dec. 30, has succeeded in shutting the federal courthouse doors on Mr. Hamcian and 150 other Guantanamo detainees whose cases are pending at various levels of the federal court system.

If that proved to be the case, the result would be "a nightmare scenario," a group of prominent law professors told the Supreme Court in one of the briefs. "The keys to the courthouse will be placed in the exclusive control of the executive," the brief says, creating "the legal equivalent of incommunicado detention of Japanese aliens in a relocation camp in Idaho." The professors were Burt Neuborne and Norman Dorsen of New York University, Judith Resnik of Yale, and Frank Michelman and David Shapiro of Harvard.

Another brief, filed by the Center for National Security Studies, a civil liberties group, and the Constitution Project, a bipartisan study group, asserts flatly that if the new law, the Detainee Treatment Act of 2005, does in fact strip the Supreme Court of jurisdiction over the Harridan case, then the law is unconstitutional.

The Bush administration has not yet responded to such assertions; its brief is not due until early next month. But it appears both from the president's statement upon signing the measure, which originated as Section 1005 of a military spending bill, and from motions the administration has filed in the lower courts that government lawyers do take the view that the new law applies to pending cases and that the justices must dismiss the Hamdati appeal.

Linda Greenhouse, "Detainee Case Hits on Limits of Presidency," The New York Times. Copyright © 2006 by The New York Times. Reprinted with permission provided by PARS International Corp.

When he signed the bill into law, Mr. Bush added a written statement that said "the executive branch shall construe Section 1005 to preclude the federal courts from exercising subject matter jurisdiction over any existing or future action, including applications for writs of habeas corpus, described in Section 1005."

The section provides that "no court, justice or judge shall have jurisdiction to hear or consider" habeas corpus petitions or "any other action" that relates to "any aspect of the detention" of individuals in military custody at the Navy base at Guantanamo Bay.

Justices, 5-3, Broadly Reject Bush Plan to Try Detainees

Linda Greenhouse

The Supreme Court on Thursday repudiated the Bush administration's plan to put Guantanamo detainees on trial before military commissions, ruling broadly that the commissions were unauthorized by federal statute and violated international law.

"The executive is bound to comply with the rule of law that prevails in this jurisdiction," Justice John Paul Stevens, writing for the 5-to-3 majority, said at the end of a 73-page opinion that in sober tones shredded each of the administration's arguments, including the assertion that Congress had stripped the court of jurisdiction to decide the case.

A principal flaw the court found in the commissions was that the president had established them without Congressional authorization.

The decision was such a sweeping and categorical defeat for the administration that it left human rights lawyers who have pressed this and other cases on behalf of Guantanamo detainees almost speechless with surprise and delight, using words like "fantastic," "amazing" and "remarkable."

Michael Ratner, president of the Center for Constitutional Rights, a public interest law firm in New York that represents hundreds of detainees, said, "It doesn't get any better."

President Bush said he planned to work with Congress to "find a way forward," and there were signs of bipartisan interest on Capitol Hill in devising legislation that would authorize revamped commissions intended to withstand judicial scrutiny.

The ruling marked the most significant setback yet for the administration's broad expansions of presidential power.

The courtroom was, surprisingly, not full, but among those in attendance there was no doubt they were witnessing a historic event, a defining moment in the ever-shifting balance of power among branches of government that ranked with the court's order to President Richard M. Nixon in 1974 to turn over the Watergate tapes, or with the court's rejection of President Harry S. Truman's seizing of the nation's steel mills, a 1952 landmark decision from which Justice Anthony M. Kennedy quoted at length.

Linda Greenhouse, "Justices, 5-3, Broadly Reject Bush Plan to Try Detainees," The New York Times. Copyright © 2006 by The New York Times. Reprinted with permission provided by PARS International Corp.

Senator Arlen Specter, Republican of Pennsylvania and chairman of the Judiciary Committee, introduced a bill immediately and said his committee would hold a hearing on July 11, as soon as Congress returned from the July 4 recess. Mr. Specter said the administration had resisted his effort to propose similar legislation as early as 2002.

Two Republican senators, Lindsey Graham of South Carolina and Jon Kyl of Arizona, said in a joint statement that they were "disappointed" but that "we believe the problems cited by the court can and should be fixed."

"Working together, Congress and the administration can draft a fair, suitable and constitutionally permissible tribunal statute," they added.

Both overseas and in the United States, critics of the administration's detention policies praised the decision and urged Mr. Bush to take it as an occasion to shut down the Guantanamo prison camp in Cuba.

"The ruling destroys one of the key pillars of the Guantanamo system," said Gerald Staberock, a director of the International Commission of Jurists in Geneva. "Guantanamo was built on the idea that prisoners there have limited rights. There is no longer that legal black hole."

The majority opinion by Justice Stevens and a concurring opinion by Justice Kennedy, who also signed most of Justice Stevens's opinion, indicated that finding a legislative solution would not necessarily be easy. In an important part of the ruling, the court held that a provision of the Geneva Conventions known as Common Article 3 applies to the Guantanamo detainees and is enforceable in federal court for their protection.

The provision requires humane treatment of captured combatants and prohibits trials except by "a regularly constituted court affording all the judicial guarantees which are recognized as indispensable by civilized people."

The opinion made it clear that while this provision does not necessarily require the full range of protections of a civilian court or a military court-martial, it does require observance of protections for defendants that are missing from the rules the administration has issued for military commissions. The flaws the court cited were the failure to guarantee the defendant the right to attend the trial and the prosecution's ability under the rules to introduce hearsay evidence, unsworn testimony, and evidence obtained through coercion.

Justice Stevens said the historical origin of military commissions was in their use as a "tribunal of necessity" under wartime conditions. "Exigency lent the commission its legitimacy," he said, "but did not further justify the wholesale jettisoning of procedural protections."

The majority opinion was joined by Justices David H. Souter, Ruth Bader Ginsburg and Stephen G. Breyer, who wrote a concurring opinion focusing on the role of Congress. "The court's conclusion ultimately rests upon a single ground: Congress has not issued the executive a blank check," Justice Breyer said.

The dissenters were Justices Clarence Thomas, Antonin Scalia and Samuel A. Alito Jr. Each wrote a dissenting opinion.

Justice Scalia focused on the jurisdictional issue, arguing that Congress had stripped the court of jurisdiction to proceed with this case, *Hamdan v. Rumsfeld*, No. 05-184, when it passed the Detainee Treatment Act last December and provided that "no court, justice, or judge" had jurisdiction to hear habeas corpus petitions filed by detainees at Guantanamo Bay.

The question was whether that withdrawal of jurisdiction applied to pending cases. The majority held that it did not.

Justice Thomas's dissent addressed the substance of the court's conclusions. In a part of his opinion that Justices Scalia and Alito also signed, he called the decision "untenable" and "dangerous." He said "those justices who today disregard the commander in chief's wartime decisions" had last week been willing to defer to the judgment of the Army Corps of Engineers in a Clean Water Act case. "It goes without saying that there is much more at stake here than storm drains," he said.

Chief Justice John G. Roberts Jr. did not take part in the case. Last July, four days before Mr. Bush nominated him to the Supreme Court, he was one of the members of a three-judge panel of the federal appeals court here that ruled for the administration in the case.

In the courtroom on Thursday, the chief justice sat silently in his center chair as Justice Stevens, sitting to his immediate right as the senior associate justice, read from the majority opinion. It made for a striking tableau on the final day of the first term of the Roberts court: the young chief justice, observing his work of just a year earlier taken apart point by point by the tenacious 86-year-old Justice Stevens, winner of a Bronze Star for his service as a Navy officer in World War II.

The decision came in an appeal brought on behalf of Salim Ahmed Hamdan, a Yemeni who was captured in Afghanistan in November 2001 and taken to Guantanamo in June 2002. According to the government, Mr. Hamdan was a driver and bodyguard for Osama bin Laden. In July 2003, he and five others were to be the first to face trial by military commission. But it was not until the next year that he was formally charged with a crime, conspiracy.

The commission proceeding began but was interrupted when the federal district court here ruled in November 2004 that the commission was invalid. This was the ruling the federal appeals court, with Judge Roberts participating, overturned.

Lt. Cmdr. Charles Swift, Mr. Harridan's Navy lawyer, told The Associated Press that he had informed his client about the ruling by telephone. "I think he was awe-struck that the court would rule for him, and give a little man like him an equal chance," Commander Swift said. "Where he's from, that is not true."

The decision contained unwelcome implications, from the administration's point of view, for other legal battles, some with equal or greater importance than the fate of the military commissions.

For example, in finding that the federal courts still have jurisdiction to hear cases filed before this year by detainees at Guantanamo Bay, the justices put back on track for decision a dozen cases in the lower courts here that challenge basic rules and procedures governing life for the hundreds of people confined at the United States naval base there.

In ruling that the Congressional "authorization for the use of military force," passed in the days immediately after the Sept. 11 attacks, cannot be interpreted to legitimize the military commissions, the ruling poses a direct challenge to the administration's legal justification for its secret wiretapping program.

Representative Adam Schiff, a California Democrat who has also introduced a bill with procedures for trying the Guantanamo detainees, said the court's refusal to give an open-ended ruling to the force resolution meant that the resolution could not be viewed as authorizing the National Security Agency's domestic wiretapping.

Perhaps most significantly, in ruling that Common Article 3 of the Geneva Conventions applies to the Guantanamo detainees, the court rejected the administration's view that the article does not cover followers of Al Qaeda. The decision potentially opened the door to challenges, by those held by the United States anywhere in the world, to treatment that could be regarded under the provision as inhumane.

Justice Stevens said that because the charge against Mr. Hamdan, conspiracy, was not a violation of the law of war, it could not be the basis for a trial before a military panel.

JOSE PADILLA, A U.S. CITIZEN ARRESTED IN CHICAGO AND ACCUSED OF PLOTTING TO EXPLODE A DIRTY BOMB.

AT ISSUE

Can an American citizen captured in the U.S. be denied access to American courts?

2002
May — Arrested in Chicago.
June — Declared an enemy combatant, he is held in South Carolina with no criminal charges and is denied access to a lawyer.
Dec. — A federal judge rules that while the president can detain enemy combatants, Mr. Padilla must be allowed to meet with a lawyer.

2003
Dec. — An appellate panel rules that the president cannot indefinitely hold a citizen arrested on U.S. soil as an enemy combatant.

2004
Feb. — The Supreme Court agrees to hear the case.
June — The Supreme Court rules 5 to 4 that Mr. Padilla filed his case in the wrong jurisdiction and must refile.

2005

March— A federal judge says the president overstepped his authority by holding Mr. Padilla for three years without filing criminal charges.

Sept. — An appellate panel overturns the ruling, saying the president can detain him.

Nov. — The administration drops his enemy combatant status and brings criminal charges just days before a deadline to file arguments with the Supreme Court.

2006

April — The Supreme Court denies a request by Mr. Padilla to hear his case and he remains in civilian custody. Three justices who voted not to hear the case write that the court stands ready to intervene should Mr. Padilla's status change.

RASUL V. BUSH

Shafiq Rasul, a British citizen captured in Afghanistan, and other detainees at the Guantanamo facility.

DECIDED IN 2004

AT ISSUE

Can noncitizens held as unlawful enemy combatants be denied access to American courts?

Fall 2001 — Captured in Afghanistan.

2002

Jan. — Mr. Rasul arrives at the Guantanamo Bay facility.

Feb. — Lawyers file a case on behalf of several Guantanamo detainees, including Mr. Rasul.

July — A federal judge says the detainees cannot contest their detention because they are not citizens and the Guantanamo Bay facility is outside the United States.

2003

March — A federal appeals panel says federal courts do not have jurisdiction over the base in Cuba.

Nov. — The Supreme Court agrees to hear the case.

2004

March — Mr. Rasul is released; the case continues on behalf of other detainees.

June —The Supreme Court rules 6 to 3 that the courts do have jurisdiction over Guantanamo and that detainees must be allowed to challenge their detention.

2005

Jan. — In trying to apply the Supreme Court ruling, two federal judges reach opposite conclusions on whether Guantanamo detainees have a right to have federal courts examine their detentions.

Sept. — An appellate panel hears arguments in an appeal of the two January cases.

2006

March — The Bush administration argues before an appellate panel that more than 200 Guantanamo detainee lawsuits should be dismissed in the wake of the Detainee Treatment Act.

HAMDAN V. RUMSFELD

Salim Ahmed Hamdan, a former driver for Osama bin Laden, captured in Afghanistan
DECIDED YESTERDAY.

AT ISSUE

Are the military tribunals legal? And does a December 2005 law strip the courts of jurisdiction in the case?

Fall 2001 — Captured in Afghanistan by Afghan forces allied with the United States. 2002 During 2002 Mr. Hamdan arrives at the Guantanamo facility.

2003

July — One of six prisoners designated eligible for trial by military tribunal.

Dec. — A military lawyer is appointed to represent Mr. Harridan in his tribunal.

2004

Aug. — The military tribunal begins.

Nov. — A federal judge halts the tribunal, ruling that it violates military law and obligations under the Geneva Conventions, which require that detainees be treated as prisoners of war unless a special tribunal determines they are not.

2005

July — An appellate panel that includes Judge John G. Roberts Jr., who is later named to the Supreme Court, overturns the ruling, allowing the tribunals.

Nov. — The Supreme Court agrees to hear the case.

2006

March — The Supreme Court hears the case, with Chief Justice Roberts recusing himself.

July — The Supreme Court rules 5 to 3 that the tribunals violate military law and the Geneva Conventions. The court says the Detainee Treatment Act does not apply to pending cases.

Schools Improve After Lawsuit, Study Says

Carla Rivera

Three years after the settlement of a class-action lawsuit brought on behalf of California's poorest students, a new study has found that teaching and learning conditions in the state's lowest-performing schools have improved: More children are receiving textbooks, school facilities are in better repair and more teachers have proper credentials.

The report, scheduled to be released Monday, is the first comprehensive assessment of the impact of *Williams v. California*, which resulted in a package of laws requiring county superintendents to visit the lowest-achieving schools to monitor the availability of textbooks and the physical condition of buildings as well as to determine if teachers—particularly those in classrooms with large numbers of English-learners—are properly assigned.

The ACLU Foundation of Southern California and Public Advocates, which prepared the report and were co-counsel for the plaintiffs, found progress in all areas, although some counties and individual districts, such as Los Angeles Unified, still fell behind statewide averages.

Some education groups that have been monitoring the settlement criticized the adequacy of complaint procedures and the depth of teacher training. They pointed to figures in the report, such as that 20,000 classes with substantial numbers of English-learners still did not have teachers with the proper training to provide instruction. They also noted that there is no evidence the settlement has helped to close the achievement gap between poor students and non-native English-speakers and their white counterparts.

During the study period from 2004 to 2006, students statewide received more than 88,000 new textbooks and instructional materials, nearly 3,000 emergency campus repairs were funded and the percentage of fully credentialed teachers increased from 90% to 92%.

"Williams set a floor, not a ceiling, for providing all students a meaningful opportunity to learn, and while work still remains to be done to reach these basic standards in some schools, the significant improvements in all three key areas targeted by Williams demonstrate that clear standards, combined with targeted funds and effective accountability systems, can

Carla Rivera, "Schools Improve After Lawsuit, Study Says," Los Angeles Times. Copyright © 2007 by Los Angeles Times Syndicate. Reprinted with permission.

make a positive difference in our children's classrooms," said Brooks Allen, the ACLU of Southern California attorney overseeing the settlement's implementation.

The Williams suit was filed in May 2000 by several civil rights organizations, which argued that tens of thousands of minority students were being denied an equal education when compared with their suburban counterparts. A settlement was announced in August 2004, and legislation outlining the conditions of the agreement was signed into law a month later by Gov. Arnold Schwarzenegger. The new standards and most accountability systems—including a complaint process—apply to ail public schools. All districts must perform self-evaluations to ensure compliance.

The lowest-performing schools on the 2006 Academic Performance Index receive additional funds and oversight, with mandatory annual inspections, some of which are unannounced.

The settlement holds the state responsible for ensuring compliance and provides $1 billion to accomplish its goals, including an $800-million emergency repair program. Districts are required, for example, to address textbook deficiencies no later than eight weeks after the start of school and the county office of education can request that the state purchase the books, with the costs deducted from the district

The report, conducted by UCLA researchers, looked at four segments of the state—Los Angeles County, the Bay Area, Sacramento County, and the Central Valley—and statewide trends. Among the key findings:

- The proportion of low-performing schools with insufficient textbooks dropped from 20% in 2005 to 13% in 2006.
- Although 62% of the state's lowest-performing schools needed some type of repair in 2005, that number fell to 47% the following year.
- Teachers who were assigned to classes with 20% or more English-learners and lacked proper training dropped from 30% in 2005 to 13% in 2006.
- In Los Angeles County, which has 80 school districts and 1.7 million students, the percentage of low-performing schools with insufficient textbooks dropped from 22% to 14% during the study period and the county showed improvements in other areas as well. One concern, though, was the number of low-performing schools with at least some teachers assigned to classrooms for which they were not qualified or credentialed, which fell from 83% to 70%, but still far exceeded the statewide figure of 53%.

The County Office of Education Supt Darline P. Robles acknowledged that it remains a challenge for schools to hire properly credentialed teachers for classrooms of limited-English speaking students.

"Unfortunately, there has been declining enrollment in some schools and teachers with English-learner credentials may have been let go," said Robles, whose office is required to review 598 schools under the Williams settlement "The report does reflect progress made by schools and school districts to implement not only the legal parts of law but the spirit of it."

According to the report, 69% of all improperly assigned teachers in the state were reported in one district—Los Angeles Unified, where district officials said they have focused "laser-like" attention on improving the numbers, with intensive training for current staff and mandatory English-learner certificates for new hires. In fact, out of 35,000 teachers in the district, only 2,700 now lack proper certificates, said Deborah Ignagi, the district's interim administrator of certificated employment operations.

"We look at Williams as a real positive thing that has held us more closely accountable in making real progress," said Ignagni.

The report cites instances in which the settlement has dramatically improved education, such as at Frank D. Parent Elementary School in the Inglewood Unified School District. When the Williams suit was in litigation, said the report, the school did not provide enough books for students to take home, 43% of teachers lacked full credentials, and school bathrooms were filthy and regularly lacked toilet paper. Students in grades 6 through 8 did not have science books or lab equipment.

Now, according to the report, "students' access to textbooks both at home and at school has increased as has students' access to a corps of committed and highly qualified teachers. In addition, the school is maintained in good repair, consistent with the new Williams standard."

Principal Gary Gregory agreed that the school has been transformed and credits much of that improvement to the lawsuit settlement Teachers and staff have been trained to spot problems and report them immediately, and everyone stays on their toes because the campus can receive unannounced visits, he said.

"What's very positive is that our district takes this as a top priority and that has made it very easy," said Gregory. "We use as leverage our school being a Williams school and they are very quick to accommodate."

While lauding the overall intent of the settlement, some advocacy groups say much remains to be done. Gabriel Medel, a member of the group Parents For Unity, which has been monitoring the settlement, said responses to complaints, for example, often drag out or are disregarded. In one instance, a promise to buy books at one L.A. Unified school resulted in students receiving copies of chapters. In another, a girls' gym closed by a fire still has not been repaired and school officials have been unresponsive to parents' concerns. Another school purportedly refused to enroll an English-learner, claiming it lacked sufficient resources.

"The system is working when parents are well-informed," Medel said, "but it still doesn't have the full effect in changing the landscape for children's needs."

Discussion Questions

1. What is judicial policymaking?

2. How does judicial policymaking differ from other modes of policymaking?

3. How can courts "correct" political failures?

4. Are these specific examples appropriate uses of judicial power or should the courts defer to the elected branches?

5. Do they violate the "logic of the triad"?

6. If so, what are the bases of legitimacy for judicial policymaking?

7. How would you have ruled in these cases?

8. What are the implications of these readings for the judicial appointment process? Should it be more or less politicized?

C. The Limits on Law and Courts

Promising is one thing; delivering is quite another. The next set of readings explores several constraints of the courts' ability to resolve disputes and make policy: namely, doctrinal, institutional and cultural constraints. At the end of this section, additional study materials are provided that cut across the materials on doctrinal, institutional and cultural constraints. These materials, especially the concepts of dynamic versus constrained courts, are crucial for organizing the readings into a broader debate.

1. Doctrinal Constraints

C ourts and judicial power are creatures of the law. As such, although doctrinal constraints are far from perfect, the law itself can potentially serve to limit the courts' power.

ADDITIONAL RECOMMENDED MATERIALS:

Lief Carter and Thomas F. Burke, *Reason in Law* (2007)

Ronald Dworkin, *Taking Rights Seriously* (1978)

Howard Gillman, "What's Law Got to Do With It? Judicial Behavioralists Test the 'Legal Model' of Judicial Decision Making," *Law & Social Inquiry* 26(2) (2001): 465-504.

Herbert M. Kritzer and Mark Richards, "The Influence of Law in the Supreme Court's Search and Seizure Jurisprudence," *American Political Science Review* 37(4): 827-840.

Gordon Silverstein, *Law's Allure* (2009)

Of Creon and Captain Vere

Robert Cover

I

Antigone's star has shown brightly through the millennia. The archetype for civil disobedience has claimed a constellation of first-magnitude emulators. The disobedient—whether Antigone, Luther, Gandhi, King, or Bonhoeffer—exerts a powerful force upon us. The singular act, the risk, the dramatic appeal to a juster justice, all contribute to the high drama of the moment and the power of the actor's role. No wonder, then, that such men and women are celebrated in literature and history. No wonder that a great psychiatrist like Erikson, upon embarking on a venture in history and biography, chose Luther and Gandhi as his first subjects.

Yet, in a curious way, to focus upon the disobedient and the process of disobedience is to accept the perspective of the established order. It is a concession that it is the man who appeals beyond law that is in need of explanation. With the sole exception of Nazi atrocities, the phenomenon of complicity in oppressive legal systems (oppressive from the actor's own perspective) has seldom been studied.[1] Thus, Creon is present only as a foil for Antigone,

---

1   Complicity with the Nazi regime has been the object of much study. But at least the transatlantic emphasis has been an analysis of responsibility on the command and policy initiative *level* in a genocidal situation. Some attempts have been made to associate legal positivism—especially in its Kelsenian form—with the atrocities. H. L. A, Hart has vigorously and convincingly argued that positivism has no necessary relationship to such amoral and immoral judicial conduct. Indeed, he has demonstrated how the English positivists, and most especially Bentham, urged the analytical distinction between law as it is and law as it ought to be and stressed the human origins of law in order to be able to effectively measure the law against an external standard for reform purposes. (In Bentham's case the external standard was, of course, utility. But one need not accept the utilitarian basts of morality to accept the necessity of the analytical distinction.) See, e.g., H. L. A. Hart, "Positivism and the Separation of Law and Morals," 71 *Harvard Law*

Robert Cover, Justice Accused: Antislavery and the Judicial Process, pp. 42376. Copyright © 1975 by Yale University Press. Reprinted with permission.

not himself the object of the artist's study of human character. In *Antigone* note the curious one-dimensional character of the King. How he comes to make his law and at what cost in psychic terms is not treated at all. Indeed, Creon's first conflict is not between right and law, but between his son and his pride. And even in the midst of that conflict he betrays his singular obtuseness to the complexity of the situation he created by crying filial impiety and anarchy in one breath. He is astounded by the possibility of Haemon's sympathy to an affront to authority. Much of the simplicity of Creon lies in the choice of a tyrant as model for legal system. The making of law and its applications are wholly confined to a single will unconstrained by any but the most personal of considerations such as the feelings and actions of a son.

Melville's Captain Vere in *Billy Budd* is one of the few examples of an attempt to portray the conflict patterns of Creon or Creon's minions in a context more nearly resembling the choice situations of judges in modern legal systems, Billy Budd, radical innocence personified, is overwhelmed by a charge of fomenting mutiny, falsely levied against him by the first mate Claggart. Claggart seems to personify dark and evil forces. Struck dumb by the slanderous charges, Billy strikes out and kills the mate with a single blow. Captain Vere must instruct a drumhead court on the law of the Mutiny Act as it is to be applied to Billy Budd—in some most fundamental sense "innocent," though perpetrator of the act of killing the first mate. In what must be, for the legal scholar, the high point of the novella, Vere articulates the "scruples" of the three officers (and his own) and rejects them.

> How can we adjudge to summary and shameful death a fellow creature innocent before God, and whom we feel to be so?—Does that state it aright? You sign sad assent. Well, I too feel that, the full force of that. It is Nature. But do these buttons that we wear attest that our allegiance is to Nature? No, to the King.

And, but a few paragraphs farther on, Vere asks the three whether "occupying the position we do, private conscience should not yield to that imperial one formulated in the code under which alone we officially proceed."

In Vere's words we have a positivisms condensation of a legal system's formal character. Five aspects of that formalism may be discerned and specified: First, there is explicit recognition of the role character of the judges—a consciousness of the formal element. It is a uniform, not nature, that defines obligation. Second, law is distinguished from both the transcendent and the personal sources of obligation. The law is neither nature nor conscience. Third, the law is embodied in a readily identifiable source which governs transactions and occurrences

---

Review 593 (1958). While I argue within that a thoroughgoing legal positivism was one of the many factors that determined the complicity of the antislavery judge in the system of law that he himself considered immoral, it is but one such factor. Moreover, I shall also argue that the same jurisprudential perspective contributed to the most radical of the opposition viewpoints with regard to slave law.

of the sort under consideration: here an imperial code of which the Mutiny Act is a part. Fourth, the will behind the law is vague, uncertain, but *clearly not* that of the judges. It is here "imperial will" which, in (either eighteenth- or) nineteenth-century terms as applied to England, is not very easy to describe except through a constitutional law treatise. But, in any event, it is not the will of Vere and his three officers. Fifth, a corollary of the fourth point, the judge is not responsible for the content of the law but for its straightforward application.

> For that law and the rigor of it, we are not responsible. Our vowed responsibility is in this: That however pitilessly that law may operate in any instances, we nevertheless adhere to it and administer it.

These five elements are part of Vere's arguments. But *Billy Budd* is a literary work and much that is most interesting about Vere is not in what he says but in what he is, in overtones of character. For example, we have intimations from the outset of a personality committed to fearful symmetries. His nickname, derived from Marvell's lines:

> Under the discipline severe
> Of Fairfax and the starry Vere

suggests an impersonal and unrelaxed severity. And his intellectual bent, too, reinforces this suggestion of rigidity. He eschewed innovations "disinterestedly" and because they seemed "insusceptible of embodiment in lasting institutions." And he lacked "companionable quality." A man emerges who is disposed to approach life institutionally, to avoid the personal realm even where it perhaps ought to hold sway, to be inflexibly honest, righteous, and duty bound.

It is this man who, seeing and appreciating Budd's violent act, exclaimed, "Struck dead by an angel of God! Yet the angel must hang." And, characteristically, it is Vere who assumes the responsibility of conveying the dread verdict to the accused. Melville's speculations on that "interview" are revealing. He stresses the likelihood that Vere revealed his own full part in the "trial." He goes on to speculate that Vere might well have assumed a paternal stance in the manner of Abraham embracing Isaac "on the brink of resolutely offering him up in obedience to the exacting behest." Such a religious conviction of duty characterizes our man. Neither conventional morality, pity, nor personal agony could bend him from a stern duty. But in Vere's case the master is not God but the King. And the King is but a symbol for a social order.

Righteous men, indeed, suffer the agonies of their righteousness. Captain Vere betrayed just such agony in leaving his meeting with Billy Budd. But there is no indication that Vere suffered the agony of doubt about his course. When Billy died uttering "God Bless Captain Vere," there is no intimation that the Captain sensed any irony (whether intended or not) in the parting benediction. If Captain Vere is Abraham, he is the biblical version, not Kierkegaard's shadow poised achingly at the chasm.

Melville has been astonishingly successful in making his readers ask dreadful questions of Vere and his behavior. What deep urge leads a man to condemn unworldly beauty and innocence? To embrace, personally, the opportunity to do an impersonal, distasteful task? How reconcile the flash of recognition of "the angel must die" and the seizing of the opportunity to act Abraham, with declared protestations, unquestionably sincere, that only plain and clear duty overcomes his sense of the victim's cosmic innocence? We have so many doubts about a man who hears and obeys the voice of the Master so quickly, and our doubts are compounded when it is a harsh social system that becomes the Lord.

I venture to suggest that Melville had a model for Captain Vere that may bring us very close to our main story. Melville's father-in-law was Chief Justice Lemuel Shaw of the Massachusetts Supreme Judicial Court. A firm, unbending man of stern integrity, Shaw dominated the Massachusetts judicial system very much as Captain Vere ran his ship. The Chief Justice was a noted, strong opponent to slavery and expressed his opposition privately, in print, and in appropriate judicial opinions. Yet, in the great causes célèbres involving fugitive slaves, Shaw came down hard for an unflinching application of the harsh and summary law. The effort cost Shaw untold personal agony. He was villified by abolitionists. I cannot claim that Vere is Lemuel Shaw (though he might be), for there is no direct evidence. I can only say that it would be remarkable that in portraying a man caught in the horrible conflict between duty and conscience, between role and morality, between nature and positive law, Melville would be untouched by the figure of his father-in-law in the Sims Case, the Latimer affair, or the Burns controversy. We know Melville's predilection to the ship as microcosm for the social order. He used the device quite plainly with respect to slavery in *Benito Cereno*.

The fugitive slave was very Budd-like, though he was as black as Billy was blonde. The Mutiny Act admitted of none of the usual defenses, extenuations, or mitigations. If the physical act was that of the defendant, he was guilty. The Fugitive Slave Act similarly excluded most customary sorts of defenses. The alleged fugitive could not even plead that he was not legally a slave so long as he was the person *alleged* to be a fugitive. The drumhead court was a special and summary proceeding; so was the fugitive rendition process. In both proceedings the fatal judgment was carried out immediately. There was no appeal.

More important, Billy's fatal flaw was his innocent dumbness. He struck because he could not speak. So, under the Fugitive Slave Acts, the alleged fugitive had no right to speak. And, as a rule, slaves had no capacity to testify against their masters or whites, generally. Billy Budd partakes of the slave, generalized. He was seized, impressed, from the ship *Rights of Man* and taken abroad the *Bellipotent*. Aboard the *Bellipotent* the Mutiny Act and Captain Vere held sway. The Mutiny Act was justified because of its necessity for the order demanded on a ship in time of war. So the laws of slavery, often equally harsh and unbending, were justified as necessary for the social order in antebellum America. Moreover, the institution itself was said to have its origin in war.

But most persuasive is Vere and his dilemma—the subject matter of this book. For, if there was a single sort of case in which judges during Melville's lifetime struggled with the moral-formal dilemma, it was slave cases. In these cases, time and again, the judiciary paraded its helplessness before the law; lamented harsh results; intimated that in a more perfect world, or at the end of days, a better law would emerge, but almost uniformly, marched to the music, steeled themselves, and hung Billy Budd.

Of course, *Billy Budd,* like any great work of literature, exists on many levels. I would not deny the theology in the work, nor the clash of elemental good and elemental evil in Budd and Claggart. But the novella is also about a judgment, within a social system, and about the man who, dimly perceiving the great and abstract forces at work, bears responsibility for that judgment. It is about starry-eyed Vere and Lemuel Shaw.

2

The rest of this book is not about literature, but about Lemuel Shaw and many judges like him. It is the story of earnest, well-meaning pillars of legal respectability and of their collaboration in a system of oppression—Negro slavery. 1 have chosen to analyze at length only the dilemma of the antislavery judge—the man who would, in some sense, have agreed with my characterization of slavery as oppression. It was he who confronted Vere's dilemma, the choice between the demands of role and the voice of conscience. And it was he who contributed so much to the force of legitimacy that law may provide, for he plainly acted out of impersonal duty.

In a static and simplistic model of law, the judge caught between law and morality has only four choices. He may apply the law against his conscience. He may apply conscience and be faithless to the law. He may resign. Or he may cheat: He may state that the law is not f what he believes it to be and, thus preserve an appearance (to others) of conformity of law and morality. Once we assume a more realistic model of law and of the judicial process, these four positions become only poles setting limits to a complex field of action and motive. For in a dynamic model, law is always becoming. And the judge has a legitimate role in determining what it is that the law will become. The flux in law means also that the law's content is frequently unclear. We must speak of direction and of weight as well as of position. Moreover, this frequent lack of clarity makes possible "ameliorist" solutions. The judge may introduce his own sense of what "ought to be" interstitially, where no "hard" law yet exists. And, he may do so without committing the law to broad doctrinal advances (or retreats).

In a given historical context the way in which judges are likely to respond to the moral-formal dilemma is going to be determined by a wide variety of intellectual and institutional variables. Judges, more than most men, are conscious of the baggage of the past. Thus, the traditions that they inherit will be important. For both slavery and the v judicial role in antebellum America the judge had a library of works that influenced the idiom in which he thought. The nature of that intellectual tradition is my first inquiry. I shall examine the natural law tradition on slavery as it stood in the late eighteenth century. I shall then explore the actual uses of principled preferences for liberty in the first thirty or forty years of the nineteenth century. This exploration will delineate the areas of accepted usage of preference for liberty in judicial opinion and the areas where the judge could move the law in the direction of freedom. I shall then explore the sorts of demands that were made upon the judiciary to go beyond those accepted areas and the judicial refusal to do so. That refusal will be traced on the cognitive level to carefully formulated ideas about the judicial function that are themselves the products of a heritage of conflict over the values that ought to govern judging. The dialectical context for the judge's response was not constant, and it is necessary to examine responses to many demands varying, in part, with the ideology of the lawyers and the movements they represented.

Finally, I shall confront directly the question of personality. With Captain Vere we have the sense that it is not logic alone that leads him to his response. So, with Lemuel Shaw, John McLean, Joseph Story, and others, we must inquire into the internal forces that produced an almost uniform response of role fidelity. The theory of cognitive dissonance provides a suggestive framework for integrating the uniform response, the personalities of these men, and the professional and intellectual milieu in which they worked.

Make no mistake. The judges we shall examine really squirmed; were intensely uncomfortable in hanging Billy Budd. But they did the job. Like Vere, they were Creon's faithful minions. We must understand them—as much as Antigone—if we are to understand the processes of injustice.

2005 Legislative Summary
Gulf Coast Relief
Alex Wayne

STATUS

H urricane Katrina which devastated New Orleans and the coasts of Louisiana, Mississippi and Alabama in August prompted Congress to quickly pass more than $82 billion for recovery and rebuilding in the Gulf Coast region in September (PL 109-81, PL 109-62), In addition, lawmakers introduced more than 180 House and Senate bills and resolutions addressing specific issues and needs—including eduction, housing, health concerns and aid for displaced workers—incurred after Katrina, and then Hurricane Rita, hit the Gulf Coast, Several became law, but lawmakers also included Katrina-specific provisions in the fiscal 2006 budget reconciliation and Defense appropriations bills.

SYNOPSIS

Lawmakers representing the Gulf Coast pressed for an expensive expansion of Medicaid, the shared state-federal health insurance program for the poor. Katrina simultaneously displaced hundreds of thousands of people and eliminated their homes and jobs, something that some politicians feared would leave the evacuees without access to health care.

Many lawmakers also saw a need for new flexibility in the distribution of education dollars. Among the evacuees were hundreds of thousands of schoolchildren who were forced to find new schools far from home. Politicians worried that the federal money intended for the children's old schools would not follow them to their new ones—particularly private schools, which in some cases offered free or discounted tuition to Katrina victims.

To deal with health care, Senate Finance Chairman Charles E. Grassley, R-Iowa, and Max Baucus of Montana, the panel's senior Democrat, wrote a bill (S 1716) that would have expanded Medicaid. Their measure would have opened Medicaid to practically anyone who

Alex Wayne, "2005: Legislative Summary: Gulf Coast Relief," CQ Weekly. Copyright © 2006 by CQ Roll Call, Inc. Reprinted with permission.

lived in a state hit by Katrina, and it would have promised full federal funding for those states' Medicaid programs. But at a cost of nearly $9 billion, many conservatives rejected it.

So Grassley used a package of spending cuts ordered by the fiscal 2006 budget resolution (H Con Res 95) to carry a scaled-down version of his Katrina Medicaid bill. The new provision left out language offering Medicaid aid to states that were hosting, victims, and at $1.8 billion, its price tag was more palatable to conservatives.

Meanwhile, Michael B. Enzi, R-Wyo. *chairman* of the Senate Health, Education, Labor and Pensions (HELP) Committee, al: used the budget reduction bill for Katrina aid. He offered an amendment that would provide $1.2 billion in assistance for schools that took in Katrina victims, whether the institutions are public, private or religious.

Teachers' unions opposed the measure, fearing it *amounted* to a school voucher program that would lead to money being drained from public schools to private ones. But Enzi carefully wrote his measure to attract Democratic support, including fro Edward M. Kennedy of Massachusetts, ranking Democrat on HELP and a staunch voucher opponent who argued that the crisis demanded greater flexibility in education spending. Enzi also had a foil in a competing measure by John Ensign, R-*He* that critics called a voucher program. Ensign's amendment was defeated on a 31-68 vote, clearing the way for Enzi's measu to be adopted by voice vote.

The House version of the budget reconciliation bill did not include any provisions addressing education aid for Katrina victims. But the final version of the bill (S 1932), which the House is expected to clear after it returns Jan. 31, included $2.1 billion for Medicaid relief for Katrina victims.

Education aid, meanwhile, ended up in the fiscal 2008 Defense spending bill (HR 2883). The $1.8 billion provision includes $750 million to help damaged schools reopen, $845 million to reimburse schools hosting Katrina evacuees and $200 million to aid in rebuilding colleges on the Gulf Coast.

In the weeks and months after Hurricane Katrina, Congress also cleared several bills addressing specific needs of the Gulf Coast, They include:

- HR 3650 (PL 109-83)—to allow a federal court to move its proceedings when emergency conditions leave no venue with its jurisdiction available. The hurricane closed three federal courthouses in the region, including the home of the U.S. Court c Appeals for the 5th Circuit, Signed into law Sept. 9,

- HR 804 (PL 109-64)—to prevent federal agencies from considering flood mitigation payments as income. Signed into law Sept, 20.

- HR 3869 (PL 109-85) and HR 4133 (PL 109-108)—to boost the borrowing authority of the Federal Emergency Manager™ Agency to pay federal flood insurance claims. Signed into law Sept. 20 and Nov. 21.

- HR 3189 (PL 109-88)—to allow the Education Department to waive the repayment requirement for displaced students receiving Pell grants, Signed into law Sept. 21.

- HR 3688 (PL 109-87)—to allow the Education Department to waive repayment requirements for students who receive campus-based aid and have been displaced from their institution because of a natural disaster. Signed into law Sept. 21.

- HR 3672 (PL 109-88)—to temporarily waive work requirements and time limits imposed under the Temporary Assistance Needy Families program for families displaced by the hurricane. Signed into law Sept. 21.

- HR 3781 (PL 109-72)—to give more flexibility for a Labor Department program that provides temporary disaster relief and training of up to six months to individuals who take part in projects that assist victims of a disaster, Signed into law Sept. 23.

- HR 2132 (PL 109-78)—to allow the Education Department to waive student loan rules during a war or national emergency Signed into law Sept. 30.

- HR 3884 (PL 109-82)—to give preferences to hurricane-affected states in receiving additional funds from the Rehabilitate Services Administration. Signed into law Sept. 30,

- HR 3971 (PL 109-91)—to provide $500 million to Louisiana, Alabama and Mississippi to help pay unemployment benefits for their residents, The measure also extended until Dec. 31 a program that provides transitional Medicaid coverage for recipients leaving welfare and moving into work, and another that provides grants to groups that teach abstinence-only sex education. A program to assist low-income seniors with Medicare premiums was be extended through Sept. 30, 2007. Signed into law Oct. 20.

LEGISLATIVE ACTION:

House adopted the conference report on HR 2883 (H Rept 109-359), 308-106, on Dec. 19.

House adopted the conference report on S 1932 (H Rept 109-362), 212-206, on Dec. 19.

Senate voted, 51-50, on Dec, 21 to approve S 1932 with three provisions stricken from the language of the conference repc sending it back to the House for final action.

Senate cleared HR 2863, 93-0, on Dec. 21

Katrina Panel Indicts Response

Tim Starks

More than four years after the Sept. 11 terrorist attacks, the nation remains woefully unprepared to handle major catastrophe a select House panel created to investigate the government's response to Hurricane Katrina concluded in a report released last week.

With a review by the Bush administration due later this month and a Senate report to follow in March, Congress is working to come up with ways to ensure the federal government is better prepared for the next major disaster.

The report released Feb. 15 by the Republican-dominated House panel is a blistering indictment of the government response at every level. It has already triggered legislative proposals ranging from an overhaul of contracting during disasters to the potentially contentious proposal to remove the Federal Emergency Management Agency (FEMA) from the Homeland Securi Department,

"If 9-11 was a failure of imagination, then Katrina was a failure of initiative," according to the report. "It was a failure of leadership."

But it also has touched off partisan bickering that, in an election year, could make cooperation on major issues difficult. The conclusions of the panel put the White House on the defensive and emboldened Democratic critics.

'The federal response to Katrina is a glaring example of the culture of corruption, cronyism and incompetence that has marked the Republican leadership in Washington, D.C.," said House Minority Leader Nancy Pelosi, D-Calif, fitting the report release into one of the party's election year themes. Democrats had boycotted the panel, pressing instead for an independent investigation.

The panel's findings assessed blame at the state, local and federal level. But it is the federal response where lawmakers will focus their attention. Among the report's findings on the federal government response:

Tim Starks, "Katrina Panel Indicts Response," CQ Weekly. Copyright © 2006 by CQ Roll Call, Inc. Reprinted with permission.

- The White House should have realized Aug. 29, the day the storm made landfall, that the levees had broken, causing the flooding that did the majority of the damage. Instead, it discounted some of the information it had received.

The committee said it was hampered in assessing the response of the president and top aides who were with him at the time at his ranch in Crawford, Texas, because the White House refused to turn over some e-mails and other data the panel had requested.

The White House's decision to withhold documents and communications raising concerns about executive privilege leaves the select Committee no choice but to find, based on the information we have received, that a failure of initiative plagued the White House as well," states the report.

- Homeland Security Secretary Michael Chertoff should have declared Katrina an "incident of national significance" at least two days prior to landfall, when the National Weather Service predicted a category 4 or 5 hurricane would strike New Orleans. Doing so would have sped the deployment of federal resources to the region.

Chertoff should not have sent Michael D. Brown, who was FEMA's director at the time, to serve as the "principal federal official" at the disaster scene. Instead, he should have picked someone who had undergone required training to he such. Before landfall, Chertoff should have convened an interagency group to examine the potential consequences of He lacked the disaster experience to provide "adequate advice and counsel" to the White House, the report concludes,

- A slow exodus of senior FEIVIA employees left, the agency and the Homeland Security Department without "adequate train* and experienced staff for the Katrina response." The lack of readiness of the agency's national emergency response teams hindered the federal response., the report said.

"Numerous officials and operators, from state and FEMA directors to local emergency managers told the same story: If members of the state and federal emergency response teams are meeting one another for the first time at the operations center, then you should not expect a well-coordinated response."

Local and state officials also failed in aspects of the , response, the committee found.

While the evacuation of the general population went well, later mandatory evacuations by local officials led to unnecessary deaths. Over-hyped proclamations by local officials about the extent of the disaster and the chaos in New Orleans, widely publicized by the *media*, delayed the arrival of relief teams because of fears for their safety, according to the report.

After excerpts of the select panel's draft report leaked to the media, the Bush administration and Chertoff—who had endured weeks of scathing criticism from everyone from the Government Accountability Office to Brown—mounted a damage control campaign.

At a conference of emergency management officials, the White House's homeland security and counterterrorism adviser previewed some of the findings of the administration's own review of the response, then launched into a defense of what President Bush did during the unfolding disaster.

"I reject outright any suggestion that President Bush was anything less than fully involved," said the adviser, Frances Fragos Townsend. "He received regular briefings, had countless conversations with federal, state and local officials and took extraordinary steps prior to landfall."

Republicans in Congress, too, fired back at Pelosi and other Democrats who sought political advantage from the report.

"Once again, House Democrat leaders are putting politics before progress at the expense of the families impacted by Hurricane Katrina," said Majority Leader John A. Boehner, R-Ohio. Instead of working in a constructive fashion to address key problems in the response to Katrina at all levels of government, House Democrats have abdicated their responsibility to the American people by refusing to participate in a bipartisan investigation."

Democrats renewed their calls for an independent investigation because, they said, the panel failed to gain possession of important White House documents. But Thomas M. Davis III, R-Va., who chaired the panel, said the committee received more than enough information to complete its review.

Democrats also called on Chertoff to step down. In the job for a year, Chertoff spent the week of the report's release proposing new reforms for FEMA and accepting ultimate blame for the poor response while saying he was let down by Brown. Brown had said he went over Chertoff s head to speak with the White House in the storm's aftermath.

"I am responsible for the Department of Homeland Security," Chertoff said in testimony to a Senate panel Feb, 15. "I'm accountable and accept responsibility for the performance of the entire department, the bad and the good. I also have the responsibility to fix what's wrong,"

The Senate Homeland Security and Governmental Affairs Committee grilled Chertoff at its final hearing in its investigation and will soon prepare a report that will present specific recommendations, But some lawmakers have already begun preparing legislation to address the response to Katrina.

The House Transportation and Infrastructure Committee will soon begin moving legislation expected to call for the Homeland Department to relinquish control of FEMA. The House Appropriations Subcommittee on Homeland Security will likely look to boost funding for the embattled agency.

Meanwhile, the House Government Reform Committee will consider a move to overhaul contracting procedures during disasters. And the House Armed Services Committee will take action to improve the coordination between the Defense Department and other governmental bodies.

Among the ideas lawmakers floated, the most controversial was to remove FEMA from the Homeland Security Department.

In 2002, the Bush administration folded the agency into one of the newly created department's four divisions, this one responsible for emergency preparedness and response.

A move to extract the agency could spark a turf fight on Capitol Hill because several committees would have jurisdiction over any legislation addressing the agency's status.

After Katrina ravaged the Gulf Coast last August, many lawmakers called anew for FEMA to be made a separate agency. Senate Rules Chairman Trent Lott R-Miss., joined the chorus by announcing he would introduce a bill separating the agency.

Bill Shuster, R-Pa., who sat on the House select panel on Katrina, and chairs a Transportation and Infrastructure subcommittee with oversight of FEMA, said his panel almost certainly would recommend restoring the agency's independence. The idea has drawn support from other members of the select Katrina panel, particularly those from Gulf states threatened by hurricanes.

Both leaders of the Senate panel investigating Katrina—Chairwoman Susan Collins, R-Maine, and Joseph I. Lieberman of Connecticut, the ranking Democrat—have said they are not inclined to recommend FEMA's return to independence.

And the chairman of the House Homeland Security Committee said that while he believes FEMA's autonomy within the department should be strengthened, the agency should not be broken out as an independent entity.

'The consensus after 9/11 was that FEMA should be a part of the department," said Peter T. King, R-N.Y. "We don't want to always be responding to the last disaster."

In Court Ruling on Floods, More Pain for New Orleans

Adam Nossiter

There is disappointment but little surprise here at a federal judge's grudgingly absolving the Army Corps of Engineers of liability in the flooding of New Orleans after Hurricane Katrina.

Although the decision, issued Wednesday, was sharply critical of the corps, the judge's finding has if anything only hardened the ill feelings against the government that have hung over this city since the storm.

The plaintiffs in the class-action suit dismissed by the judge were many of the hundreds of thousands of people who filed claims here against the corps last year because of the levee breaches that flooded the city. They lined up in cars and on foot and jammed the streets around the agency's district headquarters, acting out what has been a loudly spoken article of faith since the days in 2005 when water covered 80 percent of New Orleans and ruined the homes of thousands: the corps—not nature, not a record-breaking storm surge and not local politics or local negligence—was to blame.

The judge, Stanwood R. Duval Jr. of the Federal District Court here, a son of South Louisiana, heartily seconded that notion on Wednesday, suggesting that the corps was guilty of "gross incompetence." But Judge Duval said he was powerless to rule favorably on the lawsuit because the Flood Control Act of 1928 granted legal immunity to the government in the event of failure of flood control projects like levees.

Kathy Gibbs, a corps spokeswoman, said the agency agreed with the dismissal, but declined further comment because other suits over Hurricane Katrina damage are pending, The Associated Press reported.

Local reaction to the ruling was muted. In part because the judge said last year that he would probably have to find the corps immune from damages, expectations appear to have been low, even as bitterness over the losses festered along with a desire to fix blame on the agency.

Adam Nossiter, "In Court Ruling on Floods, More Pain for New Orleans," The New York Times. Copyright © 2008 by The New York Times. Reprinted with permission provided by PARS International Corp.

"There was almost a general understanding that—guess what?—they're exempt from prosecution," said Bari Landry, president of the Lakeview Civic Improvement Association, in a neighborhood devastated by the failure of the flood walls.

"We knew there was a very good chance this would not go forward," Ms. Landry said. "I'm not at all surprised."

Ms. Landry was one of some 350,000 people who filed claims. The lawyers who brought the suit dismissed Wednesday represented about 65,000 of those claimants. They said Thursday that they would appeal, arguing that the corps was not protected by the 1928 law's immunity clause, largely because a change it had made to its flood protection plan for New Orleans had not been authorized by Congress.

If Judge Duval's conclusion provided no comfort, his language did, echoing in legal terminology what has been strong criticism of the corps by activists, politicians and the local media.

"While the United States government is immune for legal liability for the defalcations alleged herein, it is not free, nor should it be, from posterity's judgment concerning its failure to accomplish what was its task," the judge wrote. "This story—50 years in the making—is heart-wrenching. Millions of dollars were squandered in building a levee system with respect to these outfall canals which was known to be inadequate by the corps's own calculations."

Though the ruling spotlighted many missteps by the corps over the years, it made little of other possible factors, including culpability of former local officials overseeing levees and drainage, and particularly their rejection of the corps' original plan for floodgates on the drainage canals that so devastated the city.

Supporters of the claimants applauded Judge Duval's language, suggesting that it might yet fuel their cause. "What we've had so far is just a suspicion," said Joseph Bruno, a lawyer in the case. "You now have a U.S. federal district judge who's had a chance to evaluate the facts and draw legal conclusions. Now you've got a determination where a guy says, 'Look, but for the nuances of the statute, these people will be called on to pay.'"

Sandy Rosenthal of the activist group Leeves.org said: "Clearly Judge Duval is frustrated by what he had to do. It's outrageous these levees were fragile. He and I agree the corps was responsible for the failure of the levees. It's a positive thing that Judge Duval outlined all those things in his statements."

The text of Judge Duval's opinion is online at nytimes.com/katrina.

Discussion Questions

1. What is "judicial can't"?

2. Why did the judge refuse to rule in favor of the flood victims? Did he think that the Army Corps of Engineers had acted reasonably?

3. Compare these readings with those on judicial policy-making. What are some the differences between the law governing cases of "judicial can't" versus the law governing cases like *Brown v. Board*?

2. Institutional Constraints

Doctrine is not the only source of constraint on the courts' ability to resolve disputes and make policy effectively. Courts are also limited by institutional constraints, both with respect to how the courts themselves are organized ("internal" institutional constraints) and how they relate to other political actors ("external" institutional constraints). So, for example, it is often said that, unlike Congress, courts cannot choose what issues it will address. Instead, they must rely on litigants to bring them cases to set their agenda. In addition, even if a case is filed, courts lack the power of the sword and purse to implement their decisions. These readings aim to explore these constraints.

Additional recommended materials:

William Eskridge, Jr., "Reneging on History? Playing the Court/Congress/President Civil Rights Game," *California Law Review* 79 (1991):613-84

Louis Fisher. "The Legislative Veto: Invalidated, It Survives," Law and Contemporary Problems 56 (1993): 273-92

Frontline: The Last Abortion Clinic (a documentary on state strategies aimed at limiting access to abortions)

Donald Horowitz, *The Courts and Social Policy* (1977)

Melnick, R. Shep, *Between the Lines: Interpreting Welfare Rights* (1994)

The Dynamic and the Constrained Court

Gerald N. Rosenberg

W hat is the role of U.S. courts in producing significant social reform? When and under what conditions will U.S. courts be effective producers of significant social reform? When does it make sense for individuals and groups pressing for such change to litigate? What kinds of effects from court victories can they expect? Which view best captures the reality of American politics? Given the alleged success of the social reform litigation of the last four decades, and Americans' attachment to the Dynamic Court view, it is tempting to suggest that it *always* makes sense for groups to litigate. On the other hand, our attachment to the vision of the Constrained Court, as well as a knowledge of legal history, can suggest that courts can *never* be effective producers of significant social reform. But "always" and "never" are claims about frequency, not conditions. To fully understand the role of the courts in producing significant social reform, we must focus on the latter.

Many scholars have turned their attention to the questions this litigation activity raises. However, their findings remain unconnected and not squarely centered on whether, and under what conditions, courts produce significant social reform. Some writing has focused on the determinants of winning court cases rather than on the effects of court decisions. Galanter (1974), for example, asks "why the 'haves' come out ahead" and suggests that the resources and experience available to established and on-going groups provide an advantage in litigation. Similarly, Handler (1978), while exploring outcomes as well as the resources available to litigants, stresses the latter too. While these and similar works provide interesting theories about winning cases, that is a different question from the effects courts have on political and social change.

On the outcome side, there are numerous individual studies. Unfortunately, they tend to focus narrowly on a given issue and refrain from offering hypotheses about courts and change.[1]

---

1   For example, see the studies excerpted and compiled in Becker and Feeley (1973). A more theoretical work, although unfortunately not focused on important political and social change,

Gerald Rosenberg, "The Dynamic and the Constrained Court," The Hollow Hope, pp. 9-27. Copyright © 1991 by University of Chicago Press. Reprinted with permission.

More self-consciously theoretical case studies have examined admittedly non-controversial areas (Rebell and Block 1982), the need for federal pressure to improve race relations (Hochschild 1984), or have suggested so many hypotheses (one hundred and thirty-five of them) as to be of little practical help (Wasby 1970, 246-66). Finally, the extensive law review literature on institutional reform either lacks evidence or focuses on individual cases with little or no attempt to generate hypotheses.[2] While much of this work is well done, it does not address the larger question.

In the bulk of this chapter, I flesh out the two views. My aim is to make each view plausible, if not enticing. Then, critically examining evidence for their plausibility, I develop a set of constraints and conditions under which courts can produce significant social reform. These suggest that both views oversimplify court effectiveness.

STRUCTURAL CONSTRAINTS: THE LOGIC OF THE CONSTRAINED COURT VIEW

The view of courts as unable to produce significant social reform has a distinguished pedigree reaching back to the founders. Premised on the institutional structure of the American political system and the procedures and belief systems created by American law, it suggests that the conditions required for courts to produce significant social reform will seldom exist. Unpacked, the Constrained Court view maintains that courts will generally not be effective producers of significant social reform for three reasons: the limited nature of constitutional rights, the lack of judicial independence, and the judiciary's inability to develop appropriate policies and its lack of powers of implementation.

The Limited Nature of Rights

The Constitution, and the set of beliefs that surround it, is not unbounded. Certain rights are enshrined in it and others are rejected. In economic terms, private control over the allocation and distribution of resources, the use of property, is protected (Miller 1968). "Rights" to certain minimums, or equal shares of basic goods, are not. Further, judicial discretion is bound by the norms and expectations of the legal culture. These two parameters, believers in the Constrained Court view suggest, present a problem for litigators pressing the courts for significant social reform because most such litigation is based on constitutional claims that rights are being denied.[3] An individual or group comes into a court claiming it is being denied

---

is Johnson and Canon (1984).

2   For representative examples, see Aronow (1980); Eisenberg and Yeazell (1980); Monti (1980); Note (1980); Note (1975).

3   Sometimes, however, court cases deal not in the language of constitutional rights but in the world of statutory interpretation. While many of the constraints suggested below are applicable

some benefit, or protection from arbitrary and discriminatory action, and that it is *entitled* to this benefit or that protection. Proponents of the Constrained Court *view* suggest that this has four important consequences for social reformers.

First, they argue, it limits the sorts of claims that can be made, for not *all* social reform goals can be plausibly presented in the name of constitutional rights. For example, there are no constitutional rights to decent housing, adequate levels of welfare, or clean air, while there are constitutional rights to minimal governmental interference in the use of one's property. This may mean that "practically significant but legally irrelevant policy matters may remain beyond the purview of the court" (Note 1977, 436). Further, as Gordon (1984, 111) suggests, "the legal forms we use set limits on what we can imagine as practical outcomes." Thus, the nature of rights in the U.S. legal system, embedded in the Constitution, may constrain the courts in producing significant social reform by preventing them from hearing many claims.

A second consequence from the Constrained Court perspective is that, even where claims can be made, social reformers must often argue for the establishment of a new right, or the extension of a generally accepted right to *a* new situation. In welfare rights litigation, for example, the Court was asked to find a constitutional right to welfare (Krislov 1973). This need to push the courts to read the Constitution in an expansive or "liberal" way creates two main difficulties. Underlying these difficulties is judicial awareness of the need for predictability in the law and the politically exposed nature of judges whose decisions go beyond the positions of electorally accountable officials. First, the Constitution, lawyers, judges, and legal academics form a dominant legal culture that at any given time accepts some rights and not others and sets limits on the interpretation and expansion of rights. Judicial discretion is bound by the beliefs and norms of this legal culture, and decisions that stray too far from them are likely to be reversed and severely criticized. Put simply, courts, and the judges that compose them, even if sympathetic to social reform plaintiffs, may be unwilling to risk crossing this nebulous yet real boundary.[4] Second, and perhaps more important, is the role of precedent and what Justice Traynor calls the "continuity scripts of the law" (Traynor 1977, 11). Traynor, a justice of the California Supreme Court for twenty-five years, Chief Justice from 1964 to 1970, and known as a judge open to new ideas, wrote of the "very caution of the judicial process" (1977, 7). Arguing that "a judge must plod rather than soar," Traynor saw that the "greatest judges" proceed "at the pace of a tortoise that steadily makes advances though it carries the past on its back" (1977, 7, 6). Constrained by precedent and the beliefs of the dominant legal culture, judges, the Constrained Court view asserts, are not likely to act as crusaders.

---

here as well, when elected officials have acted to produce significant social reform, the conditions under which courts operate are dramatically changed.

4   As Diver (1979, 104) puts it, a "judge's actions must conform to that narrow band of conduct considered appropriate for so antimajoritarian an institution."

Third, supporters of the Constrained Court view note, as Scheingold (1974) points out, that to claim a right in court is to accept the procedures and obligations of the legal system. These procedures are designed, in part, to make it difficult for courts to hear certain kinds of cases. As the Council for Public Interest Law (CPIL) puts it, doctrines of standing and of class actions, the so-called political question doctrine, the need to have a live controversy, and other technical doctrines can "deter courts from deciding cases on the merits" (CPIL 1976, 355) and can result in social reform groups being unable to present their best arguments, or even have their day in court. Once in court, however, the legal process tends to dissipate significant social reform by making appropriate remedies unlikely. This can occur, McCann (1986, 200) points out, because policy-based litigation aimed at significant social reform is usually "disaggregate[d] ... into discrete conflicts among limited actors over specific individual entitlements." Remedial decrees, it has been noted, "must not confuse what is socially or judicially desirable with what is legally required" (Special Project 1978, 855). Thus, litigation seldom deals with "underlying issues and problems" and is "directed more toward symptoms than causes" (Harris and Spiller 1976, 26).

Finally, it has long been argued that framing issues in legally sound ways robs them of "political and purposive appeal" (Handler 1978, 33). In the narrow sense, the technical nature of legal argument can denude issues of emotional, widespread appeal. More broadly, there is the danger that litigation by the few will replace political action by the many and reduce the democratic nature of the American polity. James Bradley Thayer, writing in 1901, was concerned that reliance on litigation would sap the democratic process of its vitality. He warned that the "tendency of a common and easy resort" to the courts, especially in asking them to invalidate acts of the democratically accountable branches, would "dwarf the political capacity of the people" (Thayer 1901, 107). This view was echoed more recently by McCann, who found that litigation-prone activists' "legal rights approach to expanding democracy has significantly narrowed their conception of political action itself" (McCann 1986, 26). Expanding the point, McCann argued that "legal tactics not only absorb scarce resources that could be used for popular mobilization ... [but also] make it difficult to develop broadly based, multiissue grassroots associations of sustained citizen allegiance" (McCann 1986, 200). For these reasons, the Constrained Court view suggests that the nature of rights in the U.S. constrains courts from being effective producers of significant social reform. Thus,

Constraint I: The bounded nature of constitutional rights prevents courts from hearing or effectively acting on many significant social reform claims, and lessens the chances of popular mobilization.

Limits on Judicial Independence—The Institutional Factor

As the colloquy between Justice Jackson and U.S. Attorney Rankin illustrates, reformers have often turned to courts when opposition to significant social reform in the other branches has prevented them from acting. Thus, much significant social reform litigation takes place in the context of stalemate within, or opposition from, the other branches. For courts to be effective in such situations, they must, logically, be independent of those other branches. Supporters of the Constrained Court view point to a broad array of evidence that suggests the founders did not thoroughly insulate courts or provide them with unfailing independence.[5]

To start, the appointment process, of course, limits judicial independence. Judges do not select themselves. Rather, they are chosen by politicians, the president and the Senate at the federal level. Presidents, while not clairvoyant, tend to nominate judges who they think will represent their judicial philosophies. Clearly, changing court personnel can bring court decisions into line with prevailing political opinion (and dampen support for significant social reform).[6] Thus, the Constrained Court perspective sees the appointment process as limiting judicial independence.

Judicial independence requires that court decisions, in comparison to legislation, do not invariably reflect public opinion. Supporters of the Constrained Court view note, however, that Supreme Court decisions, historically, have seldom strayed far from what was politically acceptable (McCloskey 1960, 223-24).[7] Rather than suggesting independence, this judicial unwillingness to often blaze its own trail perhaps suggests, in the words of Finley Peter Dunne's Mr. Dooley, that "the supreme court follows the election returns" (Dunne 1901, 26).[8]

In at least two important ways, the Constrained Court view suggests, Congress may constrain court actions. First, in the statutory area, Congress can override decisions, telling the courts they misinterpreted the intent of the law. That is, Congress may rewrite a provision to meet court objections or simply state more clearly what it meant so that the courts' reading

---

5   For a clear theoretical discussion of the notion of judicial independence, see Shapiro (1981), chapter 1.

6   In terms of producing significant social reform, the appointment process may be overemphasized. To the extent that the Constrained Court view is correct, appointing judges intent upon significant social reform won't lead to greater court contributions to it because the other structural constraints render courts impotent as producers of significant social reform. Thus, the appointment process only serves a negative role.

7   More specifically, comparing the Court's opinions with those of the public on issues in 146 decisions over the years 1935-1986, Marshall found consistency nearly two-thirds of the time (Marshall 1989, chap. 4). In the period 1969-84, all but two of the years of the Burger Court, the Court's opinions were consistent with the public's over 70 percent of the time (Marshall 1985).

8   In the wake of Mr. Dooley's comments, after the Supreme Court abruptly switched sides and upheld New Deal legislation, Felix Frankfurter wrote the following to Justice Stone: "I must confess I am not wholly happy in thinking that Mr. Dooley should, in the course of history turn out to have been one of the most distinguished legal philosophers" (quoted in O'Brien 1985, 22).

of the law is repudiated.[9] Second, although Congress cannot directly reverse decisions based on constitutional interpretations, presumably untouchable by the democratic process, it may be able to constrain them by threatening certain changes in the legal structure. A large part of the reason, of course, is the appointment process. But even without the power of appointment, the Court may be susceptible to credible threats against it. Historical review of the relations of the Court to the other branches of the federal government suggests that the Court cannot for long stand alone against such pressure. From the "Court-packing" plan of FDR to recent bills proposing to remove federal court jurisdiction over certain issues, court-curbing proposals may allow Congress to constrain courts as producers of significant social reform (Nagel 1965; Rosenberg 1985; cf. Lasser 1988).

American courts, proponents of the Constrained Court view claim, are particularly deferential to the positions of the federal government. On the Supreme Court level, the solicitor general is accorded a special role. The office has unusual access to the Court and is often asked by the Court to intervene in cases and present the government's position. When the solicitor general petitions the Court to enter a case, the Court almost invariably grants the request, regardless of the position of the parties.[10] The government is also unusually successful in convincing the Court to hear cases it appeals and to not hear those it opposes.[11] The solicitor general's access to the Court carries over to the winning of cases. Historically, the solicitor general (or the side the government is supporting when it enters a case as amicus) wins about 70 percent of the time (Scigliano 1971; Ulmer and Willison 1985). It appears that the federal government has both extraordinary access to and persuasive abilities with the Court (Ducat and Dudley 1985; Dudley and Ducat 1986).

That does not comport with notions of independence and a judicial system able to defy legislative and political majorities. Thus, the Constrained Court view's adherents believe,

---

9   Modern examples include Grove City College v. Bell (1984), which limited the fund cut-off provisions of Title IX. In the spring of 1988 Congress, over President Reagan's veto, enacted the Civil Rights Restoration Act which overturned the decision. A similar case occurred with General Electric v. Gilbert (1976), where the Supreme Court held that an employer's disability plan that excluded pregnancy from its coverage did not violate Title VII of the 1964 Civil Rights Act. Congress responded in 1978 by amending the law to prohibit such exclusion. More generally, in the period 1944-60, Congress rewrote courts' decisions fifty times (Wasby 1978b).

10   In the years 1969-83, the solicitor general petitioned to enter 130 cases without the consent of the parties. The Court granted access in 126 of those cases (97 percent) (Ulmer and Willison 1985).

11   While the Court agrees to hear, on average, about 7 or 8 percent of cases appealed to it (13 or 14 percent not including petitions from prisoners), the solicitor general's petitions are accepted almost three-quarters of the time. When the solicitor general opposes an appeal, the Court rarely accepts the case, doing so, for example, in only 4 percent of the cases during the 1969-83 period (Ulmer and Willison 1985).

Constraint II: The judiciary lacks the necessary independence from the other branches of the government to produce significant social reform.

Implementation and Institutional Relations

For courts, or any other institution, to effectively produce significant social reform, they must have the ability to develop appropriate policies and the power to implement them. This, in turn, requires a host of tools that courts, according to proponents of the Constrained Court view, lack. In particular, successful implementation requires enforcement powers. Court decisions, requiring people to act, are not self-executing. But as Hamilton pointed out two centuries ago in *The Federalist Papers* (1787-88), courts lack such powers. Indeed, it is for this reason more than any other that Hamilton emphasized the courts' character as the least dangerous branch. Assuaging fears that the federal courts would be a political threat, Hamilton argued in *Federalist 78* that the judiciary "has no influence over either the sword or the purse; no direction either of the strength or of the wealth of the society; and can take no active resolution whatever. It may truly be said to have neither FORCE nor WILL, but merely judgment; and must ultimately depend upon the aid of the executive arm even for the efficacy of its judgments" *(The Federalist Papers* 1961, 465). Unlike Congress and the executive branch, Hamilton argued, the federal courts were utterly dependent on the support of the other branches and elite actors. In other words, for Court orders to be carried out, political elites, electorally accountable, must support them and act to implement them. Proponents of the Constrained Court view point to historical recognition of this structural "fact" of American political life by early Chief Justices John Jay and John Marshall, both of whom were acutely aware of the Court's limits.[12] President Jackson recognized these limits, too, when he reputedly remarked about a decision with which he did not agree, "John Marshall has made his decision, now let him enforce it."[13] More recently, the unwillingness of state authorities to follow court orders, and the need to send federal troops to Little Rock, Arkansas, to carry them out, makes the same point. Without elite support (the federal government in this case), the Court's orders would have been frustrated. While it is clear that courts can stymie change (Paul 1960), though ultimately not prevent it (Dahl 1957; Nagel 1965; Rosenberg 1985), the Constitution, in the eyes of the Constrained Court view, appears to leave the courts few tools to insure that their decisions are carried out.

---

12 Having been the nation's first Chief Justice, Jay refused the position in 1801, telling President Adams that he lacked faith that the Court could acquire enough "energy, weight and dignity" to play an important role in the nation's affairs (quoted in McCloskey 1960, 31). And *Marbury* v. *Madison,* if nothing else, demonstrates Marshall's acute awareness of the Court's limits.

13 Supposedly made in response to the Supreme Court's decision in *Worcester* v. *Georgia* (1832).

If the separation of powers, and the placing of the power to enforce court decisions in the executive branch, leaves courts practically powerless to insure that their decisions are supported by elected and administrative officials, then they are heavily dependent on popular support to implement their decisions. If American citizens are aware of Court decisions, and feel duty-bound to carry them out, then Court orders will be implemented. However, proponents of the Constrained Court view point out that survey data suggest that the American public is consistently uninformed of even major Supreme Court decisions and thus not in a position to support them (Adamany 1973; Daniels 1973; Dolbeare 1967; Goldman and Jahnige 1976). If the public or political elites are not ready or willing to make changes, the most elegant legal reasoning will be for nought.

This constraint may be particularly powerful with issues of significant social reform. It is likely that as courts deal with issues involving contested values, as issues of significant social reform do almost by definition, they will generate opposition. In turn, opposition may induce a withdrawal of the elite and public support crucial for implementation. Thus, proponents of the Constrained Court view suggest that the contested nature of issues of significant social reform makes it unlikely that the popular support necessary for implementation will be forthcoming.

A second claim made by proponents of the Constrained Court view about courts effectively implementing decisions is that the legal system is a particular type of bureaucracy that has few of the advantages and many of the disadvantages of the ideal Weberian type. For example, important components of the Weberian bureaucracy include a hierarchical command structure, a clear agenda, little or no discretion at lower levels, stated procedures, job protection, positions filled strictly by merit, area specialization, and the ability to initiate action and follow-up. While on the surface the U.S. judicial system is hierarchical, has stated procedures, and provides job protection, closer examination under a Constrained Court microscope complicates the picture. For example, although orders are handed down from higher courts to lower ones, there is a great deal of discretion at the lower levels. Decisions announced at the appellate level may not be implemented by lower-court judges who disagree with them or who simply misunderstand them. Similarly, procedures designed to prevent arbitrary action may be used for evasion and delay. Further, unlike the ideal bureaucratic type, courts lack a clear agenda and any degree of specialization. Rather, judges and clerks go from case to case in highly disparate fields. This means that area expertise and planning, often crucial in issues involving significant social reform, are seldom present, making it uncertain that the remedy will be appropriate to the problem. In terms of initiation and follow-up, the nature of the legal bureaucracy puts barriers in the way of courts. For example, courts cannot initiate suits but must wait for litigants to approach them. Because stated procedures must be followed, because courts have small staffs, and because the legal system requires individuals rather than courts to initiate proceedings, appellate courts may never know whether their decisions have been implemented. Follow-up is difficult because it may be years by the time appellate judges discover an incident (or pattern) of non-implementation, through a case working its way up to them. Finally, the insulated "above politics" position of courts limits judges in cutting deals and actively politicking in support of a decision. The distance between the ideal Weberian bureaucracy and the American judiciary is so large, proponents of the Constrained Court view might argue, that even if courts actively promote significant social reform, they cannot easily achieve the results their decisions command.[14]

Through the eyes of the Constrained Court view, the decentralized nature of the judicial system may constrain courts from producing significant social reform for several reasons. In a nutshell, the structure of courts opens the possibility for bias and misinterpretation to influence lower-court decisions. Further, the entrepreneurial nature of many lawyers makes it difficult for groups seeking significant social reform through the courts to present a coherent strategy. And the nature of the legal bureaucracy makes delay endemic. These claims merit brief attention.

The American judicial system vests considerable discretion in lower-court judges. Only rarely do appellate courts issue final orders. In almost all cases, they remand to the trial court for issuance of the final order. This leaves lower-court judges with a great deal of discretion. The objective judge will conscientiously attempt to follow the higher court's orders. However, misinterpretation of those orders, especially if they are vague, is possible. Further, the biased judge has a myriad of tools with which to abuse discretion. These include the "delay endemic to legal proceedings" (CPIL 1976, 355), narrow interpretation, and purposeful misinterpretation. In this kind of case, litigants must follow procedure and re-appeal the case to the higher court for help, further delaying change.

This structural aspect of the American judicial system, those in the Constrained Court camp argue, may pose a particular problem for litigants seeking significant social reform. Bias and misinterpretation aside, it may be difficult for groups seeking reform to present a coherent strategy. Access to the legal system can be gained in any one of hundreds of courts (in the federal system) by any one of hundreds of thousands of lawyers. In particular, as Cowan (1976), Tushnet (1987), and Wasby (1983, 1985) note, interest groups planning a litigation strategy may find themselves faced with a host of cases not of their doing or to their liking. There is no way to prevent other lawyers, individuals, and groups from filing cases. And if these cases are not well-chosen and well-argued, they may result in decisions that wreak havoc with the best-laid plans. Thus, groups are sometimes on the defensive, forced to disassociate themselves from the legal arguments of purported allies and sometimes even to oppose them.

Although in practice federal judges have life tenure, this does not mean they are free from constraints. In asking for significant social reform, litigants are asking judges to reform

_____

14 In an empirical study of four important cases, Horowitz supports this line of reasoning and concludes that effective implementation aimed at reforming institutions requires information and knowledge that judges don't have and political compromises that they ought not to make. See Horowitz (1977), especially chapters 2 and 7. Interestingly, a much less elaborate version of this argument was made in 1963 (Friendly 1963, 791-92). For a critical review of Horowitz, see Wasby (1978a).

existing institutions. However, judges may be unwilling to take on this essentially non-judicial task. To the extent that lower-court judges are part of a given community, ordering massive change in their community may isolate them and threaten the respect of the court. Also, the judicial selection process for lower federal court judges, is designed to select people who reflect the mores and beliefs of the community in which the court sits (Chase 1972). Therefore, adherents to the Constrained Court view argue, it is unlikely that lower-court judges will be predisposed to support significant social reform if the community opposes it.

The opportunity for delay that is built into the judicial bureaucracy constrains courts in several ways. First, through constant appeals, motions, and the use of other procedures, parties under court order to implement significant social reform can gain time. For example, when threatened with a lawsuit over prison conditions, a state corrections director replied: "a lawsuit is twenty-six months away. We could buy some time" (Cooper 1988, 259). Second, parties opposed to change can initiate their own lawsuits, using the courts to challenge and invalidate legislative, administrative, or other judicial action. In the environmental field both Wenner (1982, 1988) and Hays (1986) note that industry has systematically relied on courts to delay change. For those opposed to reform, delay can allow for changes in political and economic conditions, leading to reversals of the ordered reform. Thus, the opportunity for delay inherent in the legal bureaucracy, believers in the Constrained Court view argue, makes courts poor institutions for producing significant social reform.

A further obstacle for court effectiveness, assert believers in the Constrained Court view, is that significant social reform often requires large expenditures. Judges, in general prohibited from actively politicking and cutting deals, are not in a particularly powerful position to successfully order the other branches to expend additional funds. "The real problem" in cases of reform, Judge Bazelon wrote, "is one of inadequate resources, which the courts are helpless to remedy" (Bazelon 1969, 676). While there may be exceptions where courts seize financial resources, they are rare precisely because courts are hesitant to issue such orders which violate separation of powers by in effect appropriating public funds. Even without this concern, courts "ultimately lack the power to force state governments [or the federal government] to act" (Frug 1978, 792) because if governments refuse to act, there is little courts can do. They are unlikely to hold governors, legislators, or administrators in contempt or take other dramatic action because such action sets up a battle between the branches that effectively destroys any chance of government cooperation. Thus, judges are unlikely to put themselves in such no-win situations. Further, the "limits on government resources are no less applicable in the courtroom than outside of it" (Frug 1978, 788). As Frug asserts, "the judicial power of the purse will, in the final analysis, extend no further than a democratic decision permits" (Frug 1978, 794).

The claims of the Constrained Court view about the judiciary's lack of tools, and its dependence on others to implement its decisions, can be illustrated by one kind of significant social reform, the wholesale reshaping of bureaucracies. Recent work suggests that courts encounter particular difficulties when they try to reshape highly complicated institutions and bureaucracies.[15] For example, Frug contends that given the number of variables involved, these kind of institutions are "too complex to be administered under court orders" (Frug 1978, 789). Even supporters of the competence of courts note the importance of the complexity of large organizations to court effectiveness (Note 1977), and realize that litigation in such cases requires "some relatively elaborate rearrangement of the institution's mode of operation" (Eisenberg and Yeazell 1980, 468). More specifically, successful reshaping requires the acquiescence, if not the support, of administrators and staff. This presents several problems. First, without the support of political leaders, there is little incentive for administrators to risk their jobs to implement court orders. In the Alabama mental health litigation, for example, the acting superintendent of the Partlow facility was fired for cooperating with the plaintiffs during the remedy hearings (Cooper 1988, 195). In such cases, staff will be especially reluctant to help implement changes. In addition, rigid insistence on conformity to rules such as court orders "breeds distrust, destruction of documents, and an attitude that T won't do anything more than I am absolutely required to do'" (Christopher Stone, quoted in McCann 1986, 229-30). In other words, changes required by outsiders, such as courts, may be "strongly resisted" (Special Project 1978, 837) by administrators and staffs, who, as one study suggested, "have a practically limitless capacity to sabotage reform" (Diver 1979, 94). And if administrators and staffs don't act voluntarily, there is little judges can do. While courts do have the power to cite recalcitrant bureaucrats for contempt, the use of such coercive power tends to make martyrs out of resisters and to strengthen the resolve of others to prevent change (Diver 1979, 99; Special Project 1978, 839). Thus, both administrators and staffs have to be won over by the judge for courts to be effective, and judges may not be in a very good position to receive such support. Such rearrangement is difficult for courts, the logic of the Constrained Court view suggests, because they lack the resources to gain adequate understanding of the intricacies of reform and the tools to insure compliance.

Another aspect of the Weberian ideal type involves specialization and expertise. It is plausible that courts' remedial decrees would be more effective if they took into account "the internal and external factors affecting bureaucratic behavior" (Note 1980, 537). Yet, even proponents of court competence realize that "no single judge" has "the resources, inclination, or the time to pursue this sort of detailed and extensive analysis" (Aronow 1980, 759). This analysis has been seconded by several activist judges. Judge Frank M. Johnson, for example, has written that "judges are trained in the law. They are not penologists, psychiatrists, public administrators, or educators" (Johnson 1981, 274). Similarly, Justice Traynor has pointed out that such analysis pulls judges far from their training: "A judge is constrained by training, experience, and the office itself not to undertake responsibilities that belong to the legislature" (Traynor 1977, 8). This means, Constrained Court view supporters claim, that judges often have incomplete knowledge of the resources available or of the power dynamics

---

15   Golann and Fremouw (1976); Harris and Spiller (1976); Kalodner and Fishman (1978); Note (1977); Special Project (1978).

of the institution or bureaucracy that appears before them. A common result is that judicial reform decrees may lack a realistic sense of available resources. For example, in the *Wyatt* case, one of the principal attorneys for the plaintiffs demanding reform of Alabama's mental health facilities concluded that the standards adopted by the court required "staffing of the institutions with more professionals than there are in the State of Alabama" (Halpern 1976, 85). Similarly, Yudof suggests that "lawyers and judges frequently fail to distinguish between altering the behavior of an individual and altering the behavior of an institution" (Yudof 1981, 444). Thus, it has been suggested that "the realities of the institutional reform suit correspond neither to the talents of most judges nor to the attributes of traditional adjudication" (Kirp and Babcock 1981, 317).

It may also be the case that the effective implementation of significant social reform requires long-term planning and serious consideration of costs. Courts, it has been suggested, are not constituted to be effective at either of these. Judges, McCann suggests, are "largely bound to episodic case-by-case remedies for complex social problems at odds with the long-term supervisory capacities necessary for effective means-oriented planning" (McCann 1986, 226). Further, if "taking political reform seriously requires taking economics seriously as well" (McCann 1986, 164), then litigation may provide little help for two reasons. First, litigation, by its piecemeal nature, "discourages a comprehensive economic orientation" (McCann 1986, 168). Second, of course, judges are not trained economists, and litigators are limited to legal, rights-oriented forms of argument, not economic analysis. Courts, it can be argued, are not structured to produce significant social reform. Thus, proponents of the Constrained Court view propose,

> Constraint III: Courts lack the tools to readily develop appropriate policies and implement decisions ordering significant social reform.

To sum up, the Constrained Court view holds that litigants asking courts for significant social reform are faced with powerful constraints. First, they must convince courts that the rights they are asserting are required by constitutional or statutory language. Given the limited nature of constitutional rights, the constraints of legal culture, and the general caution of the judiciary, this is no easy task. Second, courts are wary of stepping too far out of the political mainstream. Deferential to the federal government and potentially limited by congressional action, courts may be unwilling to take the heat generated by politically unpopular rulings. Third, if these two constraints are overcome and cases are decided favorably, litigants are faced with the task of implementing the decisions. Lacking powerful tools to force implementation, court decisions are often rendered useless given much opposition. Even if litigators seeking significant social reform win major victories in court, in implementation they often turn out to be worth very little. Borrowing the words of Justice Jackson from another context, the Constrained Court view holds that court litigation to produce significant social reform may amount to little more than "a teasing illusion like a munificent bequest in a pauper's will" (*Edwards* v. *California* 1941, 186).

COURT EFFECTIVENESS: THE LOGIC OF THE DYNAMIC COURT VIEW

The three constraints just presented are generated from the view of courts as unable to produce significant social reform. That view appears historically grounded and empirically plausible. Yet, on reflection, it has two main difficulties. First, it seems to overstate the limits on courts. After all, since the mid-twentieth century or so courts have been embroiled in controversies over significant social reform. Many lawyers, activists, and scholars have acted or written with the belief that the constraints are weak or non-existent and can easily be overcome. Indeed, the whole modern debate over judicial activism makes no sense if the Constrained Court view is correct. If courts are as impotent as the constraints suggest, then why has there been such political, academic, and judicial concern with the role of courts in modern America? Theory and practice are unaligned if the Constrained Court view is entirely correct. Second, examined carefully, its claim is that courts are *unlikely* to produce significant social reform; it does not deny the possibility. However, that doesn't help us understand when, and under what conditions, courts can produce significant social reform. The Constrained Court view is not the complete answer.

The Dynamic Court view may help. It maintains that courts can be effective producers of significant social reform. Its basic thrust is that not only are courts not as limited as the Constrained Court view suggests, but also, in some cases, they can be more effective than other governmental institutions in producing significant social reform. As Aryeh Neier puts it, "[s]ince the early 1950s, the courts have been the most accessible and, often, the most effective instrument of government for bringing about the changes in public policy sought by social protest movements" (Neier 1982, 9). The constraints of the Constrained Court view, then, may oversimplify reality.

Political, Institutional, and Economic Independence

Proponents of the Dynamic Court view argue that the Constrained Court view entirely misses key advantages of courts. At the most fundamental level, key to the Dynamic Court view is the belief that courts are free from electoral constraints and institutional arrangements that stymie change. Uniquely situated, courts have the capacity to act where other institutions are politically unwilling or structurally unable to proceed. For example, one of the great strengths of courts is the ability to act in the face of public opposition. Elected and appointed officials, fearful of political repercussions, are seldom willing to fight for unpopular causes and protect the rights of disliked minorities. Courts, free of such electoral accountability, are not so constrained. From civil rights to women's rights, from protecting the rights of the physically and mentally challenged to ensuring that criminal defendants are treated constitutionally, the courts have acted where other institutions have refused. Justice Brennan, concurring in a 1981 prison reform case, summarized this view: "Insulated as they are from political pressures, and charged with the duty of enforcing the Constitution, courts are in the strongest position to insist that unconstitutional conditions be remedied, even at significant financial cost" *(Rhodes* v. *Chapman* 1981, 359).

The ability of courts to act is particularly clear with issues of significant social reform. With such issues, entrenched interests often have the institutional base to prevent change in other political bodies. In civil rights in the 1950s, for example, as the colloquy between Justice Jackson and Assistant Attorney General Rankin reflects, the key position of Southern Democrats in Congress virtually insured that no civil rights legislation would be forthcoming. If change was to come, proponents of the Dynamic Court view argue, it could come only from the courts. Similarly, examining school desegregation in the years 1968-72, Hochschild argues that "were it not for the courts, there would be little reduction in racial isolation [in the public schools]"(Hochschild 1984, 134). And with re-apportionment, legislators from malapportioned districts had no incentive to reform the electoral system and vote themselves out of office, until the courts acted. In other words, the Dynamic Coon view proposes that courts are free from the obstacles that lead to "a partial failure of executive or legislative government institutions to do their jobs in a satisfactory and legal way" (CPIL 1976, 208).

A similar argument applies to bureaucratic and institutional change. Proponents of the Dynamic Court view suggest that insulation, institutional inertia stemming from routinized procedures, and group pressure make it difficult for non-judicial institutions to reform themselves. Looking at "entrenched bureaucracies," environmental lawyer Victor Yannacone saw "self-perpetuating, self-sufficient, self-serving bureaus [which] are power sources unto themselves, effectively insulated from the people and responsible to no one but themselves" (Yannacone 1970b, 185). Where there is little incentive to change, it is only an outside force such as a court, uninvolved in daily operations, that may have the will to force change. Organizations contemplating reform also must confront the desires of their constituencies. "In the face of pressures from many diverse constituencies and interests," Aronow writes, "it is unlikely that even public institutions headed by cooperative administrators will reform themselves without the outside coercive force of the court providing the impetus for specific change" (Aronow 1980, 751). Courts simply do not face such pressures. Court decisions will not adversely affect the court's ongoing relations with elected officials, interest groups, financial backers, and the like, whose cooperation is essential for getting work done, far the simple reason that courts are not structured to need or maintain such ongoing relations. Courts do not depend on carefully worked out institutional arrangements because they do not specialize in any one area. Unlike bureaucracies and large institutions, the parties they deal with vary from case to case. Here, too, courts are uniquely situated.

The "inadequacy" of the political process is an essential basis for the Dynamic Court view because "policy formulation in our society is too often 3 one-sided affair—a process in which only the voices of the economically or politically powerful are heard" (CPIL 1976, 8). In the legislative and executive branches, not all affected interests are heard and not all voices carry the same weight. The predictable result of this systematic exclusion of the "public" is that "government agencies cannot adequately represent all facets of live public interest" (CPIL

1976, 172). However, courts, it is contended, can rectify this exclusion because, "unlike the hierarchical statist view of entrenched elite rule, the judicial view guarantees the independence of citizen groups contending for influence within the adversary process" (McCann 1986, 116). Neither access nor influence depends on connections or position. Access to all affected interests is guaranteed by judicial rules, and influence depends on strength of argument, not political position. As William F. Butler of the Environmental Defense Fund put it, "all it takes is one person with a good legal argument that can convince a judge and that's that" (quoted in McCann 1986, 208). The judiciary, with "no corrupting links to anyone," affords "equality of both access and influence to citizens" more "completely" than any "other institutional form" (McCann 1986, 118, 116). And this means that it is able to respond to social reform claims of ordinary citizens where other institutions are not (Sax 1971, 57, 112, 231). As Justice Neely of West Virginia puts it, American courts alleviate the "more dangerous structural deficiencies of the other institutions of democratic government" and thus are the "central institution in the United States which makes democracy work" (Neely 1981, xiii, xi).

The underlying claim here of the Dynamic Court view is that access and influence are not dependent on economic and political resources. The kind of professional lobbying that is required to be effective in influencing bureaucracies or enacting legislation is not necessary for winning court cases. Groups lacking key resources can use courts not only directly to change the law but also to strengthen their voices within the other branches of government and authoritatively present their positions. Thus, proponents of the Dynamic Court view claim, courts offer the best hope to poor, powerless, and unorganized groups, those most often seeking significant social reform.

The judicial process may also provide a powerful forum for gathering and assessing information. In contrast to legislative and bureaucratic proceedings, wide participation in legal proceedings makes it likely that the full range of relevant information will be brought to bear on the final decree. Where crucial information is being withheld, or is hard to obtain, the judicial process of discovery, supported by the coercive powers of the court, may help bring it to light. Further, the adversarial process insures that information will be rigorously assessed before it takes the status of "fact." Thus, as Chayes points out, the information that the Court has "will not be filtered through the rigid structures and preconceptions of bureaucracies" (Chayes 1976, 1308). Judges, then, are in a strong position to act. As Cavanagh and Sarat put it, it is "difficult to see how any other institutional actor [than the judge] is better equipped to become informed of the ramifications of comparable decisions" (Cavanagh and Sarat 1980, 381-82).

Influence accompanies access in legal proceedings because judges must respond to legal arguments and provide reasons for their opinions. Unlike in other institutions, arguments cannot be ignored or dismissed without discussion. Judges, in contrast to elected or other appointed officials, cannot easily duck the tough issues. Further, judges are limited by the Constitution, statutes, and precedent in the kind of responses they can make. A judge's dislike or disapproval of actions provides insufficient grounds to support a legal decision.

This means, of course, that the positions of unpopular and politically weak groups, denied access to and influence with administrative, executive, and legislative branches, must be taken seriously by the courts.

To sum up, proponents of the Dynamic Court view assert that courts have the ability to act when other institutions won't, because judges are electorally unaccountable and serve with life tenure. Unencumbered by electoral commitments and political deal-making, and protected from recrimination, they can act to fulfill the constitutional mandate. Thus, as Fiss puts it, courts can produce significant social reform because the judicial office is "structured by both ideological and institutional factors that enable and perhaps even force the judge to be objective—not to express his preferences or personal beliefs, or those of the citizenry, as to what is right or just, but constantly to strive for the true meaning of the constitutional value" (Fiss 1979, 12-13). Courts, then, can provide an escape from the pathologies of rigid bureaucracies, ossified institutions, and a reluctant or biased citizenry.

Courts as Catalysts—Indirect Effects of the Dynamic Court

In striving for the "true meaning of the constitutional value," courts base decisions on principle. Unlike legislatures or executives, courts do not act out of calculations of partisan preference. This means, proponents of the Dynamic Court view suggest, that courts can point the way to doing what is "right." They can remind Americans of our highest aspirations and chide us for our failings. Courts, Bickel suggests, have the "capacity to appeal to men's better natures, to call forth their aspirations, which may have been forgotten in the moment's hue and cry" (Bickel [1962] 1986, 26). For Rostow, the "Supreme Court is, among other things, an educational body, and the Justices are inevitably teachers in a vital national seminar" (Rostow 1952, 208). Bickel agrees, viewing courts as "a great and highly effective educational institution" (Bickel [1962] 1986, 26). In the Dynamic Court view, the courts have important indirect effects, educating Americans and heightening their understanding of their constitutional duty.

Court decisions also have indirect effects, proponents of the Dynamic Court view suggest, through dramatizing issues and spurring action. Courts can provide publicity for issues and serve as a "catalyst" for change (Halpern 1976, 75). Where the public is ignorant of certain conditions, and political elites do not want to deal with them, court decisions can "politicize issues that otherwise might have remained unattended" (Monti 1980, 237). This may put public pressure on elites to act. Indeed, litigation may "often" be "the best method of attracting public attention to institutional conditions and of publicly documenting abuses" (Neier 1982, 29). By bringing conditions to light, and showing how far from constitutional or statutory aspirations practice has fallen, court cases can provide a "cheap method of pricking powerful consciences" (Note 1977, 463).[16] Thus, litigation "serves as a catalyst,

---

16 A small sampling of such claims includes Halpern (1976, 75); Handler (1978, 209); and Scheingold (1974, 9).

not a usurper, of the legislative process" (Sax 1971, 157). This ability to dramatize may be particularly effective with custodial institutions such as hospitals, prisons, and mental institutions where court cases have brought inhumane conditions to light.[17] As Sax puts it, "courts can be used to bring matters to legislative attention, to force them upon the agendas of reluctant and busy representatives" (Sax 1971, xviii).

In addition, court action may invigorate and encourage groups to mobilize and take political action (Scheingold 1974, 131, 148; McCann 1986, 108). In both civil rights and women's rights, for example, the federal courts are often seen as having served this role. As Yannacone told a conference audience:

> Every piece of enlightened social legislation that has come down in the past 50 or 60 years has been preceded by a history of litigation (applause) in which trial lawyers somewhere around the country have forcibly focussed the attention of the legislature on the inadequacies of existing legislation (Yannacone 1970a, 77).

Thus, proponents of the Dynamic Court view assert that judicial decisions have important extra-judicial effects.

Another way in which courts may indirectly produce significant social reform is by facilitating negotiations. As an external force unbeholden to involved interests, courts are free to act. They can provide a neutral forum where parties can work out their differences. Also, the threat of litigation can serve as a "basic political resource" (Grossman and Sarat 1981, 89). That is, rather than expend money, time, and energy defending against a lawsuit and countering the publicity it generates, parties may find it more palatable to negotiate. Without the threat of lawsuits, Cavanagh and Sarat suggest, many institutions would "never get to the bargaining table" (Cavanagh and Sarat 1980, 405). Where institutions are incapable of internal reform, and there is ineffective public or interest group-pressure, courts may provide a prod.

For the proponents of the Dynamic Court view, then, courts have powerful indirect effects. Their politically neutral position allows them to teach Americans about the meaning of their constitutional obligations. Court decisions can change opinions, generate media coverage, and inspire action. They can provide the necessary nudge to start the reform process. In other words, they have a unique and important kind of potency.

Evolving Procedures

Much of the Constrained Court view's plausibility comes from Constraint III, the courts' supposed lack of implementation powers. Contrary to this view, however, proponents of the Dynamic Court view assert that not only are courts in a unique position to act, but they also have the "demonstrated ability to evolve new mechanisms and procedures" to cope with the

---

17   Halpern (1976, 75); Harris (1976, 57); Neier (1982, 29); Note (1975, 1349-50).

complexities of significant social reform litigation (Cavanagh and Sarat 1980, 373). One such mechanism is court appointments of special masters to fill in many of the courts' structural weaknesses. Special masters can survey and gather information, talk with interested parties, hold hearings, conduct investigations, draft and float potential remedial decrees, and generally serve as the eyes and the ears of the judge (Aronow 1980). In other words, they can perform many duties helpful to finding an agreeable solution, duties that would appear unseemly if performed by the judge. They are able to do this, Aronow maintains, while retaining "court-like detachment and independence" (Aronow 1980, 766). Aronow and others argue that to the extent that courts have lacked tools to effectively implement remedial decrees in the past, the problem is well on the way to being solved.

Other changes, it is suggested, that have allowed courts to overcome the obstacles suggested by the Constrained Court view include the court's retention of jurisdiction, the creation of monitoring commissions, and the active engagement of the judge (Chayes 1976; Fiss 1979). These steps are designed to allow the court to closely follow the implementation process. If court decrees are not being implemented, or if unforeseen circumstances render parts of decrees inappropriate, these mechanisms allow for speedy correction. For example, if judges retain jurisdiction, then any of the parties can immediately return to court if the decree is not being implemented or if changing circumstances require its modification. Similarly, monitoring commissions can inform the judge of implementation progress and alert the court to the need for further action. And, of course, the mere availability of these tools can influence the behavior of the parties. With these kind of tools readily at hand, possibly recalcitrant parties may think twice before violating remedial decrees. Even with the uncertainties of institutional reform litigation, courts can create effective tools.

Why the "Haves" Come Out Ahead

Speculations of the Limits of Legal Change

Marc Galanter

A TYPOLOGY OF PARTIES

Because of differences in their size, differences in the state of the law, and differences in their resources, some of the actors in the society have many occasions to utilize the courts (in the broad sense) to make (or defend) claims; others do so only rarely. We might divide our actors into those claimants who have only occasional recourse to the courts (one-shotters or OS) and repeat players (RP) who are engaged in many similar litigations over time. The spouse in a divorce case, the auto-injury claimant, the criminal accused are OSs; the insurance company, the prosecutor, the finance company are RPs. Obviously this is an oversimplification; there are intermediate cases such as the professional criminal. So we ought to think of OS-RP as a continuum rather than as a dichotomous pair. Typically, the RP is a larger unit and the stakes in any given case at€ smaller (relative to total worth). OSs are usually smaller units and the stakes represented by the tangible outcome of the case may be high relative to total worth, as in the case of injury victim or the criminal accused. Or, the OS may suffer from the opposite problem: his claims may be so small and unmanageable (the shortweighted consumer or the holder of performing rights) that the cost of enforcing them outruns any promise of benefit...

Let us refine our notion of the RP into an "ideal type" if you will—a unit which has had and anticipates repeated litigation, which has low stakes in the outcome of any one case, and which has the resources to pursue its long-run interests. (This does not include every real-world repeat player; that most common repeat player, the alcoholic derelict, enjoys few of the advantages that may accrue to the RP. His resources are too few to bargain in the short run or take heed of the long run.) An OS, on the other hand, is a unit whose claims are too large (relative to his size) or too small (relative to the cost of remedies) to be managed routinely and rationally.

Marc Galanter, "Why the 'Haves' Come Out Ahead: Speculations on the Limits of Legal Change," Law and Society Review, vol. 9, no. 1. Copyright © 1974 by John Wiley & Sons, Inc. Reprinted with permission.

We would expect an RP to play the litigation game differently from an OS. Let us consider some of his advantages:

1. RPs, having done it before, have advance intelligence; they are able to structure the next transaction and build a record. It is the RP who writes the form contract, requires the security deposit, and the like.
2. RPs develop expertise and have ready access to specialists.[1] They enjoy economies of scale and have low start-up costs for any case.
3. RPs have opportunities to develop facilitative informal relations with institutional incumbents.
4. The RP must establish and maintain credibility as a combatant. His interest in his "bargaining reputation" serves as a resource to establish "commitment" to his bargaining positions. With no bargaining reputation to maintain, the OS has more difficulty in convincingly committing himself in bargaining.[2]
5. RPs can play the odds. The larger the matter at issue looms for OS, the more likely he is to adopt a minimax strategy (minimize the probability of maximum loss). Assuming that the stakes are relatively smaller for RPs, they can adopt strategies calculated to maximize gain over a long series of cases, even where this involves the risk of maximum loss in some cases.
6. RPs can play for rules as well as immediate gains. First, it pays an RP to expend resources in influencing the making of the relevant rules by such methods as lobbying. (And his accumulated expertise enables him to do this persuasively.)
7. RPs can also play for rules in litigation itself, whereas an OS is unlikely to. That is, there is a difference in what they regard as a favorable outcome. The larger the stake for any player and the lower the probability of repeat play, the less likely that he will be concerned with the rules which govern future cases of the same kind. ... On the other hand, the player with small stakes in the present case and the prospect of a series of similar cases ... may be more interested in the state of the law.

   ... [If we were to assume] that the institutional facilities for litigation were overloaded and settlements were prevalent, [w]e would then expect RPs to "settle" cases where they expected unfavorable rule outcomes. Since they expect to litigate again, RPs

---

1   Ironically, RPs may enjoy access to competent paraprofessional help that is unavailable to OSs. Thus the insurance company can, by employing adjusters, obtain competent and experienced help in routine negotiations without having to resort to expensive professionally qualified personnel.

2   An offsetting advantage enjoyed by some OSs deserves mention. Since he does not anticipate continued dealings with his opponent, an OS can do his damnedest without fear of reprisal next time around or on other Issues. (The advantages of those who enjoy the luxury of singlemindedness are evidenced by some notorious examples in the legislative arena, for instance, the success of prohibitionists and of the gun lobby.) Thus there may be a bargaining advantage to the OS who (a) has resources to damage his opponent; (b) is convincingly able to threaten to use them. An OS can burn up his capital, but he has to convince the other side he is really likely to do so. Thus an image of irrationality may be a bargaining advantage. ... An OS may be able to sustain such an image in a way that an BP cannot. ...

Figure 3: A Taxonomy of Litigation by Strategic Configuration of Parties

Initiator, Claimant

	One-Shotter	Repeat Player
One-Shotter (Defendant)	Parent v. Parent (Custody) Spouse v. Spouse (Divorce) Family v. Family Member (Insanity Commitment) Family v. Family (Inheritance) Neighbor v. Neighbor Partner v. Partner OS vs OS I	Prosecutor v. Accused Finance Co. v. Debto Landlord v. Tenant I.R.S. v. Taxpayer Condemnor v. Property Owner RP vs OS II
Repeat Player (Defendant)	WelfareClient v. Agency Auto Dealer v. Manufacturer Injury Victim v. Insurance Company Tenant v. Landlord Bankrupt Consumer v. Creditors Defamed v. Publisher OS vs RP III	Union v. Company Movie Distributor v. Censorship Board Developer v. Suburban Municipality Purchaser v. Supplier Regulatory Agency v. Firms of Regulated Industry RP vs RP IV

can select to adjudicate (or appeal) those cases which they regard as most likely to produce favorable rules. On the other hand, OSs should be willing to trade off the possibility of making "good law" for tangible gain. Thus, we would expect the body of "precedent" cases—that is, cases capable of influencing the outcome of future cases—to be relatively skewed toward those favorable to RP... In [stipulating] that RPs can play for rules, I do not mean to imply that RPs pursue rule-gain as such. If we recall that not all rules penetrate (i. e., become effectively applied at the field level), we come to some additional advantages of RPs.

8. RPs, by virtue of experience and expertise, are more likely to be able to discern which rules are likely to "penetrate" and which are likely to remain merely symbolic commitments. RPs may be able to concentrate their resources on rule-changes that are likely to make a tangible difference. They can trade off symbolic defeats for tangible gains.

9. Since penetration depends in part on the resources of the parties (knowledge, attentiveness, expert services, money), RPs are more likely to be able to invest the matching resources necessary to secure the penetration of rules favorable to them.

...What this analysis does is to define a position of advantage in the configuration of contending parties and indicate how those with other advantages tend to occupy this position of advantage and to have their other advantages reinforced and augmented thereby. This position of advantage is one of the ways in which a legal system formally neutral as between "haves" and "have-nots" may perpetuate and augment the advantages of the former

We may think of litigation as typically involving various combinations of OSs and RPs. We can then construct a matrix such as Figure 1 and fill in the boxes with some well-known if only approximate American examples.

(We ignore for the moment that the terms OS and RP represent ends of a continuum, rather than a dichotomous pair.)

On the basis of our incomplete and unsystematic examples, let us conjecture a bit about the content of these boxes:

Box I: OS vs. OS

The most numerous occupants of this box are divorces and insanity hearings. Most (over 90 per cent of divorces, for example) are uncontested. A large portion of these are really pseudo-litigation, that is, a settlement is worked out between the parties and ratified in the guise of adjudication. When we get real litigation in Box I, it is often between parties who have some intimate tie with one another, fighting over some unsharable good, often with overtones of "spite" and "irrationality." Courts are resorted to where an ongoing relationship is ruptured; they have little to do with the routine patterning of activity. The law is invoked ad hoc and instrumentally by the parties. There may be a strong interest in vindication, but neither party is likely to have much interest in the long-term state of the law (of, for instance, custody or nuisance). There are few appeals, few test cases, little expenditure of resources on rule-development. Legal doctrine is likely to remain remote from everyday practice and from popular attitudes.

Box II: RP vs. OS

The great bulk of litigation is found in this box—indeed every really numerous kind except personal injury cases, insanity hearings, and divorces. The law is used for routine processing of claims by parties for whom the making of such claims is a regular business activity. Often the cases here take the form of stereotyped mass processing with little of the individuated attention of full-dress adjudication. Even greater numbers of cases are settled "informally" with settlement keyed to possible litigation outcome (discounted by risk, cost, delay).

The state of the law is of interest to the RP, though not to the OS defendants. Insofar as the law is favorable to the RP it is "followed" closely in practice (subject to discount for RP's transaction costs). Transactions are built to fit the rules by creditors, police, draft boards and other RPs. Rules favoring OSs may be less readily applicable, since OSs do not ordinarily plan the underlying transaction, or less meticulously observed in practice, since OSs are unlikely to be as ready or able as RPs to invest in insuring their penetration to the field level.

Box III: OS vs. RP

All of these are rather infrequent types except for personal injury cases which are distinctive in that free entry to the arena is provided by the contingent fee.[3] In auto injury claims, litigation is routinized and settlement is closely geared to possible litigation outcome. Outside the personal injury area, litigation in Box III is not routine. It usually represents the attempt of some OS to invoke outside help to create leverage on an organization with which he has been having dealings but is now at the point of divorce (for example, the discharged employee or the cancelled franchisee). The OS claimant generally has little interest in the state of the law; the RP defendant, however, is greatly interested.

Box IV: RP vs. RP

Let us consider the general case first and then several special cases. We might expect that there would be little litigation in Box IV, because to the extent that two RPs play with each other repeatedly, the expectation of continued mutually beneficial interaction would give rise to informal bilateral controls. This seems borne out by studies of dealings among businessmen and in labor relations. Official agencies are invoked by unions trying to get established and by management trying to prevent them from getting established, more rarely in dealings between bargaining partners. Units with mutually beneficial relations do not adjust their differences in courts. Where they rely on third parties in dispute-resolution, it is likely to take a form (such as arbitration or a domestic tribunal) detached from official sanctions and applying domestic rather than official rules.

However, there are several special cases. First, there are those RPs who seek not furtherance of tangible interests, but vindication of fundamental cultural commitments. An example would be the organizations which sponsor much church-state litigation. Where RPs are contending about value differences (who is right) rather than interest conflicts (who gets what) there is less tendency to settle and less basis for developing a private system of dispute-settlement.

Second, government is a special kind of RP. Informal controls depend upon the ultimate sanction of withdrawal and refusal to continue beneficial relations. To the extent that withdrawal of future association is not possible in dealing with government, the scope of informal

---

3   Perhaps high volume litigation in Box III is particularly susceptible to transformation into relatively unproblematic administrative processing when RPs discover that it is to their advantage and can secure a shift with some gains (or at least no losses) to OSs. Cf. the shift from tort to workman's compensation in the industrial accident area ... and the contemporary shift to no-fault plans in the .automobile injury area.

controls is correspondingly limited. The development of informal relations between regulator agencies and regulated firms is well known. And the regulated may have sanctions other than withdrawal which they can apply; for instance, they may threaten political opposition. But the more inclusive the unit of government, the less effective the withdrawal sanction and the greater the likelihood that a party will attempt to invoke outsides allies by litigation even while sustaining the ongoing relationship. This applies also to monopolies, units which share the government's relative immunity to withdrawal sanctions. RPs in monopolistic relationships will occasionally invoke formal controls to show prowess, to give credibility to threat, and to provide satisfactions for other audiences. Thus we would expect litigation by and against government to be more frequent than in other RP vs. RP situations. There is a second reason for expecting more litigation when government is a party. That is, that the notion of "gain" (policy as well as monetary) is often more contingent and problematic for governmental units than for other parties, such as businesses or organized interest groups. In some cases courts may, by proffering authoritative interpretations of public policy, redefine an agency's notion of gain. Hence government parties may be more willing to externalize decisions to the courts. And opponents may have more incentive to litigate against government in the hope of securing a shift in its goals.

A somewhat different kind of special case is present where plaintiff and defendant are both RPs but do not deal with each other repeatedly (two insurance companies, for example). In the government/monopoly case, the parties were so inextricably bound together that the force of informal controls was limited; here they are not sufficiently bound to each other to give informal controls their bite; there is nothing to withdraw from! The large one-time deal that falls through, the marginal enterprise—these are staple sources of litigation.

Figure 4: A Typology of Legal Specialists

Lawyer

	Specialized by Party	Specialized by Field and Party	Specialized by Field
Client RP	"House Counsel" or General Counsel for Bank, Insurance Co., etc. Corporation Counsel for Government Unit	Prosecutor Personal Injury Defendant Staff Counsel for NAACP Tax Labor/Management Collections	Patent
Client OS	"Poverty Lawyers" Legal Aid	Criminal Defense Personal Injury Plaintiff	Bankruptcy Divorce

Where there is litigation in the RP vs. RP situation, we might expect that there would be heavy expenditure on rule-development, many appeals, and rapid and elaborate development of the doctrinal law. Since the parties can invest to secure implementation of favorable rules, we would expect practice to be closely articulated to the resulting rules. ...

LAWYERS

What happens when we introduce lawyers? Parties who have lawyers do better. Lawyers are themselves RPs. Does their presence equalize the parties, dispelling the advantage of the RP client? Or does the existence of lawyers amplify the advantage of the RP client? We might assume that RPs (tending to be larger units) who can buy legal services more steadily, in larger quantities, in bulk (by retainer) and at higher rates, would get services of better quality. They would have better information (especially where restrictions on information about legal services are present). Not only would the RP get more talent to begin with, but he would on the whole get greater continuity, better record-keeping, more anticipatory or preventive work, more experience and specialized skill in pertinent areas, and more control over counsel.

One might expect that just how much the legal services factor would accentuate the RP advantage would be related to the way in which the profession was organized. The more members of the profession were identified with their clients (i. e., the less they were held aloof from clients by their loyalty to courts or an autonomous guild) the more the imbalance would be accentuated. The more close and enduring the lawyer-client relationship, the more the primary loyalty of lawyers is to clients rather than to courts or guild, the more telling the advantages of accumulated expertise and guidance in overall strategy.

What about the specialization of the bar? Might we not expect the existence of specialization to offset RP advantages by providing OS with a specialist who in pursuit of his own career goals would be interested in out-comes that would be advantageous to a whole class of OSs? Does the specialist become the functional equivalent of the RP? We may divide specialists into (1) those specialized by field of law (patent, divorce, etc.), (2) those specialized by the kind of party represented (for example, house counsel), and (3) those specialized by both field of law and "side" or party (personal injury plaintiff, criminal defense, labor). Divorce lawyers do not specialize in husbands or wives, nor real-estate lawyers in buyers or sellers. But labor lawyers and tax lawyers and stockholders-derivative-suit lawyers do specialize not only in the field of law but in representing one side. Such specialists may represent RPs or OSs. Figure 2 provides some well-known examples of different kinds of specialists:

Most specializations cater to the needs of particular kinds of RPs. Those specialists who service OSs have some distinctive features:

First, they tend to make up the "lower echelons" of the legal profession. ... (Of course the correlation is far from perfect; some lawyers who represent OSs do not have these characteristics and some representing RPs do. ...)

Second, specialists who service OSs tend to have problems of mobilizing a clientele (because of the low state of information among OSs) and encounter "ethical" barriers imposed by the profession which forbids solicitation, advertising, referral fees, advances to clients, and so forth.

Third, the episodic and isolated nature of the relationship with particular OS clients tends to elicit stereotyped and uncreative brand of legal services. ...

Fourth, while they are themselves RPs, these specialists have problems in developing optimizing strategies. What might be good strategy for an insurance company lawyer or prosecutor—trading off some cases for gains on others—is branded as unethical when done by a criminal defense or personal injury plaintiff lawyer. It is not permissible for him to play his series of OSs as if they constituted a single RP.

Conversely, the demands of routine and orderly handling of a whole series of OSs may constrain the lawyer from maximizing advantage for any individual OS. ...

Figure 5: Why the "Haves" Tend to Come Out Ahead

Element	Advantages	Enjoyed by
PARTIES	—ability to structure transaction —specialized expertise, economies of scale —long-term strategy —ability to play for rules —bargaining credibility —ability to invest in penetration	—repeat players, large, professional*
LEGAL SERVICES	—skin, specialization, continuity	—organized, professional,* wealthy
INSTITUTIONAL FACILITIES	—passivity —cost and delay barriers —favorable priorities	—wealthy, experienced, organized —holders, possessors —beneficiaries of existing rules —organized, attentive
RULES	—favorable rules —due process barriers	—older, culturally dominant —holders, possessors

The existence of a specialized bar on the OS side should overcome the gap in expertise, allow some economies of scale, provide for bargaining commitment and personal familiarity. But this is short of overcoming the fundamental strategic advantage of RPs—their capacity to structure the transaction, play the odds, and influence rule-development and enforcement policy.

Specialized lawyers may, by virtue of their identification with parties, become lobbyists, moral entrepreneurs, proponents of reforms on the parties' behalf. But lawyers have a cross-cutting interest in preserving complexity and mystique so that client contact with this area of law is rendered problematic. Lawyers should not be expected to be proponents of reforms which are optimum from the point of view of the clients taken alone. Rather, we would expect them to seek to optimize the clients' position without diminishing that of lawyers. ...

INSTITUTIONAL FACILITIES

We see then that the strategic advantages of the RP may be augmented by advantages in the distribution of legal services. Both are related to the advantages conferred by the basic features of the institutional facilities for the handling of claims: passivity and overload.

These institutions are passive, first, in the sense that [they are] "reactive"—they must be mobilized by the claimant—giving advantage to the claimant with information, ability to surmount cost barriers, and skill to navigate restrictive procedural requirements. ... The presiding official acts as umpire, while the development of the case, collection of evidence and presentation of proof are left to the initiative and resources of the parties. Parties are treated as if they were equally endowed with economic resources, investigative opportunities and legal skills. Where, as is usually the case, they are not, the broader the delegation to the parties, the greater the advantage conferred on the wealthier, more experienced and better organized party.

... In several ways overload creates pressures on claimants to settle rather than to adjudicate:

- by causing delay (thereby discounting the value of recovery);
- by raising costs (of keeping the case alive);
- by inducing institutional incumbents to place a high value on clearing dockets, discouraging full-dress adjudication in favor of bargaining, stereotyping and routine processing;
- by inducing the forum to adopt restrictive rules to discourage litigation.

Thus, overload increases the cost and risk of adjudicating and shields existing rules from challenge, diminishing opportunities for rule-change. This tends to favor the beneficiaries of existing rules.

Second, by increasing the difficulty of challenging going practice, overload also benefits those who reap advantage from the neglect (or systematic violation) of rules which favor their adversaries.

Third, overload tends to protect the possessor—the party who has the money or goods—against the claimant. For the most part, this amounts to favoring RPs over OSs, since RPs typically can structure transactions to put themselves in the possessor position.

Finally, the overload situation means that there are more commitments in the formal system than there are resources to honor them—more rights and rules "on the books" than can be vindicated or enforced. There are, then, questions of priorities in the allocation of resources. We would expect judges, police, administrators and other managers of limited institutional facilities to be responsive to the more organized, attentive and influential of their constituents. Again, these tend to be RPs.

Thus, overloaded and passive institutional facilities provide the setting in which the RP advantages in strategic position and legal services can have full play.

RULES

We assume here that rules tend to favor older, culturally dominant interests. This is not meant to imply that the rules are explicitly designed to favor these interests, but rather that those groups which have become dominant have successfully articulated their operations to pre-existing rules. To the extent that rules are evenhanded or favor the "have-nots," the limited resources for their implementation will be allocated, I have argued, so as to give greater effect to those rules which protect and promote the tangible interests of organized and influential groups. Furthermore, the requirements of due process, with their barriers or protections against precipitate action, naturally tend to protect the possessor or holder against the claimant. Finally, the rules are sufficiently complex and problematic (or capable of being problematic if sufficient resources are expended to make them so) that differences in the quantity and quality of legal services will affect capacity to derive advantages from the rules.

Thus, we arrive at Figure 3 which summarizes why the "haves" tend to come out ahead. It points to layers of advantages enjoyed by different (but largely overlapping) classes of "haves"—advantages which interlock, reinforcing and shielding one another. ...

STRATEGIES FOR REFORM

Our categorization of four layers of advantage (Figure 3) suggests a typology of strategies for "reform" (taken here to mean equalization—conferring relative advantage on those who did not enjoy it before). We then come to four types of equalizing reform:

- rule-change,
- improvement in institutional facilities,
- improvement of legal services in quantity and quality,
- improvement of strategic position of have-not parties.

... [Here Professor Galanter sketches some of the possible ramifications of change on each of these four levels. We have included only the discussion relating to the improvement of the strategic position of the "have-not parties."]

The reform envisaged here is the organization of "have-not" parties (whose position approximates OS) into coherent groups that have the ability to act in a coordinated fashion, play long-run strategies, benefit from high-grade legal services, and so forth.

One can imagine various ways in which OSs might be aggregated into RPs. They include (1) the membership association-bargaining agent (trade unions, tenant unions); (2) the assignee-manager of fragmentary rights (performing rights associations like ASCAP); (3) the interest group-sponsor (NAACP, ACLU, environmental action groups). All of these forms involve upgrading capacities for managing claims by gathering and utilizing information, achieving continuity and persistence, employing expertise, exercising bargaining skill and so forth. These advantages are combined with enhancement of the OS party's strategic position either by aggregating claims that are too small relative to the cost of remedies (consumers, breathers of polluted air, owners of performing rights); or by reducing claims to manageable size by collective action to dispel or share unacceptable risks (tenants, migrant workers). A weaker form of organization would be (4) a clearing-house which established a communication network among OSs. This would lower the costs of information and give RPs a stake in the effect OSs could have on their reputation. A minimal instance of this is represented by the "media ombudsman"—the "action line" type of newspaper column. Finally, there is governmentalization—utilizing the criminal law or the administrative process to make it the responsibility of a public officer to press claims that would be unmanageable in the hands .of private grievants.

An organized group is not only better able to secure favorable rule changes, in courts and elsewhere, but is better able to see that good rules are implemented. It can expend resources on surveillance, monitoring, threats, or litigation that would be uneconomic for an OS. Such new units would in effect be RPs. Their encounters with opposing RPs would move into Box IV of Figure 1. Neither would enjoy the strategic advantages of RPs over OSs. One possible result, as we have noted in our discussion of the RP v. RP situation, is delegalization, that is, a movement away from the official system to a private system of dispute-settlement; another would be more intense use of the official system.

Many aspects of "public interest law" can be seen as approximations of this reform. (1) The class action is a device to raise the stakes for an RP, reducing his strategic position to that of an OS by the stakes more than he can afford to play the odds on, while moving the claimants into a position in which they enjoy the RP advantages without having to undergo the outlay for organizing. (2) Similarly, the "community organizing" aspect of public interest law can be seen as an effort to create a unit (tenants, consumers) which can play the RP game. (3) Such a change in strategic position creates the possibility of a test-case strategy for getting rule-change. Thus "public interest law" can be thought of as a combination of community organizing, class action and test-case strategies, along with increase in legal services. ...

IMPLICATIONS FOR REFORM: THE ROLE OF LAWYERS

We have discussed the way in which the architecture of the legal system tends to confer interlocking advantages on overlapping groups whom we have called the "haves." To what extent might reforms of the legal system dispel these advantages?

Our analysis suggests that change at the level of substantive rules is not likely in itself to be determinative of redistributive outcomes. Rule change is in itself likely to have little effect because the system is so constructed that changes in the rules can be filtered out unless accompanied by changes at other levels. In a setting of overloaded institutional facilities, inadequate costly legal services, and unorganized parties, beneficiaries may lack the resources to secure implementation; or an RP may restructure the transaction to escape the thrust of the new rule. Favorable rules are not necessarily (and possibly not typically) in short supply to "have-nots;" certainly less so than any of the other resources needed to play the litigation game. Programs of equalizing reform which focus on rule-change can be readily absorbed without any change in power relations. The system has the capacity to change a great deal at the level of rules without corresponding changes in everyday patterns of practice or distribution of tangible advantages. Indeed rule-change may become a symbolic substitute for redistribution of advantages.

The low potency of substantive rule-change is especially the case with rule-changes procured from courts. That courts can sometimes be induced to propound rule-changes that legislatures would not make points to the limitations as well as the possibilities of court-produced change. With their relative insulation from retaliation by antagonistic interests, courts may more easily propound new rules which depart from prevailing power relations. But such rules require even greater inputs of other resources to secure effective implementation. And courts have less capacity than other rule-makers to create institutional facilities and re-allocate resources to secure implementation of new rules. Litigation then is unlikely to shape decisively the distribution of power in society. It may serve to secure or solidify symbolic commitments. It is vital tactically in securing temporary advantage or protection, providing leverage for organization and articulation of interests and conferring (or withholding) the mantle of legitimacy. The more divided the other holders of power, the greater the redistributive potential of this symbolic/tactical role.

Our analysis suggests that breaking the interlocked advantages of the "haves" requires attention not only to the level of rules, but also to institutional facilities, legal services and organization of parties. It suggests that litigating and lobbying have to be complemented by interest organizing, provisions of services and invention of new forms of institutional facilities.

The thrust of our analysis is that changes at the level of parties are most likely to generate changes at other levels. If rules are the most abundant resource for reformers, parties capable of pursuing long-range strategies are the rarest. The presence of such parties can generate effective demand for high grade legal services—continuous, expert, and oriented to the long run—and pressure for institutional reforms and favorable rules. This suggests that we can roughly surmise the relative strategic priority of various rule-changes. Rule-changes which relate directly to the strategic position of the parties by facilitating organization, increasing the supply of legal services (where these in turn provide a focus for articulating and organizing common interests) and increasing the costs of opponents—for instance authorization of class action suits, award of attorneys' fees and costs, award of provisional remedies—these are the most powerful fulcrum for change. The intensity of the opposition to class action legislation and autonomous reform-oriented legal services such as California Rural Legal Assistance indicates the "haves" own estimation of the relative strategic impact of the several levels.

The contribution of the lawyer to redistributive social change, then, depends upon the organization and culture of the legal profession. We have surmised that court-produced substantive rule-change is unlikely in itself to be a determinative element in producing tangible redistribution of benefits. The leverage provided by litigation depends on its strategic combination with inputs at other levels. The question then is whether the organization of the profession permits lawyers to develop and employ skills at these other levels. The more that lawyers view themselves exclusively as courtroom advocates, the less their willingness to undertake new tasks and form enduring alliances with clients and operate in forums other than courts, the less likely they are to serve as agents of redistributive change. Paradoxically, those legal professions most open to accentuating the advantages of the "haves" (by allowing themselves to be "captured" by recurrent clients) may be most able to become (or have room for, jnore likely) agents of change, precisely because they provide more license for identification with clients and their "causes" and have a less strict definition of what are properly professional activities.

Do the characteristic advantages of RPs flow from their position in a structure for litigation, or from their position in a predominantly extra-adjudicatory distributive order? Are very well-to-do OSs in a very much different position from a typical RP? Or are poor RPs in a different position from the typical OS? If not, is there any significance whatsoever in the OS/ RP distinction? Perhaps organizing RP units out of have-not OSs works, when it does work, not by virtue of changing the group's strategic position with respect to litigation, but rather by changing its relative power in the largely extra-ad judicatory political and economic orders.

Discussion Questions

1. What is the "constrained court view"?

2. What is the "dynamic court view"?

3. What is a "repeat player" versus a "one shotter"? What are the advantages of a repeat player?

4. How might the uneven distribution of legal resources limit the courts' opportunities to make policies and correct political failures?

3. Cultural (and Economic) Constraints

Like any policy-maker, courts must persuade parties to comply with their decisions. This task is often complicated by resistant subcultures who are hostile to the courts or unwilling to support the necessary laws designed to address a policy problem.

Additional recommended materials:

Nathan Glazer, "On Subway Graffiti in New York," *The Public Interest* (Winter 1979): 3-11
Mary Ann Glendon, *Rights Talk: The Impoverishment of Political Discourse* (1991)
To Kill a Mocking Bird (1962) (a movie about an African-American wrongly accused in the South)

Civil Rights

James Q. Wilson and John DiIulio

I n 1830 Congress passed a law requiring all Indians east of the Mississippi River to move to the Indian Territory west of the river, and the army set about implementing it. In the 1850s a major political fight broke out in Boston over whether the police department should be obliged to hire an Irish officer. Until 1920 women could not vote in most elections. In the 1930s the Cornell University Medical School had a strict quota to limit the number of Jewish students who could enroll. In the 1940s the army, with the approval of President Franklin D. Roosevelt, removed all Japanese-Americans from their homes in California and placed them in relocation centers far from the coast.

In all such cases some group, usually defined along racial or ethnic lines, was denied access to facilities, opportunities, or services that were available to other groups. Such cases raise the issue of civil rights. That issue is not whether the government has the authority to treat different people differently, but only whether such differences in treatment are "reasonable." All laws and policies make distinctions—for example, the tax laws require higher-income people to pay taxes at a higher rate than lower-income ones—but not all distinctions are defensible. The courts have long held that classifying people on the basis of their income and taxing different classes at different rates is quite permissible because such classifications are not arbitrary or unreasonable and they are related to a legitimate public policy (that is, raising revenue). Increasingly, however, the courts have said that classifying people on the basis of their race or ethnicity is unreasonable—these are suspect classifications—and while not every law making such classifications will be ruled unconstitutional, they all will be subject to especially strict scrutiny.

Given the theory of policy-making developed so far in this book, it may seem surprising that certain groups, particularly those that constitute only a small minority of the population, should require any special protection at all. We have seen how easy it is for many small groups—businesses, occupations, unions—to practice client politics. They can obtain some special advantage (a grant, a license, a subsidy) or avoid some threatened regulation because, being small, they find it easy to organize and to escape general public notice. Yet Native Americans, blacks, Japanese-Americans, and Mexican-Americans are also relatively small

James Q. Wilson & John DiIulio, "The Civil Rights Movement," American Government , pp. 545-561. Copyright © 1995 by Cengage Learning, Inc. Reprinted with permission.

groups whose demands seemingly place little burden on the majority population. Despite this, they have been more often the victims than the clients of the policy-making process.

To explain the victimization of certain groups and the methods by which they have begun to overcome that victimization, we shall consider chiefly the case of black Americans. Black-white relations have in large measure defined the problem of civil rights in this country; most of the landmark laws and court decisions have involved black claims. The strategies employed by or on behalf of blacks have typically set the pattern for the strategies employed by other groups. At the end of this chapter we shall look at the related but somewhat different issue of women's rights.

THE BLACK PREDICAMENT

Though constituting more than 12 percent of the population, blacks until fairly recently could not in many parts of the country vote, attend integrated schools, ride in the front seats of buses, or buy homes in white neighborhoods.

One reason is that the perceived costs of granting these demands were not widely distributed among the public at large but instead were concentrated on some relatively small, readily organized, immediately affected group. Citizens generally may not feel threatened if a black moves into Cicero, Illinois; goes to school at Little Rock Central High School; or votes in Neshoba County, Mississippi—but at one time most whites (and even now some whites) in Cicero, Little Rock, and Neshoba County felt deeply threatened. In the language of this book civil rights in these places was not a matter of client politics but of competitive or interest-group politics. This was especially the case in those parts of the country, notably in the Deep South, where blacks were often in a majority. There the politically dominant white minority felt keenly the potential competition for jobs, land, public services, and living space posed by large numbers of people of another race. But even in the North, black gains often appeared to be at the expense of lower-income whites who lived or worked near them, not at the expense of upper-status whites who lived in suburbs.

The interest-group component of racial politics put blacks at a decided disadvantage: they were not allowed to vote at all in many areas, they could vote only with great difficulty in others, and even in those places where voting was easy, they often lacked the material and institutional support for effective political organizations. If your opponent feels deeply threatened by your demands and in addition can deny you access to the political system that will decide the fate of those demands, you are, to put it mildly, at a disadvantage. Yet from the end of Reconstruction down to the 1960s—for nearly a century—many blacks in the South found themselves in just such a position.

A second reason why the restrictions on black Americans continued for so long is that majoritarian politics worked to the disadvantage of blacks. Because of white attitudes, this was the case even when white and black interests were not directly in competition. To the dismay of those who prefer to explain political action by economic motives, people often attach greater importance to the intangible costs and benefits of policies than to the tangible ones. Thus, even though the average black represented no threat to the average white, antiblack attitudes—racism—produced some appalling actions. Between 1882 and 1946, 4,715 people, about three-fourths of them blacks, were lynched in the United States. Some lynchings were carried out by small groups of vigilantes acting with much ceremony, but others were the actions of frenzied mobs. In the summer of 1911 a black charged with murdering a white man in Livermore, Kentucky, was dragged by a mob to the local theater, where he was hanged. The audience, which had been charged admission, was invited to shoot the swaying body (those in the orchestra seats could empty their revolvers, those in the balcony were limited to a single shot).

Though public opinion in other parts of the country was shocked by such events, little was done: lynching was a local, not a federal, crime. It obviously would not require many lynchings to convince blacks in these localities that it would be foolhardy to try to vote or enroll in a white school. And even in those states where blacks did vote, popular attitudes were not conducive to blacks' buying homes or taking jobs on an equal basis with whites. Even among those professing to support equal rights, a substantial portion opposed black efforts to obtain them and federal action to secure them. In 1942 a national poll showed that only 30 percent of whites thought that black and white children should attend the same schools; in 1956 the proportion had risen to 49 percent, still less than a majority. (In the South white support for school integration was even lower—14 percent favored it in 1956, about 31 percent in 1963.) As late as 1956 a majority of southern whites were opposed to integrated public transportation facilities. Even among whites who generally favored integration, there was in 1963 (before the ghetto riots) considerable opposition to the black civil-rights movement: nearly half of the whites who were classified in a survey as moderate integrationists thought that demonstrations hurt the black cause; nearly two-thirds disapproved of actions taken by the civil-rights movement; and over a third felt that civil rights should be left to the states.

In short the political position in which blacks found themselves until the 1960s made it difficult for them to advance their own interests with any feasible legislative strategy: their opponents were aroused, organized, and powerful. Thus, if those interests were to be championed in Congress or state legislatures, blacks would have to make use of white allies. Though some such allies could be found, they were too few to make a difference in a political system, such as the one found in Congress, that gives a substantial advantage to strongly motivated opponents of any new policy. For that to change, one or both of two things would have to happen: additional allies would have to be recruited (a delicate problem, given that many white integrationists disapproved of aspects of the civil-rights movement), or the struggle would have to be shifted to a policy-making arena in which the opposition enjoyed less of an advantage.

Partly by plan, partly by accident, black leaders followed both of these strategies simultaneously. By publicizing their grievances, but above all by developing a civil-rights movement that (at least in its early stages) dramatized the denial of essential and widely accepted liberties, blacks were able to broaden their base of support in both elite and public opinion and thereby

Critical Thinking: The Black College Predicament

Until the Supreme Court desegregation rulings, blacks in most parts of the South could attend only segregated, all-black colleges. After a long struggle, blacks won admission to previously all-white colleges and universities.

This left an unanswered question: What should happen to the previously all-black schools, some of which had a long and illustrious history of providing education? Theoretically, whites would be free to enroll in traditionally black schools just as blacks were free to enter all-white ones, but in fact, very few whites applied to the all-black schools. Moreover, some black educators believe that attending a predominately black school is helpful to many black students, just as some female educators believe that going to an all-women college makes sense for many female students. The United Negro College Fund raises money for predominately black colleges.

But the Supreme Court, having ruled that separate schools are inherently unequal, opposed segregation. In 1992, it decided that the state-funded maintenance in Mississippi of eight universities, some of which were predominately black, was uncon- stitutional/ This ruling challenges public funding for all colleges and universities that have a predominately minority or female enrollment.

Should black colleges be abolished? Should colleges serving specific groups be banned even when no one is excluded from attending any school on the basis of race? Should blacks or women who prefer a more segregated environment be forced to attend mostly white and coeducational schools?

United States v. Fordice, 112 S.Ct. 2727 (1992)

to raise civil-rights matters from a low to a high position on the political agenda. By waging a patient, prolonged, but carefully planned legal struggle, black leaders shifted the key civil-rights decisions from Congress, where they had been stymied for generations, to the federal courts.

After this strategy had achieved some substantial successes—after blacks had been enfranchised and legal barriers to equal participation in political and economic affairs had been lowered—the politics of civil rights became more conventional. Blacks were able to assert their demands directly in the legislative and executive branches of government with reasonable (though scarcely certain) prospects of success. Civil rights became less a matter of gaining entry into the political system and more one of waging interest-group politics within that system. At the same time the goals of civil-rights politics were broadened. The struggle to gain entry into the system had focused on the denial of fundamental rights (to vote, to organize, to obtain equal access to schools and public facilities); since that entry the dominant issues have been manpower development, economic progress, and the improve- ment of housing and neighborhoods.

THE CAMPAIGN IN THE COURTS

The Fourteenth Amendment was both the opportunity and the problem. Adopted in 1868, it *seemed* to guarantee equal rights for all: "No state shall make or enforce any law which shall abridge the privileges or immunities of citizens of the United States; nor shall any state deprive any person of life, liberty, or property, without due process of law; nor deny to any person within its jurisdiction the equal protection of the laws."

The key phrase was "equal protection of the laws." Read broadly, it might mean that henceforth the Constitution would be color-blind: no state law could have the effect of treating whites and blacks differently. Thus a law segregating blacks and whites into separate schools or neighborhoods would be unconstitutional. Read narrowly, "equal protection" might mean only that blacks and whites had certain fundamental legal rights in common, among them the right to sign contracts, to serve on juries, or to buy and sell property, but otherwise they could be treated differently.

Historians have long debated which view Congress held when it proposed the Fourteenth Amendment. What forms of racial segregation, if any, were still permissible? Segregated trains? Hotels? Schools? Neighborhoods?

The Supreme Court took the narrow view. Though in 1880 it declared unconstitutional a West Virginia law requiring juries to be composed only of white males, it decided in 1883 that it was unconstitutional for Congress to prohibit racial discrimination in public accommodations such as hotels. The difference between the two cases seemed, in the eyes of the Court, to be this: serving on a jury was an essential right of citizenship that the state could not deny to any person on racial grounds without violating the Fourteenth Amendment, but registering at a hotel was a convenience controlled by a private person (the hotel owner), who could treat blacks and whites differently if he or she wished.

The major decision that was to determine the legal status of the Fourteenth Amendment for over half a century was *Plessy v. Ferguson.* Louisiana had passed a law requiring blacks and whites to occupy separate cars on railroad trains operating in that state. When Adolph Plessy, who was seven-eighths white and one-eighth black, refused to obey the law, he was arrested. He appealed his conviction to the Supreme Court, claiming that the law violated the Fourteenth Amendment. In 1896 the Court rejected his claim, holding that the law treated both races equally even though it required them to be separate. The equal-protection clause guaranteed political and legal but not social equality. "Separate-but-equal" facilities were constitutional because if "one race be inferior to the other socially, the Constitution of the United States cannot put them on the same plane."

"Separate but Equal"

Thus began the separate-but-equal doctrine. Three years later the Court applied it to schools as well, declaring in *Camming v. Richmond County Board of Education* that a decision in a

Georgia community to close the black high school while keeping open the white high school was not a violation of the Fourteenth Amendment because blacks could always go to private schools. Here the Court seemed to be saying that not only could schools be separate, they could even be unequal.

What the Court has made, the Court can unmake. But to get it to change its mind requires a long, costly, and uncertain legal battle. The National Association for the Advancement of Colored People (NAACP) was the main organization that waged that battle. Formed in 1909 by a group of whites and blacks in the aftermath of a race riot, the NAACP did many things—lobbying in Washington and publicizing black grievances, especially in the pages of *The Crisis,* a magazine edited by W. E. B. Du Bois—but its most influential role was played in the courtroom.

It was a rational strategy. Fighting legal battles does not require forming broad political alliances or changing public opinion, tasks that would have been very difficult for a small and unpopular organization. A court-based approach also enabled the organization to remain nonpartisan.

But it was a slow and difficult strategy. The Court had adopted a narrow interpretation of the Fourteenth Amendment. To get it to change its mind would require the NAACP to bring before it cases involving the strongest possible claims that a black was unfairly treated under circumstances sufficiently different from those of earlier cases so that the Court could either distinguish the new cases from the old ones or find some grounds for changing its mind.

The steps in that strategy were these: First, persuade the Court to declare unconstitutional laws creating schools that were separate but obviously unequal. Second, persuade it to declare unconstitutional laws supporting schools that were separate but unequal in not-so-obvious ways. Third, persuade it to rule that racially separate schools were inherently unequal and hence unconstitutional.

Can Separate Schools Be Equal?

The first step was accomplished in a series of court cases stretching from 1938 to 1948. In 1938 the Court held that Lloyd Gaines had to be admitted to an all-white law school in Missouri because no black law school of equal quality existed in that state. In 1948 the Court ordered the all-white University of Oklahoma Law School to admit Ada Lois Sipuel, a black, even though the state planned to build a black law school later. For education to be equal, it had to be available now. It still could be separate, however: the university admitted Ms. Sipuel but required her to attend classes in a section of the state capitol, roped off from other students, where she could meet with her law professors.

The second step was taken in two cases decided in 1950. Heman Sweatt, a black, was treated by the University of Texas Law School much as Ada Sipuel had been treated in Oklahoma: "admitted" to the all-white school but relegated to a separate building. Another black, George McLaurin, was allowed to study for his Ph.D. in a "colored section" of the all-white University of Oklahoma. The Supreme Court unanimously decided that these arrangements were unconstitutional because, by imposing racially based barriers on the black students' access to professors, libraries, and other students, they created unequal educational opportunities.

The third step, the climax of the entire drama, began in Topeka, Kansas, where Linda Brown wanted to enroll in her neighborhood school but could not because she was black and the school was by law reserved exclusively for whites. When the NAACP took her case to the federal district court in Kansas, the judge decided that the black school that Linda could attend was substantially equal in quality to the white school that she could not attend. Thus denying her access to the white school was constitutional. To change that, the lawyers would have to persuade the Supreme Court to overrule the district judge on the grounds that racially separate schools were unconstitutional even if they were equal. In other words, the separate-but-equal doctrine would have to be overturned by the Courts.

It was a risky and controversial step to take. Many states, Kansas among them, were trying to make their all-black schools equal to those of whites by launching expensive building programs. If the NAACP succeeded in getting separate schools declared unconstitutional, the Court might well put a stop to the building of these new schools. Blacks could win a moral and legal victory but suffer a practical defeat— the loss of these new facilities. Despite these risks the NAACP decided to go ahead with the appeal.

BROWN V. BOARD OF EDUCATION

On May 17, 1954, a unanimous Supreme Court, speaking through an opinion written and delivered by Chief Justice Earl Warren, found that "in the field of public education the doctrine of 'separate but equal' has no place" because "separate educational facilities are inherently unequal" *Plessy v. Ferguson* was overruled, and "separate but equal" was dead.

The ruling was a landmark decision, but the reasons for it and the means chosen to implement it were as important and as controversial as the decision itself. There were at least three issues. First, how would the decision be implemented? Second, on what grounds were racially separate schools unconstitutional? Third, what test would a school system have to meet in order to be in conformity with the Constitution?

Implementation The *Brown* case involved a class-action suit; that is, it applied not only to Linda Brown but to all others similarly situated. This meant that black children everywhere now had the right to attend formerly all-white schools. This change would be one of the most far-reaching and disputatious events in modern American history. It could not be effected overnight or by the stroke of a pen. In 1955 the Supreme Court decided that it would let local federal district courts oversee the end of segregation by giving them the power to approve or disapprove local desegregation plans. This was to be done "with all deliberate speed."

In the South "deliberate speed" turned out to be a snail's pace. Massive resistance to desegregation broke out in many states. Some communities simply defied the Court; some sought to evade its edict by closing their public schools. In 1956 over one hundred southern members of Congress signed a "Southern Manifesto" that condemned the *Brown* decision as an "abuse of judicial power" and pledged to "use all lawful means to bring about a reversal of the decision."

In the late 1950s and early 1960s the National Guard and regular army paratroopers were used to escort black students into formerly all-white schools and universities. It was not until the 1970s that resistance collapsed and most southern schools were integrated. The use of armed force convinced people that resistance was futile; the disruption of the politics and economy of the South convinced leaders that it was imprudent; and the voting power of blacks convinced politicians that it was suicidal. In addition federal laws began providing financial aid to integrated schools and withholding it from segregated ones. By 1970 only 14 percent of southern black schoolchildren still attended all-black schools.

The Rationale As the struggle to implement the *Brown* decision continued, the importance of the rationale for that decision became apparent. The case was decided in a way that surprised many legal scholars. The Court could have said that the equal-protection clause of the Fourteenth Amendment makes the Constitution, and thus state laws, color-blind. Or it could have said that the authors of the Fourteenth Amendment meant to ban segregated schools. It did neither. Instead it said that segregated education is bad because it "has a detrimental effect upon the colored children" by generating "a feeling of inferiority as to their status in the community" that may "affect their hearts and minds in a way unlikely ever to be undone." This conclusion was supported by a footnote reference to social-science studies of the apparent impact of segregation on black children.

Why did the Court rely on social science as much as or more than the Constitution in supporting its decision? Apparently for two reasons. One was the justices' realization that the authors of the Fourteenth Amendment may *not* have intended to outlaw segregated schools. The schools in Washington, D.C., were segregated when the amendment was proposed, and when this fact was mentioned during the debate, it seems to have been made clear that the amendment was not designed to abolish this segregation. When Congress debated a civil-rights act a few years later, it voted down provisions that would have ended segregation in schools. The Court could not easily base its decision on a constitutional provision that had, at best, an uncertain application to schools. The other reason grew out of the first. On so important a matter the chief justice wanted to speak for a unanimous court. Some justices did not agree that the Fourteenth Amendment made the Constitution colorblind. In the interests of harmony the Court found an ambiguous rationale for its decision.

Desegregation versus Integration That ambiguity led to the third issue. If separate schools were inherently unequal, what would "unseparate" schools look like? Since the Court had not said that race was irrelevant, an "unseparate" school could be either one that blacks and whites were free to attend if they chose or one that blacks and whites in fact attended whether they wanted to or not. The first might be called a desegregated school, the latter an integrated school. Think of the Topeka case. Was it enough that there was now no barrier to Linda Brown's attending the white school in her neighborhood? Or was it necessary that there actually be black children (if not Linda, then some others) going to that school together with white children?

As long as the main impact of the *Brown* decision lay in the South, where laws had prevented blacks from attending white schools, this question did not seem important. Segregation by law (**de jure segregation**) was now clearly unconstitutional. But in the North, laws had not kept blacks and whites apart; instead all-black and all-white schools were the result of residential segregation, preferred living patterns, informal social forces, and administrative practices (such as drawing school-district lines so as to produce single-race schools). This was often called segregation in fact (**de facto segregation**).

In 1968 the Supreme Court settled the matter. In New Kent County, Virginia, the school board had created a "freedom-of-choice" plan under which every pupil would be allowed without legal restriction to attend the school of his or her choice. As it turned out, all the white children chose to remain in the all-white school, and 85 percent of the black children remained in the all-black school. The Court rejected this plan as unconstitutional because it did not produce the "ultimate end," which was a "unitary, nonracial system of education." In the opinion written by Justice William Brennan, the Court seemed to be saying that the Constitution required actual racial mixing in schools, not just the repeal of laws requiring racial separation.

This impression was confirmed three years later when the Court considered a plan in North Carolina under which pupils in Mecklenburg County (which includes Charlotte) were assigned to the nearest neighborhood school without regard to race. As a result about half the black children now attended formerly all-white schools, with the other half attending all-black schools. The federal district court held that this was inadequate and ordered some children to be bused into more distant schools in order to achieve a greater degree of integration. The Supreme Court, now led by Chief Justice Warren Burger, upheld the district judge on the grounds that the court plan was necessary to achieve a "unitary school system."

This case—*Swann v. Charlotte-Mecklenburg Board of Education*—pretty much set the guidelines for all subsequent cases involving school segregation. The essential features of these rules are:

- To violate the Constitution, a school system, by law, practice, or regulation, must have engaged in discrimination. Put another way, a plaintiff must show an intent to discriminate on the part of the public schools.
- The existence of all-white or all-black schools in a district with a history of segregation creates a presumption of intent to discriminate.
- The remedy for past discrimination will not be limited to freedom of choice, or what the Court called "the walk-in school." Remedies may include racial quotas in the assignment of teachers and pupils, redrawn district lines, and court-ordered busing.
- Not every school must reflect the social composition of the school system as a whole.

Relying on *Swann,* district courts have supervised redistricting and busing plans in localities all over the nation, often in the teeth of bitter opposition from the community. In Boston

Chronology of Major Events in the Civil Rights Movement, 1955-1968

Dec. 5, 1955	Blacks in Montgomery, Alabama, begin yearlong boycott of bus company; the Reverend Martin Luther King, Jr., emerges as leader.
Feb. 1, 1960	First sit-in demonstration. Black students at North Carolina Agricultural and Technical College sit in at dime-store lunch couter in Greensboro.
May 4, 1961	Freedom rides begin as blacks attempt to ride in white sections of interstate buses. Violence erupts, a bus is burned, U.S. marshals are dispatched to restore order.
Sept. 30, 1962	Violence greets effort of James Meredith, a black, to enroll in University of Mississippi.
Apr. 3, 1963	Demonstrations by blacks begin in Birmingham, Alabama; police retaliate.
June 12, 1963	Medgar Evers, Mississippi state chairman of NAACP, murdered in Jackson.
Aug. 28, 1963	March on Washington by 250,000 whites and blacks.
Fall 1963	Blacks boycott schools in several northern cities to protest *de facto* segregation.
June 1964	Three civil-rights workers killed in Neshoba County, Mississippi.
Summer 1964	First ghetto riots by blacks in northern cities, beginning in Harlem on July 18.
Jan. 2, 1965	King begins protest marches in Selma, Alabama; police attack marchers in February and March.
Aug. 11, 1965	Black riots in Watts section of Los Angeles and on West Side of Chicago.
June 6, 1966	James Meredith shot (but not killed) while on protest march in Mississippi.
Summer 1966	Black ghetto riots in Chicago, Cleveland, New York, and other cities; King leads protest marches in Chicago.
Summer 1967	Riots or violent demonstrations in 67 cities.
Apr. 4, 1968	Martin Luther King, Jr., murdered in Memphis, Tennessee.

Key Provisions of Major Civil Rights Laws

1957   **Voting** Made it a federal crime to try to prevent a person from voting in a federal election. Created the Civil Rights Commission.

1960   **Voting** Authorized the attorney general to appoint federal referees to gather evidence and make findings about allegations that blacks were being deprived of their right to vote. Made it a federal crime to use interstate commerce to threaten or carry out a bombing.

1964   **Voting** Made it more difficult to use devices such as literacy tests to bar blacks from voting.

Public accommodations Barred discrimination on grounds of race, color, religion, or national origin in restaurants, hotels, lunch counters, gasoline stations, movie theaters, stadiums, arenas, and lodging houses with more than five rooms.

Schools Authorized the attorney general to bring suit to force the desegregation of public schools on behalf of citizens.

Employment Outlawed discrimination in hiring, firing, or paying employees on grounds of race, color, religion, national origin, or sex.

Federal funds Barred discrimination in any activity receiving federal assistance.

1965   **Voter registration** Authorized appointment by the Civil Service Commission of voting examiners who would require registration of all eligible voters in federal, state, and local elections, general or primary, in areas where discrimination was found to be practiced or where less than 50 percent of voting-age residents were registered to vote in 1964 election. The law was to have expired in 1970, but Congress has since extended it; it will expire in 2007.

Literacy tests Suspended use of literacy tests or other devices to prevent blacks from voting.

1968   **Housing** Banned, by stages, discrimination in sale or rental of most housing (excluding private owners who sell or rent their homes without the services of a real-estate broker).

Riots Made it a federal crime to use interstate commerce to organize or incite a riot.

1972   **Education** Prohibited sex discrimination in education programs receiving federal aid.

1988   **Discrimination** If any part of an organization receives federal aid, no part of that organization may discriminate on the basis of race, sex, age, or physical handicap.

1991   **Discrimination** Made it easier to sue over job discrimination and collect damages; overturned certain Supreme Court decisions.

the control of the city schools by a federal judge, W. Arthur Garrity, lasted for more than a decade and involved him in every aspect of school administration.

One major issue not settled by *Swann* was whether busing and other remedies should cut across city and county lines. In some places the central-city schools had become virtually all black. Racial integration could be achieved only by bringing black pupils to white suburban schools or moving white pupils into central-city schools. In a series of split-vote decisions the Court has announced this rule: intercity court-ordered busing will only be authorized when it has been shown that the suburban areas as well as the central city have in fact practiced school segregation. Where that cannot be shown, such inter-city busing will not be required. The Court was not persuaded that intent had been proved in Atlanta, Detroit, Denver, Indianapolis, and Richmond, but it was persuaded in Louisville and Wilmington, and so intercity busing was ordered in the last two cities but not in the first five.

The importance that the Court attaches to intent means that if a school system that was once integrated becomes all-black as a result of whites' moving to the suburbs, the Court will not require that district lines constantly be redrawn or new busing plans adopted to adjust to the changing distribution of population. This in turn means that as long as blacks and whites live in different neighborhoods for whatever reason, there is a good chance that some schools in both areas will be heavily of one race. If mandatory busing or other integration measures cause whites to move out of a city at a faster rate than they otherwise would (a process often called "white flight"), then efforts to integrate the schools may in time create more single-race schools. Ultimately integrated schools will exist only in integrated neighborhoods or where the quality of education is so high that both blacks and whites want to enroll in the school even at some cost in travel and inconvenience.

Mandatory busing to achieve racial integration has been a deeply controversial program and has generated considerable public opposition. Surveys show a majority of people oppose it. As recently as in 1992, 48 percent of whites in the Northeast and 53 percent of southern whites felt that it was "not the business" of the federal government to ensure "that black and white children go to the same schools." Presidents Nixon, Ford, and Reagan opposed busing; all three supported legislation to prevent or reduce it, and Reagan petitioned the courts to reconsider busing plans. The courts refused to reconsider, and Congress has passed only minor restrictions on busing.

The reason why Congress has not followed public opinion on this matter is complex. It has been torn between the desire to support civil rights and uphold the courts and the desire to represent the views of its constituents. Because it faces a dilemma, Congress has taken both sides of the issue simultaneously.

During the 1970s the House of Representatives would pass bills restricting busing, whereupon the Senate would amend them by allowing busing if ordered by a court. The result was no policy at all. In 1981 the Senate approved a bill forbidding federal judges from ordering busing except in very narrow circumstances, but it never became law. Although a House version of these bills was adopted in 1982, it, too, never became law. Throughout the 1980s Congress did enact laws forbidding the use of federal funds to bus schoolchildren

Figure 19.2 Growing Support Among Southern Democrats in Congress for Civil-Rights Bills

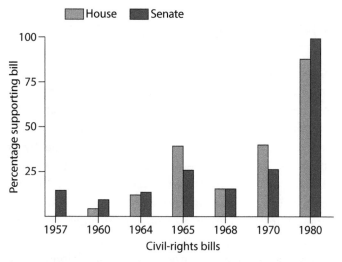

SOURCES: Congressional Quarterly, *Congress and the Nation*, vols. I, II, III, VII.

Table 19.2 Increase in Number of Black Elected Officials

TABLE 19.1   Increase in Number of Black Elected Officials

Office	1970	1991
Congress and state legislatures	182	476
City and county offices	715	4,493
Judges and sheriffs	213	847
Boards of education	362	1,629
Total	1,472	7,445

SOURCES: *Statistical Abstract of the UnitedStates, 1990, 260; Statistical Abstract of the United States, 1992,267.*

for purposes of racial integration; these laws had little effect, however, since a judge could still order states and cities to pay the costs. By the late 1980s busing was a dying issue in Congress, in part because no meaningful legislation seemed possible and in part because popular passion over busing had somewhat abated.

Then, in 1992, the Supreme Court made it easier for local school systems to reclaim control of their schools from the courts. In DeKalb County (a suburb of Atlanta), the schools had been operating under court-ordered desegregation plans for many years. Despite this effort full integration had not been achieved, largely because the neighborhoods increasingly had become either all-black or all-white. The Court held that the local schools could not be held responsible for segregation solely caused by segregated living patterns and so the courts would relinquish their control of the schools.

THE CAMPAIGN IN CONGRESS

The campaign in the courts for desegregated schools, though slow and costly, was a carefully managed effort to alter the interpretation of a constitutional provision. But to get new civil-rights laws out of Congress required a far more difficult and decentralized strategy, one that was aimed at mobilizing public opinion and overcoming the many congressional barriers to action.

The first problem was to get civil rights on the political agenda by convincing people that something had to be done. This could be achieved by dramatizing the problem in ways that shocked the consciences of those whites who were not racists but who were ordinarily indifferent to black problems. Brutal lynchings of blacks provided such shocks, but lynchings were becoming less frequent in the 1950s and obviously black leaders had no desire to provoke more lynchings just to get sympathy for their cause.

Those leaders could, however, arrange for dramatic confrontations between blacks claiming and whites denying some obvious right. Beginning in the late 1950s these confrontations began to occur in the form of sit-ins at segregated lunch counters and "freedom rides" on segregated bus lines. At about the same time, efforts were made to get blacks registered to vote in counties where whites had used intimidation and harassment to prevent it.

The best-known demonstration occurred in 1955-1956 in Montgomery, Alabama, where blacks, led by a young minister named Martin Luther King, Jr., boycotted the local bus system after it had a black woman, Rosa Parks, arrested because she refused to surrender her seat on a bus to a white man.

These early demonstrations were based on the philosophy of **nonviolent civil disobedience**—that is, peacefully violating a law, such as one requiring blacks to ride in a segregated section of a bus, and allowing oneself to be arrested as a result.

But the momentum of protest, once unleashed, could not be centrally directed or confined to nonviolent action. A rising tide of anger, especially among younger blacks, resulted in the formation of more militant organizations and the spontaneous eruption of violent demonstrations and riots in dozens of cities across the country. From 1964 to 1968 there were in the North as well as the South four "long, hot summers" of racial violence.

The demonstrations and rioting succeeded in getting civil rights on the national political agenda, but at a cost: many whites, opposed to the demonstrations or appalled by the riots, dug in their heels and fought against making any concessions to "lawbreakers," "troublemakers," and "rioters." In 1964 and again in 1968 over two-thirds of the whites interviewed in opinion polls said that the civil-rights movement was pushing too fast, had hurt the black cause, and was too violent.

In short there was a conflict between the agenda-setting and coalition-building aspects of the civil-rights movement. This was especially a problem since, in the 1960s, conservative southern legislators still controlled many key congressional committees that had for years been the graveyard of civil-rights legislation. The Senate Judiciary Committee was dominated by a coalition of southern Democrats and conservative Republicans, and the House Rules Committee was under the control of a chairman hostile to civil-rights bills, Howard Smith of Virginia. Any bill that passed the House faced an almost certain filibuster in the Senate. Finally, President John F. Kennedy was reluctant to submit strong civil-rights bills to Congress.

Four developments made it possible to break the deadlock. First, public opinion was changing. Between 1959 and 1965 the proportion of southern whites who said that they were willing to have their children attend a school that was half black more than doubled (though it was still less than a majority), while the proportion of northern whites giving the same answer was high (over 60 percent) throughout that period. About the same change could be found in attitudes toward allowing blacks equal access to hotels and buses. Of course support in principle for these civil-rights measures was not necessarily the same as support in practice; nonetheless there clearly was occurring a major shift in popular approval of at least the principles of civil rights. At the leading edge of this change were young, college-educated people.

Second, certain violent reactions by white segregationists to black demonstrators were vividly portrayed by the media, especially television, in ways that gave to the civil-rights cause a powerful moral force. In May 1963 the head of the Birmingham police, Eugene "Bull" Connor, ordered his men to use attack dogs and high-pressure fire hoses to repulse a peaceful march by blacks demanding desegregated public facilities and increased job opportunities. The pictures of that confrontation (such as the one shown above) created a national sensation and contributed greatly to the massive participation, by whites and blacks alike, in the "March on Washington" that summer. About a quarter of a million people gathered in front of the Lincoln Memorial to hear the Reverend King deliver a stirring and widely hailed address, often called the "I Have a Dream" speech. The following summer in Neshoba County, Mississippi, three young civil-rights workers (two white and one black) were brutally murdered by Klansmen aided by the local sheriff. When the FBI identified the murderers, the effect oil national opinion was galvanic: no white southern leader could any longer offer persuasive opposition to federal laws protecting voting rights when white law-enforcement officers had killed students working to protect those rights. And the next year a white woman, Viola Liuzzo, was shot and killed while driving a car used to transport civil-rights workers. Her death was the subject of a presidential address.

Third, President John F. Kennedy was assassinated in Dallas, Texas, in November 1963. Many people originally (and wrongly) thought that he had been killed by a right-wing conspiracy; even after the assassin was caught and revealed to have left-wing associations, the shock of a president's murder in a southern city helped build support for the efforts by the new president, Lyndon B. Johnson (himself a Texan), to obtain passage of a strong civil-rights bill as a memorial to the slain president.

Fourth, the 1964 elections not only returned Johnson to office with a landslide victory, but also sent a huge Democratic majority to the House and retained the large Democratic margin in the Senate. This made it possible for northern Democrats to outvote or outmaneuver southerners in the House.

The cumulative effect of these forces led to the enactment of five civil-rights laws between 1957 and 1968. Three (1957, 1960, and 1965) were chiefly directed at protecting the right to vote; one (1968) was aimed at preventing discrimination in housing; and one (1964), the most far-reaching of all, dealt with voting, employment, schooling, and public accommodations.

The passage of the 1964 act was the high point of the legislative struggle. Liberals in the House had drafted a bipartisan bill, but it was now in the House Rules Committee, where such matters had often disappeared without a trace. In the shock of Kennedy's murder a discharge petition was filed, with President Johnson's support, to take the bill out of committee and bring it to the floor of the House. But the Rules Committee, without waiting for a vote on the petition (which it probably realized that it would lose), sent the bill to the floor, where it passed overwhelmingly. In the Senate an agreement between Republican Minority Leader Everett Dirksen and President Johnson smoothed the way for passage in several important respects. The House bill was sent directly to the Senate floor, thereby bypassing the southern-dominated Judiciary Committee. Nineteen southern senators began an eight-week filibuster against the bill. On June 10, 1964, by a vote of seventy-one to twenty-nine, cloture was invoked and the filibuster ended—the first time in history that a filibuster aimed at blocking civil-rights legislation had been broken.

Since the 1960s congressional support for civil-rights legislation has grown—so much so, indeed, that labeling a bill a civil-rights measure, once the kiss of death, now almost guarantees its passage. For example, in 1984 the Supreme Court decided that the federal ban on discrimination in education applied only to the "program or activity" receiving federal aid and not to the entire school or university. In 1988 Congress passed a bill to overturn this decision by making it clear that antidiscrimination rules applied to the entire educational institution and not just to that part (say, the physics lab) receiving federal money. When President Reagan vetoed the bill (because, in his view, it would diminish the freedom of church-related schools), Congress overrode the veto. In the override vote *every* southern Democrat in the Senate and almost 90 percent of those in the House voted for the bill. This was a dramatic change from 1964, when over 80 percent of the southern Democrats in Congress voted against the Civil Rights Act (see Figure 19.2).

This change partly reflected the growing political strength of southern blacks. In 1960 less than one-third of voting-age blacks in the South were registered to vote; by 1971 more than half were, and by 1984 two-thirds were. In 1991 over seven thousand blacks held elective office in the South (see Table 19.1). But this was only half of the story. Attitudes among white political elites and members of Congress had also changed. This was evident as early as 1968, when Congress passed a law barring discrimination in housing even though polls showed that only 35 percent of the public supported the measure.

Mexico's Drug War

Violence Too Close to Home

Jonathan Broder

Mexico's illegal drug trade used to be relatively civilized, made up of small-time traffickers who smuggled marijuana and heroin into the United States and the corrupt officials who accepted their bribes to look the other way. Both sides followed certain unwritten rules: The officials forbade the traffickers from selling their wares inside Mexico and from arming themselves too extravagantly. Kidnapping was out of bounds. If a drug trafficker felt compelled to eliminate a rival, Mexican officials encouraged him to do so discreetly—preferably north of the border, where the investigation would be a problem for law enforcement in the United States, not Mexico.

Such conditions seem almost quaint compared with the violence that wracks the country today. Mexico's drug gangs have added South American cocaine and methamphetamine to their exports, and they earn as much as $39 billion a year from sales in the United States. They also peddle plenty of the drugs to Mexicans. To protect their profits, the cartels have taken advantage of openings in U.S. gun-control laws to stock up on military-grade assault rifles, grenade launchers, bazookas and even heavy machine guns, smuggling them back into Mexico for fire-fights with government forces and rival gangs. The cartels also operate helicopters, jet planes and small submarines for use in smuggling.

Since the beginning of 2007, the drug war has claimed the lives of about 7,500 people—almost double the number of U.S. troops killed in Iraq since 2003. The dead include more than 200 American citizens, some of whom were probably involved in the drug business but also others who were innocent bystanders caught in the cross-fire.

Using a combination of bribes and extreme cruelty that includes gruesome tortures and beheadings, the drug cartels have corrupted or intimidated police and magistrates, taking effective control over a growing number of towns and rural areas south of the border. The gangs also have moved north into Arizona and other states, where kidnappings, gun battles and executions among rival cartel members are becoming increasingly common.

Jonathan Broder, "Mexico's Drug War: Violence Too Close to Home," CQ Weekly. Copyright © 2009 by CQ Roll Call, Inc. Reprinted with permission.

With an approving nod from the United States, Mexican President Felipe Calderon has thrown his army into the fight against the cartels, but the well-armed gangs are fighting back. And according to some U.S. officials and experts, the drug barons are winning.

In Washington, where policy debates involving Mexico have been confined mostly to trade and immigration for the past two decades, sudden awareness of the drug war has produced some alarming assessments. Retired Gen. Barry McCaffrey, who was the drug czar in the Clinton White House, warned recently that unless the Mexican government gains control of the drug gangs, the United States could, within a decade, be confronting on its southern border a "narco-state"—meaning an area controlled by drug cartels. The Pentagon envisions an even worse scenario: Mexico and Pakistan, it says, are the countries most at risk of swiftly collapsing into "failed states"—those whose central governments are so weak they have little practical control over most of their territory.

Beset as he is at home by the credit crisis and plunging economy, President Obama's response to the chaos in Mexico has so far been to continue some George W. Bush administration policies while beginning a search for others. He is expected to focus on possible regional approaches when he attends a Summit of the Americas in Trinidad and Tobago next month.

Experts on the region, though, say the magnitude of the drug war in Mexico and its danger to the United States far exceed the reach of existing federal policies, perhaps even the policies the new administration is considering, such as stepped-up military aid and regional cooperation.

Uncontrolled drug violence in Mexico, these experts say, might result in tens of thousands of refugees surging across the border, adding to the estimated 12 million immigrants already in the country illegally. U.S. drug officials say that a narco-state in Mexico could turn the ungoverned territory along the border into a permanent springboard for Mexican drug traffickers smuggling their goods north into California, Arizona, New Mexico, and Texas. And economic analysts say that should the Mexican government completely collapse, it would jeopardize oil exports from Mexico, from which the United States receives a third of its supply.

"Any descent by Mexico into chaos," the Pentagon's Joint Forces Command wrote in November, "would demand an American response based on the serious implications for homeland security alone."

SCRAMBLE FOR SOLUTIONS

A more likely result than such a complete descent into chaos, some authorities on the region say, is that Mexico becomes an "informal" narco-state, where the current democratic government continues but the drug cartels wield great influence behind the scenes. Such a development would not increase the flow of illegal immigrants into the United States, they say.

Whatever the assessment, the climate of violence in Mexico has spooked many former U.S. officials, as well as current members of the administration and Congress. Some have proposed their own dramatic solutions, topped off by the suggestion of Duncan Hunter, a staunchly conservative Republican who gave up his Southern California House seat last year after a brief run for president, to build a wall along the entire 2,000-mile border with Mexico.

The administration has not spelled out any major new policies on Mexico; the White House Web site, chock full of policy prescriptions for dozens of issues, says not a word about illegal drugs and little about Mexico.

In the short term at least, the new president has decided to keep alive his predecessor's program that provides Mexico with training, equipment and intelligence aid to fight the drug gangs. The economic stimulus package Obama pushed to enactment this winter includes funds to help bolster border security and curb the flow of guns from the United States into Mexico. And he has ordered his top homeland security advisers to work side-by-side with the National Security Council to address not only terrorism, but also other security threats such as organized crime and narco-trafficking.

Meanwhile, in advance of the annual pilgrimage of thousands of American college students to spend their spring vacations at the beaches and bars of Cancun, Mazatlan and Puerto Vallarta, the State Department has issued a travel alert warning of the increased Mexican drug violence and kidnapping. The alert, guaranteed to terrify parents if not students, said U.S. travelers have been trapped in firefights between government forces and drug gangs that have resembled "small unit combat."

Administration officials, including Attorney General Eric H. Holder Jr., sound confident that the gangs can be defeated and the violence quelled, even if they have no bold new plans to make that happen. After a major federal drug bust late last month involving suspected Mexican traffickers, Holder declared, "We can provide our communities the safety and the security that they deserve only by confronting these dangerous cartels head-on, without reservation. We can do that, and we will do that."

"These cartels," he said, "will be destroyed."

The situation in Mexico will be high on the agenda at next month's meeting in Trinidad, where Obama is expected to seek a multilateral approach aimed at cutting drug supplies in South and Central America while trying to reduce demand for drugs in the United States— just the sort of progress that has eluded the government since the "war on drugs" got under way in the Nixon administration nearly four decades ago.

Some Latin American leaders, including former presidents of several countries, have called for a different approach—decriminalizing marijuana, the most popular recreational drug of their citizens and also the region's biggest illicit export to the United States. In the past, Obama has said that American law enforcement agencies should stop prosecuting marijuana users because it would save precious resources to combat more-serious crimes; he does not favor legalizing the drug, however.

Experts on Latin America say that unless Obama commits more money and aid to the fight in Mexico, the drug cartels could turn the Southwest frontier into a lawless borderland. "U.S. complacency about the troubles in Mexico is very dangerous," warned Moises Nairn, a former Venezuelan minister of trade and industry and now the editor of Foreign Policy magazine.

"You don't want a narco-state to become your neighbor. It's an illusion that you can have a border that can protect you."

A WEAK NEIGHBOR

When Calderon first deployed 6,500 Mexican troops to take on the drug cartels in December 2006, the traffickers were operating primarily in the seven northern Mexican states. Today, the cartels' reach has spread to 18 of Mexico's 32 states, and Calderon is deploying 45,000 troops—a quarter of his entire army—to confront them.

It is a war marked by spectacular violence. Drug gangs sometimes behead government officials and members of rival gangs, then post videos of the executions on the Internet. Hundreds of people have simply disappeared. The fate of some of the missing became clear in January, when Mexican authorities arrested a man who admitted disposing of 300 kidnap victims for the drug gangs by liquefying their bodies in large vats of industrial solvents. The arrested man, Santiago Meza Lopez, was known as *El Pozolero*—the Stew Maker.

Mexican drug violence has touched at least one U.S. lawmaker personally. Last June, a relative by marriage of Texas Democrat Silvestre Reyes, the chairman of the House Select Intelligence Committee, was seized by gunmen in Ciudad Juarez, the violent and corrupt Mexican city across the border from El Paso. After being notified by Reyes' staff, U.S. Immigration and Customs Enforcement (ICE) agents helped arrange the relative's return after her family paid a $32,000 ransom. (There was no suggestion the kidnapping was related to Reyes' position in Congress.)

Such reports have been increasingly common in Mexico for more than a year now. But in Washington, where Bush administration officials were focused primarily on the Middle East, few mentioned Mexico's troubles until after Obama won the presidency in November. Only then did military and intelligence officials for the first time describe the events as a national security threat.

In its report that month on likely challenges facing U.S. forces in the future, the Pentagon's Joint Forces Command explained why it had included Mexico as a country that faced the risk of sudden collapse.

"The Mexican possibility may seem less likely, but the government, its politicians, police and judicial infrastructure are all under sustained assault and pressure by criminal gangs and drug cartels," the report said. "How that internal conflict turns out over the next several years will have a major impact on the stability of the Mexican state."

Just before he departed in January as director of the CIA, Michael V. Hayden listed the threat the drug gangs pose to Mexico's stability as one of top challenges facing Obama. He urged the president to strengthen ties with Mexican intelligence to deal with the situation there. "As bad as it is—and it is bad," Hayden said, "there's an opportunity here."

Even Obama's director of national intelligence, Dennis C. Blair, has chimed in, telling Congress last month that the Mexican government already has lost control over some parts of its country. "The corruptive influence and increasing violence of Mexican drug cartels," Blair told the Senate Select Intelligence Committee on Feb. 12, "impedes Mexico City's ability to govern parts of its country."

Latin America specialists who have been following events in Mexico say it's about time U.S. officials paid more attention to their southern neighbor.

"The United States has ignored Mexico and its needs and realities," said Nairn. "More people have been beheaded in Mexico this year than in Iraq. The battles being fought in Mexico may be more important for the average U.S. citizen than those being fought in Baqubah," the scene of heavy Iraqi insurgent activity.

Mexican officials bristle at the dire forecasts for their country. "The suggestion that Mexico is remotely close to a failed state or is heading in that direction is analytically flawed and therefore simply wrong," Arturo Sarukhan, Mexico's ambassador to the United States, said in a statement. "Mexico is today a country with solid institutions, a consolidating and pluralistic democracy, a vibrant civil society, and, despite the global recession, strong economic fundamentals."

In a separate interview, Sarukhan argued that the heavy toll from the armed confrontations in Mexico is, if anything, a sign of his government's strength and determination to confront the cartels, which, he adds, have grown increasingly desperate under the army's assault. "The violence," Sarukhan said, "is an indication that they're feeling the pressure and against the ropes."

Many U.S. experts on Mexico also reject what George W. Grayson, a Mexico scholar at the College of William & Mary, called the "overstated" tone of the recent warnings about Mexico.

"The army is still loyal to the regime," said Grayson. "Most workers get up and go to their jobs every day, and the major production facilities around the country continue to turn out goods and services."

Allyson Benton, a Mexico City-based analyst for the Eurasia Group, an international risk analysis firm, said flatly, "Mexico is not a failed state and will not become one."

But, these regional analysts add, Mexico suffers from serious institutional weaknesses, including a police force and judiciary that have been thoroughly corrupted by the bribes the drug cartels are offering. The scope of the corruption was driven home last November, when Noe Ramirez Mandujano, Mexico's top anti-drug official, was arrested for allegedly pocketing $450,000 a month from drug traffickers.

"By any measure, the cartels are winning," despite the Mexican army's offensive, Grayson said. "They're active in more states now. They're involved in a broader array of criminal activities. They're certainly getting incredible publicity for their brutal executions, and they're making lots of money."

Despite such violence and corruption, though, Grayson and other Latin America experts do not believe Mexico's government will completely collapse.

"What we're seeing are not the symptoms of a failed state," Nairn said. But, he added, "I do believe that Mexico is a country at risk. The government may lose control of certain enclaves."

Ted Galen Carpenter, vice president for defense and foreign policy studies at the libertarian Cato Institute, says the growing influence of the cartels, which now provide the money to fund the campaigns of some Mexican politicians, makes it more likely the country will become "an informal narco-state model in which the cartels become the power behind the throne."

MORE U.S. ASSISTANCE NEEDED

For McCaffrey, the former drug czar, that kind of scenario is bad enough. He has called on Obama to waste no time in developing a plan, with the money to pay for it—a "resourced strategy"—that is "appropriate for the dangers we face."

Right now, Obama's strategy consists of continuing the Bush administration program dubbed the Merida Initiative—a three-year, $1.4 billion effort to fund training and equipment for Mexican law enforcement to fight drug trafficking and organized crime. The program, named for the Yucatan capital where Bush and Calderon met in March 2007, also includes greater cooperation between U.S. and Mexican intelligence services. In December, just before leaving office, Bush implemented the plan, making the first $197 million available to Mexico.

The $787 billion stimulus bill that Obama signed included roughly $600 million for border security, including $40 million to help local law enforcement officials "combat criminal narcotic activity" along the border.

"The recent escalation of violence along the southern border demands our immediate attention," said Senate Homeland Security Chairman Joseph I. Lieberman, a political independent from Connecticut. "To deal with the spillover of violence into U.S. territory, we must assess border security programs and plans in place, and we must review the readiness of federal, state and local law enforcement."

Homeland Security Secretary Janet Napolitano has vowed to work closely with the Mexican government against the drug gangs through intelligence sharing. She also has said she is reviewing a plan by the Bush administration to rush U.S. troops to the border if there is a surge of refugees trying to escape the drug violence.

"We don't want to militarize the border," Napolitano said last month in her first appearance before the House Homeland Security Committee. But she acknowledged the need for what she called a "contingency plan to deal with worst-case scenarios."

McCaffrey says he wants to see funding for the Merida program increased significantly and its implementation speeded up.

"The proposed U.S. government spending in support of the government of Mexico is a drop in the bucket compared to what we have spent in Iraq and Afghanistan," he noted in a December study of Mexico's drug war. "The stakes in Mexico are enormous. We cannot afford to have a narco-state as a neighbor."

McCaffrey also wants to see Obama step up cooperation with Mexico on cross-border law enforcement. Mexican officials have tried to organize the 10 U.S. and Mexican border states for this effort, but McCaffrey says cooperation remains "inadequate," largely because U.S. officials suspect some of their Mexican counterparts are secretly working for the cartels.

Meanwhile, lawmakers from border states have long maintained that the solution to keeping Mexican drugs and drug violence from crossing the Rio Grande is a huge increase in border security. At last month's House Homeland Security panel hearing, Republican Michael McCaul of Texas, who was previously a federal prosecutor with a specialty in national security and counterterrorism, urged Napolitano to "consider, along with the Merida Initiative, also funding on our side of the border for increased Border Patrol, ICE" agents and more local police.

Noting that Texas Gov. Rick Perry had asked for 1,000 federal troops to beef up security along the border, McCaul characterized the situation in Mexico as "a state of war."

Administration officials say the Department of Homeland Security will move ahead with a Bush administration plan to build 670 miles of fencing and barriers at critical crossing points along the U.S.-Mexican border, and that the administration also wants to implement Bush's plan for an electronic fence along the entire 2,000 miles of the border. The $1 billion project, which combines sensors, radar, thermal imaging equipment, unmanned aircraft and software to provide border officials with a picture of border entries in real time, has been plagued by delays and logistical problems.

The majority of congressional Democrats, as well as Republicans from states along the border, prefer deploying surveillance technology over building physical fences, which, they say, separate people and breed resentment on both sides of the border.

GROWING CALLS FOR LEGALIZATION

Administration officials say that, at the April summit in Trinidad, Obama will be eager to listen to new policy ideas about regional security.

Some of the ideas, however, promise to be controversial. In advance of the summit, a group of respected Latin American leaders, including the former presidents of Mexico, Colombia and Brazil, urged current leaders to consider decriminalizing the personal use of marijuana. In a Feb. 11 statement, the group said decades of government attempts to halt the production and trafficking of illegal drugs have failed. Implicit in the statement was that the United States should consider decriminalization as well, in the belief that it would obviate the need for much of the criminal behavior.

"We are further than ever from the announced goal of eradicating drugs the statement said. Meanwhile, "most of the damage associated with cannabis use—from the indiscriminate arrest and incarceration of consumers to the violence and corruption that affect all of society—is the result of the current prohibitionist policies."

The statement is the latest in a trend among regional leaders to openly challenge Washington's four-decade war on drugs. In October, Honduran President Manuel Zelaya called for the legalization of drugs as a way to stop drug-trafficking violence. In Argentina, the government of President Cristina Fernandez de Kirchner is promoting the decriminalization of drug use. Even Mexico's Calderon has suggested the legalization of small amounts of marijuana and cocaine.

According to Juan Carlos Hidalgo, a Latin America specialist at the Cato Institute, several factors are behind the Latin American calls for a different approach to the drug war. Left-leaning governments that already have strained relations with the United States are less concerned about ruffling its feathers. In other countries, free-trade agreements with the United States have made them feel less vulnerable to losing their wide-open economic relationship as punishment for speaking out.

But most important, Hidalgo says, Latin American governments are feeling increasingly overwhelmed by the problems of drug-related violence and corruption. "Many now regard the U.S. war on drugs as a threat to their own stability," he said.

The view Obama expressed in the campaign—decriminalize marijuana use but don't legalize it—would mean federal and state agents would tolerate personal marijuana use but still go after dealers and traffickers.

There is virtually no chance Congress will relax federal anti-drug laws drugs anytime soon. Current and former U.S. drug officials recoil at the suggestion, pointing out that the United States tried that already.

Michael Braun, a former chief of operations at the Drug Enforcement Administration, notes that the worst period of addiction in American history was the 19th century, when opiates and cocaine were generally legal, socially accepted and widely used. Indeed, the popular Sears & Roebuck catalogues of the 1890s offered a syringe and a small amount of cocaine for $1.50. Three years after the enactment of a law to regulate these drugs in 1915, Congress determined that roughly 1 percent of Americans were drug users. Today, 8 percent of Americans—about 20 million—use drugs according to government figures.

Braun acknowledges that despite law enforcement and treatment strategies that have reduced drug use in the United States, the problem is never going to disappear. After all, he notes ruefully, the United States remains the world's largest market for illegal drugs.

And unless Calderon—with help from Obama—wins the drug war in his country, the Mexican cartels will continue to supply that market, bribing or killing those who dare to stand in their way. McCaffrey warns that time is not on the side of Obama or Calderon. Since he took office in 2006, Calderon's public support has dwindled as ordinary Mexicans lose faith in the country's corrupt judicial system. Citing another symptom of Mexico's despair, McCaffrey also noted "increasing discussion of legalization of drugs or acquiescence in the drug trade, which used to be presumed to be a U.S., not Mexican problem."

It is far too early to say how Calderon's crusade against the drug traffickers will end. But Nairn, who is also the author of "Illicit," a 2005 book about the challenges posed by the gangs that smuggle drugs and other contraband across the globe, provides some sobering context as Washington policy makers watch the direction of Mexico's drug war.

"As I was researching the book, I did not find one country—including the United States—where the government could claim that it was winning against these guys," Nairn said. "So if the most powerful country in the world, with all its money, technology and good government, cannot do it, why should we expect Mexico to succeed?"

Karoun Demirjian contributed to this story.

Back at the Henry Horner Homes

Alex Kotlowitz

CHICAGO—When a friend of mine takes the elevated train home to Oak Park, a western suburb here, she makes a point of sitting away from the window. She worries she might get hit by gunfire while passing the Henry Horner Homes project

Pharoah Walton, age 9, lives in Henry Horner. For him the shooting is so frequent and intrusive that he's learned over the years to look both ways before running when he hears gunfire.

Our inner-city neighborhoods, particularly public housing projects have become islands of violence, isolated both geographically and In spirit from the rest of us. Delivery trucks and taxis dare not venture into these embattled neighborhoods, which are cordoned off by boulevards and highways rather than by walls or rivers. Many residents don't have telephones; there aren't even any supermarkets within walking distance. There is, say residents, a feeling of terrible aloneness.

Most disturbing, however, is how little we know or care about what happens on the inner-city reefs. Most of us are like my friend, for whom the neighborhood is a blur and the violence a momentary but passing threat.

Local newspapers and television news programs rarely report on stabbings and shootings at Henry Horner. Even the police, who must deal with it daily, don't record it all. Joseph Gardner, a former executive at the Chicago Housing Authority, the landlord for the city's approximately 40,000 public housing units, concedes that "after 4:30 the gang run these developments."

Indeed, they do. I regularly visited Henry Horner Homes over a period of three months to report an Oct. 27 page one story of a 12-year-old's almost daily confrontation with violence. I have remained friends with Lafeyette Walton and his family and just a few weeks ago met a 17-year-old friend of theirs. Later that night he was gunned down and killed.

Adam Kotlowitz, "Back at the Henry Horner Homes," Wall Street Journal. Copyright © 1987 by Dow Jones & Company, Inc. Reprinted with permission.

It's hard to avoid trouble at the project. This summer 14-year-old Lolita Strong miraculously survived an errant bullet that lodged in her skull. One mother won't let her three young children play on the playground's rusted Jungle Gym. Instead, she moves all her furniture to the side and the living room becomes their "outside."

The police are overwhelmed by the problem and, perhaps, a bit fearful themselves. One foot patrolman told me he won't go above the first floor in Henry Horner's high-rises without a partner. After a big gun battle early in the summer in which young gang members shot at each other from building to building like battleships at sea. I called the police department's central headquarters to ask what was on record about the shoot-out. I was told that if such combat took place, the newspapers would have written about it and the city's top police officials would have discussed it at their morning briefing. Thus it must not have happened.

But it did. I arrived at Henry Horner within half an hour of the shooting and, over the next few weeks, talked with residents (both children and parents), community workers and policemen—all of whom recounted the battle.

The city's response to the growing violence has been muted at best. Henry Horner residents say the only contact they have with local politicians is around election time—and even then it's nominal. Chicago narrowly averted losing control of the Housing Authority to the federal government in a power struggle that all but neglected the needs of the CHA's tenants. But Sen. Bill Bradley (D., N.J.) on a recent trip to Chicago visited five mothers from henry Horner to discuss what might be done about the violence. The women asked for tighter security, better screening of tenants and a police phone number they could call with anonymous tips.

The CHA's Mr. Gardner requested a meeting with me last month at which, in a kind of cathartic exercise, he reeled off the agency's frustration in trying to diminish the violence in the projects. In August, the agency replaced its security guards with off-duty police officers, he said, but funds for the program ran out in October. "CHA as a landlord can't solve this problem by itself," he sighed. As for Mr. Gardner, at the end of our meeting he said that he was leaving the agency the following week to run for a seat on the commission that oversees the city's sewage disposal.

Some compare Henry Horner and other such communities with war zones like Beirut and Norther Ireland. And there are similarities. In Belfast, for example, the IRA "kneecaps" people who have disobeyed its laws. In the projects, people are shot for disobeying the gangs' rules.

But there is one major difference: In Beirut and Northern Ireland, adults—and children—can direct their anger and bitterness toward political targets, with some long-shot aim of change. In Henry Horner no such opponent or dream exists.

When the apartment next to the Waltons was firebombed this fall, there was no public outrcy. No political leader came forth to say that this must stop. The news media didn't run major stories on the terrorist attack. The police didn't come out in full force. Even the local residents took it in stride. In the jargon of Henry Horner, just another apartment was "cocktailed."

Henry Horner is not an anomaly. In a memo to his staff, John Calhoun, executive director of the National Crime Prevention Council, wrote of a recent visit to Detroit, a city whose neighborhoods have become virtual battlefields: "When I worked on the streets with kids in the '60s, there was also the grinding poverty visible in Detroit, perhaps more, but there was a difference. People were on the sidewalk and in the streets; the church was still a powerful voice; whatever shred of family existed spoke with authority. There was hope. Facing the Detroit [of today], I was frightened—not for my safety, but for the future of these children. ... The kids are colossally, terribly alone."

Says a mother at Henry Horner Homes: "Bringing up a child where I do, you can lose them." Indeed, we've already lost entire communities.

Within days after my story on Lafeyette Walton came out, the family heard that the gangs were angry about the article. So Lafeyette's mother, LaJoe, panicked and took Lafeyette, Pharoah and her four-year-old triplets to her sister's house in a nearby neighborhood.

"Then I had time enough to think," she recalls. "What am I running for if I ain't done nothing? I was afraid when I left, I was just mostly hurting when I came back." The gangs, thank God, have not harmed the Waltons. But Mrs. Walton says she stays up nights worrying about her children. So might we all.

Bronx Child's Fatal Fall Retraces Sad Pattern

Samuel G. Freedman

From a rear courtyard where rats roam, to a roof strewn with hypodermic needles, 1015 Boynton Avenue in the Bronx is a horror. Some of its problems can only be experienced. Some can be quantified in statistics assembled by the city: 605 housing code violations; $95,000 overdue in taxes, $25,000, in arrears to the city for emergency repairs.

But the six-story brick building, listed as being owned by Nat Raso of White Plains, would probably have remained one more anonymous eyesore in the Clason Point neighborhood had not a 5-year-old resident, Santo Morello, fallen five stories to his death Monday.

Next to his body, his neighbors found the window bar that was supposed to have prevented just such a tragedy. His mother later told friends she had never received the nuts and bolts to anchor the bars in place, even after asking the landlord.

COMMON ELEMENTS

What happened at 1015 Boynton Avenue, and what led up to it, provides a case history that authorities say is typical of such incidents. There have been more than 60 falls this year, six in the last week of hot, muggy weather. In the most recent accident, a mentally handicapped 8-year-old girl, Jennifer Rios, injured her head and right eye Tuesday when she fell from an unguarded window of her family's first-floor apartment at 37 First Avenue in Manhattan.

Most of the falls from windows involve both a neglectful landlord and an impoverished, single-parent family, according to Charlotte Spiegel, the director of the Window Falls Prevention Program of the City Health Department. The Boynton Avenue incident had both elements.

The death of Santo Morello illustrates the failure of the city's 10-year-old law requiring landlords to install window bars in every apartment where a child younger than 10 lives—provided the tenant requests them by certified letter.

Samuel Freedman, "New York Child's Fatal Fall Retraces Pattern," The New York Times. Copyright © 1986 by The New York Times. Reprinted with permission provided by PARS International Corp.

It also raises questions about whether a more stringent window-bar law, enacted two weeks ago and to be enforced beginning in mid-September, can be effective; for all the statute's tough language, no inspectors are assigned solely to its compliance.

Mr. Raso—who is registered with the City Department of Housing Preservation and Development as the owner of 1015 Boynton Avenue—could not be reached for comment Wednesday. He did not return several messages left on the answering machine of his White Plains office. Nor could a reporter find him at 745 East 178th Street in the Tremont section of the Bronx, an apartment building he owns and has sometimes listed as his business address.

Amid Mr. Raso's silence, his tenants gave their version of the demise of 1015 Boynton. Until the early 1980's, they said, the building had been a functional, if Spartan, structure in a poor, largely Hispanic neighborhood Just north of the Bruckner Expressway.

BROKEN ELEVATOR, EXPOSED WIRES

But shortly after Mr. Raso's company, the J.A.M. Development Corporation, bought the building on Jan. 12, 1983, the pace of repairs fell behind the frequency of problems, the tenants said. The building today does not bear the usual marks of abuse by tenants—urine-soaked hallways, filthy apartments—but betrays longtime neglect in its broken elevator, exposed wires, unpainted walls and missing fixtures.

The local police say that with 1015 Boynton's front-door lock broken, narcotics dealers use the lobby as a marketplace for heroin and cocaine. Many addicts, in turn, climb onto the roof to use the drugs, as is evident from the spent needles, burnt matches and empty cocaine vials lying on the tar.

"The landlord doesn't fix anything," Gladys Bajandas, a resident for 20 years said in Spanish through an interpreter. "He just comes to take the rent."

In Miss Bajandas's $196-a-month apartment, a 3-by-4-foot chunk of plaster has fallen from the bathroom ceiling. An L-shaped piece several feet long is missing from the bedroom wall. There is a hole several inches in diameter in the wall of her son Antonio's bedroom.

'RATS AS BIG AS FOOTBALLS'

"This building's a shambles," said Richard Acosta, a 23-year-old who is unemployed and who has lived in 1015 Boynton since 1979. "The elevator's always messed up. Some people got windows, some don't. The lights in the hallway don't work. You look around the back, we got rats as big as footballs."

The general neglect includes the matter of window bars, the tenants said.

"Just about everyone in the building has little kids and you can count on one hand the ones with bars," said Maggie Nazario, a 23-year-old assistant in a medical clinic who has a 2-year-old son.

In that respect, the Morellos were luckier than most of the 70 families in 1015 Boynton. Their apartment at least had window bars, albeit without the bolts and butterfly nuts to secure them. The superintendent, David Sirra, said Mr. Raso had never supplied him with the hardware and drill needed to install the bars.

MAKESHIFT SOLUTION

The Morellos, like the other residents in the building with bars, could only expand the bars to fit in their metal window frames. In such a position, only an overlap of about a quarter of an inch of metal on each side holds the bars in place. They can be dislodged either by pressure—such as a child leaning against them—or by sliding the edges of the bars back toward the middle.

For many residents, Santo's death confirmed the fears they harbored for their own children. "I was by my window cleaning when Santo was falling," said Maria Santiago, who lives with children aged 8, 4 and 1 in a fourth-floor apartment. "He was screaming, 'Mommy!' I just started crying. I haven't been able to sleep yet."

New York City housing inspectors have cited the owners of 1015 Boynton for 605 code violations in the building, some dating as far back as 1978, but "the bulk" since Mr. Raso bought the building, according to Roz Post, director of public information for the City Department of Housing Preservation and Development.

SUPERINTENDENT ASKS FOR HELP

Seventy-two of the violations were for such "immediately hazardous" conditions as rodents and 331 more for "hazards" including broken glass. Mr. Raso also owes the city $95,000 in principal and interest on taxes that date to 1982, according to Finance Department records. Housing officials said he also remained $25,870 in arrears in repaying the city for making emergency repairs on the building.

Mr. Sirra said he was unable to correct all the problems in 1015 Boynton by himself, and most tenants tended to agree.

"I know what has to be done," said Mr. Sirra, who lives in the building. "But I don't have the materials or the people to do it with. A few months ago, Raso told me he'd get someone to help me. For a couple of days, I did have a couple of men. Since then, I haven't seen anybody."

Faced with such an impasse, one tenant and the city have turned to the courts. Carmen Sanchez, a resident of 1015 Boynton, is now suing Mr. Raso in Civil Court in the Bronx, seeking various repairs to her apartment. And on July 25—three days before Santo died—the city filed legal briefs in State Supreme Court seeking to seize 1015 Boynton from Mr. Raso. The case is pending.

But when it comes to enforcement of the window-bar law, futility has frequently been the rule throughout the city, officials acknowledge.

The old law required a landlord to install the bars only if a tenant requested them in a certified letter. Many landlords simply claimed they had never received such a letter, Ms. Spiegel, of the window-fall program, said.

"It wasn't a conscionable defense," she said. "But it was a defense."

In addition, city authorities often could not locate the offending owner, said Nicholas Titakis, the director of the Administrative Tribunal of the Health Department. The tribunal hears cases of health code violations.

As a result, the Health Department brought charges against 757 landlords in 1985, and had to dismiss the cases against 113 of them. The dismissal rate of about 15 percent contrasts with a figure of 2.5 percent in all other cases heard by the tribunal, Mr. Titakis said.

FAMILY AS A FACTOR

Yet the physical condition of 1015 Boynton reflects only part of the pathology common to falls from windows. The other component to most cases is the victim's family.

"The profile of these families is a troubled one," Ms. Spiegel said. "Single parents, subsisting on welfare, children with illnesses. It's the same kind of household in which you see lead-poisoning cases."

That was the situation at 1015 Boynton. Santo's mother, Zorado, is an unmarried 20-year-old who had two children younger than 5. Santo fell out of the window, friends of the family said, while his mother was at the stove cooking him cereal, her back turned.

The friends said Miss Morello was still in shock yesterday and could not speak to a reporter. "She just keeps saying, 'My son, my son, my son,'" said Mercedes Semiday, a friend of Miss Morello's.

The outlines of Miss Morello's life fit at least a half-dozen other residents of 1015 Boynton. A visitor who enters a few apartments is likely to find an infant being diapered, one or two small children playing and an indoor laundry line strung with tiny clothes.

Some of the women work at jobs in garment factories, others live on welfare. Many said they had had children by several different men. The only woman who said she had a husband asked a reporter not to give her name, lest she lose her welfare payments.

"Some of the mothers just leave their kids upstairs and go to hang out downstairs all day," said Beverly Santiago, a 21-year-old business school student with a 2-year-old son.

Gazing at the windows of 1015 Boynton, one sees curtains, plants, a few window bars—and hardly any air-conditioners. Nor do the apartments have cross-ventilation. This, too, helps explain why falls from windows tend to be a plague on the poor, city officials say.

"It gets tremendously hot inside," said Mary Acosta, who works in a linen factory. "Any child that's looking for a little bit of air is going to look for an open window."

That leaves the question of how much difference, if any, the new window-bar law will make. Under the statute, it is up to the landlord to find out which tenants are eligible for the window bars and then to install them. The law carries a penalty of up to six months in jail and a $500 fine.

Ms. Spiegel maintained that compliance with the law would be good. "From the volume of calls we're getting about it," she said, "it looks like' the landlords are going to carry the ball and run. There's a feeling the time for delay is over."

But no Health Department inspector, she added, will be responsible solely for monitoring compliance with the law. Rather, the department will depend on reports from several hundred inspectors already responsible for investigating lead poisoning and pest control. Department officials, Ms. Spiegel said, will also ask clients at the city's 20 child health stations if they have the window bars.

Mayor Koch defended that system. "You have to live within your budget and try to maximize your resources," he said at City Hall yesterday.

Discussion Questions

1. Did *Brown v. Board* result in widespread desegregation in the South? If not, why not?

2. Why has the "war on drugs" largely failed both here and abroad?

3. Why did the landlords in New York fail to comply with the basic safety rules for the benefit of their tenants?

4. Can the law, even when vigorously enforced, overcome a resistant subculture? If not, what are the implications for judicial power?

Summary of Key Differences Between the Constrained Court View ("CCV") Versus Dynamic Court View ("DCV")

Points of Tension	CCV	DCV
Core Metaphor for American Politics	Principal agent (where the elected branches are the principals and courts are agents)	Independent political forums (where all the branches are engaged in a tug-of-war)
Doctrinal Constraints	Strong	Weak
Key External Institutional Features	<ul><li>Appointment power</li><li>Legislative checks<ul><li>- Overrides/Threat of overrides</li><li>- Power over Jurisdiction</li><li>- Power over budget</li></ul></li></ul>	<ul><li>Limited removal power</li><li>Life tenure/Guaranteed salary</li><li>Sluggish lawmaking process</li><li>Vague laws</li><li>Uniformed principals</li></ul>
Key Internal Institutional Features	<ul><li>Passivity</li><li>Fragmentation</li><li>Lack of the power of the sword and purse</li></ul>	<ul><li>Broad standing rules</li><li>Politically appointed judges</li><li>Extensive injunctive powers</li></ul>
Cultural Constraints	Strong (Court must persuade within dominant cultural norms)	Weak (Court can draw on pliable American Creed to set agendas and frame debates)
Conception of Politics	<ul><li>Distributive (politics is a zero sum game about who gets what, when, where)</li></ul>	<ul><li>Constitutive (politics as an ongoing dialogue among groups about the framing of problems and possible situations)</li></ul>

Do you agree with this characterization of these views? If not, why not?

1. In what ways do the constrained and dynamic court views conflict?
2. In what ways do they talk past one another?
3. Which of these views do you think is more accurate? How would you test these competing views?

PART II
The American Legal System

Having explored the general role of law and courts in society, the second part of the readings takes a closer look at the American legal system with an eye towards assessing the Dynamic and Constrained Court debate. It is worth stressing that the Dynamic versus Constrained Court debate is **NOT** a debate about whether the American legal system is "good" or "bad"; it concerns the degree to which American courts determine U.S. policy. For example, you may prefer courts to be "constrained," and play a secondary role in the policy-making process but believe that, in practice, American courts are "dynamic" and improperly impinge on the elected branches' policy-making prerogatives. Conversely, you may wish the courts were more active in the process but believe that they have a limited role in making policy.

DO NOT CONFUSE NORMATIVE JUDGMENTS ABOUT WHAT COURTS SHOULD DO WITH EXPLANATORY ANALYSIS OF WHAT COURTS TEND TO DO IN PRACTICE. In Part IV of the reader, we'll consider whether the American legal system serves democratic values. In this section, however, the focus is on what the courts do.

A. The American Legal System

An Overview

We begin with a general overview of the federal and state legal court systems in the United States. In reviewing this material, consider how American courts (especially federal courts) are organized.

ADDITIONAL RECOMMENDED MATERIALS:

A Civil Action (movie starring John Travolta about a famous tort case)

Robert A. Carp, Ronald Stidham, and Kenneth Manning, *Judicial Process in America* (2007 Seventh Edition)

Howard Gillman, *The Votes that Counted* (2001)

Anthony Lewis, *Gideon's Trumpet* (1964)

Judicial Politics in the United States

Mark C. Miller

STRUCTURE OF COURTS IN THE UNITED STATES

This chapter will examine the structure of the third branch of government at both the federal and state levels in the United States. The federal court and state court systems have overlapping jurisdictions and share the same geographical space, though of course the state courts are really fifty-one separate court systems defined by individual state constitutions and state statutes (the District of Columbia courts function like a slate court system for these purposes, even though the District is not a state with all of the concomitant rights and privileges). We begin with a discussion of the general differences between trial courts and appellate courts. Then we will turn to a discussion of some of the differences between the structure of the federal courts and the state courts. The chapter will conclude with a discussion of the limits of federal jurisdiction because the state courts can, and do, hear many more cases than the federal courts.

Before we dive into the differences between trial courts and appellate courts, we should start with a discussion of the concept of jurisdiction. In this context, **jurisdiction** means the power or authority of a court to hear a certain type of case. Jurisdiction can be vertical, meaning that a lower court must decide a case before a higher court can review that decision. Jurisdiction can also be horizontal, meaning that some courts can only hear cases regarding certain subject matters. These are often referred to as **limited jurisdiction courts**. For example, in some states, housing courts can only hear cases regarding landlord-tenant issues. Juvenile courts in most states can only hear cases regarding delinquency, neglect and abuse of children, or child custody issues. At the federal level, the U.S. Court of Federal Claims will only hear monetary claims against the federal government, the U.S. Tax Court only hears certain federal tax cases, and the Foreign Intelligence Surveillance Court will only grant warrants for intelligence surveillance. **General jurisdiction courts** can hear a wide variety of criminal, civil, and administrative law cases. All of the regular federal courts and many state courts are courts of general jurisdiction.

Mark C. Miller, "Structure of Courts in the United States," Judicial Politics in the United States, pp. 29-54. Copyright © 2015 by Perseus Books Group. Reprinted with permission.

Jurisdiction can also be geographical, meaning that courts can only hear cases within a certain geographical boundary. For example, the Municipal Court of Boston can only hear certain types of disputes arising within the city limits. Thus, the term *jurisdiction* can also be used as a synonym for venue, meaning the geographical area over which the court has the authority to hear cases. The state court systems generally have open jurisdiction, meaning that almost all cases can be filed in some specific court in the state, while the jurisdiction for federal courts is limited by federal statutes. Only cases that meet at least one of the four current tests for federal jurisdiction can be heard in federal trial courts; this will be addressed in more detail toward the end of the chapter. Jurisdiction questions clearly affect whether a certain case can be heard in a federal court, in a state court, or in either court system.

TRIAL COURTS VERSUS APPELLATE COURTS

In this section, we will discuss the specific characteristics of trial courts and appellate courts, as well as the differences between the two. Figure 2.1 shows the general organization of the contemporary federal and state court systems, as well as the relationship between those two systems. Because each state structures its own court system according to its own constitution and statutes, Figure 2.1 assumes a simplified generic state court system organization, consisting of state supreme courts at the top, followed by state appellate courts, and then state trial courts. Some states have very complicated court systems, while others are quite simple in their organization, as will be discussed in more detail later in this chapter. The U.S. district courts, the U.S. courts of appeals, and the U.S. Supreme Court are the three courts in the federal court system.

Trial Courts and Questions of Fact

Cases and litigants enter all the court systems through the trial courts. In Figure 2.1, the trial courts are the bottom row on both the federal and state sides of the chart (federal trial courts are known as U.S. district courts). In many parts of the world these trial courts are called "courts of first instance," American trials are public events, open to the press and to the general public. In the United States, trial courts in both the federal and state systems usually use a single judge to hear a case. In rare circumstances, a U.S. district court may use a three-judge panel to hear a case if such a panel is required by a federal statute for a specific type of lawsuit, such as certain civil rights cases.[1]

At a civil or criminal trial, each party is represented by its own attorneys. The lawyers examine witnesses and present evidence in order to assist the court in determining the facts of the dispute or crime. The lawyers present the facts in the most favorable light for their clients, and the jury {if there is one) determines whose presentation of the facts is most correct. If there is no jury, then the judge hands down the verdict in the case, that is, the decision of which side's presentation of facts serves as the legal outcome for the dispute. In

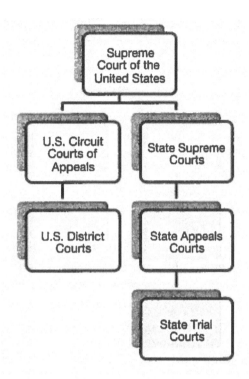

FIGURE 6: The State and Federal Court Systems in the United States

Note: While state supreme courts are the highest interpreters of pure issues of state law, these state courts must follow the precedents handed down by the U.S. Supreme Court. Thus, the state supreme courts are listed below the U.S. Supreme Court because they are considered lower courts for precedential purposes.

other words, the verdict announces who wins and who loses, based on the facts the jury or the judge believe to be true. In a criminal case, after a guilty verdict the judge also hands down the sentence because criminal sentencing is a matter of law handled by the judge in almost all criminal cases except capital punishment cases. In a capital punishment case, the jury first decides the verdict, and then, after hearing more evidence relevant to the sentencing phase, the jury determines if the convicted defendant should receive the death penalty or life imprisonment.[2] (See Chapter 5 for more on the criminal justice system.)

The main purpose of trial courts, therefore, is to determine questions of fact. The judge is responsible for determining any questions of law (defined below), as well as questions of fact if there is no jury. But if there is a jury present, then it is solely the jury's responsibility to determine questions of fact. In most states, the judge gives the jury instructions that limit the jurors, deliberations to the facts of the case.[3] When focusing on questions of fact, trial courts are only concerned about the specific case before them. The loser at trial has the right to appeal the decision to a first-level appellate court. The only exception is that the prosecutor in a criminal case generally cannot appeal a finding of not guilty.

Appellate Courts and Questions of Law

Appellate courts are where appeals are filed. In Figure 2.1, the trial courts are at the bottom of both sides of the chart. All the courts above the trial courts in the chart are appellate courts. There may be multiple appellate courts in any given court system.

Lawyers communicate their appeals in writing to appellate courts, and appellate courts issue their decisions in written opinions. In three-tier court systems, the loser at the lower appellate court can then appeal to a higher appellate court. Some appellate courts have a **mandatory docket**, meaning that they must hear every appeal filed with them. This is true of all first-level appellate courts, including the U.S. courts of appeals and many state intermediate appeals courts. The U.S. Supreme Court, however, has a **discretionary docket**, meaning that it decides which appeals to hear and which ones to reject. Some state supreme courts also have a discretionary docket. The U.S. Supreme Court is the highest appellate court in the country, and its decisions serve as binding precedent for all lower federal and state courts. The U.S. Supreme Court only accepts about 2 percent of the more than ten thousand appeals presented to it each year for full argument.

The state supreme courts are the highest interpreters of state constitutions and of matters that are purely issues of state law. For example, when the Massachusetts Supreme Judicial Court declared that the state constitution provided the right of same-sex marriage, that case was not heard by the U.S. Supreme Court because there was deemed to be no federal issue in that case. Thus, the Massachusetts Supreme Judicial Court was the last word on the issue of same-sex marriage under its state constitutional provisions. (See Chapter 7 for more details about the appellate court process.)

Appellate courts serve a variety of purposes. One purpose of all appellate courts in the United States is to correct errors of law at trial.[4] Although appellate courts in the United States generally accept the facts as determined at the trial in the lower-level trial courts, they review the legal rulings made by the trial courts to determine if the trial judges have correctly applied the law to the facts of the case.[5] In other words, the appellate courts make sure that the trial judge did not misinterpret the law. Every litigant has the right to at least one appeal in order to make sure that there were no legal errors at trial. The error correction function of appellate courts also ensures that the law is being applied consistently across all courts and judges.

A second purpose of appellate courts is to answer questions of law. **Questions of law** are much broader than questions of fact and are issues that will arise in other future cases. In order to answer the questions of law before them, appellate courts must interpret multiple sources of law, such as constitutions, statutes, and agency decisions. The court's answer to a question of law, and especially the reasoning for that answer, is what is known as **precedent** (a concept you might recall from Chapter 1). When appellate courts answer questions of law, they set precedent for all future cases in the courts below them.

Let us look at an example of questions of fact and questions of law that occurred in the same case. In the original O. J. Simpson criminal trial in California in 1995, the main question of fact in the case was whether or not Simpson had actually killed his former wife and her boyfriend. Part of the evidence in the case involved a bloody glove that was thought to have been used during the murders. The police and prosecutors argued that Simpson left the bloody glove at the crime scene. The question of fact here was fairly simple—did the glove actually belong to Simpson? In the words of Simpson's defense lawyer, Johnnie L. Cochran, "If it doesn't fit, then you must acquit."

The questions of law were more complicated in this case, regarding in part whether DNA evidence should be admissible in any court The question of law was whether technology had advanced to the point where DNA evidence was trustworthy and reliable enough for use at trial. The Simpson trial was interrupted because the law regarding this issue was unclear at the time. The Supreme Court of California then decided that DNA evidence was scientifically reliable and there-fore could be used as evidence at trial. This is a question of law because the decision of the California Supreme Court was binding precedent for all lower courts in the state and applied to all future cases, including the O. J. Simpson murder trial. Although the California Supreme Court's decision was not binding precedent for other courts in other jurisdictions, almost every state and federal court soon followed the California court's decision that DNA evidence is trustworthy enough to be admitted as evidence at trial. This is an example of persuasive precedent, a concept introduced in Chapter 1. After the decision of the California Supreme Court on this question of law, the trial of O. J. Simpson resumed. Simpson was acquitted of these murders, although he did eventually lose a wrongful-death civil suit brought by the relatives of the murdered individuals. Recall that the burden of proof in civil cases is much lower than it is in criminal trials.

Appellate Court Opinions

Appellate courts issue their rulings in writing. An appellate court decision has two parts: the outcome of the case and the reasoning. The outcome means who wins the case and who loses, and so is most important to the parties involved, but the reasoning of the majority becomes binding precedent for all lower courts in the judicial hierarchy because it answers the specific question of law in the case.

There are several types of appellate opinions. Recall that all appellate courts have multiple judges hearing the case. **The majority opinion** reflects the majority outcome and the majority reasoning. In other words, the majority opinion is the one that receives the majority of the votes on the appellate court. On the U.S. Supreme Court, for example, the majority opinion gets at least five votes among the nine justices. The majority opinion states who wins and who loses, and the reasoning behind the majority opinion becomes the precedent from the case ruling. The **holding** in a case is the legal doctrine that the majority opinion articulates, a concise statement of the precedent the ruling has created. A **concurrence** agrees with the majority outcome, but for different reasons. The **dissenting opinion** is the minority's preferred outcome and the minority's reasoning for that outcome. On the U.S. Supreme Court, for example, a dissent gets four or fewer votes among the nine justices. On a three-judge panel on the U.S. courts of appeals, a majority opinion would get two votes, while the dissent would get one vote.

A **plurality opinion** does not get a majority vote on the court but may become the controlling precedent under certain circumstances, such as if the opinion gets some combination of five votes in the U.S. Supreme Court. For example, in *Regents of the University of California* v, *Bakke* (1978), Justice Lewis F. Powell's plurality opinion became the controlling precedent for the Supreme Court in affirmative action cases. While Justice Powell was the lone justice to sign on to his opinion in its entirety, he did get five votes for each part of the opinion, making it the opinion of the Court. In his opinion, Justice Powell said that race and sex quotas are unconstitutional in the absence of a finding of past intentional discrimination by the specific university or employer in question. This part of Powell's opinion received the votes of four conservative justices plus his own. But the other half of the opinion, where Justice Powell said that race and sex could be considered among other factors in educational admissions and employment, received the votes of four liberal justices plus his own. While the whole of Powell's plurality opinion technically only got one vote, it nevertheless became the opinion of the Court because he got five votes for each portion of his decision.

FEDERALISM AND THE AMERICAN COURT SYSTEMS: A HISTORICAL OVERVIEW

This chapter will now turn to the differences between the state and federal court systems. Recall that there are really fifty-one different state court systems, but for convenience this section will compare the federal court system with a generic state court system. Every state has both a federal court system and a state court system within its borders, with overlapping jurisdictions. We have both state and federal court systems in our country because state courts existed well before the U.S. Constitution of 1789 called for the creation of the federal court system. In many ways, the federal courts were superimposed upon the existing state court structures. The organization and structure of the court systems in the United States are extremely complicated in part because of our unique system of federalism. Most other federalist governments around the world have chosen to have one unified court system, like the one in Canada, instead of having two separate court systems, as we have in the United States.

At this point, a general definition of federalism would be helpful. To understand federalism, we must compare it with other approaches used around the world. There are three basic choices about how to structure the relationship between the national government and regional governments: unitary, federal, and confederal. **Federalism** is the division of power between the national government and the regional governments (in the United States, these are the states). In a federal system, the national government is supreme over the regional governments, although the regional governments retain certain powers. Article VI of the U.S. Constitution contains a **Supremacy Clause**, which, when read in conjunction with the Fourteenth Amendment, clearly indicates that we have a federal system in which the states are legally inferior to the national government. The British Empire at the time of the American Revolution was a **unitary system**, where all power was centralized in the national government in London. **Confederal systems** mean that there is a division of power between the national government and the regional governments, with the regional governments being supreme. Confederal systems will be discussed in more detail later in this chapter. The U.S. Constitution and various federal statutes spell out the structure of the federal court system, while the state constitutions and state statutes generally establish the structure of the state courts.

The Articles of Confederation

The existing state court systems were first created in colonial times. Because the original thirteen states were founded as British colonies, the colonists brought the English common law notions of law and courts with them. Each colony set up its own court system with its own rules and procedures. After the American Revolution, the state court systems remained much as they had been prior to independence.

After the Declaration of Independence in 1776, the national government of the United States first functioned under the **Articles of Confederation**. This confederal system of government divided power between the national government and the states, but the states were considered supreme, with limited power given to the central government. Note that under the Articles of Confederation we did not have a president or a Supreme Court. Congress was the only institution of the central government. Each state maintained its own state court system under the Articles of Confederation, and there were no national or federal courts at all during this period. The state constitutions determined the jurisdiction and procedures to be followed in each state judicial system, including the number and levels of courts available to the state's citizens.

During the Civil War, the southern states experimented with another confederal system, known as the Confederate States of America. The state courts remained intact during the Civil War and most of Reconstruction, although the judges during Reconstruction were mostly unionists loyal to the north.[6] There were great variations among the colonial court systems, the state court systems that existed right after the Revolution, and the post-Civil War courts. These differences among the state courts continue today.

The U.S. Constitution of 1789

The Articles of Confederation proved unworkable, and the Constitutional Convention created a new system of government that included federalism as a key component. The new Constitution created a national executive (the president), a new bicameral legislature (the U.S. Congress), and a new Supreme Court of the United States. Article III of the U.S. Constitution stated that a Supreme Court of the United States would be created and left it to Congress to determine how to structure the remaining parts of the new federal court system.

Note that Article III of the Constitution of 1789 is silent about the state court systems. The existing state court systems are mentioned only indirectly in the Constitution's Article IV, where the Full Faith and Credit Clause states that "Full Faith and Credit shall be given in each State to the public Acts, Records, and judicial proceedings of every other State." Some scholars also argue that Article IV's Guarantee Clause, which requires that the states have a republican form of government, also implies that the states should have separate court systems. Thus, when the states ratified the U.S. Constitution of 1789, they did not give up their separate and unique state judicial systems. These court systems continued to be defined by the state constitutions and state statutes. The new Constitution merely superimposed a new layer of federal courts on the existing state courts.

In the Judiciary Act of 1789, Congress established the basics of the federal court system that still exist today. Today, the federal courts have a three-tier structure, with the U.S. Supreme Court at the top of the judicial pyramid. The decisions of the U.S. Supreme Court are binding precedent for all the lower federal courts and under most circumstances for all the state courts. In *Fletcher v. Peck* (1810), the Supreme Court ruled that its power of judicial review extended to determining the constitutionality of state laws. In *Cooper v. Aaron* (1958), the U.S. Supreme Court reaffirmed that it is the final arbiter of the U.S. Constitution under the Supremacy Clause.

Some have argued that one of the greatest responsibilities of the U.S. Supreme Court under the U.S. Constitution of 1789 is to protect the federal government from the states. After giving itself the power of judicial review in its decision in *Marbury v. Madison* (1803), the Supreme Court worked hard to consolidate federal power at the expense of the states. For example, in *McCulloch v. Maryland* (1819), the Court declared that the states had no power to tax the newly created national bank, because the power to tax was the power to destroy. Hie Civil War was fought in part over issues of federalism. Originally, the Bill of Rights applied only against the power of the federal government. However, after World War II, the U.S. Supreme Court began using the Fourteenth Amendment to apply most of the Bill of Rights to the states in a process known as **Incorporation**. Incorporation was done in a piecemeal fashion by the U.S. Supreme Court over an extended period of time, and, by today, most of the elements of the Bill of Rights limit state power as well as federal power. Over time, many justices have been concerned about the states improperly encroaching on federal power. Justice Oliver Wendell Holmes supported this idea of protecting the federal government from the states when he wrote, "I do not think the United States would come to an end if we lost our power to declare an Act of Congress void. I do think the Union would be imperiled if we could not make that declaration as to the law of the several States."[7] Issues of federalism remain a great concern for the U.S. Supreme Court as it tries to figure out when the national government can overrule the states and when the states should retain powers of their own.

THE FEDERAL COURT SYSTEM

This next section will examine in more detail the workings of the federal court system. We will first look at the U.S. district courts, followed by the U.S. court of appeals, and then the U.S. Supreme Court. We will also discuss specialized federal courts and federal judicial agencies.

Federal Trial Courts: The U.S. District Courts

Unlike the great variation found in the state court systems, the federal courts are quite uniform in their structure. The federal trial court is called the U.S. district court, and there are ninety-four federal districts in the United States today. Almost all federal cases begin in the U.S. district courts. Every state has at least one U.S. district court, and the larger states may include several districts. Puerto Rico, the District of Columbia, and several of the U.S. territories also have their own U.S. district courts. A few districts have only one or two judges, but some have as many as thirty. Congress decides how many judges will serve in any given district; in 2013 there were 677 judges authorized to sit on the various U.S. district courts around the country. Just like their counterparts on the U.S. courts of appeals and the U.S. Supreme Court, judges on the U.S. district courts are appointed by the president and confirmed by the U.S. Senate for life terms. Many U.S. district courts also have **federal magistrate judges**, selected by a majority vote by the regular judges assigned to the district. These magistrate judges serve an eight-year term and assist the regular federal judges, mostly with highly complex litigation.

U.S. Circuit Courts of Appeals

The U.S. circuit courts of appeals are the intermediate appellate courts in the federal system. Figure 2.2 shows the current boundaries of the U.S. circuit courts of appeals. There are twelve regional circuit courts of appeals, plus the Court of Appeals for the Federal Circuit. The Court of Appeals for the Federal Circuit has nationwide jurisdiction to hear appeals in specialized cases, such as those involving patent laws and cases decided by the Court of International Trade and the Court of Federal Claims. The smallest circuits (the Second, Fifth, Seventh, and Eleventh Circuits) include three states, while the largest circuit court, the Ninth Circuit, includes nine states plus several federal territories. In 1997, the circuit courts heard a total of more than fifty thousand cases; in 2004 they received more than fifty-six thousand appeals,[8] and in 2005 they heard more than sixty-eight thousand cases.[9] There were a total of 179 judgeships authorized for these courts in 2013. The smallest circuit, the First Circuit, has six judges, while the largest circuit, the Ninth Circuit, has twenty-eight judges. Like all other regular federal judges, judges on the U.S. courts of appeals are appointed by the president and confirmed by the U.S. Senate for life terms. The types of cases that the circuit courts hear vary by region—for example, the Second, Fifth, and Ninth

FIGURE 7: Map of the U.S. Circuit Courts of Appeals

Source: Administrative Office of the United States Courts.

Circuits tend to hear many immigration appeals, given the large number of immigrants in the areas serviced by those courts.[10]

The existing U.S. courts of appeals system was created in 1891, although the U.S. Congress has changed the boundaries for some of the circuits on various occasions since then. For example, in 1980, for both political and management reasons Congress split the old Fifth Circuit into two new circuits—the current Fifth Circuit includes the states of Texas, Louisiana, and Mississippi, while the new Eleventh Circuit covers the states of Florida, Georgia, and Alabama.[11]

These federal appellate courts have a mandatory docket, meaning that they must hear all appeals that come to them.[12] The U.S. circuit courts of appeals hear appeals from the U.S. district courts and from many federal administrative agencies.[13] These courts use panels of three randomly selected judges to hear most cases, although it is possible for a losing party to request that the entire court (or a subset of fifteen judges on large circuits such as the Ninth Circuit) rehear a case, in what is known as an *en banc* review, after the three-judge panel has rendered its decision.[14] In order for an *en banc* hearing to occur, a regular judge on the circuit must first endorse the litigant's request, and then a majority of the regular judges on the circuit must vote for the *en banc* review.[15] Because the Supreme Court hears so few cases each year, the U.S. courts of appeals serve as the last word on many federal law questions. These courts also correct errors of law made by federal trial judges and administrative agencies.[16]

These intermediate federal appellate courts have undergone several name changes over their history, as well as changes in their basic makeup and structure. Originally the U.S. circuit courts were composed of a combination of judges from the U.S. district courts and the U.S. Supreme Court. These borrowed judges rode circuit, meaning that they literally traveled around the states in the circuit, hearing appeals from the lower federal courts as well as having some trial jurisdiction. The Judiciary Act of 1891, however, created the current system of freestanding U.S. courts of appeals with their own judges. The old circuit courts were finally abolished in 1911, though we continue to use *circuit courts* as a colloquial name for the U.S. courts of appeals.[17] Traditionally, researchers did not pay as much attention to the judicial decision making on the U.S. courts of appeals as they did to the U.S. Supreme Court, but more and more scholars are now studying these intermediate federal appellate courts.[18]

The Supreme Court of the United States

The highest court in the United States is of course the Supreme Court of the United States. This court today has nine justices, who are appointed by the president and confirmed by the U.S. Senate for life terms. The exact number of justices on the Supreme Court is determined by Congress, not by the U.S. Constitution. In the nineteenth century the number of justices varied over time, but Congress eventually settled on nine in 1869, during Reconstruction. In what is known as his court-packing plan, President Franklin D. Roosevelt unsuccessfully proposed almost doubling the size of the Supreme Court when the Court kept declaring his New Deal programs to be unconstitutional.[19] This was one of the few votes in Congress that FDR lost in his many years in office. Today, having nine justices on the Supreme Court seems to be constitutionally enshrined in the minds of Americans even though that number does not appear in the Constitution itself.

The chief justice of the United States, often referred to as the first among equals,[20] is appointed by the president and confirmed by the Senate whenever that specific seat is vacant. Only rarely does a president nominate someone already sitting on the Supreme Court for this position, although Chief Justice Rehnquist was an associate justice when President Reagan elevated him to the chief justice position.[21] There is no requirement that the president appoint someone to the U.S. Supreme Court who has previously served as a judge on any court. For example, prior to being appointed as chief justice, Earl Warren served as governor of California. Justice Elena Kagan served as the U.S. solicitor general and before that as the dean of Harvard Law School, but she had never held a judgeship before being appointed to the Supreme Court.

As mentioned earlier, the U.S. Supreme Court creates binding precedent that ail the other lower courts in both the state and federal court systems must follow. The U.S. Supreme Court also has administrative responsibilities over all other federal courts, overseeing many of the day-to-day activities of the lower courts.[22] The Judiciary Act of 1925 repealed most of the mandatory jurisdiction of the Supreme Court, thus almost completely allowing it to control its own caseload. With its discretionary docket, today's U.S. Supreme Court refuses to hear about 98 percent of the cases brought to it.[23] The power of judicial review allows appellate courts and especially the U.S. Supreme Court to declare the actions of other political actors to be unconstitutional. Taken together, the ability of appellate courts to make precedent and their power of judicial review makes American appellate courts very strong policy makers.

Specialized Federal Courts

In addition to the regular district courts, there are several other types of specialized federal trial courts. Each district has special **bankruptcy courts**, which are separate units of the district courts. Unlike most other types of disputes, bankruptcy cases cannot be heard in the state courts. They must be heard only in special bankruptcy courts attached to the regular U.S. district courts, and in 2008 and 2009 more than a million bankruptcy cases were filed each year.[24] **Bankruptcy judges** are appointed by the majority of the regular federal judges who sit on the U.S. district court, and they serve fourteen-year terms. There are now more than three hundred federal bankruptcy judges in the United States.

The Court of International Trade has jurisdiction over cases involving international trade and customs issues, and the United States Court of Federal Claims has jurisdiction over most claims for money damages against the United States, disputes over federal contracts, and unlawful takings of private property by the federal government, among a variety of other claims against the U.S. government. There is also a special U.S. Tax Court that hears cases involving the Internal Revenue Service, although this special court does not have a monopoly over these disputes because they are often heard in other federal trial courts as well.[25] Most of the judges on these courts are so-called **Article II judges**, because they do not have the life terms enjoyed by their regular judicial colleagues. Life-term judges are referred to as **Article III judges**.

Another specialized federal court is the Foreign Intelligence Surveillance Court, which approves warrants for federal law enforcement and intelligence personnel conducting investigations into suspected terrorism and other illegal activities occurring on U.S. soil. Its judges are borrowed from the regular U.S. district courts and serve only part-time on this court.[26] The military justice system has its own appeals court, known as the United States Court of Appeals for the Armed Forces, and its own rules of procedure. This court exercises worldwide appellate jurisdiction over members of the armed forces on active duty and other individuals subject to the Uniform Code of Military Justice. It is composed of five civilian judges appointed for fifteen-year terms by the president with the advice and consent of the Senate.[17]

Federal Judicial Agencies

Another important aspect about the structure of the federal courts is the existence of federal judicial agencies of various types. These agencies and bodies generally serve the needs of the federal judiciary and provide necessary assistance to the federal courts. The **Judicial Conference of the United States** (not to be confused with the private meetings of the justices at the Supreme Court discussed in Chapter 7) is the committee that voices the collective views of the federal judiciary to the outside world—in other words, it is the policy-making arm for all federal courts. The U.S. Judicial Conference often presents the positions of the federal judiciary to Congress on legislative matters including budgets, security for judges, courthouse construction issues, and judicial workload crises caused when there are many judicial vacancies because the U.S. Senate is slow in confirming new federal judges. Within the judiciary, this group also produces recommendations that the lower federal courts must follow in order to standardize and thus improve judicial administration throughout the nation. The Judicial Conference was first created in 1922 at the urging of Chief Justice William Howard Taft, and Congress changed its name to the current one in 1948. The chief justice of the United States is the head of the U.S. Judicial Conference, and its members include federal judges from both the U.S. courts of appeals and the U.S. district courts.

Founded in 1939, the **Administrative Office of the United States Courts** (AO) serves as staff for the Judicial Conference. The Administrative Office also provides research, administrative, legal, financial, management, program, and information technology services to the federal judiciary. The AO communicates the views of the judiciary to the president and Congress, thus serving an unofficial lobbying function for federal judges collectively. The Administrative Office employs lawyers, public administrators, accountants, systems engineers, analysts, architects, statisticians, and other types of professional individuals.

Another federal judicial agency is the **Federal Judicial Center** (FJC). This agency provides training and research for the federal judiciary in a wide range of areas, including court administration, case management, budget and finance, human resources, and court technology. In the United States, all judges are drawn from the legal profession, and, because there is no "judge school" like there is in a number of European countries, many of them have no experience with the day-to-day problems and issues that judges face. Thus, the FJC attempts to fill this gap, both for new judges and for long-serving members of the federal judiciary. The FJC also provides assistance and training to judges from around the world who want to learn more about the U.S. legal system. This work of the FJC is discussed in more detail in Chapter 13.

The final federal judiciary agency, the **United States Sentencing Commission**, is somewhat of a hybrid agency. One of the major purposes of the Sentencing Commission is to recommend federal sentencing guidelines to Congress, which must then enact these suggestions into law. The Sentencing Commission also advises Congress and the executive branch about effective and efficient crime policy in general, and the agency collects and analyzes a broad range of information on federal crime and sentencing issues. The U.S. Sentencing Commission is treated as an independent agency housed in the judicial branch of government, but it serves the needs both of Congress and of the federal courts. Currently the Sentencing Commission has seven members who are appointed by the president and confirmed by the Senate for six-year terms. At least three of the commissioners must be federal judges, and no more than four may belong to the same political party.

Congress first created the U.S. Sentencing Commission in the Sentencing Reform Act of 1984, in order to limit the discretion of federal judges in their criminal sentencing decisions, and the first set of federal sentencing guidelines was put into place in 1987. Congress was concerned that federal criminal sentences were not uniform across the decisions made by a single judge, judges serving on the same court, or courts across the country. Congress was also concerned about appearing to be tougher on crime. Thus, the federal sentencing guidelines system was designed to eliminate disparities in federal criminal sentences. Although the Supreme Court had found the federal sentencing guidelines to be constitutional in *Mistretta v. United States* (1989), later in *United States v. Booker* (2005) the Court ruled that these guidelines were merely advisory and could not be treated as mandatory restrictions on the discretion of federal judges. More details about the criminal trial process can be found in Chapter 5.

THE STATE COURT SYSTEM

We will now turn to an examination of the various state courts. When Americans encounter a court firsthand, usually as a juror or as a litigant, it is almost always a state trial court in a state judicial system. Over 98 percent of all legal cases today are heard in the state courts. There are more than sixteen thousand courts in the state judicial systems, and they process approximately a hundred million cases per year. The state courts employ more than thirty thousand judicial officers (including judges and others) and many more support staff. Through its state constitution and other laws, each state can decide how to structure its own court system, including how many types of courts the system will have and which courts will have the jurisdiction to hear what types of cases.[28]

Once a case begins in either a state court system or the federal court system, it usually stays in that system unless a federal trial court grants a writ of habeas corpus (discussed in more detail in Chapter 5) or the U.S. Supreme Court eventually agrees to hear the case. The states employ a variety of selection methods for their judges, although most states use some type of election system. These different state judicial selection processes will be explored in more detail in Chapter 3.

The Structure of State Courts

Some states employ a very simple structure for their state courts, while other states have a very complex system. Figure 2.3 shows a generic state court structure, one that is fairly straightforward in organization. Note that this three-tier system is quite similar to the federal court structure. During the nineteenth century, almost no states had a three-tier state court system, but by the twentieth century most states had added new intermediate courts of appeals to help reduce the caseload of the state supreme courts. This change allowed state supreme courts to focus more on cases that involved important public policy issues, while the intermediate courts of appeals handled the more routine error correction functions of appellate courts.[29] California is a state that follows a simple federal-style three-tier court structure, as shown in Figure 2.4. The one exception to this is that death penalty cases skip the courts of appeals and go directly to the California Supreme Court after the death penalty is imposed by a jury in a trial court. On the other hand, some states have chosen to have a more complicated

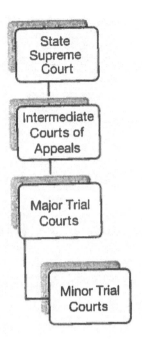

FIGURE 8: A Generic State Court Structure

FIGURE 9: Structure of California State Courts

Note: All death penalty cases go directly from the trial courts to the California Supreme Court.

court structure for their state courts. Figure 2.5 illustrates the extremely complex state court structure in Massachusetts. In the Bay State, there is the traditional three-tier system, but it is complicated by the fact that the Superior Court is the court of first instance (initial trial court) for some cases. Other cases start in one of the other trial courts and are then referred

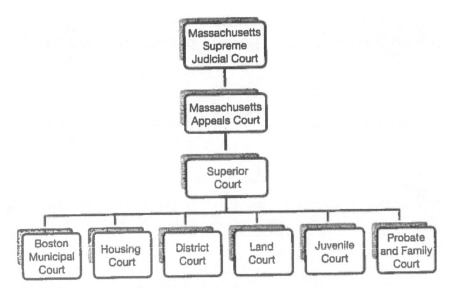

FIGURE 10:13 Structure of the Massachusetts State Court System

Note: For some major cases the Superior Court is the entry-level initial trial court, and for some cases the Superior Court serves as a review court after preliminary hearings are held in other trial courts.

to the Superior Court after a preliminary hearing; in these cases, the Superior Court acts more like an appellate court. At times, two different trial courts could simultaneously have jurisdiction over a case, resulting in judges having to take the time to sort out whether a case actually belongs before their bench. The Massachusetts structure can be confusing even for lawyers with some experience in this extremely complicated state court system.

Because each state has its own court structure, state trial courts can have a variety of names and jurisdictions. Some of these courts hear only major cases, while other courts hear both major and minor disputes. Some of these trial courts hear a broad range of cases, while others hear only very specialized ones.[30] States might also have both trial courts of general jurisdiction and courts of limited jurisdiction. Depending on the state, these courts may carry such names as *municipal courts, district courts, superior courts, county courts, juvenile courts, probate courts, family courts, housing courts,* or even *drug courts.* In the state of New York some of the trial courts are called *supreme courts,* which is very confusing because in almost every other state the supreme court is at the top of the judicial pyramid, not at its bottom or entry point. The original *Law and Order* TV series was set in New York City and therefore used New York nomenclature, setting its fictional trials in the "supreme courts" of New York City.

Although each state court system is unique, based on the states own constitution and statutes, there is a certain similarity in the structures of many regular state court systems, which is not surprising given that states frequency borrow ideas from each other. Nevertheless, even though the states may have formal statewide rules on how to administer the courts, local judges often follow their own norms and practices in overseeing their courtrooms. Thus, even where there is a centralized judicial administration, local judges have considerable freedom to run their own courts as they see fit.[31]

The American Bar Association and others have recommended that states simplify their court structures.[32] Part of the court unification movement involved putting state court administration in the hands of professionals supervised by the state supreme courts. The idea was to promote efficiency and to protect the independence of state courts from undue legislative control.[33] This court unification movement failed in many states. For example, in Massachusetts traditionally clerk magistrates who worked for the judges obtained their jobs through a patronage system, and individual clerks were hired by legislators or by the governor instead of by the judges for whom they worked. Most of the clerk magistrates kept their jobs for life because the judges had no right to dismiss them.[34] Even after a patronage scandal erupted in Massachusetts in 2012, when a number of probation officials were indicted for racketeering, bribery, and mail fraud because they created a deceptive hiring system that allowed them to give jobs to their friends, relatives, and political supporters, the state has yet to change dramatically the system for hiring these clerk magistrates.[35]

One category of specialized state trial courts is worth mentioning in more depth. **Juvenile courts** are special courts designed to handle issues of juvenile delinquency and neglect, and they are structured much differently than courts for adults. First created in Chicago in 1899, these courts serve multiple purposes.[36] In most states, the juvenile courts deal with issues of juvenile delinquency as well as problems of neglect and abuse of children. They may also deal with issues of child custody. These courts tend to close their proceedings to the public in order to protect the children's privacy and the confidentiality of the matters at hand, and they usually do not follow the same rules of procedure as the regular courts. One of the most important U.S. Supreme Court decisions in the area of juvenile justice is *In re Gault* (1967). In this case, the Court ruled that while some flexibility in procedures was necessary in juvenile courts, minors still had a number of due process rights in these courts, including the right to an attorney in many situations.[37] The standard in this court even in juvenile delinquency cases is the best interests of the child. As one expert on juvenile justice concludes, "The general purpose of juvenile court acts is to ensure the welfare of the juveniles while protecting their constitutional rights in such a way that removal from the family unit is accomplished only for a reasonable cause and in the best interests of the juvenile and society."[38] Thus, most juvenile courts are more concerned with rehabilitation goals than are most judges in so-called adult courts.

State Appellate Courts

Most states have two levels of appellate courts, an intermediate court of appeals and a state supreme court. In many states, the first-level court of appeals is regional and may be referred to as an intermediate appeals court, while the state supreme court is the top court in the state, hearing appeals from the various regional courts of appeals. In eleven states, cases still go immediately from the trial courts to the state supreme court because the state does not have an intermediate appeals court.[39]

Most state intermediate-level appellate courts hear cases in panels of three judges, while most state supreme courts have seven judges who all sit for every case the court hears, though some states use five and a few use nine. Texas and Oklahoma each have two supreme courts, one for criminal appeals and another for appeals in civil cases. The top courts in the states of Maryland and New York are called the "court of appeals," while every other state calls their court of last resort the "supreme court." The National Center for State Courts, headquartered in Williamsburg, Virginia, coordinates a great deal of research and data dealing with the various state court systems.

There are some issues that bypass the state trial courts and go directly to state appellate courts or, more commonly, to the state supreme courts as part of their original jurisdiction. For example, cases involving disciplining of judges and attorneys often go directly to the state supreme courts after initial administrative proceedings by a bar disciplinary board. For states that allow advisory opinions, that is, opinions on the constitutionality of legislation before it goes into effect, these requests come from the state legislature or the governor and go directly to the state supreme court. Some state supreme courts also have original jurisdiction over certain types of writs.[40]

The state supreme courts are the final interpreters of the state constitutions and the courts of last resort under state law. In *Hortonville Joint School District No. 1. v. Hortonville Education Association* (1976), the U.S. Supreme Court clearly stated, "We are, of course, bound to accept the interpretation of [state] law by the highest court of the State."[41] Even though the state supreme courts are the last word on state law, the truth is that only a minuscule number of cases from state appeals courts are ever reviewed by state supreme courts, and only a tiny fraction of rulings by state supreme courts are ever heard by the U.S. Supreme Court.[42] Thus, state appellate courts retain a certain amount of decisional autonomy.

The state supreme courts have the last word on questions of state law because the U.S. Supreme Court will hear only cases that involve a federal issue of some sort.[43] The U.S. Supreme Court will not review a decision of a state supreme court if the ruling is based on adequate and independent state law grounds. In other words, if a case raises both state and federal law issues, the U.S. Supreme Court will not hear the case if the state law issues are adequate to settle the dispute. For example, *Fox Film Corp. v. Muller* (1935) involved a contract dispute between a filmmaker and an individual who had promised to show one of the company's films. The U.S. Supreme Court refused to hear the suit because the case could be decided based purely on state law. Even though Fox Film Corporation asked the Court to review the case based on both federal and state law claims, the Court ruled that it would not hear the case because the state law issues were an adequate and independent ground for ending the dispute. However, in *Michigan v. Long* (1983), a case dealing with the police finding drugs in the defendant's car, the U.S. Supreme Court took the case because it ruled that the Michigan Supreme Court was in reality exclusively using federal law and federal precedents in its decision and not basing its ruling on purely state law grounds. This case clarified the somewhat confusing doctrine of adequate and independent state grounds for deciding cases. As Alan Tarr, a judicial scholar, has described the effects of the adequate and independent state law doctrine, "State rulings based on state statutes, the common law, or state constitutions are altogether immune from federal judicial scrutiny, unless a 'federal question' is raised or unless the case falls within the federal courts' diversity jurisdiction."[44]

The state supreme courts hear many constitutionally based cases each year. State supreme courts vary a great deal in how they interpret their state constitutions, in part because state constitutions range in size from eight thousand words (similar to the size of the U.S. Constitution) to two hundred thousand words.'[45] State supreme courts collectively hear around two thousand constitutional cases each year, while the U.S. Supreme Court hears on average only about thirty. Many argue that scholars have not paid enough attention to the importance of the state supreme courts in shaping American law. According to Neal Devins and Nicole Mansker, experts on state constitutional law, "State supreme courts have eclipsed the U.S. Supreme Court in shaping the meaning of constitutional values."[46]

State supreme courts and state laws are free to provide more protection to individual rights and liberties than is found in the U.S. Constitution because the U.S. Constitution only provides a minimum, or floor, level of such rights.[47] Starting in the early 1970s, many state courts became much more liberal than their federal counterparts. Many civil liberties and social reform interest groups started bringing cases in state courts because they felt that the state courts would provide various constitutional protections that the more conservative federal courts would not.[48] For example, the states can bar discrimination on the basis of sexual orientation even though there are no federal laws prohibiting such discrimination. The state courts were also the forum for rulings that required the states to equalize their funding for public schools across the state. The U.S. Supreme Court had ruled in *San Antonio Independent School District v. Rodriguez* (1973) that, since there is no federal right to an education, it would not hear cases asking for equalized funding for public schools. Thus, the state supreme courts can provide a greater level of constitutional protection on various issues by interpreting their state constitutions more broadly than the U.S. Supreme Court interprets the U.S. Constitution. This is especially true today in some states in the areas of abortion, gay rights, takings, school financing, religious liberty, tort reform, and some criminal procedure protections.[49]

The state supreme courts also have a much harder time avoiding more controversial decisions because they generally do not have the various technical avoidance techniques available to the federal courts.[50] Of course, since the U.S. Supreme Court only hears about 2 percent of the requests for appeals each year, in many cases the decision of the state supreme court is the last word even if there might be a federal issue in the case.

LIMITATIONS OF THE FEDERAL COURT SYSTEM

In this section, we discuss some of the limitations of the federal justice system, including federal jurisdiction requirements and case and controversy restrictions.

Federal Jurisdiction

Unlike the state courts, which generally have open jurisdiction and have some courts that can hear almost any case, the jurisdiction of the federal courts is limited, which is why federal courts hear many fewer cases than state courts. Congress determines the jurisdiction of the federal courts, and for a case to be heard in a federal court it must meet at least one of the four current tests for **federal jurisdiction**:

1. If the U.S. government is a party to the case, then the case must be heard in the federal courts. This means that all federal crimes are tried in the federal courts (the U.S. government is the prosecutor), and all civil cases involving the federal government must be heard in federal court. Bankruptcy cases must also be heard in federal courts. The U.S. government does not appear in state courts.
2. If there is a federal issue in the case involving a federal source of law (e.g., the U.S. Constitution, federal statutes, a presidential executive order, or a federal agency decision), then the plaintiff has the choice of whether to file the case in the federal courts or in state courts. If a state judge hears the case, then he or she must apply federal precedents.
3. In a so-called diversity case, where there are parties from different states in a civil case worth more than $75,000, then the plaintiff has the choice of filing the case in state courts or in the federal courts. If a federal judge hears the case, it is quite likely that he or she will be applying state precedents to the dispute.
4. The Class Action Fairness Act of 2005 created another test for federal jurisdiction. When the parties are from different states and the total amount in controversy exceeds $5 million, then the federal courts may consolidate various individual cases into a single federal class action lawsuit. This new legislation was sought by large nationwide corporate interests, such as drug manufacturers, who felt that they were not being treated fairly when they faced large numbers of lawsuits in numerous state courts concerning a common issue or dispute. Thus, they wanted their cases to be heard only in federal courts.

Since Congress has created these four tests for federal jurisdiction, it is an open question whether Congress can also refuse to allow the federal courts to hear certain types of cases. That controversy will be discussed in more detail in Chapter 10.

Cases and Controversies

In addition to the federal jurisdiction requirements discussed above, federal cases must meet the requirements of having an actual case and controversy, as required by Article III of the Constitution. In some ways, these requirements are internal checks on the courts' power of judicial review. Very early in our constitutional history, the U.S. Supreme Court ruled that it and the other federal courts would never provide advisory opinions. An **advisory opinion** is an opinion on the constitutionality of legislation before that legislation goes into effect.

This is the main way for a case to reach the constitutional court of France, for example. In Canada, these are called reference cases. One of the most famous reference cases in Canada came after the national parliament asked the Supreme Court of Canada to decide whether Quebec could secede from the confederation. The Canadian Supreme Court spelled out what must be negotiated before the province could secede.[51] Opponents of advisory opinions often argue that the advisory opinion procedure subordinates the courts to the legislature or to the executive because, even though the courts cannot usually refuse to issue an advisory opinion, the other branches are under no obligation to follow the court's advice.[52]

Some state supreme courts do offer advisory opinions to their legislative or executive branches. Of the ten states that currently have advisory opinion procedures in place, six were among the original thirteen British colonies.[53] For example, after the Massachusetts Supreme Judicial Court ruled in *Goodridge v. Department of Public Health* (2003) that same-sex couples had the same right to marry as opposite-sex couples, the Massachusetts legislature asked the court for an advisory opinion about whether civil unions, then in use in Vermont, would satisfy the court's ruling. The Massachusetts Supreme Court responded by saying that separate was never equal, thus clarifying that, when the court said same-sex couples had the right to marry, marriage meant marriage, and civil unions would not be sufficient.

As part of its case and controversy doctrines, the Supreme Court of the United States has ruled that cases filed in federal courts must also meet certain other threshold requirements in order to abide by the Constitution's Article III case and controversy requirement. The lawsuit must be filed in the right place, known as the proper **venue**, and in the right court with the proper jurisdiction. First, the Court will not allow the federal courts to hear cases that are **collusive**, where there is no actual dispute. *Muskrat v. United States* (1911) can be considered such a case. In this case, the U.S. Congress passed legislation that authorized certain Native Americans to bring a lawsuit to determine the constitutionality of specific laws allocating tribal lands. However, when David Muskrat and J. Henry Dick did just that, the Supreme Court ruled that there was no real controversy in the case and disallowed the suit The parties to the case heard in federal court must have **standing**, meaning that the party filing the case suffered an actual harm from the dispute. In other words, standing means that the case is filed by the right party. In *Frothingham v. Mellon* (1923), the U.S. Supreme Court ruled that taxpayers do not have standing to challenge federal spending decisions. This rigid prohibition on taxpayer standing was eased somewhat by the Court in *Flast v. Cohen* (1968), when the Court ruled that taxpayers might have standing in certain narrow circumstances such as challenges under the First Amendments Establishment Clause. However, the Court seemed to return to a highly restricted view of taxpayer standing in *Arizona Christian School Tuition Organization v. Winn* (2011), when the Court refused to allow taxpayers to challenge an Arizona tax credit program that provides tax credits for contributions to tuition even at religious schools. At times, Congress can give plaintiffs standing to sue, such as when it allowed environmental groups to sue on behalf of the spotted owl and other endangered species.

The timing of the case must also be correct for the case to be heard in federal court. If the controversy is already resolved, then the dispute is **moot**, because the courts will not hear hypothetical cases. However, at times this doctrine is treated as flexible. For example, the Supreme Court in *Roe v. Wade* (1973) ruled that the question of whether or not a woman could choose to have an abortion was not moot, despite the fact that the plaintiff in the case had already had the baby, because she could get pregnant again and the issue would recur for other women who could not get their cases heard during the nine months of a pregnancy. If the case is not **ripe**, it means that it has been filed too early. Often in administrative law cases, the court will require that all administrative proceedings be exhausted before a federal court can hear the case.

Another threshold doctrine is somewhat more complicated and harder to define. The Supreme Court has said that the federal courts should not hear **political questions**. This generally means that the courts should not settle disputes that are better handled by a different branch of government. Many foreign policy issues have been determined to be political questions, better handled by the other branches of government. This doctrine can also be quite flexible. In *Baker v. Carr* (1962), and to a lesser degree in *Reynolds v.* Sims (1964), the Supreme Court held that legislative redistricting issues were not political questions because only courts could grant relief to voters who felt that the legislative district lines in place at the time were violating their equal protection rights by giving urban representatives many more constituents than rural representatives had. In other words, because the legislatures would not handle the redistricting themselves, only the courts could change the current system, and so the issue was not a political question.

CHAPTER SUMMARY

This chapter examined the basic structure of the courts in the United States. It began with a discussion of the broad differences between trial courts and appellate courts, as well as the differences between questions of fact and questions of law. The chapter then turned to a deeper examination of the federal courts and the state courts, looking at the specifics of the organizations and jurisdictions of trial courts and appellate courts in both systems. The chapter also defined the work of the federal judicial agencies, which assist federal judges in their work. The chapter ended with a discussion of the limitations of federal courts, from federal jurisdiction requirements to case and controversy requirements. Both types of requirements, often referred to as threshold requirements, must be met before a federal court will hear a case.

FOR FURTHER READING

Baum, Lawrence. 2011. *Specializing the Courts*. Chicago: University of Chicago Press.

Bernard, Thomas J. 1992. *The Cycle of Juvenile Justice*. New York: Oxford University Press.

Klarman, Michael J. 2004. *From Jim Crow to Civil Rights: The Supreme Court and the Struggle for Racial Equality*. New York: Oxford University Press.

Langer, Laura. 2002. *Judicial Review in State Supreme Courts: A Comparative Study.* Albany: State University of New York Press.

O'Brien, David M. 2011. *Storm Center: The Supreme Court in American Politics.* 9th edition. New York: W. W. Norton.

Powe, Lucas A., Jr. 2000. *The Warren Court and American Politics.* Cambridge, MA: Belknap Press.

Rosenberg, Gerald N. 1991. *The Hollow Hope: Can Courts Bring About Social Change?* Chicago: University of Chicago Press.

Rowland, C. K., and Robert A. Carp. 1996. *Politics and Judgment in Federal District Courts.* Lawrence: University Press of Kansas.

Sunstein, Cass R. 2009. *A Constitution of Many Minds: Why the Founding Document Doesn't Mean What It Meant Before.* Princeton, NJ: Princeton University Press.

Tushnet, Mark. 2003. *The New Constitutional Order.* Princeton, NJ: Princeton University Press.

Discussion Questions

1. How are the courts organized in the United States?

2. What values and policy goals does this institutional structure seem to promote?

3. Who is likely to win in this system? Who is likely to lose?

4. Are courts more or less likely to be dynamic in this system? Why or why not?

B. The American Legal System

Historical and Comparative Perspectives

To place the American legal system into sharper focus, it is useful to consider historical and comparative perspectives. This section of the reader examines how the American legal system has changed over time, and how it differs from those in other industrialized democracies.

ADDITIONAL RECOMMENDED MATERIALS:

Seymour Martin Lipset, *American Exceptionalism* (1996), pp. 17-23

Robert Kagan, *Adversarial Legalism: The American Way of Law* (2001), pp. 6-14

Thomas F. Burke, Lawyers, *Litigation and Legal Rights: The Battle over Litigation in American Society* (2002)

Sean Farhang, *The Litigation State* (2010)

American Exceptionalism

Seymour Martin Lipset

INTRODUCTION

The American difference, the ways in which the United States varies from the rest of the world, is a constant topic of discussion and in recent years, of concern. Is the country in decline economically and morally? Is Japan about to replace it as the leading economic power? Why does the United States have the highest crime rate, the most persons per capita in prison? Does the growth in the proportion of illegitimate births of single-mother families reflect basic changes in our moral order? Why is our electoral turnout rate so low?

Americans once proudly emphasized their uniqueness, their differences from the rest of the world, the vitality of their democracy, the growth potential of their economy. Some now worry that our best years as a nation are behind us. Americans distrust their leaders and institutions. The public opinion indicators of confidence in institutions are the lowest since polling on the subject began in the early sixties. These concerns suggest the need to look again at the country in comparative perspective, at the ways it differs from other economically developed nations. As I have frequently argued, it is impossible to understand a country without seeing how it varies from others. Those who know only one country know no country.

The idea of American exceptionalism has interested many outside the United States. One of the most important bodies of writing dealing with this country is referred to as the "foreign traveler" literature. These are articles and books written by visitors, largely European, dealing with the way in which America works as compared with their home country or area. Perhaps the best known and still most influential is Alexis de Tocqueville's *Democracy in America.* The French aristocrat came here in the 1830s to find out why the efforts at establishing democracy in his native country, starting with the French Revolution, had failed while the American Revolution had produced a stable democratic republic. The comparison, of course, was broader than just with France; no other European country with the partial exception of Great Britain was then a democracy. In his great book, Tocqueville is the first to refer to the

Seymour Martin Lipset, American Exceptionalism, pp. 17-23. Copyright © 1996 by W. W. Norton & Company, Inc. Reprinted with permission.

United States as exceptional—that is, qualitatively different from all other countries. He is, therefore, the initiator of the writings on American exceptionalism.

The concept could only have arisen by comparing this country with other societies. Tocqueville looked at the United States through the eyes of someone who knew other cultures well, particularly that of his native country, but also to some considerable degree Great Britain. *Democracy in America* deals only with the United States and has almost no references to France or any other country, but Tocqueville emphasized in his notes that he never wrote a word about America without thinking about France. A book based on his research notes, George Pierson's *Tocqueville and Beaumont in America,* makes clear the ways in which Tocqueville systematically compared the United States and France. At one point, he became sensitive to the fact that America was a very decentralized country, while France was reputed to be the opposite. Tocqueville commented that he had never given much thought to what centralization in France meant since as a Frenchman, he did what came naturally. He then wrote to his father, a prefect of one of the regional administrative districts, and asked him to describe the concentration of political power in France. His father apparently sat down and wrote a lengthy memorandum dealing with the subject.

When Tocqueville or other "foreign traveler" writers or social scientists have used the term "exceptional" to describe the United States, they have not meant, as some critics of the concept assume, that America is better than other countries or has a superior culture. Rather, they have simply been suggesting that it is qualitatively different, that it is an outlier. Exceptionalism is a double-edged concept. As I shall elaborate, we are the worst as well as the best, depending on which quality is being addressed.

The United States is exceptional in starting from a revolutionary event, in being "the first new nation," the first colony, other than Iceland, to become independent. It has defined its *raison d'être* ideologically. As historian Richard Hofstadter has noted, "It has been our fate as a nation not to have ideologies, but to be one." In saying this, Hofstadter reiterated Ralph Waldo Emerson and Abraham Lincoln's emphases on the country's "political religion," alluding in effect to the former's statement that becoming American was a religious, that is, I ideological act. The ex-Soviet Union apart, other countries define themselves by a common history as birthright communities, not by ideology.

The American Creed can be described in five terms: liberty, egalitarianism, individualism, populism, and laissez-faire. Egalitarianism, in its American meaning, as Tocqueville emphasized, involves equality of opportunity and respect, not of result or condition. These values reflect the absence of feudal structures, monarchies and aristocracies. As a new society, the country lacked the emphasis on social hierarchy and status differences characteristic of postfeudal and monarchical cultures. Postfeudal societies have resulted in systems in which awareness of class divisions and respect for the state have remained important, or at least much more important than in the United States. European countries, Canada, and Japan have placed greater emphasis on obedience to political authority and on deference to superiors.

Tocqueville noted, and contemporary survey data document quantitatively, that the United States has been the most religious country in Christendom. It has exhibited greater acceptance of biblical beliefs—and higher levels of church attendance than elsewhere, with the possible exception of a few Catholic countries, such as Poland and Ireland, where nationalism and religion have been interwoven. The American religious pattern, as Tocqueville emphasized in seeking to account for American individualism, is voluntary, in other words, not state-supported. All denominations must raise their own funds, engaging in a constant struggle to retain or expand the number of their adherents if they are to survive and grow. This task is not incumbent upon state-financed denominations.

The United States, as elaborated in chapter Two, is the only country where most church-goers adhere to *sects,* mainly the Methodists and Baptists, but also hundreds of others. Elsewhere in Christendom the Anglican, Catholic, Lutheran, and Orthodox *churches* domi-nate. The churches are hierarchical in structure and membership is secured by birthright. Parishioners are expected to follow the lead of their priests and bishops. Sects, by contrast, are predominantly congregational; each local unit adheres voluntarily, while the youth are asked to make a religious commitment only upon reaching the age of decision. Churches outside of the United States historically have been linked to the state; their clergy are paid by public authorities, their hierarchy is formally appointed or confirmed by the government, and their schools are subsidized by taxes.

American Protestant sectarianism has both reinforced and been strengthened by social and political individualism. The sectarian is expected to follow a moral code, as determined by his/her own sense of rectitude, reflecting a personal relationship with God, and in many cases an interpretation of biblical truth, one not mediated by bishops or determined by the state. The American sects assume the perfectibility of human nature and have produced a moralistic people. Countries dominated by churches which view human institutions as corrupt are much less moralistic. The churches stress inherent sinfulness, human weakness, and do not hold individuals or nations up to the same standards as do the sectarians who are more bitter about code violations.

The strength of sectarian values and their implications for the political process may be seen in reactions to the supreme test of citizenship and adherence to the national will, war. State churches have not only legitimated government, for example, the divine role of kings; they have invariably approved of the wars their nations have engaged in, and have called on people to serve and obey. And the citizens have done so, unless and until it becomes clear their country is being defeated. Americans, however, have been different. A major anti-war movement sprang up in every conflict in which the United States has been involved, with the notable exception of World War II, which for the country began with an attack. Americans have put primacy not to "my country right or wrong," but rather to "obedience to my conscience." Hence, those who opposed going to war before it was declared continued to be against it after Congress voted for war.

Protestant-inspired moralism not only has affected opposition to wars, it has determined the American style in foreign relations generally, including the ways we go to war. Support for a war is as moralistic as resistance to it. To endorse a war and call on people to kill others and die for the country, Americans must define their role in a conflict as being on God's side against Satan—for morality, against evil. The United States primarily goes to war against evil, not, in its self-perception, to defend material interests. And comparative public opinion data reveal that Americans are more patriotic ("proud to be an American") and more willing to fight if their country goes to war than citizens of the thirty or so other countries polled by Gallup.

The emphasis in the American value system, in the American Creed, has been on the individual. Citizens have been expected to demand and protect their rights on a personal basis. The exceptional focus on law here as compared to Europe, derived from the Constitution and the Bill of Rights, has stressed rights against the state and other powers. America began and continues as the most anti-statist, legalistic, and rights-oriented nation.

The American Constitution intensifies the commitment to individualism and concern for the protection of rights through legal actions. The American Bill of Rights, designed to protect the citizenry against the abuse of power by government, has produced excessive litigiousness. It has fostered the propensity of Americans to go to court not only against the government, but against each other. The rights of minorities, blacks and others, women, even of animals and plants, have grown extensively since World War II through legal action.

The American disdain of authority, for conforming to the rules laid down by the state, has been related by some observers to other unique American traits, such as the highest crime rate, as well as the lowest level of voting participation, in the developed world. Basically, the American revolutionary libertarian tradition does not encourage obedience to the state and the law. This point may be illustrated by examining the results when the American and Canadian governments tried to change the system of measurements and weights to metric from the ancient and less logical system of miles and inches, pounds and ounces. A quarter century ago, both countries told their citizens that in fifteen years, they must use only metric measurements, but that both systems could be used until a given date. The Canadians, whose Tory-monarchical history and structures have made for much greater respect for and reliance on the state, and who have lower per capita crime, deviance, and litigiousness rates than Americans, conformed to the decision of their leaders and now follow the metric system, as anyone who has driven in Canada is aware. Americans ignored the new policy, and their highway signs still refer to miles, weights are in pounds and ounces, and temperature readings are in Fahrenheit.

An emphasis on group characteristics, the perception of status in collectivity terms, necessarily encourages group solutions. In Europe, the emphasis on explicit social classes in postfeudal societies promoted class-consciousness on the part of the lower strata and to some extent *noblesse oblige* by the privileged. The politics of these countries, some led by Tories such as Disraeli and Bismarck, and later by the lower-class-based, social democratic left, favored policies designed to help the less affluent by means of state solutions such as welfare, public housing, public employment, and medical care. Americans, on the other hand, have placed greater stress on opening the door to individual mobility and personal achievement through heavy investment in mass education.

The cross-national differences are striking. This country has led the world by far in the proportion of people completing different levels of mass education from early in the nineteenth century, first for elementary and high schools, later for colleges and graduate institutions. While America has long predominated in the ratio of those of college and university age attending or completing tertiary education, the numbers and proportions involved have been massive since World War II. A report on the proportion of 20- to 24-year-olds in higher education, as of 1994, indicates that it is almost double, 59 percent, in the United States to that in most affluent European countries and Japan: the Netherlands (33%), Belgium (32%), Spain (32%), France (30%), Germany (30%), Japan (30%), and Austria (29%). And America spends a greater proportion of its gross domestic product (GDP) on education, 7.0 percent, than does the European Union, 5.3 percent, or Japan, 5.0 percent.

Conversely, European countries have devoted a much larger share of their GNP, of their public funds, to bettering the living conditions of their working classes and the less privileged generally. The European social democrats have had frequent opportunities to hold office since the 1930s. To transform the situation of the working class, they have emphasized group improvement policies, such as public housing, family allowances and state medicine. Until recently, however, they preserved a class-segregated educational system with elite high schools and failed to focus on the expansion of university education.

American values were modified sharply by forces stemming from the Great Depression and World War II. These led to a much greater reliance on the state and acceptance of welfare and planning policies, the growth of trade unions and of class divisions in voting. While these changes continue to differentiate the contemporary United States from the pre-Depression era, the prosperous conditions which characterized most of the postwar period led the population to revert in some part to the values of the founders, especially distrust of a strong state. Support for diverse welfare entitlement policies has declined; trade union membership has dropped considerably, from a third to a sixth of the employed labor force; and class-linked electoral patterns have fallen off. Americans remain much more individualistic, meritocratic-oriented, and anti-statist than peoples elsewhere. Hence, the values which form the context for public policy are quite different from those in other developed countries, as the results of the 1994 congressional elections demonstrated.

These differences can be elaborated by considering the variations between the American Constitution and those of "most other liberal democracies ... [which contain] language establishing affirmative welfare rights or obligations." Some writers explain the difference by the fact that except for the American, almost all other constitutions were drawn up since World War II and, therefore, reflect a commitment to the welfare state, to upgrading the bottom level. But as Mary Ann Glendon has emphasized,

> The differences long predate the postwar era. They are legal manifestations of divergent, and deeply rooted, cultural attitudes toward the state and its functions. Historically, even eighteenth- and nineteenth-century continental European constitutions and codes acknowledged state obligations to provide food, work, and financial aid to persons in need. And continental Europeans today, whether of the right or the left, are much more likely than Americans to assume that governments

have affirmative duties. ... By contrast, it is almost obligatory for American politicians of both the right and the left to profess mistrust of government.

In much of the writing on the subject, American exceptionalism is defined by the absence of a significant socialist movement in the United States. This again is a comparative generalization, emphasizing that socialist parties and movements have been weaker in the United States than anywhere else in the industrialized world, and also that the membership of trade unions has been proportionately smaller than in other countries. Analysts have linked those facts to the nature of the cjass system as well as to attitudes toward the state. Where workers are led by the social structure to think in fixed class terms, as they are in postfeudal societies, they have been more likely to support socialist or labor parties or join unions. But class has been a theoretical construct in America. The weakness of socialism is undoubtedly also related te the lower legitimacy Americans grant to state intervention and state authority. I discuss these matters in chapter Three, which deals with trade unions and socialism.

Courts and the Political Process: Jack W. Peltason's Contributions to Political Science

By Robert A. Kagan

Political events have a disconcerting habit of outflanking political scientists' theories. We often seem like a team of near-sighted detectives, stooping to search for clues concerning an unsolved mystery, oblivious to a crime wave that is breaking behind our backs, transforming the political landscape. Thus, when I recently set out to re-read Jack Peltason's *Federal Courts in the Political Process*, published in 1955, I half expected to encounter a kind of time capsule, a description of a judicial system far removed from the contemporary hyperactive legal scene. Since 1955, American legislatures and courts have become immensely more ambitious. Law now penetrates more deeply into society, covering problems that rarely surfaced in Eisenhower-era courts, from medical malpractice and sexual harassment to leaking underground storage tanks, abortion rights, and the demarcation of electoral districts. In consequence, judicial politics has become a far more intense, higher-stakes, and controversial arena.

In 1955, except for a handful of southern desegregation cases, the decisions of American school administrators and police officers rarely were successfully challenged in court. By the 1970s, in contrast, judges were micromanaging school bus routes, reshaping state prison systems, and forging a constitutional code of evidence-gathering for hundreds of municipal police departments. Between 1960 and 1980, civil rights cases against government in federal courts increased from 280 a year to about 27,000.[1]

In 1955, courts were so deferential to governmental agencies that administrative law was the dullest subject in law school. By the early 1980s, in contrast, more than 80 percent of

---

1   Peter Schuck, *Suing Government: Citizen Remedies for Official Wrongs* (Princeton: Yale University Press, 1983), 199–202. In the same period, federal court appellate cases involving constitutional issues grew sevenfold. Robert A. Kagan, "Constitutional Litigation in the United States," in *Constitutional Courts in Comparison*, ed. R. Rogowski and T. Gawron (Gummersbach, Germany: Theodor Heuss Academie, 1987).

Robert Kagan, Courts and the Political Process: Jack W. Peltason's Contributions to Political Science, pp. 19-40. Copyright © 1996 by Berkeley Public Policy Press. Reprinted with permission.

the Environmental Protection Agency's new regulations were being challenged in court,[2] as was virtually every U.S. Forest Service management plan,[3] every Department of Interior lease for offshore petroleum exploration,[4] and every new federal motor vehicle safety regulation.[5]

By the 1980s and '90s, the fates of pregnant young women and their embryos hinged on year-to-year changes in the composition of the U.S. Supreme Court and the justices' attitudes about constitutional protection for abortion rights. In contrast to the 1950s, therefore, virtually every contemporary presidential nomination to the Supreme Court threatens to unleash a high-visibility partisan battle in the Senate. Changes in tort law wrought by state judges in the 1960s and '70s now produce intense interest-group clashes in state legislatures and in Congress.

Consequently, as I re-read Peltason's *Federal Courts* and his 1961 book on the southern desegregation cases, *Fifty-Eight Lonely Men,* my pencil was poised to note all the points at which his analysis had been swamped by the subsequent flood of legal activism. The book's margins, however, remained unmarked. My pencil stirred not to underline anachronisms but to copy insightful aphorisms, to record points that abet my current research, and to designate the chapters I intend to assign in my next graduate seminar. In short, Peltason's analytic apparatus is so well constructed that it still works beautifully, even though the American judicial machinery has been revved up to gear-rattling RPMs.

Peltason on American Judicial Politics

Peltason's perspective on judicial politics remains relevant because he saw courts as part of a pluralistic political process, interacting with nationwide and local political currents and with interest group activity. Both "the law" and courts are seen as politically responsive, shaped by the dash of interests, both material and ideal. But the courts, in turn, influence the balance of political power. As Peltason put it, judicial opinions—whether they are made "in accordance with law" or as a matter of judicial discretion, whether they overrule or defer to the legislature—necessarily advance certain interests and values, while subordinating others. Hence judges unavoidably participate in the struggle among political interests, "not as a matter of choice but of function."[6]

---

2   Laurence Suskind and Gerald McMahon, "The Theory and Practice of Negotiated Rulemaking," *Yale J. on Regulation* 3 (1985): 133,134.

3   The Forest Service: Tune for a Little Perestroika," *The Economist* (March 10, 1990): 28.

4   Charles Lester, "The Search for Dialogue in the Administrative State: The Politics, Policy, and Law of Offshore Oil Development," Ph.D. dissertation, University of California, Berkeley, 1991.

5   Jerry Mashaw and Daniel Harfst, *The Struggle for Auto Safety* (Cambridge: Harvard University Press, 1991).

6   Jack W. Peltason, *Federal Courts in the Political Process* (New York: Random House, 1955), 3–5.

At the same time, Peltason rightly insisted, the political impact of judicial decisions is always contingent. Because the American judiciary is unusually decentralized and politically responsive, the meaning and impact of a judicial opinion is neither self-evident nor fixed. Judicial decisions are subject to reinterpretation by other judges ("A Supreme Court decision," Peltason wrote, "is what the subordinate judges who apply it say it is"[7]), and by legal academics ("The law reviews published by law schools... do for judicial decisions what the drama critics' reviews do for a Broadway play"[8]).

Even more importantly, Peltason showed, laws and judicial decisions are energized or enervated, rendered potent or irrelevant, by subsequent interest group activity, by the balance of litigational resources among competing interests, and by the attitudes and responses of other political officials. Thus in 1960—six years after *Brown v. Bd. of Education*—not a single school desegregation suit had been filed in all of Mississippi.[9] Die-hard segregationists who bombed and attacked black Mississippi civil rights leaders literally got away with murder. Mississippi courts locked up as insane a black student who tried to enroll in the University of Mississippi.[10] Throughout the South, Peltason noted, *Brown's* impact was limited because the NAACP, which employed the handful of lawyers willing to enforce the decision, was outmanned in the courts and distracted by state legislatures' and county prosecutors' efforts to put the NAACP out of business.[11] Thus, Peltason was led to conclude, pushing the legal realists' aphorism a step further, that in the United States "The constitution... is what the judges say it is only when the judges represent the dominant interest within the community."[12]

Yet Peltason does not simplistically reduce judicial politics to play of interest-group power alone. In his view, ideas do matter in politics, and the law embodies ideas. As he emphasized in *Fifty-Eight Lonely Men,* judicial opinions, depending on how they are crafted, can either stiffen the backbone of lower court judges or leave them vulnerable to local political pressures.[13] And on occasion, "a judicial opinion is to interest-promotion what a movie star's endorsement is to a cigarette's sales."[14] Legal ideas and pronouncements, in short, can be mobilized to make some changes in the balance of power.

---

7   *Id.,* at 14.

8   *Id.,* at 27.

9   Jack W. Peltason, *Fifty-Eight Lonely Men: Southern Federal Judges and School Desegregation* (New York: Harcourt, Brace & World, 1961), 58.

10   *Id.,* at 58–59.

11   *Id.,* at 64,76.

12   *Id.,* at 55.

13   Southern federal district court judges, Peltason observed, will act forcefully to order desegregation when they receive clear mandates from the Supreme Court, even if the judge is "personally devoted to segregation." *Fifty-Eight Lonely Men*, 246. Thus, he pointed out, it was the "ambiguity of the Supreme Court's mandate" in Brown *II* that "enabled the segregation-minded judges to set the pace; it compounds the task of those judges who are willing to act more boldly." *Id.,* at 57.

14   *Federal Courts*, 11.

Peltason's emphasis on the political contingency of judicial decisions and their consequences has been reiterated in subsequent studies that describe how judicial decisions, in interaction with other branches of government, affect the evolution of policy. I think in this regard of William K. Muir, Jr., *Law and Attitude Change* (1973); Gerald Rosenberg, *The Hollow Hope: Can Courts Bring About Social Change?* (1991); R. Shep Melnick, *Between the Lines: Interpreting Welfare Rights;* Michael McCann, *Rights at Work: Pay Equity Reform and the Politics of Legal Mobilization* (1994); Robert A. Katzmann, *Institutional Disability: The Saga of Transportation Policy for the Disabled* (1986); Robert Mnookin, ed., *In The Interests of Children: Advocacy, Law Reform and Public Policy* (1985); Nelson W. Polsby, ed., *Reapportionment in the 1970s* (1971); David Kirp, John Dwyer, and Larry Rosenthal, *Our Town: Race, Housing, and the Soul of Suburbia* (1996); and Malcolm Feeley and Edward Rubin, *Judicial Policy Making: Courts and Prison Conditions Litigation* (forthcoming). These studies of judicial politics in an era of heightened activism and conflict mesh perfectly with the basic axioms of Peltason's work.

ON THE INTENSIFICATION OF AMERICAN JUDICIAL POLITICS

Peltason's interest-group pluralism perspective on judicial politics also provides a key to a set of questions that drives my current research concerning the sources and consequences of what I have come to call "adversarial legalism."

Adversarial Legalism

In recent years, a number of political scientists and legal scholars have conducted careful studies that compare a specific area of American law and policy implementation with parallel legal controls in other economically advanced democracies. The case studies cover a range of fields, from control of crime to regulation of dangerous products, unfair business practices, environmental degradation, workplace safety, nursing home care, and medical malpractice.[15] Typically,

---

15   See, for example, Joseph Badaracco, *Loading the Dice: A Five Country Study of Vinyl Chloride Regulation* (Boston: Harvard Business School Press, 1985); David Bayley, *Forces of Order: Police Behavior in Japan and the United States* (Berkeley: University of California Press, 1976); John Braithwaite, *To Punish or Persuade: Enforcement of Coal Mine Safety* (Albany: SUNY Press, 1985); P. Day and R. Klein, "The Regulation of Nursing Homes: A Comparative Perspective," *The Milbank Quarterly* 65 (1987): 303; R. Brickman, S. Jasanoff and T. Ilgen, *Controlling Chemicals: The Politics of Regulation in Europe and the United States* (Ithaca: Cornell University Press, 1985); Sheila Josanoff, *Risk Management and Political Culture* (New York: Russell Sage Foundation, 1986); Steven Kelman, *Regulating America, Regulating Sweden: A Comparative Study of Occupational Safety and Health Policy* (Cambridge, Mass.: MIT Press, 1981); Lennart J. Lundqvist, *The Hare and The Tortoise: Clean Air Policies in the United States*

the studies report only minor *substantive* differences in basic legal norms and policies. On the other hand, American governmental and legal *style*—its *method* of policy-formulation, implementation, and dispute resolution—repeatedly is found to be virtually unique, characterized by

(1) more complex, detailed bodies of legal rules;

(2) more formal, adversarial procedures for resolving political and scientific disputes;

(3) more costly, litigant-dominated forms of legal contestation;

(4) more punitive legal sanctions;

(5) more frequent judicial intervention into administrative decision making;

(6) more political controversy about (and more frequent change of) legal rules and institutions; and

(7) more legal uncertainty, malleability, and unpredictability.

I attempt to summarize this cluster of legal propensities in the concept *adversarial legalism*.[16]

Within the United States, as noted at the outset of this essay, adversarial legalism has *increased* in recent decades. Opponents of economic development projects and shifts in government policy more often seek to block those changes in court. National expenditures have increased dramatically—much more rapidly than GNP—for legal services[17] and liability insurance. Government agencies and business firms, as well as doctors and hospitals, spend far more time and money on "defensive medicine"—costly precautions taken simply to avoid being sued. For political scientists, two questions arise:

(1) Why is adversarial legalism more intense and prevalent in the United States than in other economically advanced democracies?

(2) Why has American "adversarial legalism" increased, even as it is decried by political leaders and by a popular culture that revels in disparaging lawyer jokes?

---

and Sweden (Ann Arbor: University of Michigan Press, 1980); Gary Schwartz, "Product Liability and Medical Malpractice in Comparative Context," in *The Liability Maze*, ed. P. Huber and R. Litan (Washington, D.C.: Brookings Inst., 1991); Takao Tanase, "The Management of Disputes: Automobile Accident Compensation in Japan," Law & Society Rev. 24 (1990): 651; David Vogel, *National Styles of Regulation: Environmental Policy in Great Britain and the United States* (Ithaca: Cornell University Press, 1986); Harvey Teff, "Drug Approval in England and the United States," *Am. J. Comp. Law* 33 (1985): 567.

16   See Robert A. Kagan, "Adversarial Legalism and American Government," *J. Policy Analysis & Management* 10 (1991): 309; and in Marc K. Landy and Martin A. Levin, eds. *The New Politics of Public Policy* (Baltimore: Johns Hopkins Press, 1995).

17   Between 1960 and 1987, expenditures on lawyers in the United States grew sixfold, from $9 billion annually to $54 billion (in constant 1983 dollars), almost tripling the share of GNP consumed by legal services. R. Sander and E. D. Williams, "Why Are There So Many Lawyers? Perspectives on a Turbulent Market," *Law & Social Inquiry* 14 (1989): 431,434–35.

Peltason's political perspective points us toward the answers by reminding us that legal systems are far from autonomous. Judicial activity reflects democratic opinion and interest group pressures. Hence if adversarial legalism is more prevalent in the United States than elsewhere, and if it has increased, then that suggests that other political actors strongly supported those changes; otherwise, the judges could not get away with it. Adversarial legalism, in short, is politically constructed.

Some of that political construction, Peltason would remind us, was done in the late 18th and the 19th century. American adversarial legalism is rooted in a political culture and constitutional structure that from the nation's birth has relied on *judicially enforceable* constitutional restrictions and individual rights to constrain governmental authority. This set of arrangements invited Americans, as De Tocqueville observed, to continue politically controversial battles by means of litigation, and it propelled courts into a policymaking role.

Moreover, in the United States, both state and national bureaucracies were slow to develop, at least by European standards; hence judges, using inherited common law powers, were encouraged to take a policymaking role in the field of economic relationships."[18] Mistrustful of unresponsive legal elites, 19th century Americans insisted on political methods of selecting judges. In contrast to the professionally selected, bureaucratic, and rule-oriented judiciaries of European countries, the American bench has always been organizationally decentralized, staffed by former political activists, and highly pragmatic or policy-oriented in its approach to law. Hence American lawyers and litigants, compared to their European counterparts, are not at all shy about asking *judges* to make new policy.[19]

On the other hand, American political movements periodically have *restricted* the realm of judicial policymaking and political action. In reaction to decades of hostility from a conservative judiciary,[20] organized labor successfully lobbied Congress in the 1930s to limit judicial injunctions against strikes and to shift legal disputes about unfair labor practices from the courts into an administrative tribunal, the National Labor Relations Board. New Dealers also appointed judges who formulated doctrines that demanded judicial deference to legislative and administrative decisions—thereby squelching litigation by business interests who opposed expansion of federal regulation and taxation.

---

18   Stephen Skowronek, *Building a New American State* (New York: Cambridge University Press, 1982); Morton Horwitz, *The Transformation of American Law, 1780–1860* (Cambridge: Harvard University Press, 1977); Robert A. Kagan, " Do Lawyers Came Adversarial Legalism?" *Law dc Social Inquiry* 19 (1994): 1–62.

19   P. S. Atiyah and Robert Summers, *Form and Substance in Anglo-American Law: A Comparative Study of Legal Reasoning, Legal Theory, and Legal Institutions* (Oxford; Clarendon Press, 1987).

20   William Forbath, "Courts, Constitutions, and Labor Politics in England and America: A Study of the Constitutive Power of Law," *Law & Social Inquiry* 16 (1991): 1–34.

In sum, adversarial legalism always has opponents as well as advocates. Adversarial legalism is not the inevitable companion of rising standards of living, environmentalism, demands for racial and gender equality, or other basic trends: in European democracies, post-World War II regulatory, welfare state, and antidiscrimination programs, much like the American New Deal, relegated courts to a peripheral role in governance.

Consequently, to understand the striking growth of American adversarial legalism since the mid-1960s, it is important, following Peltason, to examine *contemporary* interest group dynamics. It is equally important to examine, I would argue, the political ideas and the governmental structures that energize and channel interest group effort.

POLITICAL CULTURE, POLITICAL STRUCTURE, AND ADVERSARIAL LEGALISM.

At the broadest level of analysis, increases in adversarial legalism can be viewed as arising from a fundamental tension in contemporary American politics:

- a *political culture* that demands comprehensive governmental protections from harm, injustice, and environmental dangers, and hence a more powerful, activist government; and
- a *set of governmental structures* based on *mistrust* of concentrated power, and hence that limit and fragment political and governmental authority.

Adversarial legalism—privately-initiated lawsuits and formal legal procedures—provides a mechanism through which interest groups can obtain and implement ambitious public policies in a "weak," structurally fragmented state.

Consider, for example, the American civil rights movement, a major wellspring of contemporary adversarial legalism. The NAACP's emphasis on *litigation*, as described by Peltason in *Fifty-Eight Lonely Men*, represented an important turn of events in American judicial politics. Historically, when American interest groups had pressed their political agendas in the courts, they asked judges to *block* political and social change. Thus in the 19th and the first third of the 20th century, business interests called upon the courts to nullify debtor-relief laws, protective labor legislation, and governmental regulations of commerce. Constitutional rights were invoked as shields against legislative policymaking. The civil rights movement, in contrast, wanted to use the Constitution as a sword, coercing government to take affirmative action against deeply entrenched discriminatory practices and to create new desegregated institutional arrangements.

Why did civil rights leaders have any reason to believe that the courts would take such a radical step? Developments in national *political culture* offered some hope. Partly because of the claims to democratic virtue engendered by the Cold War, American national political elites had become acutely sensitive to the inescapable contradiction between the egalitarian

"American creed" and the ugly reality of southern *apartheid*,[21] On the other hand, inherited *political structures*—federalism, fragmentation of governmental powers, relatively noncohesive national political parties—prevented the national political elite from outlawing school segregation. Repeatedly, southern Democrats in the Senate were able to block effective congressional civil rights legislation.

This deadlock enabled civil rights leaders to present federal judges with a powerful moral argument: if legislatures, national and state, fail to act against a nationally recognized injustice, then it is incumbent on the courts to step into the breach. Such an argument probably would not have swayed an apolitical judiciary, such as Great Britain's or France's, committed to legal formality and disinclined to engage in social problem-solving. But the American judiciary, staffed with ex-politicians, was open to arguments based on substantive justice. (When lawyers cited an ostensibly dispositive legal precedent, Chief Justice Earl Warren was said to have responded, "Yes, but is it *fair?*") Thus in 1954, the Supreme Court, focusing on the adverse social consequences of segregation, held that legally segregated schools violated the Equal Protection Clause. Moreover, because the Court's antisegregation policy was articulated as an individual, judicially enforceable constitutional right, litigation became a primary mode of policy implementation.

Building on the example of *Brown v. Board of Education,* political reformers in other fields invoked the formula for change employed in the school desegregation cases:

(a) widely publicized injustice +

(b) structural impediments (federalism and other constitutional constraints on congressional action) =

(c) organized advocacy-group demands for judicial creation of new constitutional rights +

(d) adversarial legalism as a primary mode of policy formulation and implementation.

For example, in the 1960s reformers pointed to oppressive southern state prisons, retrograde mental institutions, and abusive practices by local police departments. Their legal arguments were diverse, but their basic message was similar: if, in the face of shocking patterns of injustice, local governments refused to act, and Congress (because of the constraints of federalism) could not act, courts were obliged to take action.

In the 1960s and early 1970s, many federal judges, backed by the Warren Court, responded. They articulated new constitutional rights, issued reform orders to state legislatures, prisons, and mental institutions, and rescribed nationwide rules of criminal procedure. As in the desegregation cases, because the judges could not mandate the creation of new federal bureaucracies to implement the new rights, they sought to mobilize lawyers to do the job by means of litigation. Thus in *Gideon v. Wainwright* (1963), the Supreme Court required states

---

21   Mary Dudziak, "Desegregation as a Cold War Imperative," *Stanford L. Rev.* 41 (1988): 61; Gerald Rosenberg, *The Hollow Hope: Can Courts Bring About (Social Change?* (Chicago: University of Chicago Press, 1991), 162–69.

to give indigent defendants free defense lawyers, thereby mandating a far-flung, county-level, adversarial enforcement mechanism for the Court's new criminal procedure norms.

Put another way, the civil rights, prison reform, and criminal justice reform movements, by persuading judges to pursue institutional change by establishing legally actionable individual rights, expanded an almost uniquely American mode of governance—*private enforcement of public law by means of litigation.*

How did the judges get away with these far-reaching assertions of power? Remember that in Peltason's model of judicial politics, judges need the backing, or at least the acquiescence, of other political elites. In fact, the judge-ordered institutional reforms sometimes met with resistance. Some state governors and legislators dragged their feet in funding court-ordered prison reform. Police departments sometimes complied only superficially with the confusing constitutional rules governing searches and interrogations.

But if adversarial legalism provided a less than ideal method of reforming state and local prisons, police departments, and school systems, it remained a viable reform strategy, and indeed became even more prevalent For judicially ordered reforms enjoyed at least adequate support among *national* political and legal elites. To many political leaders in Washington, publicized revelations of police brutality and atrocious conditions in state mental hospitals were a source of national embarrassment Respected and well-organized advocacy groups, such as the American Civil Liberties Union, once armed with the new constitutional doctrines, systematically challenged noncompliant state and local decisions in federal court

Support for Warren Court mandates, of course, was far from unanimous. In 1968, presidential candidate Richard Nixon promised to appoint judges who would be "strict constructionists" and tough on crime. But constitutional doctrines are not easy to reverse when political opinion is divided. Democratic Congresses were unwilling to vote for constitutional amendments or statutes designed to reverse the Warren Court's "due process revolution." The Burger Court, bolstered by Nixon appointees, did not have enough votes to reverse Wairen Court doctrines and only whittled away at their edges. Courthouse doors thus remained open, and the judiciary remained deeply involved, through constitutional interpretation, in making policy concerning the death penalty, criminal procedure, prison crowding, treatment of the mentally ill, welfare administration, school busing, legislative district lines, and other aspects of state and local governance.

FRAGMENTED GOVERNMENT AND LEGISLATIVELY MANDATED ADVERSARIAL LEGALISM

Judge-made constitutional rulings were only one source of the expansion of adversarial legalism. Congress was equally if not more eager to promote it, for adversarial legalism promised to solve, or at least to address, a fundamental governmental problem: how to implement socially transformative legislation in a political system in which governmental authority is extremely fragmented.

During the late 1960s and 1970s, environmentalists, feminists, and advocates for consumers, the handicapped, the poor, and the aged turned not only to the courts (arguing for constitutional change) but also to Congress. Their causes were politically popular; Congress enacted the National Environmental Protection Act (1969) by a unanimous vote, the far-reaching Clean Air Act of 1970 almost unanimously.[22] On the other hand, Congress was reluctant—for political, fiscal, and constitutional reasons—to create huge federal bureaucracies to implement new nationwide regulatory programs. In many cases, primary responsibility for implementation, therefore, was assigned to state and local governmental officials.

But if governmental authority to enforce the new federal norms was to be parceled out to states and cities, how could reformers and their congressional allies be sure that the new federal norms would be energetically implemented? The answer was adversarial legalism. Congress cave private citizens and advocacy groups legal rights to appoint themselves "private attorneys general"—that is, to bring lawsuits against state and local governments for half-hearted implementation of federal laws, and in some cases to sue businesses directly for regulatory violations. Congress provided incentives, too: by 1990 Congress had enacted more than 150 one-way, fee-shifting statutes, under which plaintiffs who prevail, in whole or in part, can recover lawyers' fees from governmental and corporate defendants (although victorious defendants get no such recovery).[23]

The "private attorney general" strategy fit the fragmented American political structure. In European polities, hierarchically organized national bureaucracies are designed to ensure that local officials remain accountable to national policies. Under adversarial legalism, a decentralized, ideologically motivated array of private advocacy groups and lawyers, given access to the courts, could fulfill the accountability function.

Congress also extended the "private attorney general" concept to police the federal bureaucracy. Analyzing the public interest movement of the 1960s and 1970s, Michael McCann argues that the reformers advocated a "judicial model of democracy."[24] They wanted to expand the regulatory power of the federal government. But after 1968, they were

---

22 "David Vogel, *Fluctuating Fortunes: The Political Power of Business in America* (New York: Basic Books, 1989), Ch. 3–4.

23 R. Shep Melnick, "Separation of Powers and the Strategy of Rights," in *The New Politics of Public Policy,* ed. Marc Landy and Marin Levin (Baltimore: Johns Hopkins Press, 1995), 44; Michael Greve, "Environmentalism and Bounty Hunting," *The Public Interest* 97 (1989): 15; Karen O'Connor and Lee Epstein, "Bridging the Gap Between Congress and the Supreme Court: Interest Groups and the Erosion of the American Rule Governing Awards of Attorneys' Fees," *Western Pol. Q.* 28 (1985): 238,239–40.

24 Michael McCann, *Taking Reform Seriously: Perspectives on Public Interest Liberalism* (Ithaca: Cornell University Press, 1986), 114. For a similar account from a "public choice" perspective, see Terry Moe, "The Politics of The Bureaucratic State," in *Can the Government Govern?* ed. John Chubb and Paul Peterson (Washington, D.C.: Brookings, 1989).

concerned that federal agencies, headed by President Nixon's Republican appointees, would be subverted by regulated businesses and tight-fisted budget office officials. The reformers' solution was to demand legal rights (1) to haul federal bureaucrats into court, where they could be ordered to adhere to the original statutory intent, and (2) to participate in agency-policymaking procedures, so that public interest lawyers could challenge and ask courts to review any signs of "capture" by the regulated industry.

Just as adversarial legalism appealed to reform interests, it had special appeal to congressional Democrats in the era of "divided government" that began with the Nixon presidency in 1968. Adversarial legalism enabled Democratic legislators to take credit for enacting sweeping new laws, while letting advocacy groups, Republican administrators, and the courts struggle with the hard problems of detailed policy implementation. The Democratic Congresses enacted regulatory statutes containing highly ambitious deadlines for administrative implementation and private rights to challenge administrative inaction in the courts.[25]

The federal courts, in response, forged new legal doctrines designed to facilitate meaningful interest group participation in administrative policymaking and judicial review of administrative decisions. Federal agencies were compelled to develop more formal, quasi-judicial rule-making procedures and methods of demonstrating that their policies are rational.[26] Judges discerned "implied" statutory rights to sue government and to bring private enforcement actions, even when the original legislation was silent on the subject.[27] Lawsuits against government and appeals of governmental decisions, not surprisingly, increased apace.

Institutional fragmentation in Congress also encouraged adversarial legalism. By the late 1960s, congressional authority was splintered among many subcommittees, only weakly constrained by political party leaders. Statutes had to be painfully stitched together by shifting, issue-specific coalitions, gathering support only by offering attractive provisions to each stakeholder. The legislative output became more complex. Multisubject omnibus acts, impenetrable tax and pension laws, and the 400-page 1990 Clean Air Act resembled

25   *Taking Reform Seriously,* 112–13; Eugene Bardach and Robert A. Kagan, *Going By The Booh The Problem of Regulatory Unreasonableness* (Philadelphia: Temple University Press, 1982), Ch. 2; Martin Shapiro, *Who Guards the Guardians? Judicial Control of Administration* (Athens: University of Georgia Press, 1988); R. Shep Melnick, "Pollution Deadlines and the Coalition for Failure," in *Environmental Politics: Public Costs, Private Rewards,* ed. M. Greve and F. Smith (New York: Greenwood, 1992).

26   *Who Guards the Guardians?*

27   See *Suing Government, op. cit.* n. 1; Jeremy Rabkin, *Judicial Compulsions: How Public Law Distorts Public Policy* (New York: Basic Books, 1989) (implied private rights to sue Office of Civil Rights concerning enforcement priorities); Serge Taylor, *Making Bureaucracies Think: The Environmental Impact Strategy of Administrative Reform* (Palo Alto: Stanford University Press, 1984) (implied rights to sue for enforcement of the National Environmental Protection Act).

patchwork quilts, laden with soaring statements of purpose, legally contradictory provisions, and convoluted implementation plans. At their normative core, however, all too often one could find only a few vague phrases.[28] This style of legislation naturally magnified legal uncertainty, virtually demanding subsequent litigation and judicial reconstruction of congressional policy.

POLITICAL CONSERVATIVES AND ADVERSARIAL LEGALISM

Republican presidents and legislators, unable to prevent the enactment of new federal regulatory and welfare-state programs, also supported adversarial legalism as a mode of implementing those programs. Like the "public interest movement," the business community was mistrustful of new, more powerful federal agencies. Regulatory bureaucrats, they feared, would be ideological soulmates of environmental, consumer, or minority groups who were hostile to business and economic growth. Hence Republicans also fought for legislative provisions that would restrict administrative discretion. At their urging, statutes repeatedly instructed federal agencies to support their decisions with cost-benefit analyses and with scientific findings—which gave business firms considerable leverage in attacking regulatory decisions in court[29]

Similarly, although they could not block politically popular regulatory initiatives, conservatives' arguments against higher taxes and big government often were sufficient to block large increases in spending on federal bureaucracies. Thus Republicans joined Democrats in the basic compromise mentioned earlier—legislation that encourages litigation, rather than public expenditure, to accomplish collective goals. For example:

---

28   For a good example, see Melnick, "Separation of Powers and the Strategy of Rights," *op. cit.y* n. 23.

29   In some programs, demanding statutory analytic requirements enabled regulated businesses and proregulation advocacy groups to litigate administrative agencies into a state of near paralysis. See, e.g., John Dwyer, "The Pathology of Symbolic Legislation," *Ecology Law Quarterly* 17 (1990): 233–316; John Mendeloff, *The Dilemma of Rulemaking for Toxic Substances* (Cambridge, Mass.: MIT Press, 1987); Jeny Mashaw and Daniel Harfst, "Regulation and Legal Culture: The Case of Motor Vehicle Safety," *Yale J. on Regulation* 4 (1987): 257–316. At the same time, opponents of new economic and infrastructure projects could invoke noncompliance with demanding statutory analytic requirements to paralyze development activities. See Robert A. Kagan, "The Dredging Dilemma: Economic Development and Environmental Protection in Oakland Harbor," *Coastal Management* 19 (1991): 313–41.

- Rather than funding a public works approach to cleaning up old hazardous waste disposal sites, as most Western European nations do,[30] Congress's Superfimd statute encouraged a punitive and disastrously inefficient "first-let's-sue-the-polluters" approach.[31]
- Conservative senators' reluctance to fund a federal enforcement bureaucracy led liberal sponsors of the Truth-in-Lending Act to enact an enforcement system that relies on monetary incentives for private lawsuits against lenders.[32]
- In 1991, as case backlogs swelled at the pitifully understaffed offices of the Equal Employment Opportunity Commission, Congress's response was to encourage more private lawsuits to implement antidiscrimination laws: it enacted a law allowing plaintiffs to obtain higher money penalties, including punitive damages, in lawsuits against employers.[33]
- In 1992, the Bush administration supported enactment of the Americans ' with Disabilities Act, a sweeping law requiring "affirmative action" to employ and serve a wide array of handicapped individuals. The primary enforcement mechanism created by Congress was the private right to bring court suits (including suits for money damages) against noncomplying employers and operators of public accommodations—a strategy that requires few new federal bureaucrats and no new taxes.

---

30   Andrew Lohof, *The Cleanup of Inactive Hazardous Waste Sites in Selected Industrialized Countries* (Washington: American Petroleum Institute, 1991); R. Kopp, P. Portney, and D. DeWitt, *International Comparisons of Environmental Regulation* (Washington: Resources for The Future, 1990) (Discussion Paper QE90–22-REV).

31   The Comprehensive Environmental Response, Compensation and Liability Act (CERCLA) imposes absolute, joint and several, and retroactive liability for clean-up costs on any enterprise whose wastes found their way into the disposal site—regardless of the disposer's *share* of the wastes, regardless of whether it acted perfectly lawfully under the legal rules and containment practices prevailing at the time of disposal, regardless of any demonstrated current harm to human health. The "responsible parties" so designated then are entitled to sue other parties who had sent wastes to the same site in order to compel them to bear their fair share of (he cleanup costs. The result is virtually endless litigation and negotiation before the sites are contained. Marc Landy and Maty Hague, "The Coalition for Waste: Private Interests and the Superfimd," in *Environmental Politics: Public Costs, Private Rewards,* ed. M. Greve and F. Smith (New York: Greenwood, 1992); Thomas Church and Robert Nakamura, *Cleaning Up the Mess: Implementation Strategies in Supetjxmd* (Washington: Brookings, 1993).

32   Edward L. Rubin, "Legislative Methodology: Some Lessons From the Truth-in-Lending Act," *Georgetown L. Rev.* 80 (1991): 23.

33   Edward Potter and Ann Reesman, *Compensatory and Punitive Damages Under Title VII—A Foreign Perspective* (Washington, D.C.: Employment Policy Foundation, 1992). The American private litigation/high damage award enforcement mechanism, Potter and Reesman note, is not used in other economically advanced democracies.

Similarly, in contrast to the common perception that only political liberals have encouraged adversarial legalism, public interest law firms financed by political conservatives have pushed the Supreme Court to create new constitutional rights, such as protections against regulatory restrictions on (or "takings" of) private property, and Equal Protection Clause restrictions on race-based preferences in affirmative action programs. Activist Court rulings on both topics have propelled judges throughout the country into the business of adjudicating the validity of governmental "set-asides" for minority-owned (or ostensibly minority-owned) contractors and the decisions of local and regional zoning boards.

Even the conservative "tort reform movement" has basically sought to modulate adversarial legalism as a method of compensating accident victims, not to replace it In Western Europe, persons injured by motorcars, hospitals, hazardous products, and bumpy sidewalks turn first and almost exclusively to social insurance programs. Their medical bills are taken care of by governmentally funded national health care systems. Their lost earnings are taken care of by generous governmentally funded or mandated disability pay schemes. There usually is not much more to sue for. Any remaining "noneconomic damages" (punitive damages are unknown) are moderate in amount, awarded by professional judges according to clear legal rules—not by citizen juries, operating under vague rules.[34] Lawyering costs are a fraction of the huge toll imposed on American tort litigants.

For years, American scholars have argued for replacing tort lawsuits with claims against socially funded administrative agencies or with "no-fault" self-insurance plans. These schemes would compensate every injured person's basic economic losses, regardless of fault, in contrast to the present jury-centered litigation process, which veers wildly between overcompensation and undercompensation.[35] However, the American tort reform movement that began in the mid-1980s—led by physicians, product manufacturers, municipalities, and then-Vice President Dan Quayle—has not focused on supplanting the adversarial tort/jury system with no-fault insurance plans or administrative tribunals. Rather, the goal has simply been to make it harder for plaintiffs to obtain large damages (which tends to disadvantage the most severely injured accident victims), or to encourage more cases to settle. The current conservative-inspired tort reform movement would leave the basic structure of court-centered adversarial legalism intact

That is not to imply that liberal politicians have been supporters of radical tort reform. Democratic members of the relevant committees in state legislatures and in Congress generally

---

34   Gaiy Schwartz, "Product Liability and Medical Malpractice in Comparative Context," in *The Liability Maze,* ed. Peter Huber and Robert Litan (Washington, D.C.: Brookings Inst.,1991); Werner Pfenningsdorf and Daniel Gifford, *A Comparative Study of Liability Law and Compensation Schemes in Ten Countries and the United States* (Oak Brook, III.: Insurance Research Council, 1991).

35   "Stephen Sugannan, *Doing Away With Personal Injury Law: New Compensation Mechanisms for Victims, Consumers, and Business* (New York: Quorum Books, ; Jeffrey O'Connell, *The Lawsuit Lottery: Only the Lawyers Win* (Glencoe, 111.: The Free Press, 1979); Paul Weiler, *Medical Malpractice on Trial* (Cambridge, Mass.: Harvard University Press, 1991).

have been closely aligned with the American Trial Lawyers Association (ATLA) and its state affiliates. These organizations of plaintiffs' attorneys operate very aggressive, well-financed political action committees and fiercely (and quite effectively) oppose virtually any attempt to change the tort/jury/contingency fee system.[36]

LAWYERS AND ADVERSARIAL LEGALISM

Even aside from ATLA, the American legal profession has played a powerful role in the political construction of adversarial legalism. No other nation remotely approaches the array of special "cause lawyers" that currently operate in the United States, aggressively seeking to influence public policy and institutional development by means of innovative litigation. In no other country are lawyers so entrepreneurial in seeking out new kinds of business, so eager to challenge authority, so quick to propose new liability-expanding legal theories.

Aggressive lawyers have not been the *primary* cause of the expanding domain of judicial policymaking in the United States. Broader political currents and interest groups, as suggested earlier, were the sorcerers that called forth adversarial legalism—thereby generating demands for more legally trained apprentices. The sorcerers' apprentices, however, then became richer, better organized, more powerful, more energetic. Lawyers who believe in or profit from adversarial legalism acquired greater incentives and more opportunities to extend adversarial legalism further—and even to thwart the sorcerer's efforts to reign in it Organized activist lawyers' groups—such as the ACLU, lawyers for the disabled, antitobacco litigators, and so on—systematically push courts to extend the realm of adversarial legalism.[37] In addition to ATLA, specialized lawyer organizations, such as those who represent injured railroad workers or those who bring securities' class actions, regularly lobby legislatures (and mobilize campaign contributions) to block reforms that would reduce adversarial legalism.[38]

Perhaps more importantly, in the last few decades American law professors, judges, and lawyers elaborated legal theories that actively promote adversarial legalism—not as a

---

36 See P. Heymann and L. Liebman, "No Fault, No Fee: The Legal Profession and Federal No-Fault Insurance Legislation" in *The Social Responsibilities of Lawyers,* ed. Heymann and Liebman (Westbury, N.Y.: Foundation Press, 1988), 309; Robert A. Kagan, "Do Lawyers Cause Adversarial Legalism" *Law & Social Inquiry* 19 (1994): 1,53–58.

37 For descriptions of the role of activist lawyers in the expansion of adversarial legalism, see, e.g., Robert Curtis, "The Deinstitutionalization Story," *The Public Interest* 34 (Fall 1986); Robert Mnookin, ed., *In the Interests of Children: Advocacy, Law Reform and Public Policy* (New York: W. H. Freeman, 1985); R Shep Melnick, "Separation of Powers and the Strategy of Rights," *op. cit.* n. 23; Robert Katzmann, *Institutional Disability: The Saga of Transportation Policy for the Disabled* (Washington, D.C.: Brookings, 1986).

38 "Do Lawyers Cause Adversarial Legalism? *op. cit.* n. 36.

necessary evil but as a desirable mode of governance. Their heroic view of the judiciary's role in government is exemplified by Yale Law School professor Owen Fiss's passionate assertion:

> [W]hen one sees injustices that cry out for correction—as Congress did when it endorsed the concept of the private attorney general and as the Court of another era did when it sought to enhance access to the courts—the value of avoidance diminishes and the agony of judgment becomes a necessity. Someone has to confront the betrayal of our deepest ideals and be prepared to turn the world upside down to bring those ideals to fruition.[39]

The "confronters" Professor Fiss envisions, of course, are activist judges, the idealistic lawyers who bring the cases to court, and perhaps even the law professors who identify which injustices are intolerable and devise the remedial legal theories.

Fiss's view has not been uncontested in the law schools or in the judiciary. But on balance, in the last few decades American legal scholars and judges have become more supportive of an instrumental or even a political vision of law and the judicial role. In contrast to Great Britain, Atiyah and Summers observe in their excellent comparative analysis, "American law schools have been the source of the dominant general theory of law in America ... 'instrumentalism' . . . [which] conceives of law essentially as a pragmatic instrument of social improvement."[40] Hence American legal scholars tend to celebrate those American judges, who, like the Supreme Court in *Brown v. Board of Education,* feel authorized or even obligated to "do justice" when the other bodies of government have "failed" to ameliorate social injustice. The legal culture that law school professors instill in their students supports expanded access to courts, as well as political solutions that take the form of judicially enforceable individual rights. And that legal culture has penetrated the broader political culture to an extent that a politician who proposes policies that curtail adversarial legalism runs the risk of being attacked for "taking rights away" from the citizen.

THE FUTURE OF ADVERSARIAL LEGALISM

One might wonder if my account of the growth of adversarial legalism exemplifies the political scientist's near-sighted detective syndrome—an analysis of patterns that already are being superseded. For example, there are indications that Americans have lost patience with adversarial legalism. In 1995, Congress passed significant restrictions on securities litigation. In the last few years, a majority of state legislatures have passed litigation-restricting tort reform laws. The U.S. Supreme Court, the California Supreme Court, and the

39 Owen Fiss, "Against Settlement," *Yale L. J.* 93 (1984): 1073,1086–87.

40 P. S. Atiyah and Robert Summers, *Form and Substance in Anglo-American Law,* n. 19 *supra,* at 404,

D.C. Circuit Court of Appeals—among the primary architects, in the 1960s, of an activist judicial culture—now are dominated by proponents of judicial restraint, demanding greater deference to legislative and administrative decisions. Leading legal scholars seem attracted to ideals of "civic republicanism" and "dialogue" rather than unabridgeable legal rights. Many legal practitioners exalt compromise-oriented "alternative dispute resolution," not adversarial legalism.

Nevertheless, it is unlikely that adversarial legalism will be driven from the American scene. The tides of elite legal culture may ebb and flow, sometimes strongly supporting adversarial legalism, sometimes criticizing it. But deep-rooted political and legal structures—fragmentation of power in American governments and in American political parties—guarantee that, as in the United States described by Peltason 40 years ago, politics will be pervaded by the clash of interest groups, eager and able to influence the making and implementation of public policy. Recourse to courts always will be attractive not only to influential and entrepreneurial lawyers but also to a wide variety of groups—political and social underdogs, environmentalists, civil libertarians, and business interests. The American judiciary is highly political, strongly independent, decentralized, diverse, and armed with significant constitutional powers. It is structurally accessible to politically motivated groups, inclined toward legal creativity, and historically accustomed to exerting its powers. All that suggests that the political construction of adversarial legalism, as well as efforts to constrain it, will retain a prominent place on the American political agenda.

Discussion Questions

1. How does the American legal system differ from its counterparts abroad?

2. What are the advantages other legal systems? What are the disadvantages?

3. If adversarial legalism is so costly and unpredictable, what is its political appeal?

PART III
Law, Courts, and U.S. Policymaking

T he third part of the reader focuses on the role of law and courts in several policy areas. The readings are a bit more challenging but reinforce familiar themes.

A. Coping with Modern Technology

Regulating Hazards and the Environment

T o place the American legal system into sharper focus, it is useful to consider historical and comparative perspectives. This section of the reader examines how the American legal system has changed over time, and how it differs from those in other industrialized democracies.

ADDITIONAL RECOMMENDED MATERIALS:

Seymour Martin Lipset, *American Exceptionalism* (1996), pp. 17-23

Robert Kagan, *Adversarial Legalism: The American Way of Law* (2001), pp. 6-14

Thomas F. Burke, Lawyers, *Litigation and Legal Rights: The Battle over Litigation in American Society* (2002)

Sean Farhang, *The Litigation State* (2010)

Courts and Agencies

R. Shep Meinick

We often think of a lawsuit as a case pitting one private individual or group against another. Most of the important federal court decisions over the past half century, though, have come in cases that revolve around the authority, duties, and performance of public bureaucracies. Ever since *Brown v. Board of Education* in 1954, federal courts have been deeply involved in evaluating the practices of school systems throughout the nation. One of the most important consequences of the Warren Court's incorporation of the Bill of Rights into the Fourteenth Amendment was that federal judges became enmeshed in the difficult job of supervising the behavior of thousands of police officers and public prosecutors. Since the early 1970s, federal courts have restructured scores of state prisons, housing authorities, institutions for the mentally ill, and social service agencies. At about the same time federal judges intensified their oversight of old regulatory agencies such as the Federal Communications Commission (FCC) and the Atomic Energy Commission (AEC); started to give a "hard look" at the thousands of rules issued by new "social regulation" agencies such as the Environmental Protection Agency (EPA), the Occupational Safety and Health Administration (OSHA), and the Equal Economic Opportunity Commission (EEOC); demanded that development and natural resources bureaucracies such as the Corps of Engineers, the Federal Highway Administration, and the Forest Service pay more attention to environmental values; and scrutinized the procedures and policies of state and federal agencies that distribute health and welfare benefits. Today federal judges spend much of their time regulating the behavior of government bureaucrats, and virtually all government agencies must deal with courts on a regular basis.

These extensive judicial efforts to supervise, reform, and second-guess administrative agencies are the result of three major features of American politics since the New Deal. First and most obvious is the vast expansion of government programs and bureaucracy. Most of the programs listed above did not exist before the presidency of Franklin Roosevelt. Government agencies now touch the lives of average citizens in ways unimaginable before 1932.

R. Shep Melnick; Mark C. Miller & Jeb Barnes, eds., "Courts and Agencies," Making Policy, Making Law, pp. 89-104. Copyright © 2004 by Georgetown University Press. Reprinted with permission.

Second is the nationalization of American politics. Not only has the federal government expanded its power at the expense of state and local governments, but many differences among the states—the way they educate their children, care for the needy, or handle those accused of crimes—have become suspect. This has been particularly true for the often-peculiar practices of Southern states, which combine extremely low levels of public spending with a long history of racial discrimination. Judicial review has become a key mechanism for imposing national standards on state and local agencies.

Third is the revival of confidence in judges' ability to engage in extensive social engineering. After the constitutional revolution of 1937, many people expected the federal courts to play only a minor role in policymaking. The triumphant New Deal exalted executive power—presidential leadership combined with administrative expertise. It seemed quite possible that American courts would become as meek in their dealings with administrative agencies as the courts of Great Britain. But this was not to be. The traditional American distrust of bureaucracy and insistence upon having a "day in court" reasserted themselves. The more powerful public bureaucracy became, the more assertive the judicial response.

The sweeping nature of judicial oversight of public bureaucracy coupled with the amazing diversity of administrative agencies makes generalizing about court-agency relationships particularly perilous. After all, we are dealing not just with local, state, and national agencies but also with bodies charged with everything from teaching children to spying on foreign countries, from maintaining law and order to setting safety standards for nuclear power plants, from managing forests to establishing eligibility standards for food stamps, from building sewage treatment plants to treating mental illness. Not surprisingly, judges have handled some of these agencies well, and some poorly.

This chapter attempts to bring some order to this huge universe of controversies by examining three streams of cases: (1) federal court review of *federal* agencies; (2) federal court review of *state and local* agencies on the bases of judges' interpretation of the U.S. *Constitution;* and (3) federal court review of *state and local* agencies on the basis of judges' reading of *federal laws and regulations.*[1] These three streams have distinctive histories, rationales, and political characteristics.

STREAM ONE: THE MANY REFORMATIONS OF AMERICAN ADMINISTRATIVE LAW

In 1937, the decades-long battle between progressive reformers and conservative judges culminated in the triumph of the New Deal. The Supreme Court granted Congress the power to regulate virtually any form of commerce and to spend public monies for virtually any purpose. Henceforth, economic regulation and spending programs would survive judicial review if the Court could conceive of some plausible rationale for the policies in question—hardly a demanding standard.

Nearly as dramatic as this shift in constitutional law was the Court's new attitude toward administrative discretion and statutory interpretation. For years, indeed since the founding of the Republic, the Court had insisted that determining the meaning of federal laws was the job of federal judges, not administrators. This meant that judges would show little deference to the rules and interpretations issued by administrative agencies or even, in many cases, to their findings of fact. Protecting individual liberty and private property, judges maintained, required that administrative agencies be treated simply as another private litigant, granted no more authority and entitled to no more deference than an individual or corporation (Shapiro 1988, 36-37). To the extent judges recognized that agencies were part of government, they treated them not as essential components of a coequal branch of government but as subordinate, inferior courts—subordinate to the Supreme Court, and inferior to "real" courts.

To make regulatory agencies acceptable to federal judges, Congress often gave them the form of appellate courts. The Interstate Commerce Commission, the Federal Trade Commission, and many other "independent" regulatory commissions were multimember bodies that operated through adjudication, reviewing decisions made "on the record" by "hearing examiners." Yet this was seldom enough to placate judges hostile to administrative power. In the 1890s, for example, "the ICC suffered disastrous defeats at the hands of the Supreme Court" that "emasculated" its regulation of the railroads (Hoogenboom and Hoogenboom 1976, 35, 37). Institutional rivalry reinforced the dominant judicial understanding of the constitution of limited government.

In the years immediately following 1937, the Court's newfound deference to Congress was nearly matched by its deference to administrative agencies. Never again would the Court object to excessive delegation of legislative power to administrators. They tacitly conceded that running government programs required a substantial amount of administrative interpretation of broadly written federal statutes. They also recognized agency authority to issue general rules that have the full force of law.

Because both the jurisdiction of the federal courts and the authority of federal agencies are controlled by statutes enacted by Congress, part of the battle over judicial review of agency action took place in the legislative arena. To make a very long story short, the Roosevelt Administration wanted to give agencies broad rulemaking power subject to lenient judicial review, while Republicans, business, and their toadies in the American Bar Association wanted to require agencies to use time-consuming case-by-case adjudication subject to rigorous judicial review. After years of debate, Congress approved a compromise called the Administrative Procedures Act (APA) of 1946. The APA laid out two forms of agency action: "notice-and-comment rulemaking" in which agencies act like a legislature announcing general rules; and "formal adjudication" in which agencies act like a court deciding a particular case. A court must approve regulations produced by notice-and-comment rulemaking unless it finds them "arbitrary and capricious." Formal adjudication is subject to the somewhat more restrictive "substantial evidence" test. Congress retains authority not only to determine whether an agency must use rulemaking or adjudication, but also to invent various forms of hybrid rulemaking. Federal judges remained free to determine whether "arbitrary and capricious" means (1) a policy that is completely crazy, (2) a policy they do not particularly like, or (3) something in between (see Shapiro 1988, chap. 2).

If the APA largely codified existing practices, judicial review under it reflected the New Deal consensus. By the 1950s, federal regulators and regulated industries had reached a modus vivendi, which the courts generally accepted (Bernstein 1955). Regulation of labor-management relations by the National Labor Relations Board remained contentious, but even there the courts' role remained secondary (Shapiro 1964, chap. 3). Agencies tended to avoid ambitious rulemaking, favoring narrow adjudication and incremental change based on negotiations with representatives of the industries most directly affected. As long as agencies followed established procedures, did not expand their authority too rapidly, and avoided unethical practices, the courts were willing to go along.

Two sets of developments transformed administrative law in the late 1960s and early 1970s. The first and most obvious was the vast expansion of "social regulation"—health, safety, consumer, civil rights, and environmental regulation—enacted between 1964 and 1978. By any measure, the programs administered by the newly created EPA, OSHA, EEOC, National Highway Traffic Safety Administration, and Consumer Product Safety Commission dwarfed those of the New Deal. Their rules affected not just one or two industries, but the entire national economy. Compliance costs for a single rule could run into the billions of dollars. Some (but not all) of these statutes required administrators to balance regulatory benefits against economic costs. Some also contained "citizen suit" provisions allowing anyone, not just those directly affected by the regulation, to sue the agency for failing to perform a "non-discretionary duty." The laws of the 1970s established strict deadlines for agencies to issue hundreds of new rules. During this period, Congress also passed the National Environmental Policy Act (NEPA), which requires all federal agencies to document and to take into consideration the environmental consequences of their actions.

Never before had the stakes of regulation or judicial review of agency action been so high. Courts reviewing agency rules wanted to make sure that regulators had adequate justification for imposing billions of dollars of costs on consumers. They also insisted that the new "social regulation" agencies meet the many duties and deadlines that had been rapidly thrust upon them, and that older development-oriented agencies give greater weight to environmental protection. In the words of Judge Harold Leventhal, a principal author of what became known as the "hard look" doctrine of judicial review,

> The rule of administrative law, as applied to the congressional mandate for a clean environment, ensures that mission-oriented agencies ... will take due cognizance of environmental matters. It ensures at the same time that environmental protection agencies will take into account the congressional mandate that environmental concerns be reconciled with other social and economic objectives of our society. (Leventhal 1974, *555)*

With so much at stake, the judiciary became the governor of the governors, preventing them from going too fast or too slow, requiring them to listen to a variety of voices and to give "adequate consideration" to all "relevant factors." Given the administrative and technical complexity of the new regulation and the large number of groups engaged in these controversies, this was no easy task.

Congress encouraged the courts to conduct this augmented oversight. Those members of Congress and lobbyists who worried about the cost of regulation saw judicial review as a mechanism for blocking or at least braking agency action. Environmentalists and their congressional allies often saw judicial review as a way to prevent Republicans in the White House from subverting legislative intent, which they equated with a demand for aggressive regulation. For decades, program advocates on congressional committees (usually, but not always, Democrats) battled with the White House and with economists and political executives within the agencies. Many of these conflicts ended up in court (see Melnick 1999b, 167-74).

A second and equally important cause of the "Reformation of American Administrative Law"[2] during the late 1960s and early 1970s was a profound shift in judges' understanding of public bureaucracy and government regulation. During the New Deal, attacks on regulation and bureaucracy came primarily from business and defenders of laissez-faire economics. They maintained that unless courts constantly looked over their shoulders, regulatory bureaucracies would run roughshod over private property and individual liberty, creating massive inefficiencies along the way. Three decades later, the attack on regulation and bureaucracy came primarily from the left; government agencies, advocates of stringent regulation argued, tend to be too slow and too wedded to the status quo. Rather than threatening the hegemony of business, government regulators all too often served business interests by stabilizing and dividing up markets. In the past, regulators had failed to serve the public interest because they had been "captured" by the private interests they dealt with day after day. These timid bureaucrats resisted innovation, ignored the broader consequences of their policies, and refused to listen to the many new "public interest" groups that suddenly appeared in the second half of the 1960s. Many of these groups turned to the courts to "open up" agency deliberations to a new set of players, new issues, and new values (Stewart 1975, 1713-15; Shapiro 1988, 62-73; Melnick 1983, 9-13).

Although the arguments of these new "public-interest" litigants resonated with the egalitarianism of the Warren Court, most of the "reformation" of administrative law was the work of the lower federal courts, especially the D.C. Circuit, which by statute hears an unusually large number of important administrative law cases. One of the first signs of change came in a case challenging a decision by the Federal Power Commission (FPC) to approve a large hydroelectric project on the Hudson River. The Second Circuit ruled that the FPC could not limit its analysis to energy issues; it had to demonstrate that it had given "adequate consideration" to countervailing values, especially environmental protection. This, in turn, required the FPC to allow environmental groups to intervene in licensing proceedings *(Scenic Hudson Preservation Conference v. FPC,* 354 F.2d 608 [2d Circuit, 1965]). The next year the D.C.

Circuit ruled that a national church group could speak on behalf of the potential listeners reached by a radio station in Jackson, Mississippi. The Court warned that "unless the listeners—the broadcast consumers—can be heard, there may be no one to bring programming deficiencies or offensive overcommercialization to the attention of the [FCC] Commissioners in an effective manner." By limiting participation in licensing hearings to broadcasters, the FCC had "elected to post the Wolf to guard the Sheep" (Office of Communications, United Church of Christ v. FCC, 359 F.2d 994, at 1004-5 and 1008 [D.C. Circuit, 1966]). The author of this opinion was future Supreme Court chief justice Warren Burger.

The manifesto of the "new administrative law" appeared in a 1971 D.C. Circuit decision ordering the fledgling EPA to regulate the pesticide DDT. This is fitting because publication of Rachel Carson's famous article on the dangers of DDT is widely viewed as the beginning of the modern environmental movement. In the words of Judge David Bazelon,

> We stand on the threshold of a new era in the history of the long and fruitful collaboration of administrative agencies and reviewing courts. For many years, courts have treated administrative policy decisions with great deference, confining judicial attention primarily to matters of procedure. On matters of substance, the courts regularly upheld agency action, with a nod in the direction of the "substantial evidence" test, and a bow to the mysteries of administrative expertise. ... Gradually, however, that power has come into more frequent use, and with it, the requirement that administrators articulate the factors on which they base their decisions. Strict adherence to that requirement is especially important now that the character of administrative litigation is changing. ... [C]ourts are increasingly asked to review administrative action that touches on fundamental personal interests in life, health, and liberty. These interests have always had a special claim to judicial protection, in comparison with the economic interests at stake in ratemaking or licensing proceedings. (EDF v. Ruckelshaus, 439 F.2d 584, at 597-98 [D.C. Circuit, 1971]; internal footnotes omitted)

Bazelon's stirring rhetoric disguised the fact that he had his history backwards: in the past the economic interests of regulated industries had "always had a special claim to judicial protection"; protecting the health of the public was the special job of expert agencies. In the bad old days judges worried about administrative overzealousness. Now they worried about bureaucratic timidity and capture. It was indeed a "new era."

The first phase of the "reformation" of administrative law focused on participation. Courts would ensure "adequate consideration" of "all relevant factors" by opening up the decision-making process to a wider array of interest groups. In the words of Richard Stewart,

> Faced with the seemingly intractable problem of agency discretion, courts have changed the focus of judicial review. ... so that its dominant purpose is no longer the prevention of unauthorized intrusions on private autonomy, but the assurance of

fair representation for all affected interests in the exercise of the legislative power delegated to agencies. ... If agencies were to function as a forum for all interests affected by agency decisionmaking, bargaining leading to compromises generally acceptable to all might result, thus replicating the process of legislation. (Stewart 1975, 1712)

The courts not only broadened participation rights but also required agencies to respond fully to all reasonable criticisms of its proposals (Stewart 1975, 1717-60; Shapiro 1988,44-49).

In the second phase, the courts slowly and subtly transformed the demand for greater pluralism into a demand for what Shapiro has called "synopticism"—"a process that gathers all the facts, considers all alternatives and all the possible consequences of each, and chooses those policies with the highest probability of achieving agreed goals at least cost" (Shapiro 1988, 15). Agencies need to do more than listen to everyone; they need to come up with the most rational, most comprehensive answer. This in turn requires judges to divine exactly what it is that Congress expects the agency to do. Judge Leventhal explained that "the courts are in a kind of partnership for the purpose of effectuating the *legislative* mandates" *(Portland Cement Association v. Ruckelshaus*, 486 F. 2d 375, at 394 [D.C. Circuit, 1973]). His colleague on the D.C. Circuit, Skelly Wright, added, "our duty, in short, is to see that the legislative purposes heralded in the halls of Congress are not lost in the vast halls of the federal bureaucracy" *(Calvert Cliffs Coordinating Committee v. AEC*, 449 F.2d 1109, at 1111 [D.C. Circuit, 1971]). Judges took on the task of reading between the lines of ambiguous legislation to discover a standard for establishing how a "rational" administrator would act. Frequently they resolved controversies by emphasizing that the central purpose of a newly minted statute was to protect public health and the environment. These underlying goals trumped all other concerns (see, e.g., the cases discussed in Melnick 1983, 76-80, 129-35,157-62, 261-69).

One consequence of these new judicial demands was that the rulemaking process, once short and simple, became extremely complex and protracted. The courts told agencies to consider all "relevant" evidence, respond to all "significant" comments, and weigh all "reasonable" alternatives without giving them much guidance on what "relevant," "significant," and "reasonable" mean. Because agencies do not like losing big court cases, they reacted defensively, accumulating more and more information, responding to all comments, and covering all their bets. As a result, Pierce reports, "The time to make policy through rulemaking has been stretched to nearly a decade" (Pierce 1988, 302; see also Melnick 1992). Little wonder that agencies looked for ways to avoid the rulemaking quagmire. Some decided it would be easier to use adjudication to establish agency policy. Others set policy through interpretive rulings, internal enforcement policies, and recall orders (Mashaw and Harfst 1991, chaps. 5, 8; Pierce 1991).

A second consequence was that agencies were subject to a plethora of "action-forcing" suits based on the multiple demands and deadlines included in the new regulatory statutes.

According to a 1985 study, the EPA alone was subject to 328 statutory deadlines. Among the other findings of this report were the following:

1. Very few statutory deadlines (14 percent) have been met. ...
2. Congress imposes more deadlines on EPA than it can possibly meet. ...
3. Court-ordered deadlines almost always command top management attention at EPA. ...
4. The multiplicity of deadlines reduces EPA's ability to assign priority to anything not subject to a deadline. (Environmental Law Institute and Environmental and Energy Study Institute 1985, 11, ii, iii, v, iv; see also Rabkin 1989)

In effect, this form of policymaking transfers responsibility for setting agency priorities from top administrators to interest groups, some of which use attorneys' fees won in relatively easy "action-forcing" cases to cross-subsidize other activities.

A third consequence was that the White House, the Office of Management and Budget, and political executives in the departments and agencies lost power to congressional committees and to technical personnel within the agencies. In searching for "congressional intent," courts paid much more attention to the statements and reports of the congressional sponsors, subcommittee leaders, and committee staff who shaped the legislation than to the views of the president who signed it. Agency leaders faced strong incentives to hide political judgments behind mountains of technical data and analysis, which strengthened the bargaining position of technical personnel (and lawyers) within the bureaucracy. After all, if policymaking is to be synoptic, then the outcome cannot depend on the accident of who won the last presidential election (Shapiro 1988, chap. 5; Melnick 1985, 653).

A fourth consequence was judicial exhaustion. The rulemaking record grew longer and longer, far beyond any judge's ability to review in its entirety. Statutes, committee reports, and floor statements grew as well, with all participants in the legislative process giving the courts an earful about their "intent." Most major rules were challenged by both industry—which claimed they were too stringent—and public interest groups—who claimed they were too lenient. The issues before the court were often of mind-numbing complexity.[3] Not infrequently, the result was stalemate.

Despite the importance of these developments, the Supreme Court played a peripheral role in administrative law during most of the 1960s and 1970s. As the then-law professor Antonin Scalia put it, "As a practical matter, the D.C. Circuit is something of a resident manager, and the Supreme Court an absentee landlord" in administrative law (Scalia 1978, 371). But the high court was obviously uneasy with what it saw going on below. In a 1978 opinion, it reprimanded the D.C. Circuit for imposing on the Nuclear Regulatory Commission procedural requirements that the Supreme Court described as "judicial intervention run riot" and "border[ing] on the Kafkaesque" (*Vermont Yankee Nuclear Power Corp. v. NRDC*, 435 U.S. 519, at 557 [1978]). But the D.C Circuit quickly found new legal justifications for its previous practices (see Pierce 1989).

In 1984, the Supreme Court took a more significant step. In *Chevron v. NRDC*9 467 U.S. 837 (1984), the Court instructed the lower courts to show greater deference to administrators' interpretations of the statutes they are charged with implementing:

> If the statute is silent or ambiguous with respect to the specific issue, the question for the court is whether the agency's answer is based on a *permissible* construction of the statute. ... [A] court may not substitute its own construction of a statutory provision for a reasonable interpretation made by the administrator of an agency. (467 U.S. 843-44)

Studies of lower court response to *Chevron* indicate that deference increased for a few years, but then returned nearly to pre-*Chevron* levels (Schuck and Elliott 1990; Avila 2000). Part of the problem is that the Supreme Court has not been giving the lower courts consistent signals. On a number of occasions the Court has departed from *Chevron* without explaining why.[4] But the problem of hierarchical control goes much deeper than this: almost all general rules about judicial review leave lower courts with substantial discretion to review the adequacy of an agency's evidence and its interpretation of innumerable statutory phrases.

Whether judges appointed by Republican presidents vote differently in administrative law case than judges appointed by Democratic presidents is a topic of considerable debate. On the one hand, most administrative law decisions, even in the contentious D.C. Circuit, are unanimous. On the other hand, in a significant number of highly contentious cases, judges appointed by Democrats tend to be more sympathetic to challenges brought by "public-interest" groups, and Republicans tend to be more sympathetic to challenges brought by industry (Revesz 1997; Cross and Tiller 1998; Edwards 1998; Avila 2000). This is not surprising given the fact that many of these cases in the end come down to how much trust one has in the agency before the court, how much damage one thinks the agency might do to the economy, and how inclined one is to believe that existing business practices threaten public health and safety.

Administrative law doctrine tends to focus more on regulatory programs than on spending programs. But federal agencies that distribute such entitlements as Social Security benefits, unemployment compensation, food stamps, and health care also experienced a substantial increase in judicial scrutiny starting in the late 1960s and early 1970s. The federal courts held that those deprived of the so-called new property have a constitutional right to a "due process" hearing.[5] More important, the courts became much more willing to second-guess agencies' determination of what sorts of benefits have been promised to citizens by particular entitlement statutes (see Melnick 1994, chaps. 3, 5, 8, 10). The most dramatic example of this was the multiyear battle between the federal courts and the Reagan administration over eligibility for disability benefits (see Derthick 1990, chap. 7).

The administrative law decisions discussed in this section not only are far-reaching in their policy significance, but also play a major role in structuring relationships among the three branches of government. Yet few of them would be included in courses or books on "constitutional law." The courts try to avoid overt constitutional language when adjusting relations among the branches of the federal government. But when federal judges took on the huge task of reforming state and local bureaucracies, the constitutional dimension of the undertaking was evident to all.

STREAM TWO: CONSTITUTIONAL DUTIES

From shortly before the turn of the century until 1937, the federal courts sporadically engaged in a form of judicial activism commonly known as "Lochnerism."[6] Lochnerism placed multiple restrictions on the role of government. The Supreme Court adopted a definition of "interstate commerce" that left a considerable portion of the national economy outside the reach of Congress. Its reading of the due process, contract, and takings clauses limited the regulatory power of both the state and national governments. Somewhat haphazardly it distributed "Government Keep Out" and "No Public Trespassing" signs throughout the policy landscape.

The activism that began with *Brown v. Board of Education* in 1954 produced more complicated judicial orders. These commands took the form, "If and when you engage in governmental activity X, you must do it in the following way." For example, if a state or local government provides public education, it must do so in a racially nondiscriminatory fashion. When government seeks to imprison someone for committing a crime, it must follow judicially mandated rules of evidence. If it confines a mentally ill person to a state institution, it must abide by standards of care and habilitation laid out by the court. The Supreme Court has never unequivocally said that states must provide education, care for the mentally ill, or even law enforcement. It does not need to; with very rare exceptions, no state would ever consider withdrawing from these areas. As a result, the federal courts are frequently in the business of telling state and local agencies how and to whom they must provide a variety of goods, services, and protections.

A fundamental yet little noted feature of the most controversial decisions of the Warren Court is that they sought to change the behavior of the two largest and most decentralized sets of public bureaucracies in America: schools and police. Schools and police are decentralized not just in the sense that they tend to be locally run and financed but also in the sense that they are peculiarly resistant to centralized administrative direction. It is hard for managers either to measure the output of the patrolman and the classroom teacher, or to monitor in any meaningful way the activities in which they engage. James Q. Wilson has called these "coping" organizations—managers cannot hope to solve the core compliance problem, only cope with it as best they can (Wilson 1989, 168-71). This meant that the courts were engaged in a high-visibility, high-stakes effort to lay down general rules for those bureaucracies that are particularly resistant to control through rules.

As a consequence, judges have delved deeper and deeper into these organizations in a desperate effort to stop behavior they consider unacceptable. (It would go too far to say "to achieve their goals," because courts are seldom clear about what they want schools and police forces to do. They are much clearer about what they want them to avoid doing.) In desegregation cases, judges started with issues of school assignment. Before long, they were dealing with the hiring and placement of teachers, tracking and testing, language training, discipline, sports facilities, and, ultimately, the content of the curriculum. Judges selected sites for new schools and imposed taxes to pay for them. For example, in Kansas City, Missouri, a federal district court judge ordered the construction of seventeen new schools—including several state-of-the-art magnet schools—and major renovation of fifty-five others. The cost of the changes mandated by the court exceeded a billion and a half dollars (Wise and O'Leary 2003, 177-91). Some judges, justifiably worried about white flight, tried to desegregate public housing projects within the school district.

These extensive desegregation efforts produced innovative "structural injunctions," complex, evolving, negotiated judicial orders that "establish a long, continuing relationship between the parties and the tribunal" (Fiss 1972, 1). A prominent feature of these injunctions is their longevity: court supervision frequently persists for decades. Some desegregation cases begun in the 1960s and 1970s have yet to be terminated. Year after year the special masters and monitoring committees appointed by the court worked with plaintiff attorneys and school officials to establish educational policies and priorities (see, e.g., Sandler and Shoenbrod 2003, chap. 3). Before long, structural injunctions were being used to reform other state institutions—often by the same judge who was engaged in the desegregation of public schools.[7]

Judicial efforts to control the behavior of state and local police have relied heavily on a key element of judicial leverage: finding that the Fourteenth Amendment incorporates the Fourth and Fifth Amendments, federal judges have restricted the type of evidence police and prosecutors can use in state as well as federal court. Wielding the exclusionary rule, though, does not give judges control over those police practices that do not ordinarily culminate in a criminal prosecution. So judges have searched for other mechanisms for controlling police discretion. Starting in 1961 with *Monroe v. Pape*, the Supreme Court has allowed citizens alleging misconduct to file suit for damages in federal court against police departments.[8] In 1971, the Court authorized similar suits against federal law enforcement officials *(Bivens v. Six Unknown Agents of the Federal Narcotics Bureau*, 403 U.S. 388 [1971]).

Such tort suits give courts the opportunity to define acceptable official behavior and create incentives for compliance. In a few instances federal courts have also issued injunctions against city police departments, prohibiting them from engaging in specific practices.[9] The extent to which such remedies have actually changed police behavior for the better is, of course, the subject of considerable debate. Neither judges nor anyone else can effectively monitor what thousands of patrolman are doing on their beat each day.

In the early 1970s, a number of federal district court judges took on the difficult task of reforming two other types of public institutions: facilities for the mentally ill and retarded, and prisons. The reform effort began in the South, where the condition of those confined to these "total institutions" were particularly shocking. For state mental hospitals and facilities for the developmentally disabled, the seminal case was Judge Frank Johnson's opinion in *Wyatt v. Stickney*,[10] For prisons, the breakthrough came with Judge J. Smith Henley's decisions in Arkansas.[11] Other federal district court judges quickly followed suit. Six years after *Wyatt*, ten other states were operating under similar court orders (Frug 1978, 718 n. 15). By 1995, prisons in forty-one states plus the District of Columbia, Puerto Rico, and the Virgin Islands "had at one time or another been under comprehensive court orders, as had the entire correctional system of at least ten states" (Feeley and Rubin 1998, 13; see also Dilulio 1987, 73; 1990a).

In 2000, more than thirty state child welfare agencies were operating under court order (Sandler and Shoenbrod 2003,122). The Supreme Court did little to initiate or even encourage such intervention. Its first decision on mental health facilities did not come until 1982, when it announced a relatively deferential standard for evaluating state practices *(Youngberg v. Romeo*, 457 U.S. 307 [1982]). In prison cases also, the Supreme Court urged district court judges to exercise caution and restraint.[12]

As was the case with school desegregation, judges in institutional reform cases issued detailed structural injunctions that lasted for years, even decades, and required constant modification. Judge Johnson's orders in *Wyatt v. Stickney,* for example, included the following:

- The patient must have bathroom privileges every hour and must be bathed every 12 hours. ... There will be one toilet provided for each eight patients and one lavatory for every six patients.
- The number of patients in a multi-patient room shall not exceed six persons. There shall be allocated a minimum of 80 square feet of floor space per patient in a multi-patient room. ... Single rooms must have a minimum of 100 square feet of floor space. The area of day rooms must be at least 40 square feet per patient, for dining rooms 10 square feet per patient.
- Room temperature must remain between 83 and 68 degrees. Hot tap water must be 110 degrees. (344 F.Supp. 373, at 380-82)

To monitor compliance, Judge Johnson appointed a Human Rights Committee for each institution. When Alabama failed to meet court deadlines, he put the facilities into receivership, where they remained for years.[13] This was a pattern that recurred in state after state.

Another key feature of these institutional reform cases is that judges frequently start off with broad support from professional groups, federal agencies, and even the state administrators being sued. Judge Johnson relied on the advice of the Department of Justice, the Department of Health, Education, and Welfare, the Food and Drug Administration, the Public Health Service, and professional groups such as the American Psychological Association and the Ortho-Psychiatric Association to write his implementation orders. The defendant in *Wyatt,* the marvelously named Dr. Stonewall Stickney, agreed to 90 percent of the standards established by the court (Cooper 1988, 182). Usually, the administrators of these facilities have been battling with governors and state legislatures for years to increase funding and staffing levels. They are all too well aware of their institutions' deficiencies, and they recognize that a court order can help them get the money they so desperately need. Administrators who come to office after the initial round of litigation are particularly likely to "embrac[e] the court and its orders, using the court as justification for the reforms the new chief executive officer wants to bring about on his or her own initiative" (Wood 1990, 58).

Although "collusion" might be too strong a word to describe relations between the nominal plaintiffs and defendants, the real political struggle is almost always that between the plaintiffs and defendants on the one side and those who control the state's purse strings on the other. In their study of the Kansas City, Missouri, School District (KCMSD) desegregation case, Wise and O'Leary found that

> hundreds of small bureaucracies have formed around the issues of the case, from the purchasing of textbooks to infrastructure development. These networks of bureaucracies are not about to willingly fade away. In the end, with the KCMSD's dependence on court-driven funding has come a dependence on continued court supervision. The court has become a convenient scapegoat and a shield keeping the KCMSD from accepting responsibility. (Wise and O'Leary 2003, 187)

While judges initially intervene in order to bring about major change, over the years they inevitably become protectors of the bureaucratic status quo.

At the same time, administrators are likely to become frustrated and resentful at the resulting contraction of bureaucratic autonomy. They particularly object to what they see as the court's tendency to establish unrealistic guidelines for staff levels. Judge Johnson established staffing ratios for psychiatrists, nurses, aides, clerks, psychologists, social workers, cooks, repairmen, housekeepers, and even messengers. Administrators never came close to filling all these positions. Tension also frequently develops between advocates on court-appointed monitory committees, who wish to publicize the institution's shortcomings, and administrators, who are concerned about protecting agency morale and their own reputations. Moreover, the accumulation of court orders and consent decrees reduces the ability of incoming mayors and governors to set new priorities or to institute innovative programs (Sandler and Shoenbrod 2003, 67).

Court orders frequently include elaborate "due process" requirements to structure relations between lower level bureaucrats and clients. For the disabled, this has meant individualized treatment plans. While this can be time consuming, it is very much in tune with the professional norms of physicians, psychologists, teachers, and other social service professionals. In prisons, due process has meant an increase in the number of rules prison officials must follow, enhanced opportunities for appeal, and, as a result, significantly less autonomy for the guards who are in close daily contact with inmates. Of all the "street level bureaucrats" affected by court orders, prison guards—who spend their working hours in an unusually dangerous environment—are particularly resistant to (and angry about) judicial constraints on administrative discretion (DiIulio 1990b).

Whether or not judges have improved conditions in these state institutions is the subject of considerable debate (see the essays in Dilulio 1990a). The courts' greatest success has come in closing or sharply reducing the size of institutions for the mentally ill and retarded. Here the courts played a supporting role in the wider movement toward deinstitutionalization. Today, there is a broad political and professional consensus that only those with the most severe problems are best cared for in large, impersonal institutions. The courts helped dramatize the horrors of the "warehousing" of thousands and thousands of helpless people. Ironically, though, it is much harder for either public administrators or judges to monitor the care and treatment of those who have been deinstitutionalized. This is just the tip of a larger paradox: Judges frequently demand individualized treatment for agencies' clients. The more individualized the treatment, though, the more difficult it becomes for judges to control the behavior of street-level bureaucrats. Once judges take on the task of reforming complex bureaucratic institutions, they inevitably confront the same dilemmas that administrators face on a daily basis.

STREAM THREE: THE MANDATE STATE

Four years after *Wyatt v. Stickney*, Congress passed the Education for All Handicapped Children Act. All children with disabilities are now entitled by federal law to a "free appropriate education" as spelled out in an "individualized education program" (IEP) composed by teachers and administrators in consultation with parents. When parents disagree with an IEP, they can appeal first to an independent hearing officer and then to a federal judge. Federal funding provides less than 10 percent of the cost of this mandate; state and local governments must raise the remaining 90 percent. In 1975, Congress also passed the Developmentally Disabled Assistance and Bill of Rights Act, which included lengthy guidelines for the care and treatment of those confined to state institutions. In 1980, Congress enacted the Civil Rights of Institutionalized Persons Act, which authorized the Department of Justice to file suit against state institutions that violate the constitutional rights of patients. In short, Congress was not only actively encouraging suits such as *Wyatt v. Stickney* but was also providing judges with statutory standards to impose on state and local governments. Advocates for the disabled praised Congress for protecting human rights. State and local officials complained about a steady stream of "unfunded mandates."

Today, court orders against state and local agencies are much more likely to be based on statutory rather than constitutional claims. This reflects Congress's willingness to impose mandates on subnational governments and the lower courts' willingness to read these mandates broadly. Ironically, while state and local officials have often welcomed federal legislation as an alternative to the uncertainty of litigation, the passage of federal law has usually increased opportunities for judicial review of their activities (Melnick 1994, chap. 8). Few state or local agencies are exempt from some form of oversight by federal courts.

No federal mandate has been more important than Title VI of the Civil Rights Act of 1964. Title VI requires federal agencies to terminate funding to those who engage in racial discrimination. Title VI was originally viewed as a quick and effective administrative *alternative* to litigation: agencies could simply stop the flow of federal money rather than commence a lengthy court battle. Within a few years, though, Title VI became an important *source* of civil rights litigation. Federal courts declared that the rules issued by administrators under Title VI could be enforced through "private rights of action," that is, court suits filed by private citizens. As a result, federal administrators could write elaborate regulations defining discrimination but avoid the politically dangerous task of cutting off federal funds for state and local programs. Court enforcement usually meant injunctions specifying the steps subnational governments must take to eliminate discriminatory practices rather than termination of federal funding.

Title VI was thus transformed from an administrative enforcement mechanism for guaranteeing equal protection of the law into a judicial mechanism for enforcing federal administrative rules defining a wide variety of forms of prohibited discrimination. Because it is a rare state or local agency that does not receive some sort of federal funding, the reach of the federal courts' new authority was enormous.

What Hugh Davis Graham has called "the cloning of Title VI" soon followed (Graham 1999, 197-99). Congress, federal agencies, and federal courts forbade recipients of federal funds from discriminating on the basis of gender, disability, age, or language. In deciding the thousands of cases brought against state and local agencies, the courts spelled out the standards and procedures administrators must adopt in order to avoid judicial reprimands and large damage awards. For example, in a 1998 case involving Title IX of the Education Amendments of 1972, the Supreme Court established what the majority considered "a sensible remedial scheme" for dealing with sexual harassment of public school students by teachers *(Gebser v. Lago Vista Independent School District*, 524 U.S. 274 [1998]).

Because these mandate cases usually involve judicial enforcement of regulations issued by federal administrators, they combined the "new administrative law" doctrines described in the first section of this chapter with the effort to set national standards for the operation of state and local bureaucracies. A graphic illustration of this is the long-running civil rights case of *Adams v. Richardson*, 358 F.Supp. 97 (D.D.C. 1973). In 1973, Judge John Pratt, a federal district court judge in the District of Columbia, ruled that the federal Office of Civil Rights had failed to enforce Title VI with sufficient zeal. The original plaintiffs sought to increase efforts by the Nixon administration to desegregate southern schools. Litigants representing women's groups, Hispanic groups, and the disabled later joined the suit to demand more attention for their causes. Judge Pratt essentially placed the Office of Civil Rights in receivership, specifying how it was to divide up and utilize its enforcement resources. The federal court was thus attempting to restructure a federal agency whose job it was to restructure a large number of state and local agencies. Nearly two decade later, the *Adams* case was still going strong (see also Rabkin 1989; Halpern 1995).

Title VI and Title IX are often referred to as "cross-cutting" requirements. That is, they apply to a wide variety of state and local programs receiving federal funds. Another way federal courts supervise state and local agencies is by interpreting and enforcing the "strings" attached to individual spending programs. When Congress first started providing federal funding for such things as highway construction and public assistance, it imposed only a few restrictions on the use of federal money. Enforcement of these "strings" was lax since federal administrators hesitated to terminate funding for programs they believed were in the public interest.

Over time, the number and specificity of federal strings grew and grew. In the late 1960s the federal courts announced that they, too, had authority to enforce these statutory requirements. But they would not use the counterproductive funding cutoff. Rather, they would issue injunctions to state and local officials ordering them to comply with federal rules (Melnick 1994, 48–51, 245–49). Federal administrators frequently concluded that this was a wonderful idea, and they churned out hundreds of pages of interpretations of federal law for the courts to apply. The federal courts thus became deeply involved in the details of programs run by state welfare offices, social service departments, and natural resources agencies (see Melnick 1994; Kagan 2001, chaps. 8, 10).

In recent years, the Supreme Court has tried to reduce these forms of federal court oversight of state and local governments. It has been unwilling to find private rights of action in federal spending and civil rights laws unless Congress has made its intent explicit.[14] It has refused to enforce regulations issued by the Department of Justice under Title VI that go beyond the clear commands of the statute itself (*Alexander v. Sandoval*, 532 U.S. 275 [2001]). It has narrowed the conditions in which it will issue systemwide injunctions against state agencies (*Blessing v. Freestone*, 520 U.S. 329 [1997]). The extent to which these rules will result in a substantial decline in court supervision of state and local agencies depends both on the lower courts' willingness to follow the Supreme Court's lead and Congress's reaction to the new rules established by the judiciary.

In the cases cited in the previous paragraph, the Supreme Court established standards for lower courts in their oversight of federal agencies, which regulate state and local agencies, which in turn establish standards for the behavior of private individuals. Sound pretty convoluted? It is. Given the complexity of these chains of regulation and the immense variation among agencies and programs, it is nearly impossible to offer useful generalizations about "court-agency relations." What should be clear, though, is that this is a very strange way to run a government. It is highly unlikely that anyone who set out to design the machinery of government would ever come up with something that looks like this.

How, then, did we end up here? The best answer, I think, is that during the past fifty years public expectations of government have grown enormously, but the traditional American distrust of government and bureaucracy has become even more pronounced. On the one hand, we demand that the federal government protect the environment, expand government financed and mandated health care, maintain Social Security, promote an educational system that "leaves no child behind," ensure "homeland security," guarantee civil rights, keep inflation levels low and employment levels high, and fight poverty, crime, drug use, teen pregnancy, HIV/AIDS, and child pornography. On the other hand, most citizens believe the federal government "can't be trusted to do what is right most of the time" and even that "the federal government has become so large and powerful that it poses a threat to the rights and freedoms of ordinary citizens" (Melnick 1999a, 300-301). Trust in government continues to sink, yet demand for government services and protections continues to grow.

The result is the layer upon layer of review and litigation described in this chapter. We demand programs that require extensive bureaucracy. We distrust centralized bureaucracy, so we rely heavily on state and local agencies. But we expect these agencies to respect the basic rights of Americans and to meet minimum national standards. So we subject these agencies to substantial regulation by federal agencies. Because we do not trust these federal agencies either, we demand judicial oversight. But this often allows a single federal district court judge to try his hand at reconstructing complex institutions, which usually involves remaking the budgetary priorities of cities and states. Few people seem to like this either. So we grouse about excessive litigiousness and the fees collected by trial attorneys without doing anything serious to reduce adversarial legalism (Kagan 2001; Burke 2002). We dream of a helpful, equitable government without an intrusive, impersonal bureaucracy. But, alas, it is only a dream. When we wake up, we start suing.

NOTES

1. State courts engage in many of the forms of judicial review examined in this chapter. Most states have statutes similar to the Administrative Procedures Act, and state constitutions often contain detailed criteria for the provision of education, welfare, and social services. It would be interesting to compare state and federal courts' oversight of administrative agencies. But this is beyond the scope of this chapter or the competence of its author.
2. The phrase comes from the title of Stewart's (1975) article, which remains the most comprehensive examination of the changes in legal doctrine during this period.
3. A good example is the *Alabama Power* case described in Melnick 1983, 103-10. The initial litigation on this topic was relatively simple—or at least it seemed so at the time.
4. Leading examples include *Motor Vehicle Mfg. Association v. State Farm Mutual Auto Insurance* Co., 463 U.S. 29 (1983); *INS v. Cardozo-Fonseca*, 480 U.S. 421 (1987); and *K-Mart v. Cartier*, 486 U.S. 281 (1988). See also Merrill 1992. In two recent cases, *Chris- tensen v. Harris County*, 529 U.S. 576 (2000), and *United States v. Mead Corp.*, 533 U.S. 218 (2001), the Court seems to have backed away from Chevron in a more sustained manner.
5. *Goldberg v. Kelly*, 397 U.S. 254 (1970). The structure and timing of the hearing depend on the nature of the benefit. See, e.g., *Mathews v. Eldridge*, 425 U.S. 319 (1976). The term "new property" comes from an influential article by Reich (1964).
6. The name comes from the Supreme Court's decision in *Lochner v. New York*, 198 U.S. 45 (1905), in which it ruled that a state law restricting the number of hours bakers could work violated the workers' right to contract protected by the Fourteenth Amendment.
7. The leading example is Judge Frank Johnson of Alabama, who was simultaneously engaged in desegregating the schools of Montgomery, reforming state institutions for the mentally ill and retarded (see below), and restructuring Alabama state welfare department.

8. *Monroe v. Pape*, 365 US 167 (1961). The ruling was originally limited to state officials. It was extended to local officials in *Monnell v. New York City Department of Social Services,* 436 U.S. 658 (1978).
9. Cooper (1988) provides a detailed examination of litigation involving the Philadelphia police department in chapter 11.
10. 325 F. Supp. 582 (M.D. AL, 1972). Subsequent orders were announced at 334 F. Supp. 1341 (1971), 344 F. Supp. 373 (1972), and 344 F. Supp. 387 (1972).
11. *Holt v. Sarver*, 300 F. Supp. 825 (E.D. Ark., 1969); *Holt v. Sarver*, 309 F. Supp. 362 (1970); *Holt v. Hutto*, 363 F.Supp. 194 (1973); *Finney v. Hutto*, 410 F.Supp. 251 (1975). This litigation is examined in Cooper 1988, chap. 8.
12. E.g., *Pell v. Procunier*, 417 U.S. 817 (1974); *Wolfe v. McDonnell*, 418 U.S. 539 (1974); *Estelle v. Gamble*, 429 U.S. 97 (1976); and *Bell v. Wolfish*, 441 U.S. 520 (1979).
13. A number of studies have followed the long process of formulating and implementing the court's orders, including Cooper 1988, chap. 7; Note 1975; and Yarbrough 1981.
14. E.g., *Gonzaga University v. Doe*, 536 U.S. 273 (2002); *Gregory v. Ashcroft*, 501 U.S. 452 (1991); *Dellmuth v. Muth*, 491 U.S. 223 (1989); *Welch v. Texas Highways and Public Transportation Departments*, 483 U.S. 468 (1987); and *Pennhurst State School and Hospital v. Halderman*, 451 U.S. 1 (1981).

Versailles Borough v. McKeesport Coal & Coke Co.

R. Stewart and J. Krier

Musmanno j., July 22, 1935—The borough of Versailles, city of McKeesport and thirteen private plaintiffs have filed a bill in equity seeking an injunction against the defendant, McKeesport Coal & Coke company, a corporation of the state of Pennsylvania.

Upon conclusion of the trial, which consumed an entire month, in which 51 witnesses were heard on behalf of plaintiffs and 71 on behalf of the defense, the chancellor filed findings of fact and conclusions of law and entered a decree *nisi* in which he dismissed the bill and the case is now before us upon exceptions filed by plaintiffs.

Defendant is the owner of 2500 acres of coal of the upper Freeport vein, located in the borough of Versailles, near the southern boundary of the city of McKeesport, where, in December 1923, it erected a modern tipple and has since been engaged in the operation of a large mine.

In the process of mining, certain impurities are found in the coal veins. These impurities, known to the industry as gob, "bone" or "boney," consist of slate and coal—the coal being deposited in quarter-inch layers between laminations of slate of similar thickness. Because of these laminations of slate, the coal found in this gob is unmerchantable, although it is combustible.

It was established at the trial that wherever coal is mined, large quantities of gob are encountered, and that for every 100 tons of merchantable coal produced, 20 tons of gob are found and must be disposed of; that it is the general practice in the industry—a practice followed by defendant, to dispose of as much of its gob as possible in the underground workings of the mine, in the so-called "rooms," after the coal has been removed, and to bring the remainder to the surface. The testimony disclosed that in the operation of its mine defendant has driven through the coal seam 62 miles of entries or main haulage ways. All of the gob encountered in these entries must be brought to the surface as there is no place inside the mine where it may be stored. Thus about half of the gob produced in a mine or the equivalent by weight, of ten per cent of the coal produced, must be brought to the surface. Brought to the surface it is piled at some point near the tipple. This is the general practice (in

Copyright in the Public Domain.

fact the only method known to the industry for the disposal of this refuse), and was followed by defendant.

During the years which have intervened since it opened its mine, defendant has deposited gob on a 20 acre tract of surface, located 230 feet from its tipple. On November 3, 1933, the gob pile caught fire. At a preliminary hearing on June 11, 1934, a temporary injunction issued, enjoining the defendant from the piling of gob on the burning heap.

Immediately following the granting of the temporary injunction, the defendant started a new gob pile, adjacent to the old (the burning one). It is now depositing its mine refuse on a new heap. At the final hearing of the bill in equity, the plaintiffs asked for an injunction against the defendant from depositing gob on the new pile, or any place near to it, claiming that such act constituted a nuisance under the law, and was, therefore, properly enjoinable.

The defendant denied that the piling of gob at any place on its property in reasonable proximity to its tipple constituted a nuisance.

Plaintiffs do not dispute the testimony offered on behalf of the defense that gob is a necessary incident to coal mining; that it is something which cannot be avoided if coal is to be mined at all; that a large part of it cannot be left in the mine, but must be brought to the surface, and that in bringing it to the surface and depositing it on a gob pile close to its tipple, defendant has followed the most approved method of gob disposal—the method followed by ail the large and best managed mines. The uncontroverted testimony is that there is no feasible method of operating a coal mine without a gob pile on the surface, as no use has ever been bound for this troublesome by-product of mining; that every large coal mine has a large gob pile close to its tipple; that sooner or later these piles all ignite through spontaneous combustion; that practically every large mine in Western Pennsylvania has a burning gob pile, and that there is no known means of averting such a fire.

If we accept the uncontroverted testimony as fact, and in the absence of denial we must so accept it, then it must follow that if we enjoin the deposit of gob and the erection of gob piles, we perforce enjoin the mining of coal, for without gob and gob piles coal mines cannot be operated, since the one is a necessary and unavoidable result of the other.

Plaintiffs rely upon the maxim, *"sic utere tou ut alienam non laedas."* However, that principle is subject to the equally well-known exception, as old as the rule itself, which holds that everyone has a right to the natural use of his own land.

That the plaintiffs are subjected to annoyance, personal inconvenience and aesthetic damage by the burning of the gob pile, is not seriously disputed. ... If by decree we prohibit the defendant from mining coal, and thereby relieve the plaintiffs from all the vexation of smoke, dust and odors that come from a burning gob pile, we must consider what harm, if any, comes to those who are interested in the continued operation of the coal mine. ...

The uncontradicted testimony discloses that upon an investment of $2,561,000.00 made eleven years before this trial, not a dollar has ever been paid by defendant in dividends; no year's operation has shown a profit and the result for the entire period shows a net loss in excess of $500,000.00. Since this has been the financial experience of defendant with its gob pile located but 230 feet from its tipple, for us to decree that it must desist from further dumping near its present pile—for us to decree that it must bear the expense of purchasing additional large surface acreage at locations distant from the tipple, would be equivalent to ordering the closing down of the mine. Defendant is engaged in a lawful business. Its stockholders are entitled to a fair and reasonable return on their investments as this gob pile ignited through causes over which defendant had no control.

Four hundred and thirteen men were employed at this mine at the time of the trial. These men and their families—about two thousand people in all, are economically dependent upon this mine for subsistence. When in full operation defendant's payroll disbursement exceeds $10,000.00 per week, and although the stockholders have received no dividends, the defendant company disbursed as wages to its employees $2,801,000 during the eleven years prior to the trial. Neither directly nor indirectly will we destroy a legitimate business without cogent and adequate reason. Under testimony adduced in this case, we cannot and will not jeopardize the employment of these miners. To do so would be to cause a far greater injury than that we are asked to enjoin. Of course, if the continued operation of this mine were a serious menace to the health or lives of those who reside in its vicinity, there would be another question before us, but there is no evidence in this case to warrant the assumption that the health of anyone is being imperiled.

The only things emanating from a coal or gob fire that might be injurious to health, are the gases arising therefrom—sulphur dioxide, hydrogen sulphide and carbon monoxide. Expert witnesses testifying for both the plaintiffs and the defendant were agreed at the trial that only negligible quantities of hydrogen sulphide and carbon monoxide were present in and about the gob fire. So that the only factor to consider, so far as injurious gas is concerned, is sulphur dioxide. Mr. Holden, a witness for the plaintiffs, testified that his tests (of which he made eighty-eight) revealed an average concentration of .67 of /one part per million, and a maximum concentration of 3 parts per million. The treatise of Henderson and Haggard on noxious gases was accepted by both sides, at the trial, as a recognized authority on the effect of irritant gases. That authority states that the physiological response to various concentrations of sulphur dioxide is as follows:

Least detectable odor of sulphur dioxide	3 to 5 ppm.
Least amount causing irritation to the eyes	20 ppm.
Least amount causing immediate irritation to the throat	8 to 12 ppm.
Least amount causing coughing	20 ppm.
Maximum concentration allowable for prolonged exposure	10 ppm.
Maximum concentration allowable for short exposure(1/2 to 1 hour)	50 to 100 ppm.
Dangerous for even a short period	400 to 500 ppm.

It is to be observed here that the least amount causing immediate irritation to the throat is 8 to 12 pm, and that, without prolonged exposure, no harm is possible until the concentration reaches a density of 10 ppm., or a concentration over three times as strong as that discovered by Mr. Holden in eighty-eight tests.

A number of witnesses called by the plaintiffs, testified to complaints of irritated throats, hay fever, asthma, coughs, headaches, eye and nose irritations, all caused by the noxious effects of the smoke, dust and odors emanating from the gob pile. Some of these witnesses stated that they were under the care of physicians, but it is extraordinary that not one of these physicians was called to testify that his patient's malady was directly traceable to residential proximity to the gob pile. It is also remarkable that the head of the bureau of health of the city of McKeesport was not subpoenaed to testify to the deleterious effect of the gob fire on the health of the people in that vicinity.

An equal if not greater number of witnesses called by the defendant testified that they lived close to and adjacent to the gob fire, yet they suffered no injurious effects because of that proximity. Four men, ranging in age between twenty-two and forty-six, testified that they actually lived in shacks, on the gob pile, while it was on fire, and they declared in court that while they did not enjoy the odors and the excessive heat, yet they suffered no cough, throat or eye irritation, headache or any other ill effect. While we would hesitate to recommend the gob pile as a suitable place for a dwelling, yet, lacking evidence that these four men were salamanders, we cannot declare that the gases thrown off by this fire are sufficient in volume or density to bring about the dire results intimated by plaintiffs' witnesses and contended for by plaintiffs' counsel.

On the other hand, we cannot believe that one's health would improve by living close to the gob fire, and we cannot believe, despite testimony advanced by defendant's witnesses to the contrary, that there is no physical discomfort or annoyance caused to residents of that vicinity, by the burning mountain. In fact, our decision in this case is not based on the assumption that the people living close to the gob fire suffer no annoyance, but that the annoyance which is theirs is trivial in comparison to the positive harm and damage that would be done to the community, were the injunction asked for granted.

Much of our economic distress is due to the fact that there is not enough smoke in Pittsburgh and the Pittsburgh district. The metropolis that earned the sobriquet of the "smoky city" has not been living up to those vaporous laurels. The economic activity of the city that was known as "the workshop of the world," has decreased in proportion as its skies cleared of smoke. While smoke *per se is* objectionable and adds nothing to the outer aesthetics of any community, it is not without its connotational beauty as its rises in clouds from smoke stacks of furnaces and ovens (and even gob fires) telling the world that the fires of prosperity are burning,—the fires that assure economic security to the workingman, as well as establish profitable returns on capital legitimately invested.

If the coal mine of the defendant had been sunk in the midst of a residential district, utterly free of factories and mills, and devoid of all of those transportational facilities which create smoke, dust, dirt and grime, the complaint of the plaintiffs might have some force and effect, but the defendant's property is in the very heart of one of the most industrialized districts of Allegheny county. Within one hundred feet of the defendant's tipple, is located the galvanizing works of the National Tube company, a plant three thousand feet in length. The Columbia foundry is close by, as is also the rubbish dump of the city of McKeesport.

A garbage dump, 100 feet by 60 feet in dimensions, is located in the immediate vicinity of the gob pile. The main line of the Baltimore and Ohio railroad is but three hundred and seventy-six feet away; this is a four-track system, and over it pass approximately forty-five trains daily,—all users of bituminous coal, and all throwing off black smoke. To the north of the gob pile, within a distance ranging between three-tenths of a mile and two and six-tenths miles, there are factories and tin plate mills; the Christy Park works of the National Tube company; the national works of the National Tube company, and many other industries, with hundreds of stacks which emit black and grey smoke from the coal consumed.

The inhabitants of this district were cognizant of the industrialization of the community when they moved into it. They voluntarily took up abode in this territory, and can scarcely with consistency now be heard to voice a protest about the smoky atmosphere. One who voluntarily goes to war should not complain about cannon smoke.

Without smoke, Pittsburgh would have remained a very pretty *village*.

Sitting in equity we are compelled here to consider whether an injunction in this case might not work a greater mischief, and far greater injury, than the wrong we are asked to redress. To enjoin the piling of gob would, of course, prevent a gob fire, and the resulting smoke and dust so destructive to the aesthetic values of the community; but the philosophy of the beautiful must give way to the realities of a bread and butter existence. Furthermore, if there were no gob fire, the plaintiffs would not be free of the disturbance of smoke; they would still have the factories, mills, garbage dumps, incinerators and railroads to contend with.

We cannot enjoin the defendant for another reason, and that is because they are making a natural use of their land. ...

There is no testimony on the part of the plaintiffs that the defendant is mining its coal in an unordinary way. On the contrary, all the evidence in the case is to the effect that the methods of mining and disposing of gob employed by the defendant are the methods used in practically all mines. Every mine has its gob pile, and it was testified that practically one hundred percent of these gob piles catch fire. It was established further that at practically every mine, the rule is to pile the gob somewhere adjacent to the hole in the earth from which it is lifted to the surface.

If we enjoin the defendant company from piling its gob at that point and in that manner, we inferentially declare that all the mines in the state, at any rate in this county must not dispose of their gob in that manner, and, since no other practical method has been recommended, (we discuss this point later) we declare by implication that all coal mines must cease operating which, of course is absurd.

It was not established, nor charged at the trial, that the defendant operated its mine in negligent or inefficient manner. ...

To haul away the gob from the district by rail, would be an exorbitant expense, and would naturally result in an increased cost of coal. Furthermore, where would the gob be hauled to? and wouldn't it catch fire at that point? and wouldn't the defendant then be liable for any damage suffered by third parties, on account of that distant gob fire? A gob pile near the tipple of the mine is a natural use of the land, but there would be no legal defense to a gob fire away from the mine property.

Counsel for the plaintiffs are working on a *theory,* but we have a condition here to face. The uncontroverted testimony of the mine engineers is that gob piles are necessary incidents to all coal mining; that there is no practical method of operating a coal mine without a gob pile outside the mine; that all bituminous coal mines have gob piles; that these piles usually catch fire through spontaneous combustion. ...

We repeat that it is established that the plaintiffs are subjected to an annoyance, and the court sympathizes with them in the violence which is done to the aesthetic unities of the community. Were it not for the greater violence (by granting the injunction) which would be done to the all-too-vital necessity of living, we would gladly exercise the power that is lodged in our office to decree the banishment of those factors that are so inimical to the sensitive appreciation of the harmonious and beautiful. But we cannot give Mediterranean skies to the plaintiffs, when by doing so, we may send the workers and bread-winners of the community involved to the Black Sea of destitution.

Pennsylvania is the great industrial state of the Union. Its prosperity and leadership are entirely dependent upon its smoke producing industries. If the necessary and unavoidable smoke produced by these industries were to be enjoined, the plants could not operate, many millions of dollars in invested capital would be destroyed and many thousands of persons thrown out of gainful employment. ...

A Primer on the Socio-Legal Model of Law and Social Change

Jeb Barnes

The next reading, *Shades of Green*, provides a complex analysis of the determinants of corporate performance under environmental laws, which, like many laws regulating risk, are primarily targeted at organizations. To understand this excerpt, it is useful to place its discussion within a broader framework for understanding how formal rules are constructed and put into practice, which I call the "socio-legal model." (See Figure 1 below.)

The socio-legal model is a nested framework, which assumes that federal laws are created at the institutional level of analysis (or what some refer to as the institutional field) and that these rules are put into practice at the level of organizations (or the organizational field). We can think of this process as a multi-tiered fountain in which the law spills from the institutional level into the organizational level. The law then combines with other social and economic factors to create pressure for an organizational response. These pressures, however, are not self-executing. They must be interpreted and translated into organizational responses by particular businesses, which can have very different management styles. These management styles in turn deeply shape the specific organizational responses to the law and thus the outcomes produced at the ground level.

More specifically, federal rules are constructed through the interaction between Congress, the president, executive agencies and the courts. These rules then filter down to the organizational level and define what Gunningham and his colleagues call the "regulatory license to operate," which means the rules governing organizational behavior.

In a critical move, *Shades of Green* recognizes that the regulatory license does not operate in a vacuum at the level of organizational fields. It combines with the "economic license to operate"—basically, market pressures that effect the financial cost of compliance—and the social license to operate—social contexts that effect the level of pressure to comply with or resist the law.

Faced with this combination of regulatory, economic and social licenses, which can vary across settings, organizations must interpret these pressures and decide how to respond.

According to *Shades of Green,* different organizations have characteristic approaches towards dealing with the law, which range along the following continuum:

- laggards, who ignore or resist the law;

- reluctant compliers, who seek to do the minimum under the law;

- committed compliers, who take the law seriously and seek to go beyond what they believe to be its minimum requirements in order to create a margin for error under the law; and

- true believers, who only take the law seriously but see the underlying goals of the law as part of their core business goals and the "right" thing to do.

These different management styles yield very different responses and thus very different outcomes under the law.

Figure 1. The Socio-Legal Model

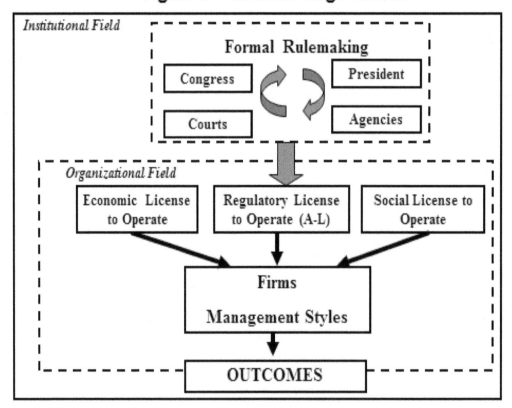

Shades of Green

Neil Gunningham et al.

O ver the past decade, a considerable literature has developed on the "greening of industry." At the heart of the field lies the question, "What are the determinants of greening?" For without an empirically grounded understanding of when and why profit-oriented businesses are willing to go beyond compliance with environmental law, or how far they are willing to do so and with what limits, it is impossible to disentangle wishful thinking and ideological exhortation from the kind of realistic expectations on which governmental and social policy can sensibly be based. Notwithstanding some valuable case studies (generally confined to environmental leaders) and some less illuminating survey evidence, adequate empirical answers have not been forthcoming. We still know little about why individual corporations behave the way they do in the environmental context, about why some companies, but not others, choose to move beyond compliance, or what motivates them to do so, about what the most important influences on environmental outcomes are, or what social policy tools are likely to prove most effective in achieving improved corporate environmental performance.

In this book, we have sought to advance the empirical understanding of these questions by studying fourteen pulp and paper manufacturing mills in British Columbia, Australia, New Zealand, and the states of Washington and Georgia in the United States. We have used a combination of qualitative and quantitative data gathered in 1998-99 to examine a number of alternative explanations for variation in "environmental performance" over time and across business corporations. We have particularly focused on the role of regulatory regimes, economic variables (such as firm-level economic incentives and resources), political and social pressures, and mental management and attitudes.

Our data and analyses have shown that the relationships between these variables and environmental outcomes are complex. This very complexity makes it desirable to both summarize and integrate our main findings, which we do in the first part of this chapter. In the second part, we explore their broader implications and lessons for social policy and regulatory design.

Neil Gunningham et al., Shades of Green: Business, Regulation and Environment, pp. 135-156. Copyright © 2003 by Stanford University Press. Reprinted with permission.

UNDERSTANDING CORPORATE ENVIRONMENTAL PERFORMANCE

To explain corporate environmental performance, we have argued, it is useful for analysts (and corporate managers themselves) to view business enterprises as simultaneously motivated and constrained by a multifaceted "license to operate." We found that corporate managers, at least in closely watched industries like pulp and paper manufacturing, viewed each facility's license to operate as including not only its regulatory permits and legal obligations but also an often-demanding "social license" and a constraining "economic license." The regulatory, economic, and social licenses are monitored and enforced by a variety of stakeholders, who commonly seek leverage by exploiting a variety of license terms. Environmental groups not only enforce the terms of the social license directly (e.g., through shaming and adverse publicity) but also seek to influence the terms of the economic license (e.g., generating consumer boycotts of environmentally damaging products) and of the regulatory license (e.g., through citizen suits or political pressure for regulatory initiatives). Thus the interaction of the different types of license often exceeds the effect of each acting alone. The terms of some legal license provisions extend the reach and impact of the social license by directly empowering social activists or by giving them access to information that they can use to pressure target enterprises. Conversely, a company that fails to respond appropriately to social license obligations risks a tightening of its regulatory license when frustrated community activists turn for help to politicians and regulators.

The terms of each strand of the "license to operate," however, often are far from clear. Moreover, proactive corporate officials sometimes can reshape some license terms-by providing information to and negotiating with regulators or environmental activists, by engaging in community outreach and education, and by scanning for technologies and procedures that simultaneously cut costs and improve the firm's environmental performance. Yet this very complexity, interactive nature, and malleability of the various license terms frustrate efforts to find objective measures of the relative stringency of one facility's license to operate as compared with another's.

Nevertheless, we attempted to examine the direct relationship between each strand of the license to operate and mill-level environmental performance. Of necessity, we could employ only rough proxies for the inherently complicated regulatory, economic, and social licenses. And we measured facilities' environmental performance—also a variegated phenomenon, consisting of action against many kinds of environmental risks—primarily by using quantitative data concerning serious kinds of water pollution and spills, which was available for most mills only for the latter part of the 1990s. This analysis, while necessarily simplistic, did produce some interesting insights into why some mills went further beyond compliance than others.

Understanding Convergence

Evaluations by government bodies and industry associations, along with our own measures, have all confirmed the same general conclusion: over the past thirty years, there has been a dramatic reduction in the polluting emissions of pulp mills in all the jurisdictions studied—on the order of 80 or 90 percent for several leading measures of water pollution in wastewater. Moreover, there has also been a considerable narrowing of differences between environmental "leaders and laggards" in levels of pollution control. All of the mills in our sample were generally in compliance with their regulatory permits; this too confirms the findings of other recent studies of the pulp and paper industry. None of the mills we studied were regulatory laggards in the sense of being ignorant of or systematic evaders of their regulatory licenses. All of the mills for which we could obtain quantifiable regulatory permit limits had gone beyond compliance, reducing the discharge of key water pollutants to levels well below those specified by their permits.

Changes in all strands of the pulp industry's license to operate, at least in economically advanced democracies, help explain both the overall decline in pollution and the general convergence of environmental performance across individual mills. Most striking, perhaps, was the convergence across the countries and the firms we studied in the *terms* of each of the individual types of license. When interviewed in 1998–99, firms with operations in more than one jurisdiction did not regard their regulatory license as being materially different in different jurisdictions. They referred to differences of enforcement style and philosophy in the different regulatory regimes, but they also observed that when the regulatory license was ratcheted more tightly in one jurisdiction, other jurisdictions commonly followed that lead. Similarly, while many mills reported that they had experienced far less social pressure in an earlier era, all now experienced some such pressure. Communities and environmental advocacy groups tended to act as de facto regulators, thereby further diluting the importance of different enforcement styles. As one mill manager put it, "the implications of failing to meet the regulations are too great from a public or market point of view, so we are more demanding on ourselves than the regulators are." Finally, the advent of globalization, and an extremely competitive world pulp market has diminished variability in the economic licenses of pulp mills. Institutional investors and financial analysts today are likely to judge all firms by common criteria.

Just as important, there has been a convergence *among* the different types of license. Just as the regulatory and social licenses have demanded tighter controls on emissions, the economic license in an increasingly competitive world market has become more demanding, pushing all the firms studied to concentrate on cutting costs and improving profits. The tougher regulator) and social licenses have substantially improved the environmental performance and attitudes of all the firms; in our sample, we did not find a single true laggard, and we found only one true Reluctant Complier.

But the economic license has simultaneously constrained how far firm* can go in a "green" direction. Due to economic constraints—especially overcapacity in the world market for pulp and the weakness of customer demand for unbleached paper or totally chlorine-free paper—none of the mills in our sample had leapt far ahead of the others by abandoning pulp bleaching or running a totally chlorine-free (TCF) operation; one mill (BC3) that had tried TCF had lost too much money in doing so and retreated. Economic license constraints helped explain why none of the firms in our sample had done the innovative engineering or made the very costly investments that would be necessary to operate a completely "closed-loop" mill, with no discharges to surrounding waterways, and why none had abandoned bleaching of paper at all as a way of reducing use of potentially polluting bleaching chemicals.

At the same time, financial markets today are more likely to react adversely to firms that get adverse publicity for regulatory noncompliance or avoiding environmental liabilities. Because both regulators and financial analysts take heed of demonstrations and protests against pulp mills, firms can justify paying heed to the social license in terms of economic risk management. The net result of accommodating to the demands of the three different types of license is that a firm can afford neither to drop too low nor aim too high: hence the considerable convergence in performance revealed by the statistics.

That convergence, however, has drifted more or less steadily toward better control of effluent in the pulp industry. The primary engine of that movement, we believe, has been periodic "tightenings" of governmental regulatory licenses. The law on the books (and in each mill's permit) is a benchmark for enforcers of both the social and economic license. Exposure of substantial legal noncompliance is taken by both community activists and professional investors as a justification for skepticism about the environmental good faith or the competence of mill managers. And that, of course, strengthens the capacity of regulatory license requirements to overcome economic license restraints.

The largest reductions in pulp mill discharge to water of harmful pollutants have stemmed from investments in expensive technologies, particularly secondary wastewater treatment facilities, oxygen delignification systems, and the substitution of chlorine dioxide for elemental chlorine as a bleaching agent (which often required construction of a chlorine dioxide plant). Economic license constraints often affected the timing of those installations, as firms often successfully argued that they should coincide with periodic rebuilding or updating of primary production equipment. But sooner or later, the regulatory license has trumped economic demands, partially through the implicit promise that all competitors would be obliged to make the same investment. And indeed, one of the most striking findings in our research has been the extent to which major investments in prevention and control technology have been made in response to pending or anticipated regulatory rules.

Understanding Variation

Convergence in environmental performance in the pulp and paper industry, while impressive, has not been complete. At the end of the twentieth century, we found significant differences among the mills we studied. The difference between best and worst performers was substantial: on some measures, such as BOD, TSS, and AOX, laggards emitted between three and four times more pollution than leaders. While some pulp mills in our sample were emitting less than 20 percent of the BOD and TSS allowed by their regulatory permits specified, others were in the 60-85 percent range. Thus we were left with an important puzzle. Why have some pulp mills done a better job in reducing pollution than others?

No simple answer emerges from our data, which point toward a complex, multivariate explanation. Corporate environmental behavior and motivation are extremely complex. They involve the interaction of numerous variables, each difficult to measure, and more resistant still to quantification, modeling, and regression analysis. Nevertheless, our interview and statistical data do generate a considerable number of insights for theories of regulation and corporate environmental behavior—relevant not just to the particular industry sector we studied but also to other highly regulated, heavily scrutinized, and mature industry sectors, and perhaps to others as well.

Variation in Firms' Licenses to Operate. Notwithstanding substantial convergence in the terms of the various license requirements, significant variation between the licenses of different mills helped explain some of the differences in their environmental performance. With respect to the *regulatory license,* for example, we found that British Columbia's lag behind the United States in requiring secondary wastewater treatment in mills at the edge of coastal waters resulted in better BOD control by those BC mills in 1998-99, on average, because their treatment facilities were newer and closer to the "state of the art." Similarly, British Columbia's more imminent and more stringent regulatory deadline for elimination of AOX discharges helps explain why BC mills, on average, had lower AOX emissions in 1998-99 than the U.S. mills in our sample. Other interfirm differences in environmental performance could be attributed at least in part to the terms of mills' particular *economic license.* For example, a mill whose products and customers were environmentally sensitive (GA2, selling paper diapers in western Europe) had low AOX discharges. Some firms operating under serious economic license limits, such as those who were cash-strapped, told us this constrained their capacity to put in place appropriate environmental technology. Conversely, mills whose corporate parents had larger sales and higher profit margins in the first half of the 1990s, a period of intense social and regulatory pressures regarding chlorine, had better technologies and better environmental performance at the end of that decade.

Different *social license* demands often appeared to be particularly powerful in influencing differences in environmental outcomes. For example, the gap between the emissions of WA2 and WA4, described earlier, was very much what one would have anticipated, given WA2's more remote, small-town location and WA4's location near the heart of a changing, more economically diversified city with lively environmental activists. In a number of cases, our interview data suggested that a painful, well-publicized encounter with a major environmental group produced a sea change in the corporate approach to the environment. More diffuse community pressure also prodded some firms to beyond-compliance measures, such as substantial expenditures on odor reduction measures. In several cases, customers' concerns, in the wake of Greenpeace's campaign in western Europe complaining about dioxin in pulp-mill effluent wedded environmental concerns with economic pressure—helping to explain lower AOX emissions on the part of some of the mills in our sample.

On the other hand, more global measures of the relationship between the different strands of the mills' license to operate did not correlate closely with contemporary variation in mill-level environmental performance. With respect to the regulatory license, for example, pulp mills' environmental performance did not consistently reflect the regulatory jurisdiction in which they operated or the type of regulatory regime they faced. On none of our measures did facilities cluster tightly by regulatory jurisdiction. Even the mills in British Columbia, where regulations called for radical reductions in AOX by the end of 2002, were not uniformly below the sample average. Notwithstanding more fearsome legal sanctions in the United States and the allegedly more legalistic U.S. approach to regulation, U.S. mills were as likely in 1998-99 to be below as above average. Similarly, we failed to detect any significant statistical relationship between regulatory jurisdiction and the extent to which pulp mills had invested in state-of-the-art pollution control or pollution-reduction technology. One reason, we conclude, is that convergence in regulatory licenses has by and large come to outweigh regulatory divergence. Just as significant, there is considerable flexibility in regulatory requirements *within* all the jurisdictions in this study, for regulators have tailored facility-level permits and informal orders to individual mills' inputs, technologies, surrounding environmental exigencies, and investment cycles.

With respect to economic variables, too, the relationships between corporate economic license and mill-level environmental performance, while suggestive in some cases, as noted above, were often inconclusive. One mill that sold pulp to be made into food containers, which one might expect to trigger especially strong market-related concerns about reducing use of elemental chlorine as a bleaching agent, operated at only 60 percent substitution, below average, and had not installed an oxygen delignification system, a leading-edge technology in reducing chlorinated organics. We discovered no significant statistical relationship, for example, between general economic conditions in the pulp industry, as measured by highs and lows in pulp prices, and various mill-level measures of pollution reduction and control of chemical spills. Similarly, we found *no* statistically significant correlation between average 1998-99 emissions and corporate economic resources, as measured by total sales or profit margin of the mill's corporate parent in 1998-99. Although mills owned by corporations with larger profit margins (ratio of income to sales) and larger annual sales income in the early 1990s generally had lower BOD, TSS, and AOX emissions late in the decade, and also had better pollution-control technology, some of those correlations did not reach the level of statistical significance. Corporate profitability in the first half of the 1990s was correlated (.62) with more ambitious environmental management style in 1998–99, but that association did not persist when we used 1995–99 measures of profitability. Some of the best-performing mills in terms of the environment were "true believers" in terms of environmental management style, despite struggling financially throughout much of the 1990s.

Finally, although a demanding social license was said by many managers to have been a trigger for certain beyond-compliance environmental measures, it is important to note that managers at different mills responded to social pressures in different ways. Some reacted to community or NGO demands with resistance rather than responsiveness. And this suggests that environmental management style—the attitudes and modes of thought that guided corporate and mill-level policy, not social pressure alone, is a key variable in determining the capacity of social pressures to shape corporate environmental performance.

Variations in Firms' Environmental Management Style. The different responses of firms to apparently similar social and regulatory pressures, plus our findings about the effects of corporate economic resources, suggest that the influence of the regulatory, economic, and social licenses on environmental performance depends on an "intervening variable"—managerial attitudes, or the combination of attitudes and executive action we call "environmental management style." When we classified each mill's environmental management style on a scale extending from Environmental Laggard through Reluctant Complier, Committed Complier, and Environmental Strategist to True Believer, and then correlated environmental management style with environmental performance, the results were striking. Average emissions for True Believers were substantially lower than those for Environmental Strategists, whose scores were substantially lower than the average for Committed Compliers, whose scores were substantially lower than the average for Reluctant Compliers.

True Believers and Environmental Strategists, we found, also tend to invest in better pollution-control technology. They also achieve larger incremental gains in environmental performance by virtue of a more dedicated approach to day-to-day environmental management (what we have called "implementation"). True Believers, we found, thus have fewer costly and environmentally harmful accidental spills of pulping chemicals. Moreover, they appear to scan more actively for win-win measures (which both improve environmental performance and cut costs). Environmental Strategists and especially True Believers also do a better job of building reputational capital with regulators and environmental activists (in local communities and nationally), which appears to pay off in attaining more flexibility in regulatory permits. In addition, True Believers and Environmental Strategists show a pattern of continued improvement in environmental performance over time, whereas Committed Compliers and Reluctant Compliers do not.

Yet firms are still constrained by the terms of their licenses. Thus environmental management style is far from omnipotent in shaping environmental performance, and it may well be shaped in part by the firm's economic situation. A firm that pushes the boundaries of its licenses too far will be punished: by regulators (if there is serious breach of the terms of a permit), by markets (if behavior goes beyond what is perceived by investors and analysts as economically rational), and by communities or NGOs (if behavior goes far beyond what is perceived as socially acceptable). As noted earlier, no mill in our sample, including True Believers, could ignore the capital constraints imposed by its economic license. And where the economic license was tight, even True Believers were not very far ahead of the Committed Compliers, for example, in adopting costly new environmental protection measures. Our data suggested that the attitudes of True Believers and Environmental Strategists resulted in incremental gains in the reliability and imaginativeness of day-to-day implementation of relatively standard corporate environmental policies, as well as a broader definition of what constituted economic gain from the installation of environmental equipment.

Moreover, although we are convinced by both our statistical and field-work data that "management matters," our methodology did not enable us to explain precisely why firms approximated one ideal type or another. As a working model, we assume that this is the outcome of interaction between external factors (e.g., license requirements) and internal factors (e.g., corporate culture). There was much to suggest that firms with different cultures behaved very differently. We were struck for example, by the behavior of a "corporate raider" that operated two mills in our sample. In each case, its attitude to the local community was confrontational in circumstances in which many other mills had gone to very substantial lengths to appease and establish trust with community groups. But to more fully tease out why different environmental management cultures arise would take a far more detailed and intensive study of a number of firms, including not just leaders (as a few studies have done) but also laggards (which are apt to refuse access to social scientists).

UNDERSTANDING CORPORATE GREENING

Our findings shed some empirical light on the literature on regulation and compliance and on the greening of industry, both of which we surveyed in Chapter 2. For example, a number of environmentalists and legal scholars presume that variation in environmental performance can be substantially explained by differences in regulatory regimes, particularly the stringency of their environmental rules and facility-level permits and the aggressiveness with which they are enforced. Yet we found that no regulatory jurisdiction is doing noticeably better or worse than the others in improving environmental performance among the pulp mills it seeks to control.

Most strikingly, the purported greater prescriptiveness and deterrence orientation of U.S. environmental regulation did not produce better environmental outcomes on the part of U.S. mills. At least in this closely watched industry, debates about coercion versus persuasive, compliance-oriented enforcement strategies are not of the essence, for once the terms of the regulatory license are established, firms have a variety of reasons to comply, over and beyond the efforts of enforcement agencies. Community and NGO vigilance in particular often has been the key to the salience and the threat, in managers' eyes, to their regulatory license, regardless of regime regulatory style.

In this industry, too, we find little empirical support for the more romantic versions of the "greengold thesis," which asserts that there is a happy coincidence between what is good for the environment and what is good for business. On the contrary, particularly with respect to investments in costly new pollution-control or pollution-reduction technologies, win-win solutions do not abound. The best example we encountered was the introduction of oxygen delignification, adopted by some mills partly because it promised operating cost reductions as well as pollution reduction. But many other mills calculated that oxygen delignification in their operations would not pay off on either dimension. Most major environmental improvements in the past few decades, such as those resulting from the installation of secondary treatment systems for wastewater and 100 percent substitution of chlorine dioxide for elemental chlorine in pulp bleaching, were driven by regulation (or anticipated regulation), since they entailed large capital investments and increases, not decreases, in operating costs, and did not result in a clear competitive advantage on the sales front. Most other new environmental technologies are extremely expensive, with no short-term payoff or demonstrable strategic advantage. Significantly, none of the companies in our sample had moved "outside the box" in terms of new bleach technologies or closed-loop production and none saw any natural market advantage in doing so.

Thus to the extent that substantial improvements of the environmental performance of the sector depend on the introduction of costly new technologies, they are not likely to be generated by economic pressure that elicits corporate scanning for win-win opportunities. That appears rather to be the comparative advantage of government regulation, which can (as it has in the pulp and paper industry) serve as a coordinating mechanism, encouraging investment in new environmental technologies by implicitly promising firms most willing to go along that that their competitors will be required to make similar investments.

On the other hand, our research indicated that firms in the pulp and paper industry enjoyed much greater opportunities to achieve win-win outcomes in terms of process and operational changes, such as diligent supervision and training that resulted in better mainte-nance and tighter process controls—which in turn reduced chemical spills, thereby minimiz-ing downtime, waste, and trouble with regulators and the community. Put another way, the "greengold" thesis had greater resonance when it came to the benefits of good housekeeping and a systematic approach to environmental management. But even in this realm, we found that *perception* was all-important. Some firms adopted vigorous environmental management and training systems and did a great deal more than was required by law, in the belief that it made good economic sense to do so, and/or because they believed it would protect the other terms of their license to operate. But other mills seemed singularly unimpressed with the idea of win-win outcomes and remained reactively driven by regulation and other social forces. It appears that management matters far more than the rhetoric of win-win.

Our research does not provide support for the various stage models of corporate greening that assert or assume that firms will go through a progression (in the view of some, a natural evolution) from laggard to compliance, to compliance plus, to environmental excellence. On the contrary, the constraints of the economic license (not least, the pressures to cut costs, the judgments of financial markets, and the unwillingness of consumers to pay a price premium for environmental excellence) are likely to keep them far short of the last of these stages. As we have seen, any company that strays too far from the terms of the economic license is likely to be brought back into line. For example, since consumers have thus far been unwilling to pay a price premium for totally chlorine-free paper, even companies that have the technology to go down this path do not use it because it is uneconomic to do so. Neither is it the case that firms will all, sooner or later, progress to at least a higher (albeit not the highest) stage of environmental performance. For notwithstanding increasing convergence in environmental performance, our study has also demonstrated substantial continuing variation and no evidence of any natural trend to higher stages of corporate greening.

On the other hand, our findings resonate with the various theories that emphasize the importance of a firm's social standing and in particular its economic stake in maintaining its reputation for environmental good citizenship. Firms in our sample, particularly larger firms with a high public profile, or even smaller ones highly dependent on the goodwill of the local community, tended to be highly sensitive to negative publicity and vulnerable to informal sanctions and shaming. And their behavior was shaped by a far broader range of stakeholders within the "organizational field" than regulators alone. Local community concern and pressure were particularly important in this respect.

Finally, our findings also lend considerable support to those who attribute importance to managerial attitude. However, whether a "greener" environmental management style derives from the sources mentioned in the literature—such as "charismatic green leadership," internal corporate culture, the nature of the firm's market niche, or other variables—was not apparent from our research, which would have had to have taken a very different form if we had sought to address such issues.

To what extent can our specific findings in this study be generalized to firms in other industries? No definitive answer can be ventured, of course. Much depends on the extent to which the other industries resemble the pulp and paper industry on at least some important dimensions.

The pulp and paper industry, for example, is subject to close environmental scrutiny, by communities as well as by regulators—especially because one component in its effluent, dioxin, has been the subject of great publicity and is particularly frightening to much of the public. It is capital-intensive and characterized by high asset specificity (that is, mills can't easily switch to other products, and companies cannot lightly abandon their huge sunk costs in current technologies). At the same time, it is intensely competitive. Firms in the Northern Hemisphere are threatened by lower-cost producers in Southeast Asia, and investors do not see the industry as a particularly attractive one; thus environmental managers have to fight especially hard for funds for beyond-compliance measures. Moreover, potential win-win innovations by one facility can be copied by others relatively easily, so that the gains from innovation may be short-lived. It is difficult for firms to capture additional market share by creating distinctive, "greener" products.

These characteristics are not unique to pulp manufacturers. To at least some extent, they are mirrored by other mature heavy industries, such as metals, chemicals, and other commodities. But it is also important to under-score the complexity of the analytical scheme we have developed to explain firm-level environmental performance. The relative tightness of the terms of a firm's regulatory, social, and economic licenses, the interaction among those license terms, and the firm's reaction to them, inevitably varies from firm to firm, as well as across industries. Thus we do not advance a crisp, highly determinative formula for predicting or explaining firms' environmental performance. Rather, our claim is that the analytic framework that arose from and pervades this study is theoretically applicable to virtually every industry, and thus can aid in comparing and understanding other regulatory contexts and firms too.

POLICY IMPLICATIONS

Our findings have a number of implications for regulatory design and social policy and suggest a number of instruments and strategies by which governments and others can most effectively change corporate environmental behavior. In analyzing the type of intervention that might be necessary, it is useful to begin by asking, "To what extent are firms likely to undertake environmental improvements voluntarily?"

Although there were a range of situations in which most of the firms we studied were willing go beyond compliance, they did so for the most part because of their perceptions of their license conditions and as a matter of risk management. Their beyond-compliance investments were mostly of the kind that we have termed "margin of safety" and "anticipatory compliance" measures, although some (in response to intense social license pressures) fell into the "good citizenship" category. It was government regulation, social pressures, and occasionally consumer action that drove environmental behavior, coupled with management's varying perceptions of the scope for win-win outcomes.

For these reasons, it would be unwise to assume that a purely voluntary approach will achieve further improvements, particularly in the case of Reluctant Compliers and Committed Compliers, which make up almost half our sample of firms. Even in the case of environmental strategists or true believers, their more ambitious good citizenship and win-win investments did not emerge across the board and were relatively limited. The evidence suggests that absent some substantial tightening of their license terms or some external shock precipitating a shift in management style, or both, many mills may simply remain at the stage of environmental progress that they have currently achieved.

In terms of regulatory design, the separate regulatory, economic, and social strands of the business enterprises' license provide a useful analytical framework for identifying the points of greatest leverage over corporate environmental performance.

Using the Regulatory License. It is important to reemphasize our finding that the largest improvements in corporate environmental controls of water discharges were associated with tightening regulatory requirements and intensifying political pressures. The big jumps in wastewater environmental performance in pulp manufacturing were the products of *regulation-driven technological change*. That is, technology changes occurred in order to meet more stringent performance standards.

As noted earlier in this chapter, further technological change is also likely to be driven by regulation. Yet governments are understandably reluctant to base performance standards on new technology that is unproven, for should the unproven technology fail, other jurisdictions will not adopt the requirement, and local industry may be put at a competitive disadvantage. More fundamentally, determining the appropriate technology on which to base a regulation is a costly and risky process for a government agency. The problems are exacerbated by information asymmetry: it is in the industry's interests to exaggerate the costs and impracticality of technological change, yet government is highly dependent on information supplied by the industry in making a determination on these matters. Thus governments are understandably reluctant to mandate substantial leaps forward in technology-based environmental performance in the absence of either major public pressure (as occurred with respect to dioxins) or the demonstrated economic viability of new technology.

Nevertheless, even without specifying more stringent performance standards, regulatory agencies are able to influence the development of new technologies by specifying their long-term goals and engaging industry officials in a dialogue about pathways and timetables for achieving them. For example, the U.S. EPA notes in the preamble to its cluster rule that it "believes that the mill of the future will approach closed-loop operations" and suggests an avenue by which this objective might be achieved.

The implied government capacity to make such technologies, once developed by leaders, mandatory for all firms provides some incentive for leaders to experiment and innovate, thereby obtaining first-mover advantages. It also provides some incentive for laggards not to fall too far behind current industry practice, so as to avoid costly retrofits if new technology becomes required. That is, regulation can stimulate greener technological innovation and adoption of innovative technology by creating a dynamic, increasingly stringent regulatory environment and decreasing uncertainty. While large shifts in the political climate toward more lenient regulation could derail the process, in recent decades, regulation in general, rather than any particular regulation, has been able to herd industry toward excellence by imposing a regulatory trajectory that forces facilities to anticipate a future of more stringent demands, in which new environmental and health impacts will have to be addressed. This effect is intensified because regulations, health and environmental concerns, and technological innovations in any jurisdiction commonly ripple through to other jurisdictions by virtue of the process of "regulatory modeling."

The "herding process" can be facilitated by the provision of good information about the relative environmental performance of regulatory leaders and laggards. For the most part, regulatory systems' performance in this regard has been disappointing. In conducting this research, for example, we faced tremendous difficulties in obtaining accurate and accessible data that could usefully be compared over time and between facilities. Good evaluations of government or corporate policy require accurate, *comparable* outcome data. Monitoring requirements can provide such data if they take into account more than the compliance of a particular facility at a particular point in time. Monitoring requirements could allow for evaluative research and policy analysis if care is taken to ensure that the data collection they require allows for comparison over time and between facilities, and if the manner in which the data are reported assures data quality and facilitates accessibility.

More broadly, some regulatory agencies have sought to nurture innovative, cost-effective solutions and to build in continuous improvement by developing a "performance track": an alternative to traditional regulation that is offered to environmental leaders who agree to implement an environmental management system, to consult with and provide information to local communities, and to achieve beyond-compliance environmental outcomes negotiated with the regulator. Underlying such approaches is the belief that such flexibility will "harness the power of competition to stimulate profitable clean technology and other environmentally beneficial innovations." For example, mill GA2 signed an agreement with the U.S. EPA under which it committed itself to maintain superior environmental performance and to serve as a benchmark for the EPA in setting effluent guidelines under the cluster rules. In return, it was given significant regulatory flexibility, as well as operational and capital cost savings, including flexible control of hazardous air pollutants, flexible air permitting for trials of new products, and fewer reporting, monitoring, and recordkeeping requirements. It was also offered greater predictability of regulatory requirements over a fifteen year period.

On the other hand, negotiating flexible permits is costly and risky for both agencies and regulated firms. Thus far, at least in the United States, they have proved feasible only in the limited number of cases where environmental and economic paybacks are sufficient to overcome their considerable cost to develop, administer, monitor, and assess, and where both agencies and facilities have sufficient reputation capital to overcome social actor opposition. WA4, for example, was able to obtain a "bubble permit" for its operations because of its heavy investments in its reputation with both regulators and social actors, while RF, already a superior environmental performer, was eager to obtain the much broader benefits described above.

Leveraging the Social License. Another central finding of our study was that business firms' social licenses provide a particularly powerful point of leverage. Community and environmental advocacy groups in particular tend to act as effective watchdogs and de facto regulators, shaming and otherwise pressuring companies into beyond-compliance environmental performance. While they can sometimes play this role in the absence of any form of state intervention, their effectiveness is enhanced by various forms of facilitative government regulation. In particular, rules that require facilities to inform the public of environmentally significant actions, and to disclose the results of monitoring, redress some of the inherent information asymmetries that occur between regulators, regulatees, and the public and allow social actors to most appropriately target their actions.

For example, in Indonesia, under the PROPER PROKASIH program, regulators rank the performance of individual facilities using surveys, a pollution database of team reports, and independent audits. An enterprise's pollution ranking is readily understandable by the public, being based on color coding (gold and green for the best performers, black, blue, and red for those not in compliance). The program has reportedly been very successful in improving the environmental performance of participating firms.[35] In our study, we found that in British Columbia, mills were particularly mindful of avoiding breaches that might result in poor standing in a periodic government-published report that functioned much as a mill-by-mill environmental scorecard. In the United States, the Toxic Release Inventory, which simply obligates firms to publish their total estimated emissions of potentially hazardous chemicals, has created strong incentives to reduce the use of such chemicals.

Moreover, our research indicates that government actions that *procedurally* empower local communities can have significant effects. In New Zealand, mills reported having become much more responsive to community environmental concerns after communities were given the legal right to challenge the terms of each facility's "consent" (permit), and thereby gained the power to delay the introduction of new processes or technology. In an Australian jurisdiction, similar effects flowed from a new law that obligated firms to prepare and comply with an environmental improvement plan, including a commitment to consultation with local communities. In Canada and the United States, the permitting process has long been open to the public and allowed for public comment on permitting decisions. Such public access has been extended in the United States through programs such as Project XL and the Environmental Leadership Program, which make it a condition for providing greater regulatory flexibility that participating companies provide information to, and consult with, local communities.

The Economic License and Environmental Performance. Turning to the economic license, we described earlier how its terms operate as a constraint on environmental leadership. Our interviews with financial institutions, industry analysts, corporate lawyers, and company officials in the pulp and paper industry suggested that the unwillingness of investment analysts and the financial community to take account of environmental issues is changing only very slowly. However, not all aspects of the economic license militate against improved environmental performance. Scholars and environmental activists have suggested that governments and NGOs can act to mitigate some of the harsher impacts of the economic license by facilitating provision of information to the market, enabling it to make more accurate evaluations as to the environmental credentials and liabilities of different firms. There is some evidence that markets do punish environmentally "bad" firms and reward "good" ones in terms of their stock price, perhaps because good environmental management may be regarded as a useful indicator of good management generally. However, other studies find no such effect. We found little evidence of this effect in our study, discovering instead that several doses of adverse publicity about one firm's environmental record had no significant effect on its stock price.

Nevertheless, governments may be able to add greater legitimacy and potency to the dissemination of relevant information to the market. For example, the U.S. Securities and Exchange Commission requires all publicly traded companies to report their environmental liabilities for both hazardous waste cleanup and environmental legal actions. However, there has been an extremely low disclosure rate. Information standards can obviously only be effective to the extent that the information they require is in fact provided.

Similarly, the launching of private efforts to improve the provision of data to the market may also have a positive impact on corporate environmental performance. For example, lists of certified "green" firms, such as the Dow Jones Sustainability Group Index (DJSI) may, over the long term, encourage small companies to strive to be listed on the index. In addition, if investing based on the DJSI provides a reasonable return on investment (as seems to be the case), such indices might lead to a less reactive approach on the part of financial analysts and provide incentives for corporate environmental leadership.

The economic license can also be influenced by consumer preferences. Were consumers to cease demanding bright white paper, pulp mills would abandon environmentally damaging bleaching technologies. In theory, that process could be accelerated through independent certification and labeling schemes that call consumers' attention to products made in environmentally preferable ways, such as unbleached paper. Realistically, however, while such labeling schemes may have value in some areas, such as the sale of up-market wines, they face a much harder task in the realm of basic commodities such as pulp or copy paper. A more promising first step, therefore, would be for governments, as major purchasers of paper products, to lead the market toward dramatic reductions in the use of bleaching chemicals by insisting on buying only (or mostly) bleach-free paper products. Similarly, in circumstances where unbleached paper is unsuitable, government could provide leadership by purchasing pulp with high recycled-paper content. However, the fickleness of government in obeying its own rules may make companies reluctant to invest heavily in such initiatives, while others (and the industry association itself) have often been involved in systematic attempts to derail such government initiatives. Despite an executive order in 1993 for the U.S. federal government to purchase recycled paper, actual purchasing behavior did not change until 1998, after a second executive order, and only after tremendous pressure to do so was applied by various environmental groups.

Policy can most directly influence the economic constraints faced by industry (and activists) by making it cheaper for industry to comply or go beyond environmental compliance (and cheaper for activists to participate in the regulatory process and obtain information). This could be done through direct subsidies, grants, tax incentives, and other transfers of money to both industry and community and environmental organizations. For example, governments can fund research consortia to find new and innovative technologies. They can also provide tax incentives for companies that install more environmentally friendly technology. And they can provide grants to activist organizations that allow them to pay staff to develop expertise or attend public hearings.

The points of leverage provided by the different strands of firms' license to operate are not, of course, mutually exclusive. Since the causes of inadequate environmental performance are complex, multifaceted, and contingent upon a range of external factors, they are unlikely to be amenable to a simple or single policy fix. Policy-makers need to employ a substantial toolkit and to leverage change at a number of different pressure points. Combinations of instruments, harnessing a broader range of social actors, are likely to provide the most promising approach. What combinations are likely to work best in what circumstances is itself a complex issue, which one of us has explored at length elsewhere.

One of our strongest findings is that management style matters. By corporate environmental management style, we should reiterate, we mean something more than the adoption of formal environmental management systems, such as ISO-14000. Environmental management style includes a set of managerial attitudes toward environmental issues and actions that go beyond the formulation and systematic implementation and evaluation of environmental policies. It includes such variables as how open and responsive managers are in dealing with regulators and environmental groups, how imaginatively and energetically they scan for win-win opportunities, and what kind of calculus they employ in evaluating the business benefits of investments in environmental improvements. What distinguished high-performing True Believers and Environmental Strategists from, say, Committed Compliers was not whether or how often they conducted systematic self-audits, or how they developed environmental management systems, but how they conceived the purpose and function of such audits or systems.

If management style is important in explaining environmental outcomes, an important policy question is whether management style is amenable to influence by the levers of public policy, and if so how? Unfortunately, government intervention on this front is risky without knowing a great deal more about *why* management attitudes in different firms approximate different ideal types. And in this regard, our research, limited to cross-sectional comparisons at one point in time, as opposed to detailed firm-by-firm histories, produced no definitive knowledge. The managers we interviewed identified a number of influences on their behavior, largely in terms of the various license conditions described earlier. But why they reacted so differently to these different pressures, we cannot say. How government policy-makers might be able to change corporate environmental management style remains an elusive, but undoubtedly important, empirical and policy issue.

Finally, our research suggests that environmental management style alone cannot guarantee superior environmental performance. Indeed the data suggest that external license factors—regulatory and social pressures, and economic constraints and resources—that both interact with (and often shape) management attitudes are crucial in determining environmental performance. If those license conditions are not congenial, measures focused on management style alone are unlikely to make a large difference. To paraphrase Marx, companies make their own history but not in circumstances of their own choosing.

Discussion Questions

1. What is the role of courts in overseeing federal agencies and administrative decision-making?

2. How has this role changed?

3. What is the proper role for the courts in overseeing federal agencies? Should they generally defer to agency expertise or vigorously review its decisions to ensure fairness?

4. How are the public policy problems of injury compensation and regulating hazards different?

5. Why did the court in the Versailles case rule against the plaintiffs? Does this case and its reasoning suggest that courts are poorly equipped to address certain types of policy issues? If so, which types and what are the alternatives to lawsuits?

6. What factors determine corporate performance under environmental laws?

B. Redressing Inequalities

Rights and Social Change

A third feature of modern pluralistic societies is the demand of minority groups for recognition and equality. Courts have obviously played a central role in the struggle over their demands. These readings provide some examples of these struggles.

ADDITIONAL RECOMMENDED MATERIALS:

Eyes on the Prize: Fighting Back (documentary on desegregation of schools in the South).

Mary L. Dudziak, *Cold War Civil Rights: Race and the Image of American Democracy* (2000).

Lauren Edelman, "Legal Ambiguity and Symbolic Structures: Organizational Mediation of Civil Rights Law," *American Journal of Sociology* (97)b 1992: 1531-76

Charles Epp, *Making Rights Real* (2009), *The Rights Revolution* (1998).

Michael McCann, *Rights at Work* (1994).

Lucas Powe, *The Warren Court and American Politics* (2000).

There Is No Harm in Climbing Stairs

P. Irons

J o Carol LaFleur, a teacher at Patrick Henry Junior High School in Cleveland, Ohio, went to see her principal, Henry E. Wilkins, on the morning of December 17, 1970. Both principal and teacher were new to their jobs; Wilkins had just taken over at the inner-city school that did not have a single white student. Jo Carol was in her first full year of teaching, assigned first to English classes and then to a "transition" class of troubled girls with emotional and educational problems. Jo Carol informed Wilkins that she was pregnant and was expecting a child the next year in July.

The principal was dismayed by news that most people would consider an occasion for congratulations. Under school-district rules, he informed Jo Carol, she could not teach after her fourth month of pregnancy, in March 1971. She would then have to go on unpaid maternity leave and could not return to her job until the semester after her child was three months old. This would keep her from teaching until January 1972. Even then, she could be assigned to any school in the city, which included some twenty junior highs. Jo Carol expressed her objections to this policy, but she returned to her classroom and nothing more happened until March 12, 1971. Wilkins then looked at his calendar and called Jo Carol to his office for another chat.

Tempers flared at the second meeting of principal and teacher. Wilkins insisted that Jo Carol sign the leave forms he thrust at her. She refused, explaining that her pregnancy did not interfere with teaching and that she wanted to complete the school year. Wilkins finally completed the form without her signature and informed Jo Carol that she was suspended from teaching. She stormed out of the office, returned to her classroom, and told her students that she would not willingly leave them.

Just five weeks after her suspension, Jo Carol faced the Cleveland school board in the federal courtroom of Judge James C. Connell. Two young lawyers, Carol Agin and Lewis Katz, had filed a complaint asking Judge Connell to hold the mandatory leave policy unlawful and to order that Jo Carol be returned to her classroom. The complaint alleged that the board's

Peter H. Irons, "There Is No Harm in Climbing Stairs," The Courage of their Convictions, pp. 307-316. Copyright © 1990 by Simon & Schuster, Inc. Reprinted with permission.

policy discriminated against women teachers and violated their "privileges and immunities" under the Fourteenth Amendment. Another pregnant Cleveland teacher, Ann Elizabeth Nelson, who taught French at Central Junior High, joined the suit with Jo Carol LaFleur. Behind the case was the Women's Equity Action League, a feminist group founded in 1968 to sponsor litigation and lobbying aimed at employment and education discrimination. Jane M. Picker, a Yale Law School graduate and professor at Cleveland—Marshall Law School, worked with WEAL and recruited Agin and Katz to try the case.

The trial before Judge Connell began on April 19, 1971, and took just two days. Crusty and conservative, Connell did not conceal his disdain for the feminist challenge to the school board's paternalism. Connell was seventy-three years old, a former county prosecutor and municipal judge appointed to the federal bench in 1954 by a fellow Republican, President Dwight Eisenhower. The school board's lawyer, Charles F. Clarke, shared Connell's party affiliation but differed in demeanor. Courtly and courteous, Clarke was a partner in Cleveland's largest corporate firm and devoted much time to community health and welfare groups; he served on the boards of the Free Medical Clinic and the Cleveland Welfare Federation. But Clarke, who also headed the national association of railroad trial lawyers, conceded nothing to his courtroom opponents and salted the trial record with objections to testimony which might damage his case.

Carol Agin and Lewis Katz challenged the mandatory leave policy as unduly rigid. An inflexible rule which banned teachers with normal pregnancies from the classroom made no sense, they argued to Judge Connell, who heard the case without a jury. Dr. Sarah Marcus presented their primary medical case against the rule. Chief of obstetrics at Women's Hospital in Cleveland since 1958, Dr. Marcus began her practice in 1923 and had treated thousands of pregnant women. She peppered her testimony with wry humor. Carol Agin first asked whether women should work during pregnancy. Women with normal pregnancies could work "up until just before they are ready to go into the hospital for delivery," Dr. Marcus answered. "I did," she added. What about physical activities like climbing stairs in schools? "I tell them to be careful and not run up the stairs all at one time, but there is no harm in climbing stairs. It is good activity."

Charles Clarke pricked himself on the doctor's sharp tongue. Unable to budge her from allowing pregnant women to continue teaching, he moved to farm work, which Dr. Marcus also approved. Clarke went on. "What about the mortality of the mothers when the babies were dropped in the field?" She obviously considered that an irrelevant question and answered curtly. Clarke took another plunge. "What about working as a steel worker," he asked, "climbing up on beams for a new steel building?" Dr. Marcus conceded that high-steel work "is hazardous, even for men." Clarke asked why she thought so. Dr. Marcus did not hide her incredulity at his question. "I watched them through the window falling off the Terminal Tower one time," she explained, "and when they got to the bottom, they weren't alive." She ended this exchange on a testy tone: "I wouldn't expect my pregnant mother to be a construction worker."

Clarke defended the board's mandatory leave policy with testimony by Mark Schinnerer, who wrote the regulation in 1952 as Cleveland's school superintendent and was now retired at the age of seventy-two. "We had some very embarrassing situations where women who were pregnant would stay too long in the classroom," he explained. Pregnant teachers "were subjected to humiliations" by students "who giggled about it." Clarke prompted Schinnerer to recall one example of student hilarity at the sight of teacher pregnancy. "It was reported that the children in the classroom in the junior high school were taking bets on whether the baby would be born in the classroom or in the hall." Schinnerer also explained why he wanted women teachers to stay at home for at least six months after childbirth. "I am a strong believer that young children ought to have the mother there" to take "tender care of the babies." Many of America's problems, he suggested, stemmed from working mothers who neglected their infants.

In the 1955 film "Blackboard Jungle," Sidney Poitier played an inner-city teacher who feared his students: "My pupils are the kind you don't turn your back on, even in class." Clarke intimated that pregnant teachers in Cleveland schools were also the likely prey of predatory students. He asked high-school superintendent Julius Tanczos how many students had assaulted teachers in the past year. Judge Connell overruled an objection to this question. School records showed a total of 256 student assaults on teachers, Tanczos stated. Clarke then asked how many guns and knives had been confiscated from students. Connell overruled another objection, and Tanczos said that forty-six guns and eighteen knives had been confiscated that year.

Clarke countered Dr. Marcus with another obstetrician, Dr. William C. Weir, whose practice spanned thirty-five years. The board's lawyer tried to turn the classroom into an emergency ward, leading the doctor through the possible complications of all nine months of pregnancy. Women in the first three months faced "spontaneous abortion, nausea and vomiting, and headaches," Dr. Weir stated. Complications in the next trimester included toxemia, which might cause convulsions, and placenta previa, resulting in serious hemorrhaging. The major complication of the third trimester, Dr. Weir said, would be spontaneous premature delivery.

Dr. Marcus had portrayed pregnant women as capable of most kinds of exertion and exercise. Dr. Weir portrayed the pregnant woman as a virtual cripple. "Her whole center of gravity changes," he stated; "her shoulders are further back, she is subject to more backaches, and due to the weight increase she is much more awkward and can't move around as quickly as she could before." Clarke then asked about the fears of pregnant women. Dr. Weir cited worries about miscarriage, labor difficulties, and abnormalities in their children. "What about an environment," Clarke continued, "in which the pregnant lady might be in fear of a physical assault?" Such fear could induce premature labor, Dr. Weir answered. Informing his witness that 256 Cleveland teachers had been assaulted by students the prior year, Clarke asked his opinion on "the wisdom and reasonableness" of the board's mandatory leave policy. "I think it is a very reasonable rule," Dr. Weir concluded.

Judge Connell agreed with Dr. Weir. His written opinion, issued on May 12, 1971, restated the testimony of Clarke's witnesses and made no mention of witnesses called by Agin and

Katz. Before adoption of the board's rule in 1952, Connell wrote, pregnant teachers "suffered many indignities" which included "children pointing, giggling, laughing and making snide remarks" about their condition. Connell cited the testimony of Julius Tanczos about assaults on teachers and confiscation of guns and knives. He then painted a grim and gruesome picture of toxemia, placenta previa, and other complications of pregnancy which could lead to hospitalization or even death. "In an environment where the possibility of violence and accident exists," Connell wrote, "pregnancy greatly magnifies the probability of serious injury."

Judge Connell brushed aside the argument that imposing a mandatory leave policy only on women violated the "equal protection" clause of the Fourteenth Amendment. Far from harming the pregnant teachers, he ruled, the board's rule was designed to protect them. Connell went back to 1908 for Supreme Court precedent, quoting at length from an opinion reflecting the paternalism of that era: "The two sexes differ in structure of body," the Court had written, "in the functions to be performed by each, in the amount of physical strength, in the capacity for long continued labor, particularly when done standing, the influence of vigorous health upon the future well-being of the race, the self-reliance which enables one to assert full rights, and in the capacity to maintain the struggle for subsistence." Six decades later, this brand of Social Darwinism still appealed to Judge Connell. He concluded that the mandatory leave policy was "entirely reasonable" and did not discriminate against pregnant teachers.

Judge Connell's old-fashioned opinion did not surprise the teachers' lawyers, who asked the federal appeals court in Cincinnati to reverse the decision. In addition to WEAL and other feminist groups, other organizations considered pregnancy leave an important issue. The American Civil Liberties Union, United Auto Workers, National Educational Association, and a federal agency, the Equal Employment Opportunity Commission, joined as "friends of the court" to support the Cleveland teachers. The three-judge panel that heard and decided the appeal included a retired Supreme Court justice, Tom (Hark, who remained on the bench and still heard an occasional case.

Judge George Edwards, a former auto worker and union lawyer who was placed on the court by President John F. Kennedy, wrote the panel's opinion in July 1972. Edwards read the trial testimony very differently than Judge Connell. He quoted Dr. Weir as admitting that many of his patients had worked past the fourth month of pregnancy without any problems. Dr. Weir's agreement that "each pregnancy is an individual matter" undermined the boards inflexible policy, Edwards noted. He did not share Connell's horror at "giggling" students: "Basic rights such as those involved in the employment relationship," Edwards wrote, "cannot' be made to yield to embarrassment."

Judge Connell had dismissed as having "no weight" the argument that the board's policy discriminated against women. Judge Edwards disagreed, finding it "a rule which is inherently based upon a classification by sex." Although male teachers could not become pregnant, "they are subject to many types of illnesses and disabilities" but not to mandatory leave rules. Finding the rule "arbitrary and unreasonable," the appellate court reversed Judge Connell

Losers in the second judicial round, the Cleveland school board asked the Supreme Court to review the case. Jo Carol LaFleur and Ann Nelson were joined by Susan Cohen, a Virginia teacher who had lost a similar case. Partly to resolve the difference between the lower federal courts, the justices voted to review both decisions and set the cases for argument on October 15, 1973. The issue of mandatory pregnancy leave reached the Supreme Court at the crest of the feminist wave. Pressure by women's groups had secured passage of "protective" laws during the Progressive era. But these laws, mostly upheld by the Supreme Court, did not give women equality with men; they reflected views of women as the "weaker" sex.

Spurred by the victories of black Americans in the 1950s, the feminist movement grew in the 1960s and gained its own victories in the early 1970s. Congress adopted the Equal Rights Amendment in 1972; more than half the state legislatures ratified the measure in the next few months. Congress approved the Equal Pay Act in 1973. The Supreme Court granted feminists their fondest wish in 1973 by upholding a right to abortion. Later that year, the Court came close to ruling that women belonged to a "suspect class" like blacks. Although the majority shied away from that holding, four justices declared their support for this position. The Burger Court, hostile to criminal defendants and the poor, seemed even more friendly to women than the Warren Court had been. Women's groups which had launched attacks on all forms of legal discrimination had every reason to feel optimistic in 1973.

The pregnancy-leave cases picked up new friends on both sides as they approached the Supreme Court. Delta Air Lines, which at that time fired pregnant stewardesses, joined the Virginia schools that had fired Susan Cohen. The Nixon administration, represented by Solicitor General Robert Bork, sided with the teachers against the school boards. Ironically, in the same month the cases were argued, Bork was badly burned in the Watergate "firestorm," when he obeyed Nixon's order to fire special prosecutor Archibald Cox.

Charles Clarke defended the Cleveland school board in the Supreme Court. Justice Blackmun, who authored the *Roe v. Wade* opinion, was "a little curious" as to why the board picked four months from conception as the time for leaving the classroom. Former superintendent Schinnerer considered that to be the time "it became apparent that the teacher was pregnant," Clarke replied. "I suspect that just as you pointed out in the *Roe* case," he told Blackmun, "medieval theology" had chosen four months as the time of "quickening" of the fetus. Schinnerer certainly reflected medieval thought about women.

Blackmun returned the argument to modern times and asked why teachers could not choose to teach until one month before giving birth. Clarke pointed to medical testimony about the "complications, disorders, and discomforts of pregnancy." Blackmun interrupted this litany of ills: Was that testimony before the Cleveland board in 1952 when it "made up this rule"? Clarke admitted it was not. The board picked the date "out of the clear blue," Blackmun suggested. Clarke could only suggest that pregnant teachers "began to swell" in the fourth month and that students might giggle at this sight.

Justice Potter Stewart wondered why the board needed a mandatory rule. Clarke replied that pregnant teachers had refused to go on unpaid leave before the rule was adopted. Teachers asked to leave after seven or eight months of pregnancy, he said, "just would not do it." Justice Blackmun followed up with a question about Jo Carol LaFleur: "Mr. Clarke, is it accurate to say that without the rule she might have finished the term without any difficulty?" Clarke conceded the point, but returned to his medical ace. "The evidence is undisputed on Dr. Weir's testimony that a schoolteacher, four months pregnant, is not an able-bodied person." Clarke did not mention Dr. Marcus, who had disputed this testimony with fifty years of experience.

With his medical testimony under question, Clarke abruptly changed his argument. "The rule was not enacted for the welfare of the teachers," he now claimed. "The rule is for the administrative convenience of the school," which could more easily replace pregnant teachers with substitutes. Despite his new legal tack, Clarke could not resist a recital of his medical horror stories. The pregnant teacher "urinates more frequently because of the pressure of the fetus on her bladder. She is more susceptible to headaches. She has the three classic fears of pregnancy, of a miscarriage, of her own death, of a deformed child."

Jane Picker, a specialist in constitutional law, took over for the teachers in the Supreme Court. She first aimed her argument at stereotypes about women. Her target was the 1908 decision that Judge Connell had cited as a "protective" measure. "Woman's frail nature historically has been an excuse for protecting her in ways which have affected her adversely," she stated. "In fact, if pregnancy is a valid reason for discriminating, we can discriminate in such a manner as to protect all women out of jobs." Picker then attacked Clarke's claim that the board's rule ensured continuity in the classroom, noting that Jo Carol LaFleur was assigned to her "transition" class to replace another pregnant teacher. "It requires the fingers of only one hand," Picker said, to count the three teachers the students met that year because of the board's policy on pregnancy. She reminded the justices that they had rejected "administrative convenience" claims in recent decisions involving women, and argued that no teacher's "employment rights should be taken away from them in order to shield children from the facts of life."

The last questions from the bench opened a new legal door. Jane Picker was first asked if this was a case "exclusively involving the Equal Protection Clause." She agreed it was. The next question was a chivalrous gesture: "You do not view it as involving the Due Process Clause at all?" The question was not academic, because recent Supreme Court opinions—including the *Roe* case—held that women had the "liberty" to make decisions about bearing and raising children under the Due Process Clause. "Your Honor," Jane Picker candidly admitted, "we did not think to plead that originally." Then she rushed through the open door and made the Due Process claim.

The Court's opinion, written by Justice Potter Stewart and handed down on January 21, 1974, ushered the teachers through the door the justices had held open for them. "This Court has long recognized," Stewart wrote, "that freedom of personal choice in matters of marriage and family life is one of the liberties protected by the Due Process Clause of the Fourteenth Amendment." Policies that acted to "penalize the pregnant teacher for deciding to bear a child" placed a "heavy burden" on constitutional rights. Stewart made a further point about the rigidity of the leave policy: "The rules contain an irrebuttable presumption of physical incompetency" of pregnant teachers. Branding such presumptions as "disfavored" by the Court, Stewart noted that the Cleveland board's medical witness, Dr. Weir, agreed "that each pregnancy was an individual matter."

Stewart's use of the "liberty" interest of the Due Process Clause, which neatly avoided questions of gender discrimination, troubled Justice Lewis Powell. Although he concurred in the result, Powell feared that broader "liberty" claims might push through the Court's open door. "As a matter of logic," he wrote, "it is difficult to see the terminus of the road upon which the Court has embarked under the banner of 'irrebuttable presumptions.' " Powell did not identify any groups which might wave this new banner, but gay and lesbian activists were among those who read the Court's opinion with interest and began to shape new legal challenges to "presumptions" that their sexual preferences were symptoms of moral or physical disease. The challenge did not reach the Court for another decade, but Powell was determined to block the road.

The Court's decision troubled two justices even more than Powell. Justice William Rehnquist wrote for himself and Chief Justice Warren Burger in dissenting. "All legislation involves the drawing of lines," Rehnquist wrote, and some people who are otherwise able to perform a function will be disadvantaged by lines that fence them out. Forcing administrators to make an "individualized determination" in each case would lead to chaos. The dissenters imagined "a twenty-year-old who insists that he is just as able to carry his liquor as a twenty-one-year-old" coming to court and waving Stewart's opinion. What really upset the dissenters, though, was the prospect of challenges to mandatory retirement laws for public employees. Rehnquist and Burger shrank at the imagined sight of older workers waving Stewart's opinion and demanding "individual determinations of physical impairment and senility."

In a sense, the *LaFleur* decision represented the high-water mark of the feminist movement in the Supreme Court. Following the decision, state laws and federal agencies barred private employers from withholding leave and disability benefits from pregnant workers. But as the feminist wave began to recede, and the Equal Rights Amendment became stalled in state legislatures, the Court stepped back from *LaFleur* and struck down such laws and regulations. Congress reacted by passing the Pregnancy Discrimination Act in 1978, which overrode the Court's restrictive rulings. Employers challenged the law and asked the Court to bail them out. But Congress had spoken loudly on the issue, and the Court decided in 1987 that a California bank must return Lillian Garland, who sued the bank, to the job she held before going on pregnancy leave, judges and lawmakers no longer giggled at pregnant women after Jo Carol LaFleur took Cleveland to court.

Eating Crow

How Shoney's, Belted By a Lawsuit, Found the Path to Diversity

Dorothy J. Gaiter

Nashville, Tenn—It wasn't so long ago that Raymond Danner shook up the staffs at his Shoney's Inc. restaurants under the theory that some of them were "too dark." Employees say he sometimes ordered managers to fire blacks if they were deemed too visible to white customers; he sometimes uttered racial slurs.

These days, Mr. Danner, now retired, gives heavily to black causes. And Shoney's, the company he co-founded, ascribes to a radically new view: The staffs *need* to be more representative of minorities in America's ever-changing business landscape.

This isn't mere bluster: Since 1989, the family-style restaurant chain has added 83 black dining-room supervisors at its Shoney's restaurants. Two of 24 vice presidents are black and an African-American sits on the company's nine member board. There were none before. From two black-owned Shoney franchises back then, there are now 13. From $2 million seven years ago, it is now spending an estimated $17 million annually to buy goods and services from minority-owned companies.

On top of that, Shoney's operates an 800 number posted in corporate offices and in its 700 Shoney's and Captain D's seafood restaurants to field complaints about racial discrimination or harassment. Recently, it fired an employee who left racial slurs on a tape recording. "We have a policy of zero tolerance," says Juanita Presley, a black lawyer and one of two employees investigating discrimination and harassment complaints.

So what took Shoney's from pariah to a company aggressively pushing workplace diversity?

A costly, attention-grabbing lawsuit; changing times; and, some think, an actual change of heart.

In April 1989, after years of complaints, civil-rights lawyers filed a class-action suit that accused Shoney's of being essentially a racist enterprise. It named more than 200 current and former executives, supervisors and managers of Shoney's who it said had disparaged blacks, blocked their promotions or fired or declined to hire them for racial reasons. Four years later, Shoney's settled the suit for a whopping $134.5 million, including lawyer and

Dorothy J. Gaiter, "Eating Crow: How Shoney's, Belted by a Lawsuit, Found the Path to Diversity," Wall Street Journal. Copyright © 1996 by Dow Jones & Company, Inc. Reprinted with permission.

administrative fees. Of that, $105 million went to pay the claims of some 20,000 employees or job applicants.

Even before settling the suit, it struck a voluntary covenant—one of three it would eventually reach—with the Southern Christian Leadership Conference, a civil-rights organization founded by the Rev. Dr. Martin Luther King Jr. and several other ministers including the Rev. Joseph E. Lowery, who currently heads it. Since then, Shoney's has pumped more than $194 million—26% more than its goals—into minority-owned companies and organizations, and into black employees' salaries.

"This is the kind of turnaround that we like to see. I've been in this business for 20 years and I've seen lots of whitewashes. This is real. Black people know this is a company where they can get ahead," says Thomas A. Warren, a Tallahassee, Fla., lawyer who helped press the class-action suit against Shoney's.

Alex Schoenbaum, Shoney's 80-year-old namesake and retired chairman, agrees: "There are a lot of people who have changed their thoughts and changed their way of doing business since this case." Mr. Schoenbaum adds: "Because it was expensive—extremely expensive."

Indeed, the settlement walloped Shoney's earnings for the fiscal year ended Oct. 31, 1992; the company posted a loss of $26.6 million after taking a $77.2 million charge to pay its share of the claims. It was certainly expensive for Mr. Danner, 71, who says he paid out of his own pocket about half of the $105 million that went to claimants.

The story of Shoney's struggle to mend its old ways touches on sensitive issues in corporate America: How does a company separate itself from a powerful chairman who built the business but who had become a lightning rod for bad publicity? How does it then change the culture that that chairman nurtured? And how does it repair the damage, rebuild and chart a new course in a field crammed with competition?

A Southern company, Shoney's was peopled with employees trying to cope with seismic, court-ordered changes in the deeply rooted ways blacks and whites interacted. At the top was Mr. Danner, described in depositions as a man with a volcanic temper whose racial sentiments seemed brazenly backward in the New South. Even today, Mr. Danner, despite agreeing to the settlement costs, says he thinks he was wrongly blamed for the company's racial culture.

The unraveling of that culture began in 1988, as saber-rattling over the lawsuit reached the highest ranks of the company. Mr. Danner was considered a business wizard who had made a fortune with his Big Boy fast-food franchises—acquired from Mr. Schoenbaum—that he operated since 1959, before the passage of federal antidiscrimination laws. In 1971, he merged with Mr. Schoenbaum's concern to form Shoney's Big Boy Enterprises Inc., building it into the nation's third-largest family-style restaurant chain. Mr. Danner became president and Mr. Schoenbaum was named chairman and chief executive. In 1976, the company assumed its current name. Mr. Danner became chairman after Mr. Schoenbaum retired from active management.

By 1988, Mr. Danner announced he was growing tired of his breakneck schedule and planned to step down as chairman after what he called a "transition year" that would help his successor, J. Mitchell Boyd, get a grip on the business. Mr. Boyd had been named CEO and vice chairman in 1986 after having spent most of his career under Mr. Danner's tutelage.

The transition year turned out to be a rocky year. "There was no affirmative action being done at all, there was no discussion of it," Mr. Boyd recalls of the time. Worried about the lawsuit, he tried to change the company with monthly sensitivity sessions for its 60 top officials. "A lot of people were born and raised in the Deep South and no matter how you slice it, culture dominates," he says. "It's a hard thing to change."

The board fought the $50,000 annual cost of the sessions, he says. Company officials showed outright contempt for them, and Mr. Danner simply declined to attend, recalls Mr. Boyd.

OPPORTUNITY CALLS

Sometime that year, Mr. Lowery recalls, a black woman who had been fired by an "abusive" manager at a Shoney's in the Atlanta area sought his help. "We picketed and got her rehired" and the manager fired. Aware of the impending lawsuit, the SCLC waded into the fray. "We're opportunists," Mr. Lowery says from the SCLC's old storefront headquarters near downtown Atlanta.

Mr. Boyd took the reins in 1989, though Mr. Danner stayed on the company's board. Then came the lawsuit, filed in U.S. District Court in Pensacola, Fla. Depositions later taken from more than 80 witnesses would prove devastating.

White managers told of how Mr. Danner told them to fire blacks if they became too numerous in restaurants in white neighborhoods; if they refused, they would lose their jobs, too. Some also said that when Mr. Danner was expected to visit their restaurant, they scheduled black employees off that day or, in one case, hid them in the bathroom. Others said blacks' applications were coded and discarded.

OBLIVIOUS TO BEHAVIOR

At first, the company was in deep denial, says Mr. Boyd, now in retirement in Florida. "The average age of the board was 72," he recalls, "and those guys just couldn't comprehend how much the world had changed. When I said it might cost $50 million to settle it, they thought that was laughable." In the board's view, "all that had happened was that Ray had said that there were too many black people in a restaurant and they couldn't see anything wrong with that."

Others saw it differently. Christine Williams, now 35, had worked for Shoney's for 16 years when she left in anger and disappointment. She says she had come there as an illiterate, teenage mother and had taught herself to read by studying the menus. She began as a salad maker and worked her way up, getting married along the way, to become well known at headquarters as a capable dining-room manager, handling schedules and supervising personnel.

But in 1989, in the culmination of many acts of humiliation, she says the company refused to assign her to manage the dining room at a Shoney's in a predominantly white neighborhood in Nashville where she had bought a home.

"They said I couldn't do it because there had never been a black dining-room manager there," Mrs. Williams recalls. 'They said it like it wasn't supposed to offend me."

She quit—and had a nervous breakdown, she says. Eventually she became part of the lawsuit; she was among one hundred or so employees who received $40,000, the highest settlement awarded to individual plaintiffs.

A NEW APPROACH

In August 1989, with the lawsuit in the courts, Shoney's began to try to change. Mr. Boyd apologized for the company's past sins, and committed Shoney's to the first of three covenants with the SCLC, promising millions of dollars toward minority contracting and recruiting. It also hired Bob Brown, a former SCLC board member, to begin helping Shoney's draft an affirmative-action program while monitoring its agreement with the SCLC.

Some at the time worried that the accord might have been a Shoney's public-relations ploy to deflect attention from, or blunt the effects of, the lawsuit. But Mr. Brown, a friend of the late Dr. King who helped resolve the historic Woolworth lunch-counters desegregation effort in the South, was convinced the new Shoney's was coming around. The covenant, he said, would serve minorities while being "good for the long-term value of the company."

Mr. Boyd also brought onto the board its first black member, Carole F. Hoover, another former adviser to Dr. King and a prominent Cleveland business woman. "I saw an opportunity to contribute, first of all, to the growth of the business and, secondly, to how African-Americans and other minorities could really be a part of that growth," she says.

Still, Mr. Boyd couldn't get the board to settle the lawsuit, despite advice from independent counsel to do so. He left in December 1989 and was succeeded by Leonard H. Roberts, the former president and CEO of Arby's Inc.

LINGERING RESISTANCE

Mr. Roberts also favored a settlement and was convinced that the new course set by Mr. Boyd made good business sense—in fact, should be accelerated. "If Shoney's had to rely upon a white, male labor pool to grow its business it was in trouble," he says. "Forget about the lawsuit; if it never existed, the company still would have changed." Nevertheless, settlement efforts failed in March 1990.

Mr. Roberts brought with him Betty Marshall, a black woman with a background in purchasing who would become Shoney's vice president for corporate and community affairs. She was unaware of the lawsuit until friends told her about it.

"I expected to see people running up and down the halls wearing white sheets," she says. Her job quickly evolved from purchasing to "helping Len communicate his vision" and administering the covenant. She was soon meeting with Shoney's purchasing agents to assess their needs while searching for minority-owned companies that could fill them. "After some matches were made," she says, "our people would come to me and say, 'Hey, those are good people. I think we can work with them.'" Suddenly it was as if Shoney's had hung out a sign that said "Guilty White Company Now Paying Blacks for Its Sins." The phones were ringing off the hooks with minority owned companies—and some white companies with token black partners—pitching their businesses.

In the interim, the board began to soften. Finally, Mr. Roberts was able to convince the company to settle—while persuading Mr. Danner to pony up a big chunk of the settlement out of his own Shoney's stock. Mr. Danner, who remains Shoney's largest individual share-holder, says he agreed to pay because he had become weary of the whole mess and the drag it was exerting on Shoney's share price. The stock, after trading in the $20 a share range, had tumbled to as low as $7.50 a share when the threat of the lawsuit first made headlines.

Mr. Roberts left in December 1992 to become president of Tandy Corp.'s Radio Shack division. Since then, Shoney has been buffeted by other forces—overly rapid expansion, expenses associated with a costly restaurant-modernization program and a general slump in the industry. Though the company returned to profitability after its 1992 litigation-related losses, it has seen its revenue flatten out since then. That year, it posted revenue of $985.2 million. In its 1995 fiscal year, it reported revenue of $1.05 billion, down 2% from $1.07 billion the year before.

Taylor H. Henry Jr., who succeeded Mr. Roberts, was himself replaced last May by C. Stephen Lynn. Mr. Lynn is a turnaround specialist who is former chairman and CEO of Sonic Corp., an Oklahoma City hamburger-restaurant chain. "Every great company has sins of the past," says Mr. Lynn, a soft-spoken man, of the challenges he faces at Shoney's. "We learn more from our defeats and shortcomings."

STILL PUZZLING

Recently in his office at Danner Co., a closely held concern that manages Mr. Danner's interests in everything from car dealerships to real estate, an amiable Mr. Danner says he is still a bit puzzled over the fuss. In his view, Shoney's old culture made sense. "My only concern is what the customer wants, making the customer happy," he says. In his deposition Mr. Danner explained that, in trying to identify why a restaurant might be underperforming, "in some cases I would have probably said that this is a neighborhood of predominantly white neighbors and we have a considerable amount of black employees and this might be the problem."

Mr. Danner has his champions. Mr. Boyd and Mr. Schoenbaum note that, when it became illegal to bar blacks from public accommodations, Shoney's was the first restaurant chain in

Tennessee to serve African-Americans. "Ray, very simply, was not a bigot," Mr. Boyd insists. "What the government was doing was social engineering and he didn't give a damn about social engineering."

Mr. Danner also has black friends, among them Francis Guess, a black Republican who served on the U.S. Commission on Civil Rights in the Reagan administration and is executive director of the Danner Foundation. Through the foundation, says Mr. Guess, Mr. Danner contributes to a number of black causes, including the Congressional Black Caucus, Urban League and some historically black colleges. Mr. Danner, his wife Judy, and son Ray Jr., 10, are life members of the National Association for the Advancement of Colored People, having joined during the course of the lawsuit. "It's just my way of giving something back to the community," Mr. Danner says.

One person who is thrilled with the outcome is Mrs. Williams, the former dining room manager. She has returned to work as a trainer-of dining-room managers—a bigger job than the one she was denied. After hearing Mr. Lynn introduce himself to the company last year, she sent him a taped message about her life and her association with Shoney's. "It's all I know," she says.

When they finally met, both recalled the meeting as emotional. People like Mrs. Williams, Mr. Lynn says, simply wanted and deserved an "opportunity to grow and prosper. She came back here and was blessed and is blessing us."

Discussion Questions

1. In the Jo Carol La Fleur case, were courts dynamic or constrained?

2. Apply the socio-legal model to the Shoney's case. What were the relevant "licenses to operate?" What was Shoney's "management style?" Was the change attributable to the settlement or other factors? How does this case make you rethink the dynamic versus constrained court debate?

PART IV
The Political Consequences of Adversarial Legalism

The march of law, courts, and litigation naturally raises questions about its consequences. In Part IV, we explore these issues.

How Policy Shapes Politics

By Jeb Barnes and Thomas F. Burke

THE QUESTION

Litigation is everywhere in American society, casting its long shadow over businesses, schools, public spaces, private lives, and nearly every aspect of government and policymaking. In recent memory, litigation has transformed how Americans finance election campaigns, how they buy health insurance, whom they can marry; it has even decided a presidential election. It has been central to struggles over civil rights, abortion, regulating tobacco, drawing electoral districts, cleaning up the environment, reforming the criminal justice system, making society more accessible to people with disabilities, and foreign policy matters such as the detention of "enemy combatants." Not every political question in the United States becomes a judicial question, as Alexis de Tocqueville claimed about 1830s America, but a remarkable share does (Silverstein 2009; Derthick 2005; Sabel and Simon 2004; Sandler and Schoenbrod 2003; Kagan 2001; Feeley and Rubin 1998; Melnick 1983,1994; Barnes and Burke 2006, 2012). According to scholars, the United States has become a "litigation state" (Farhang 2010) in which "juridification" (Silverstein 2009), "litigious policies" (Burke 2002), "adversarial legalism" (Kagan 2001), "legalization" (Sutton et al. 1994), and "legalized accountability" (Epp 2009) proliferate.

However you label it—and we will discuss our preferred label below—the expansion of legal rights and litigation evokes deep ambivalence. In the United States, the mythic qualities of law, associated with heroic lawyers such as Thurgood Marshall and Perry Mason, landmark cases such as *Brown v. Board of Education,* and cultural touchstones such as *To Kill a Mockingbird,* are a familiar aspect of the popular culture. In this view, law is majestic and godlike, transcending che pettiness of everyday life and the partisanship of politics (Ewick and Silbey 1998). In the words of Judith Shklar (1964; 111), law "aims at justice, while politics only looks to expediency. The former is neutral and objective, the latter the uncontrolled child of competing interests and ideologies. Justice is thus not only the policy of legalism, it is a policy superior to

Jeb Barnes and Thomes F. Burke, How Policy Shapes Politics, pp. 42396. Copyright © 2015 by Oxford University Press. Reprinted with permission.

and unlike any other" Steeped in this view, lawyers and legal scholars often celebrate litigation as a mechanism for vindicating and expanding individual rights, imposing accountability for the negligence and heedlessness of corporations and governmental agencies, and checking private influence on governmental rule-makers (Crohley 2008; Barnes 2009; Bogus 2001; Mather 1998).

Yet the deployment ot courts, rights, and litigation to address social problems also generates powerful criticisms. Some see litigation and the invocation of rights as a rupture of community order, a sign of social breakdown (Engel 1984). For them, increasing reliance on courts, rights, and litigation is an indication of the decline of American civilization. The "common good," they contend, has been eclipsed by the litigious society (Howard 1995); Americans have lapsed into a "culture of complaint" (Hughes 1994) in which the virtues of stoicism and grit have been replaced by the entitled whines of victims (Cole 1007). Policy analysts and political scientists, less enamored with the rhetoric of moral decline, have sought to document the more tangible downsides of litigation. They warn that it is far less efficient and predictable than other modes of policymaking, such as social insurance programs (e.g., Carroll et al. 2005; Kagan 2001; Rabkin 1989; Schuck 1986; Melnick 1983; Bardach and Kagan 1982; Horowitz 1977), and that it often leaves those harmed by violations of law to "lump" it (Abel 1987; Bumiller 1988; Haltom and McCann 2004). Litigation in this view fails both ordinary citizens, who cannot afford to use it, and organizations, which cannot efficiently plan for it.

The claims most often made about the rising prominence of courts, rights and litigation, then, tend to concern its potential cultural, administrative and economic downsides. In this book, however, we do not seek to weigh the economic costs and benefits of litigation, or its relationship to various cultural vices or virtues. Instead this book probes the *political* effects of what some have called the judicialization of public policy. To put it more precisely, we assess how the design of public policy—around courts and litigation on one hand, or through agency implementation on the other—shapes politics. We ask questions like these: *Do "judicialized" and "non-judicialized" policies differ in the interests they mobilize? The coalitions they generate? The way problems are framed? What kinds of issues do they highlight? What issues do they obscure?*

Although these questions may not be as prominent as the moral and economic concerns that are frequently voiced in popular debates about law, they also tap into deep-seated concerns about using courts, rights, and litigation to make social policy. Some worry that the appeal of litigation will divert interest groups and social movements with limited time and resources from purportedly more consequential and legitimate modes of political advocacy, such as grassroots mobilizing, coalition building, and lobbying (Rosenberg 1991). Moreover, reliance on litigation and the pursuit of legal rights is said to be self-reinforcing because it creates a template for political action that frames grievances in legalistic terms (Silverstein 2009: 69; see generally Pierson 2004). This can choke off the pursuit of comprehensive social programs, even when litigation has produced mixed policy results, as legal doctrine and individual rights displace alternative approaches to social problems. From this vantage, litigation is not only ineffective as a policy matter—a "hollow hope"—but also politically counter-productive, acting either as "flypaper" that traps groups in the courts or as a lightning rod that attracts powerful backlash and hardens opposition (Rosenberg 1991; Klarman 1994, 2004; see also Forbath 1991). Litigation and the pursuit of individual rights, it also is claimed, privatizes social problems, framing them as discrete conflicts between individuals, thus obscuring the communal dimensions of social life. The individualization inherent in litigation creates a more fragmented, less communal polity that can fail to realize common interests (e.g., Tushnet 1984; Glendon 1987, 1991; Haltom and McCann 1004; Barnes 2011).

Concerns about the expansion of law seem particularly urgent at the moment in which we write, the early twenty-first century. In the United States, we live in an era when Congress has become increasingly dysfunctional (e.g., Mann and Ornstein 2012.), making "Laws Allure" (the title of Gordon Silversteins recent book on the risks of juridification) ever more alluring. The combination of tight budgetary constraints, party polarization, narrow majorities in Congress, and divided government create a policy vacuum that court-enforced rights can fill. Disgruntled interests may feel that litigation is their only viable option for pursuing their policy agendas; elected officials may be glad to have intractable political disputes resolved elsewhere and at the expense of private litigants (Farhang 2010; Silverstein 2009; Lovell 2003; Burke 2001; Kagan 2001; Barnes 1997; Graber 1993).

Beyond the United States, the growing significance of rights, courts, and litigation is even more apparent. Over the last two decades, a bevy of comparativists and international relations scholars have been documenting rising levels of "judicialization" (Kapiszewski, Silverstein, and Kagan 2013; Ginsburg 2003; Hirschl 2004, 2008; Sweet 1999, 2000; Shapiro and Sweet 2002; Tate and Vallinder 1995), various types of "legalism" (Kelemen 2006, 2011; Bignami 2011; Kagan 1997, 2007), and "legalization" (Goldstein et. al 2001) in other nations and at the international level. The judicialization of politics, Ran Hirschl claims, "is arguably one of the most significant phenomena of late twentieth and early twenty-first century government" (Hirschl 2008: 69). The global rise of judicial power reflects a variety of possible factors, including the growth of transnational associations like the European Union (Alter 2001; Kelemen 2009) and the expansion of international human rights institutions and organizations (Sikldnk 2011; Goodale and Merry 2007; see also Epp 1998). Whatever its causes, the rising prominence of rights, courts, and litigation in politics worldwide suggests that scholars and commentators will be increasingly drawn to studying the questions raised in this book.

Our Approach

The prominence of rights, courts, and litigation in social life makes its political effects a subject of great interest, but also a challenge to study. If law is "all over," as one particularly influential article in sociolegal studies put it (Sarat 1990), how do researchers figure out what law is doing? To date, those who have been most interested in understanding what law does to politics have focused mainly on a small number of dramatic cases in which courts took center stage, usually through a ruling on the constitutionality of some statute or executive action (e.g., Rosenberg 1991; Silverstein 2009). This approach has yielded important insights into the potential political risks of relying on rights, courts, and litigation, but it can be misleading for two reasons. First, the literatures focus on high-profile constitutional cases may provide a distorted lens for viewing the effects of judicialization, which can take many forms and arise in a variety of contexts. Second, by definition, claims about the political effects of judicialization/juridification/legalization necessarily imply that politics would have been different if rights, courts, and litigation had not intervened or had intervened to a lesser degree. By not focusing more explicitly on what social scientists call the "counter-factual"—what would have happened in the absence of judicialization—the existing literature on the political risks of litigation may overstate its actual impact.

Accordingly, we start with the assumption that the best way to understand the political effects of judicialization/juridification/legalization, whether in the United States or elsewhere, is through comparison, and so in this book we compare the politics of policies that are structured around rights, courts, and litigation with policies that do not have this structure. We focus on the field of injury compensation, which, like many realms of American public policy includes a vast array of policies of diverse design, some based on litigation, others on regulation and social insurance. We first make our comparisons using a quantitative study of patterns of participation in congressional hearings on injury compensation policies, and then with three in-depth case studies.

What do we find? There are some twists and turns along the way, but we come to two fundamental conclusions. First, at least for the cases we study, many claims about the use of rights, courts, and litigation in politics seem overblown. We see, for example, litde evidence that the allure of law traps activists in its spell, or that law-focused public policies are any more difficult to reform than their bureaucratic alternatives. In many respects, then, the politics of rights and litigation does not look much different from other forms of politics.

But secondly, we find support for some of the long-standing criticisms of rights, courts, and litigation voiced by theorists, commentators, and social scientists. By organizing social issues as disputes between parties, the use of litigation does seem to individualize politics in some of the ways they have suggested. Litigation assigns fault to specific entities, and creates a complex array of winners and losers on the ground. That over time creates a distinctively fractious politics, in which interest groups associated with plaintiffs and defendants fight not only each other but among themselves as well. This pattern is particularly pronounced when we compare it to the political trajectory of social insurance policies that compensate for injuries, especially our main comparison case, Social Security Disability Insurance. There we see moments of great contention, but long periods of relative peace, and greater solidarity among interests. The bottom line, we think, is that some of the critics of judicialization/juridification/legalization are onto something when they claim that the effect of litigation is to individualize conflict over social issues, and so generate a more divisive, fractious politics.

In attempting to uncover the political effects of rights, courts, and litigation, we encountered a series of conceptual obstacles, and alas, we must begin by describing those obstacles and what we have tried to do to get around them. Discussions of concepts can be dry and technical, but to understand how we frame the rest of the book, you must first understand the reasoning behind our conceptual choices. Alter addressing these conceptual issues, the remainder of the chapter explains our case selection, summarizes our findings in greater detail, and outlines the chapters that follow.

Key Concepts and Comparisons

Our first assumption is that the central question of this book—what are the political consequences of relying on rights, courts, and litigation to address social problems?—implies a comparison between the politics of "judicialization" and "non-judicialization," or to put it more simply, between "law" and "non-law." Defining "non-judicialization" or "non-law" however, is more difficult than you might think. In Laws *Allure*, Silverstein argues that "law is different" but different from what? What is the thing that "judicialization" "juridification," "legalization," and "legal rights" are being compared to? One possibility is that a "judicialized" policy could be compared to some kind of "non-judicialized" one, but which kind? Is the normal baseline of politics legislative? Executive? Electoral? Social movement mobilization? Some combination? Or is the baseline no policy at all? So we need to know: Different from what?

There is yet another problem here, one that points to the profusion of terms used in this literature. We worry that these terms—judicialization, juridification, legalization and so on—can obscure rather than sharpen our understanding of the relationship of law and politics. When scholars argue that "law is different," they undoubtedly mean something like: courts are different from agencies or legislatures. But of course agencies and legislatures also produce law, and agency decision-making is often highly litigious. Indeed, it is hard to imagine anything in American public policy that is not connected to law and the potential threat of litigation in some way. Perhaps this point is so simple that scholars assume their readers could understand that when they write "law" they mean the kind of law produced by courts, but they rarely define the boundary of their concepts, and this creates difficulties (Burke and Barnes 2009). For example, if "law" is made up of the doctrines that appellate courts propound, what do we do with trial courc decisions, or even more importantly, the vast majority of legal claims that are disposed of or settled prior to trial? What about the ideas people have about legal rights, which may or may not have much to do with decisions that courts make? Are all these things part of whats different? Some conceptual openness about the scope of "juridification" or "judicialization" is probably inevitable given the complexity (and contested nature) ot scholarly accounts of law and rights, and the decentralized processes through which they are given meaning, but we also want to have some sense of the boundaries of these terms.

To cut through this conceptual morass, from this point forward we generally avoid formulations in this book such as "judicialization," "juridification," and "legalization." We are just not confident about how these terms should be defined. Instead, we start from the assumption that courts, like legislatures and executive branch agencies, are policymakers, and so we reject the law/politics distinction that underlies so much commentary on litigation and rights. We operate within the tradition of "political jurisprudence" pioneered by Marcin Shapiro (Shapiro 1964a, 1964b, 1966, 1968; see generally Gillman 2004), in which courts are considered comparable to other political institutions, but with their own tilts and tendencies,[4] and we heartily concur with Stuart Scheingolds insistence that *The Politics of Rights* (Scheingold 2004) be analyzed as a species of politics rather than a different kind of animal entirely. This leads us to use concepts that are comparative, but not based on static assumptions about essential features of law or courts.

Although originally designed to describe cross-national differences, we think Robert Kagans typology of policymaking processes (1991, 2001) offers a productive response to the conceptual problems we have posed for studying within-country variation, both because it is reasonably well-defined and because it is explicitly comparative. (An added benefit of using Kagan's typology is avoiding the introduction of yet another set of terms to the already confusing lexicon of judicialization/juridification/legalization.) The typology of policymaking is set forth in Table 1.1. Each cell in the box represents an ideal-type of policymaking regime, which connotes a distinct form of authority for creating and implementing policy—in this book, injury compensation policy.

The horizontal axis is the level of *formality* in defining and determining the underlying claim, meaning the degree to which decision-makers use preexisting rules in resolving disputes. The use of rules in dispute resolution involves all the paraphernalia of legal processes: precedents, records, documents, and written procedures. Informal processes, for example the use of expert administrative judgment by the Federal Reserve Board to adjust interest rates, are not closely constrained by preexisting substantive rules; the underlying policy decisions are made based on the professional judgment of its members and staff.

On the *formal* side of the horizontal axis are *adversarial legalism* and *bureaucratic legalism*. Adversarial legalism involves formal but participatory structures, meaning that the parties to the underlying dispute drive the decision-making process. In adversarial legalism, parties dominate policy construction from the bottom up; they make policy by arguing over the meaning of substantive standards and procedural rules, the application of those rules to the decision at hand, and even the fairness of the relevant rules and procedures. In the formulation and implementation of policy under adversarial legal regimes everything is a matter of dispute, and all those affected by a decision are free to participate in the disputing

Table 1.1 Four Modes of Policymaking (Kagan 2001)

Organization of Decision-Making Authority	Decision-Making Style	
	Informal	Formal
Hierarchical	Expert or political judgment	Bureaucratic legalism
Participatory	Negotiation/mediation	Adversarial legalism

process. There is an official decision-maker, but the decision-maker acts as a referee and so does not dominate the proceedings. Bureaucratic legalism, by contrast, is formal and hierarchical. It connotes a Weberian bureaucracy that centers on civil servants implementing formal rules from the top down, as in the case of social insurance programs in which government officials determine compensation according to preexisting medical criteria and payment schedules.

The structural differences between adversarial legalism and bureaucratic legalism correspond to different emphases in decision-making. In adversarial legalism, the decision-makers (judges and juries in the American civil litigation system) are not tightly bound to a centralized higher authority and so a premium is placed on particularized justice, tailoring decisions to specific circumstances. In the bureaucratic model, civil servants are bound to a centralized authority, so that emphasis is placed in the uniform application of rule across cases. As a result of these different emphases, adversarial legalism is likely to be more unpredictable and administratively costly, though also more flexible, than bureaucratic legalism (Kagan 2001).

On the *informal* side of the horizontal axis are processes in which no preexisting rules are used to resolve disputes or make policy decisions. The hierarchical version is *expert or political judgment;* the decentralized party-centered version is *negotiation/mediation.* In expert or political judgment, the expertise can be purely scientific, as when a government commission like the National Transportation Safety Board investigates the causes of an accident, or it can mix expertise with political prudence, as when the Securities and Exchange Commission decides whether to use its authority to create a rule governing some market practice. Negotiation/mediation, the bottom/left quadrant, fits any situation in which decisions must be made among roughly equal parties. Although legislatures can be highly hierarchical, many would roughly fit this cell, as each elected legislator has the right to bargain over and vote on legislation.

The cells in Kagan's table offer a way to address the "Law is Different problem. Adversarial legalism is a capacious term that we believe gets at many of the qualities that writers are referring to when they decry or praise the use of courts, litigation, and legal rights to address social problems. Further, we think negotiation/mediation, bureaucratic legalism, and expert judgment are the points of comparison implicit in criticisms of courts as detective (or commendations of them as heroic) in policymaking and implementation. Negotiation/mediation is considered the "normal" way in which policies are created through legislative deliberation, and bureaucratic legalism and expert judgment are considered the "normal" ways in which those policies are implemented by executive agencies. The combination roughly comports with textbook versions of federal policymaking in which elected lawmakers—the President and members of Congress—negotiate fundamental policy decisions, whereas issues of implementation are delegated to executive branch agencies. Commentaries about judicialization/juridification/legalization are, we think, reacting to a view that adversarial legalism is reaching into areas normally left to other less court-based modes of policymaking and dispute resolution.

Sharp-eyed readers, though, will see immediately that adversarial legalism does not mean "courts," that negotiation/mediation does not mean "legislatures" and that bureaucratic legalism does not mean "agencies"—in fact all institutions can vary in the extent they reflect these ideal-types. For example, American courts are more adversarial than European courts because they are less hierarchical, making American litigation more party-centered (Atiyah and Summers 1987; Damaska 1986). American legislatures also better fit the negotiation; mediation ideal better than typical parliaments because of their relative decentralization. Executive agencies too vary in their degree of bureaucratic legalism because they vary in the extent to which hierarchical rules structure behavior. An agency that, for example, responds to complaints, and that does not provide street-level officials much guidance in resolving those complaints, has moved away from the Weberian ideal and more toward the pole of party-centered adversarial legalism. It is important to remember that our terms represent ideal-types, which imply characteristic divisions of labor among the branches, but that in the real world, policies and institutions typically fall on a spectrum between them, not at the ends.

In fact, we believe this is another strength of the typology, particularly for studying American politics, because in the separation-of-powers, checks-and-balances American system it is hard to find pure examples of anything, be it judicial, executive, or legislative, state or federal. Policymaking and implementation in such a system, we believe, is best thought of as a dialogue among the federal branches of government and with the states (Barnes and Miller 2004; Barnes 2007a, 2013). In this context, separating out the influence of rights, courts, and litigation on American politics is particularly difficult, because it requires analysts to weigh the influence of each line in the dialogue, to try to measure how a court ruling influenced a legislature that in turn influenced an agency which in turn may have influenced the judiciary. Two of the most prominent books in the literature on the effects of law on politics, Silverstein's *Law's Allure* and Rosenberg's *Hollow Hope*, which try to isolate the effects of particular decisions such as *Brown v. Board of Education or Buckley v. Valeo*, wrestle particularly hard with this problem. Kagan's typology leads us instead to make more holistic characterizations. Instead of trying to parse the effect of a single decision in a complex, ongoing dialogue among multiple branches and levels of government, we code the design of policies as being more or less adversarial or bureaucratic, and trace how the politics within an issue area develop in the shadow of these institutional arrangements.

Our approach, then, is fundamentally comparative, but it is also multi-method, mixing quantitative and qualitative data, and developmental, analyzing change over time. We start with a quantitative analysis of 40 years of congressional hearing data on adversarial and bureaucratic injury compensation policies. These data provide a useful starting place for probing the threshold question of whether the politics of adversarial and bureaucratic legalism differ by providing a common vantage to view a key point in the ongoing policy dialogue in multiple cases. We find important cross-sectional differences between the politics of the two types of policies, which raise questions about whether (and how) these differences play out beyond congressional hearings and over time.

To explore these questions, our case studies pick up where the hearings data leave off, tracing the politics of adversarial and bureaucratic policies as they mature from creation to expansion and retrenchment, and in some instances as they become more bureaucratic or adversarial. These case studies allow us not only to explore how the politics of policies evolve over time and across multiple political institutions, but also, where appropriate, to compare the politics of different structures, adversarial and bureaucratic, within the same policy field. In adding this developmental dimension to our analysis, we build on the work of Paul Pierson (1994), who famously argues that the politics of program retrenchment differs from the politics of program creation. Pierson leaves open whether the shifting politics of policy development differs across policy types. By contrast, we explore whether "policy feedbacks"—the ways in which institutional features of policies shape politics (see generally Campbell 2006, 2012; Mettler and Soss 2004; Pierson 1993)—not only vary across different stages of development, but also vary across different types of policy designs within the same issue area. The result is a comparative developmental approach to understanding the political consequences of adversarial legalism versus bureaucratic legalism.

Case Selection

If you think about it, the critical claims made about the effects of rights, courts, and litigation—that they tend to crowd out other forms of political participation, polarize and create backlashes, get a polity stuck in unproductive policy arguments, and undermine social solidarity—are really claims about propensities, not regularities. It is easy to think of cases that support each of the claims, but also easy to think of counter-examples. *Roe v. Wade* and *Brown v. Board of Education* clearly created a political backlash, but *Loving v. Virginia*, the anti-miscegenation case, seemed to have no such effect. Similarly, gay marriage has generated considerable political contention, while the right of gay couples to adopt children has mostly slipped under the political radar (Gash 2013). Victories in litigation can create polarizing backlashes, but they can also consolidate support for legislative reform, as when states joined parents for expansion of federal special education programs, in part because they feared courts would impose unfunded judicial mandates on them (Melnick 1994). The language of rights and the use of litigation may frame social life in individualistic ways, but rights claims can be used by activists to raise consciousness about common concerns and build coalitions that bring groups together (McCann 1994; Epp 2009). So part of the problem of assessing the political effects of adversarial legalism is the familiar one of sampling. It is easy to pick cases that support your claims and easy to find cases that go against them, but not so easy to come up with a strategy for picking cases that help you generalize beyond them to get a sense of overall tilts and tendencies.

Our primary strategy for addressing this problem is comparison. We want to compare policies that are closely related and similar in important respects, but that differ in their structure, with some falling on the adversarial side of the spectrum and others on the bureaucratic side. To do this we need to sample from a policy field chat has a mix of adversarial and bureaucratic policy designs. The structure of the US. state makes this relatively easy, because it is remarkably fragmented and layered, built through the accretion of overlapping public and private programs, benefits and rights (Orren and Skowronek 2004; Hacker 2002; Berkowitz 1987). The resulting patchwork of programs and policies means that, in many areas of U.S. public policy—for example, the environment, health care, civil rights, safety regulation, and consumer protection—adversarial and bureaucratic designs operate side by side. This offers many opportunities for comparing the political consequences of different policy designs.

One such opportunity lies in the field of injury compensation, which features a vast array of overlapping public programs and private remedies, some adversarial, others bureaucratic, and still others hybrids. The overlap of many programs makes them confusing to navigate. Imagine, for example, that you fell off a ladder at work and broke your leg. You might bring any or all of the following claims: a tort lawsuit against the manufacturer of the ladder for poor design, a workers' compensation claim at either the federal or state level (depending on your job), a claim against your health insurer, and a claim for private and/or public disability insurance benefits (depending on the severity of your injury). In 1991, the Rand Institute of Civil Justice published a landmark study of this melange of injury compensation programs, audacious because it tried to estimate both the cost of all injuries in the United States and all sources of compensation. The study concluded that accident injury costs $175 billion per year—more than $300 billion in todays dollars—consisting of roughly $100 billion in direct costs and $75 billion in lost earnings (Hensler et al. 1991, Table 4.21,103). The study found that roughly 23 million people received $110 billion dollars in injury compensation each year, almost 4% of GNP at the time (102). A central finding of the study—and crucial for our purposes—was that compensation for accidents came from a variety of sources, including private insurance, employer benefits, public programs, and lawsuits (Table 4.22., 108). Given the array of policies that compensate for injury and the ways they are used, injury compensation provides promising cases for our study.

Indeed, injury compensation is almost too good, providing so many candidates tor analysis that we cannot possibly cover them all. We can, however, take advantage of the institutional variation in these policies by targeting policies that feature different levels of adversarial and bureaucratic legalism. As summarized in Table 1.2, we have selected three sets of cases. All of these cases are included in our quantitative analysis of congressional hearings and a subset of these cases involving SSDI, asbestos, and childhood vaccines are subject to in-depth case analysis.

The first set of cases includes examples of adversarial legalism: litigation over product liability, medical malpractice, and securities fraud. You may be surprised to see these forms of litigation labeled as "policies" comparable to more conventionally legislated programs like Social Security or workers' compensation. Traditionally, these forms of litigation were considered "private law" because they governed disputes between individuals and so were not thought to raise the same kinds of political or policy concerns as public law fields such as constitutional law. Today, however, what is usually labeled "tort law" is a matter of great

Table 1.2 Three Sets of Cases

Type of Case	Policy
Adversarial Legalism	Product liability, medical malpractice, and securities fraud
Bureaucratic Legalism	SSDI, the Black Lung Disability Trust Fund, and the Longshore and Harbor Workers' Compensation Act
Shifting Regimes	Vaccinc injury compensation (adversarial legalism to bureaucratic legalism), asbestos litigation (bureaucratic legalism to adversarial legalism to a layered system)

political conflict and ferment, and public policies governing tort are regularly debated at both the state and national level. (We will see in the following chapter how often Congress has held hearings to consider changes to the tort system over the past 40 years.) As with ail injury compensation policies, disputes over tort center on issues of who decides, who gets what, from whom, and how much. These forms of litigation differ from each other in interesting ways. Product liability affects a broad array of manufacturers; medical malpractice targets a group of well-organized professionals. Securities fraud litigation is an unusual case for our study because it compensates financial losses and not physical or mental injuries.

The second set of cases are characterized primarily by bureaucratic legalism: SSDI, the Black Lung Disability Trust Fund (the black lung program), and the Longshore and Harbor Workers' Compensation Act (the longshore workers' program). While all share common bureaucratic institutional features, there are some important differences. SSDI is funded from a payroll tax on workers and employers and covers disabled workers and their families. Like SSDI, the longshore workers' program is funded by a payroll tax, but unlike SSDI, only covers injured workers from a specific industry. The black lung program targets a specific category of injuries, and it is funded differently from the other programs, through a tax on products. The size of SSDI dwarfs the other programs in our sample. In 2010 alone, the SSDI trust fund paid out over $124 billion in benefits; by contrast, the longshore workers' and black lung programs paid only about $26.6 and $208 million in benefits in 2010, respectively. Finally, these policies differ on federalism; SSDI is a federal program that is pardy administered by the states while the other programs are federally administered.

The final set of cases is especially theoretically interesting for our study: injury compensation fields in which the structure of the policy shifted over time. The case of vaccine injury compensation is particularly valuable for our project because it involves an adversarial policy that was largely replaced by a bureaucratic policy, allowing for before-and-after comparisons of the politics of policies dealing with the same set of injuries. The asbestos case illustrates a more subtle pattern of development in which different types of polices are layered, so that adversarial legalism remains the dominant policy response but some bureaucratic sub-policies remain alongside tort law. If adversarial policies generate a politics different from bureaucratic policies, then we should observe changes in the politics of these fields that coincides with their change in structure. In the vaccine case, we should see a shift after bureaucratic legalism replaces adversarial legalism. In the asbestos case, we should observe a difference in the politics when activity centers on its adversarial as opposed to bureaucratic sub-policies.

Our historical case studies allow us to trace the politics of SSDI, asbestos, and vaccine policy through different stages of development, from creation through expansion and (attempted) retrenchment. They also give us the second major way we probe our questions, through within-case comparisons. Comparisons across cases are always vulnerable to the charge that what's driving differences in outcomes among the cases is not the factor that the researcher is interested in but some other unconsidered variable. Injury compensation policies have some common features, but there are many differences, say, between the history of product injury law and SSDI, and it would be problematic to assume that those differences can all be attributed to the fact that tort law is primarily adversarial and SSDI bureaucratic. By tracing developments within cases, however, we can make comparisons inside the case that are not so vulnerable to this problem. In two of our cases, covering vaccine and asbestos injury compensation, the structure of public policy shifts over time, and we take advantage of this variation by analyzing how this is related to changes in the politics of these two areas. Within the SSDI case, we compare the politics of an adversarial policy, the Americans with Disabilities Act, which addresses some of the same issues. We cannot replicate the ideal situation in social science—randomly assigning bureaucratic designs to some public policies and adversarial designs to others—but we can, by combining within-case and across-case studies, reduce some of the limitations of inductive, non-experimental research.

Our cases are not intended to be representative of the universe of injury compensation regimes within the United States, much less the universe of adversarial and bureaucratic policies. We have, for example, focused entirely on the national politics of federal programs and tort law. The vaccine case, moreover, is highly unusual in that reformers were able to replace adversarial legalism with bureaucratic legalism. We chose these examples because they provide clear examples of adversarial and bureaucratic policies in the area of injury compensation, and because they vary in several important respects: size, scope of targeted injuries, funding sources, and setting. Thus comparing patterns of politics within and across these cases should offer insight into the central question of what, if any, are the key differences between the politics of adversarial and bureaucratic legalism. We will save for our conclusion our thoughts about the possible limits on the generalizability of our cases, and the ways in which they connect to the vast literature on judicialization/juridification/legalization.

Summary of Findings

We consider four serious charges against adversarial legalism: (1) it crowds out other forms of political action, especially lobbying for legislative change, (2) it is particularly "sticky" and path-dependent, potentially locking governments into bad policies, (3) it creates polarizing backlashes, and (4) it individualizes interests, thus undermining social solidarity. We find the first three counts are overstated, at least in our cases. Adversarial legalism is either not

Crowd Out and "Flypaper Courts"

Gerald Rosenberg's *The Hollow Hope* is perhaps the most prominent critique of the use of courts to make policy within political science and law. Rosenberg's argument is largely focused on the constraints on courts as policymakers, maintaining chat courts can make social policy effectively only under very narrow circumstances. There must be precedent for the court's action; the elected branches must support the court's decisions; there must be some public support for the court's decisions and at least one of the following must be present; (1) incentives for compliance, (2) costs lor non-compliance, (3) supporting market incentives, or (4) support from local officials. Unless these conditions are met, Rosenberg argues, relying on law and courts to make policy is a "hollow hope."

Reviewers have often commented about the seeming disjunction between Rosenberg's social science approach, in which he develops the theory of the "constrained court" and lists the variables that he thinks affect its performance, and the anguished rhetoric about the pitfalls of seeking social change through law that erupts in some passages of his book and is reflected in the title. It is one thing to find that courts are constrained, but why then are they "Hollow Hopes"? Congress cannot unilaterally dictate broad social change either; to translate its formal commands into social practice, it too needs help from the other branches and levels of government and some local support, but no one would suggest that seeking legislation is an empty exercise. The answer is that Rosenberg assumes that the use of courts inevitably crowd outs other presumably more effective (and legitimate) modes of political advocacy, such as grassroots mobilization, lobbying, and coalition building. From this perspective, courts are not only a hollow hope but also "political flypaper," trapping interest groups in an expensive form of advocacy that is unlikely to yield results.

Rosenberg is certainly not alone in his concerns about the turn to adversarial legalism. In his analysis of the labor movement, William Forbath makes a parallel argument, that unions diverted resources to litigation at the expense of the broader political movement (Forbath 1991). You can compare this to the most familiar claim about the diversion of political activity from the elected branches, that it is "undemocratic," a criticism voiced both inside and outside the academy. Take for example Justice Scalias scathing dissent in *United States v. Windsor,* the divided Supreme Court decision that struck down the Defense of Marriage Act.[6] Scalia argues that judicial policymaking in the area of same-sex marriage diverted the debate from the elected branches and so tarnished the victory for advocates of gay and lesbian rights. Scalia's reasoning is that litigation channels activity away from the hard work of lobbying elected officials and members in the executive and persuading "the People."[7] For him the problem is that the judiciary is too powerful, sweeping away democratically-decided outcomes; for Rosenberg and Forbath, who clearly sympathize with the movements they are writing about, the worry is the courts and litigation are too weak. In either case, though, the critics are concerned that the turn to adversarial legalism is a turn away from other modes of politics.

In our study, however, we find no evidence that adversarial legalism "kills" politics, fixing social movements and interest groups on the pursuit of individual rights at the expense of other goals or means. Indeed, adversarial legalism seemed to fuel group mobilization, creating a more fragmented, pluralistic politics featuring more diverse interests with competing viewpoints. The high costs of litigation provided a stimulus for legislative campaigns for alternatives to litigation. The converse was also true: bureaucratic legalism did not kill *litigation*. We found a number of striking examples of interest groups using the courts to challenge the status quo within bureaucratic policies. The interest groups in our study seemed adept at moving from one institution to another, looking for levers wherever they could find them.

In part because interest groups were able to move across branches and levels of government, policymaking was shared among the branches and levels of government in our cases.[8] Elected officials often created policy designs that empowered litigants and judges, deferred to courts that developed adversarial policies, or at least invited judicial interpretation of vague or open-ended phrases (and then codified these judicially developed interpretations). Whatever the mix of adversarial and bureaucratic legalism in each case, interest groups found ways to try to influence policy. In the American system of overlapping, diversely representative forums, policymaking takes place in many forums, often at once, and American interest groups in our cases were adapted to this context, routinely combining litigation with lobbying.

Path Dependence and Framing Effects

A related charge is that adversarial legalism is particularly prone to "path dependence," so that bad or outdated policies are stuck in place, and frame political debate in ways that are problematic. The concept of path dependence has proven to be a bit like an inkblot in a Rorschach test; it means different things to different scholars. In some writings, path dependence seems merely to note that events in the past have an effect going forward, that "history matters." We prefer Paul Piersons formulation, which defines path-dependent processes as those involving "increasing returns,' meaning that with each step it gets more and more costly to get off whatever path one is on (Pierson 2004).

Life seems filled with *decreasing* returns. Your first mouthful of ice cream is much more pleasurable than the last. As more businesses move into a city, it becomes more affluent, real estate prices increase and wages rise, increasing the costs of business and reducing the appeal of the location for new ventures. A product that satisfies a lot of consumers leads rival manufacturers to develop an alternative that is even more attractive. But sometimes we see *increasing* returns, cases in which every bite of ice cream, strangely enough, tastes better and better. Silicon Valley grows richer and richer, but also more and more the place for certain companies to locate, whatever the cost. The QWERTY keyboard may or may not be the best arrangement of the keys, but as more people learn to use it, it becomes harder to sell a different design, especially if the design becomes embedded in other technologies (Pierson 2004).

Litigation is arguably somewhat like the fabled ice cream cone that gets tastier with each bite. This is certainly true for some litigants. "Repeat players" with each iteration theoretically gain over "one-shotters," as MarcGalanter posited in his classic "Why the Haves Come out Ahead" (Galanter 1974; Kritzer and Silbev 2003). Lawyers and the organizations they work for accrue expertise in how to litigate and attract new clients. They learn how best to make litigation pay, both in terms of their long-term goals but also in a more crude material sense. As the expected returns of litigation increase, interest groups may eschew other modes of advocacy, such as lobbying for new legislation, which is almost always a long shot in the lawmaking obstacle course on Capitol Hill. In contrast to the crowd out argument, in which the costs of litigation divert groups with limited resources from other modes of advocacy, the path dependence argument implies that groups come to *prefer* litigation to other modes of advocacy given its increasing returns, even when they can afford to fight in other forums.

Particular legal doctrines can also, at least theoretically, become like the ice cream cone you just cannot stop eating. Or to put it more like Gordon Silverstein (2009) would, when a public policy is juridified, the resulting accretion of precedents narrows the scope of political debate, not just in court but also in the larger political system. The idea is that legal precedents do not merely shape legal discourse but also the terms of policy debates outside the courts. As legal precedents become "givens," reform proposals that are inconsistent with them are deemed out of bounds, which limits policy options. Affirmative action becomes a matter of weighing "diversity"; abortion is framed around a woman's right to privacy. Silverstein uses campaign finance to illustrate his contention. He argues that the claim that "money is speech"—a point that was controversial at the time *Buckley v. Valeo* was decided—has become taken for granted in the politics of campaign finance, sharply delimiting the scope of reforms that are seriously considered. Silverstein explains his claim:

> When policy bounces from Congress to courts, to the administration, and back again,... the influences [of legal precedents] become more complex and often more constraining. We might think of a game of *Scrabble,* a game in which players often end up where none had originally planned or imagined. In a game of *Scrabble,* players start with a blank board, and the first player can head off in any direction he or she chooses. But slowly, over the course of the game, the players often end in one corner of the board, whereas another part of the board is totally empty.... In theory, it is still possible to move the game off in a radically different direction, but it becomes increasingly difficult (and unlikely) for that to happen (2009: 66).

Juridification, according to this claim, can lead to a highly constrained politics in which public policy debate looks like the end of a Scrabble game rather the beginning.

Silverstein's case studies focus on constitutional issues, where the institutional barriers to reversing judicial doctrines are the highest. It may be that path dependence is not so much a function of "juridification," or to use our preferred term, adversarial legalism, but merely the one form of it, American federal judicial review, in which it is hardest to reverse course once a ruling has been made. Constitutional rulings are particularly "sticky" because, as Charles Evans Hughes once said, the U.S. Constitution is what the judges say it is[9]—it is rare for a ruling to be reversed through constitutional amendment, and so difficult to recast the political debate over campaign finance or abortion in ways that would conflict with Court rulings. That said, there are reasons to believe that, U.S. constitutional law aside, adversarial legalism in all its forms should be resistant to change. The underlying dynamics of path dependence that Silverstein and Pierson identify—framing effects and increasing returns—are not wholly dependent on the existence of institutional barriers to formal revision. These dynamics are largely generated by the litigation process itself, and so apply to other forms of litigation, including common law and statutory interpretation decisions, where judicial decisions can be overridden through the passage of ordinary legislation (which itself is no mean feat).

In our study, adversarial policies were in fact prone to some degree of path dependence. The law in our cases is mostly common law, which is much easier to change than constitutional law, but still hard to reverse entirely. As a formal matter, once a legal doctrine was established, it became difficult to reform. But in our study, path dependence was hardly a unique property of adversarial legalism. Bureaucratic legal policies in our cases exhibited the same tendency: once created, agency-based programs proved hard to retrench or reform. The fact that adversarial and bureaucratic legal regimes are both formally sticky should come as no surprise. The influence of pre-existing institutional arrangements in public policymaking and administration was sketched out at least as far back as Herbert Simons *Administrative Behavior* (1947). As John Kingdon (2011: 79) once observed, policymakers of all stripes tend to "take what they are doing as given, and make small, incremental, and marginal adjustments" (see also Epp 2010). In fact, when we looked beyond the formal structures of programs and examined how the details of policies were adapted through practice over time—what Erkulwater (2006) calls "microlevel" as opposed to "macrolevel" changes—bureaucratic programs and agencies often proved *less* flexible than legal doctrines and courts, failing to adjust existing rules to new policy circumstances and political demands, and forcing stakeholders to turn to the courts, which proved remarkably adept at adjusting administrative regulations and legal doctrines to new circumstances.

Similarly, it is true, as Silverstein (2009) persuasively argues, that adversarial legalism can have powerful framing effects that preclude the consideration of various types of claims, but bureaucratic legalism also has framing effects that bound debate and cut off consideration of alternatives. As our case study of the politics of SSDI describes, attempts to change peoples understanding of the problem of disability have run up against the powerful framing that bureaucratic policies have reinforced. So, leaving aside the special case of U.S. judicial review, we found little evidence that adversarial legalism was any *more* path-dependent than bureaucratic legalism; indeed it seemed less so at the microlevel.

Backlash

Critics charge that adversarial legalism engenders strong reactions from powerful interests that lose in courts, in part because policymaking by unelected judges is seen as illegitimate, a form of judicial encroachment on the prerogatives of elected officials' turf. This argument has been made perhaps most prominently by Michael Klarman in his account of the civil rights movement. Klarmans analysis of backlash is subtle. On one hand, he argues *Brown v. Board of Education* set back the struggle for civil rights by catalyzing resistance by even relatively moderate Southern states. Litigation, in effect, eliminated the moderate middle. On the other hand, violent resistance by Southern extremists was instrumental in setting the stage for a counter-backlash at the national level. Klarmans (2012) more recent account of the fight for marriage equality is also subtle, arguing that early cases recognizing civil unions and gay marriage, like the Massachusetts litigation, engendered backlash, but the risk of backlash has ebbed as public opinion continues to swing in favor of gay marriage.

Rosenberg (1991), by contrast, makes stronger claims in connection with *Roe v. Wade,* arguing that the decision resulted in an organized counter-movement by social conservatives that has stigmatized abortion and limited access to it. In a similar vein, Mary Ann Glendon has argued that *Roe* polarized the politics of abortion, thus helping to explain why the United States continues to have such a fervent pro-choice/pro-life politics even as other nations (even largely Catholic ones) have largely resolved the issue (Glendon 1987).

Although we tend to think of the backlash argument in connection with high-profile constitutional rights, others have noted the catalytic effect of more mundane types of litigation in mobilizing opposition. A good example of this is William Haltom and Michael McCann's study of conservative and business counter-mobilization against tort law, which documents a sustained effort to shift public discourse on personal injury litigation by emphasizing one-sided and sometime false anecdotes about "frivolous lawsuits" and bogus claiming practices (Haltom and McCann 2004). Backlashes are problematic in this account partly because they divert attention from the underlying substantive issues to the propriety of judicialization itself, but also because they polarize interests and hinder compromise. The backlash argument takes many forms, but a common thread is that reliance on adversarial legalism has a potentially polarizing effect on politics.

In our cases we found lots of examples of the counter-mobilizing tendencies of adversarial legalism. Lawsuits against manufacturers for injuries purportedly caused by their products eventually stimulated massive mobilization, as one would expect. But this counter-mobilization was far more complex and variegated than is implied by the backlash literature. The targets of litigation, for example, often internally divided based on the degree of their exposure to litigation. Moreover, in some cases, by raising important issues, bringing all the parties to the table, and stimulating the building of coalitions across the plaintiff/defendant divide, litigation set the stage not for backlash but political resolution. In our cases, adversarial legalism engendered counter-mobilization but not necessary a polarizing backlash.

Individualization of political interests (and undermining of social solidarity)

A final charge is that adversarial legalism makes it harder to resolve social problems because it frames them as individual disputes and so divides interests from one another. Unlike the backlash argument, the concern is not that adversarial legalism will engender *unified* opposition but that it will Balkanize interests or internally fragment them, making the finding of common ground difficult even among groups that we might expect to be allies.

This charge takes many forms and has deep theoretical roots. A long line of political theorists, starting with Edmund Burke and Karl Marx, have critically examined how legal rights structure people's grievances and understanding of social obligations (Waldron 1987). Burke criticized the espousal of the leaders of the French Revolution of the "rights of man" as abstract, extreme, ahistorical, and so removed from the practicalities of governance. Government, he insisted, "is a contrivance of human wisdom to provide for human *wants*," and attempting to govern through abstract rights ignores the complexity of social arrangements and the intricacies of human nature (Burke 1987: 52). Marx contended that "the rights of man" are merely the rights of "egoistic man, of man separated from other men and from the community." The struggle for these political rights, Marx argued, are a symptom of the individualism and lack of social connectedness that plagues capitalist societies (Marx 1978: 43). These are very different diagnoses—and Burke and Marx were radically different thinkers—but both point to the gap between the magisterial promise of universal rights and the practical, material consequences of framing social issues as matters of rights, which they argued neglect the communal aspect of human life.

One can see echoes of these Burkean and Marxian themes in the critiques of rights that sprung up in the 1970s and 1980s, a period when the luster of social change through law began to fade in che United States. Communitarian political thinkers such as Alasdair MacIntyre, and Critical Legal Studies scholars on the left, such as Mark Tushnet and Duncan Kennedy, for all their differences, shared a basic premise: framing political conflicts as matters of legal rights (and thus channeling them through the courts and litigation process) individualizes politics, undermines social solidarity, and reinforces a narrowed and flattened view of social life (Tushnet 1984; Gabel and Kennedy 1984; Freeman 1978; MacIntyre 1981; Taylor 1998). Critics such as Wendy Brown, on similar grounds, argue that rather than emancipating citizens, rights are liable to reinscribe the very power relations they are meant to challenge (Brown 1995; Baynes 2000).

Although they start from quite different premises, we do not think it is too much of a stretch to link these legal and political theorists' commentaries to critical accounts of judicial policymaking in law and political science. The judicial policymaking literature is typically grounded in Pluralism, the interest group-focused approach to politics, rather than Marxian or Burkean themes, and so would be anathema to many radical critics of rights, but it too concerns the way in which litigation narrows and individualizes the framing of social problems. Litigation, this literature suggests, requires multi-faceted problems with many dimensions to be reduced to discrete legal disputes between individual claimants. The legalistic framing of social problems, it is contended, precludes consideration of broader concerns, and excludes some stakeholders from the deliberative process, as not all relevant parties will necessarily participate in precedent-setting lawsuits (or their settlement) (e.g., Fuller 1978; Horowitz 1977; Katzmann 1986; Melnick 1983; Derthick 2005). The process undermines the Pluralist ideal of bargaining among all affected interests.

It is admittedly a long distance from Marx to Melnick, but the common element we see is a concern about the divisive, fragmenting effects of the way in which adversarial legalism addresses social issues. And this is the concern that seems vindicated by the data in our study, which not only show a correspondence between adversarial legalism and a fractious brand of politics, but also illustrate the mechanisms that connect policy and politics.[13]

Our findings on the connection between legal policies and their politics dovetail nicely with the enormous literature on "policy feedbacks," which tend to focus on how traditional welfare programs shape politics (e.g., Schattschneider 1935; Lowi 1964; Wilson 1973; Walker 1991; Skocpol 1991; Pierson 1993, 1994, 2004; Thelen 1999; Pierson and Skocpol 2002; Mettler and Soss 2004; Mettler 2011; Campbell 2003, 2012). This literature illustrates how policies "define, arouse, or pacify constituencies" by creating incentives for political actors and by influencing beliefs about what is "possible, desirable, and normal" (Soss and Schram 2007: 113). In a widely cited review of this literature, Paul Pierson (1993) identified two general categories of policy feedbacks, resource or incentive effects (now often simply referred to as resource effects), and interpretive effects. Policies in this view provide material resources to actors that affect the way they engage in politics, but policies also frame the way social problems and actors are conceived.

We find both types of feedback mechanisms arising from the injury compensation policies in our study (Figure 1.1). First, injury policies create distinctive *distributional effects*, patterns of payout and compensation for injury that affect the material interests of the stakeholders. These distributional effects shape the stakes of interest groups in preserving or reforming the policy; this in turn affects how groups mobilize and build coalitions. Second, injury policies shape the *assignment of blame*, the framing of fault for injury. Blame assignment, in turn, affects how policymakers argue about the appropriate scheme for compensating injury.

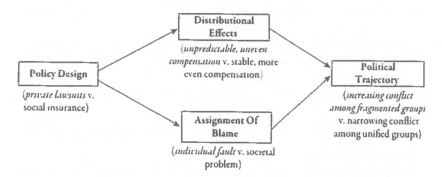

FIGURE 1.1 How policy shapes politics: injury compensation policy (*adversarial legalism* versus bureaucratic legalism)

In our cases, adversarial legalism and bureaucratic legalism created distinctive patterns of distributional and blame effects, and these effects result in distinctive political trajectories, patterns of politics over time. The distributional and blame effects of adversarial policies initially *limit* the scope of political conflict. Because adversarial legalism organizes injury compensation claims into discrete, private lawsuits, at an early stage it tends to have a privatizing effect. When there are just a few lawsuits against, say, a particular manufacturer who uses asbestos, or a particular vaccine producer, the cost and the blame for injury falls on just a few individual actors. At this stage members of Congress are disinclined to get involved, and quite willing to defer to judges who act in their traditional role as adjudicators of individual lawsuits. Even other companies in the affected industry or field fail to mobilize. They may calculate that the problem is limited to the named defendants. But as litigation expands, more and more companies and stakeholder groups become involved, and the stakes increase. At this stage, the distributional effects of adversarial legalism are powerful: as some plaintiffs and defendants win while others lose, the uneven pattern of costs and benefits generates cross-cutting interests within and across key stakeholder groups. Those most affected by litigation on the defendant side run to Congress to try to make the pain go away. Those with lower risk, even in the same field, stay on the sidelines or even fight to preserve the adversarial legal system. The distributional effects of litigation then, reduce political conflict at an early stage, but increase factionalization at a later stage.

The other mechanism, blame assignment, also shapes injury politics in a powerful way: it forces those who seek reform to reframe responsibility for injury. Where individual lawsuits frame the problem as the culpability of individual entities, would-be reformers have to recast the issue as a social problem so as to make the sins of individual actors less relevant. This is a difficult political task. The combined effect of distribution effects and blame assignment associated with adversarial legalism is to create a political trajectory of increasing intensity and factionalization.

The distributional effects and blame assignment generated by bureaucratic legalism create a strikingly different political trajectory. Here the intensity and scope of conflict diminishes over time. Our cases of bureaucratic legalism all involve social insurance in which some kind of tax is created to fund an injury compensation scheme. At creation, there is a bitter and familiar conflict over the assignment of blame: business groups and their conservative allies argue against the tax as unfair and unwarranted. If there are injuries, they contend, it is not their problem. Liberals and their allies, on the other side, argue that it is a social responsibility to provide for suffering individuals. This is a fundamental political conflict, and in two of our cases, Social Security Disability Insurance and vaccine injury compensation, it is ferocious. But once the compensation scheme in those cases is enacted, the distinctive distributional effect of bureaucratic legalism kicks in: costs are spread so widely and evenly that the incentive to mobilize against the programs dissipates. Business groups largely demobilize, and conflict over the maintenance and expansion of the programs is reduced. Moments of conflict occasionally redevelop, but they are narrower in scope and less fragmented than in our cases of adversarial legalism. Again, there is a central irony here: the same aspect of policy design chat increases conflict at the outset—the socialization of the costs of injury—over time seems to reduce conflict.

In sum, from a comparative developmental perspective, adversarial legalism and bureaucratic legalism have political trajectories that are mirror opposites. The politics of adversarial legalism commences in a decentralized fashion but becomes more pluralistic and fractious. The politics of bureaucratic legalism, by contrast, is highly polarized at the outset but over time becomes more consensual, coinciding with bureaucratic legalism's more even and predictable spreading of costs and benefits, and with the acceptance of its underlying principle of social responsibility for injury.

ROAD MAP FOR THE FOLLOWING CHAPTERS

We provide the grounds for our conclusions in the following five chapters. Chapter 2 is a quantitative analysis of patterns of congressional testimony from 1971 to 2011 on a range of adversarial and bureaucratic injury compensation policies. The data in this chapter suggest that adversarial legalism and bureaucratic legalism generate radically different types of congressional oversight. Hearings on adversarial policies, as compared to bureaucratic policies, feature more diverse types of interests, more conflicting testimony, and relatively high levels of participation by business interests. The fragmented patterns of participation and greater degree of conflict seem consistent with the concern that adversarial legalism individualizes conflict and fragments interests.

These cross-sectional findings are suggestive but only a start because they rely on the narrow prism of congressional hearings. Relatively quiet politics in Congress might mask high levels of conflict in other venues, particularly the other branches of government. Accordingly, chapters 3 through 5 feature three historical case studies of the politics of injury compensation policies. We begin with Social Security Disability Insurance, a bureaucratic policy that provides a baseline for comparison with the adversarial cases. We then turn to the asbestos case, tracing its evolving politics in several steps, first as claimants established a right to recovery, then as business interests attempted to contain their liability, resulting in a layered response to the problem of asbestos injury compensation. We end with the vaccine injury compensation case, in which an adversarial design was largely replaced by a bureaucratic design. Consistent with our quantitative analyses, these case studies suggest that the politics of adversarial legalism and bureaucratic legalism differ, but the case studies demonstrate that the differences are developmental: they lie in how patterns of conflict develop over time, with adversarial policies generating an increasing scope of conflict and bureaucratic policies tending to narrow conflict. In the concluding chapter, we summarize our findings and their limitations, and put our study in the broader context of research on law and public policy.

NOTES

1. The quote comes from an interview with a man on public assistance, and was used by Sarat to summarize an aspect of the legal consciousness of poor people on welfare, but we think it equally appropriate as a summary of the role of law in American public policy.
2. Gerhard Teubner's analysis of the concept of "juridification" demonstrates the slew of ways in which the concept has been deployed in law and social science, most of which have little to do with comparing the work of courts and legislatures. Teubner, for example, approves Jurgen Habermas's use of the concept of juridification to mark the "'constitutionalization' of the economic system," the growing use of purpose-oriented laws to regulate social life (Teubner 1987).
3. If you insist, for example, that a civil rights law like the Americans with Disabilities Act has been ineffective, is your comparison point some idealized agency-based policy that you imagine a legislature might have adopted instead, or just the conditions of people with disabilities before the ADA was adopted? On this point see Burke 1997.
4. Shapiro, for example, noted that judges are typically generalists, whereas agency officials tend to be specialists, and that courts often exercise negative power by striking down laws through judicial review as opposed to agencies, which shape policy through the promulgation of specific regulations (1968: 44).
5. We can think of our analysis as searching for patterns that are consistent across five types of comparisons: (1) cross-sectional comparisons of policies that feature different types of institutional structures (i.e., adversarial versus bureaucratic policies); (2) cross-sectional comparisons of policies that feature similar types of institutional structures but address different compensation areas (eg., asbestos litigation, vaccine litigation, medical malpractice, product liability, and securities fraud litigation); (3) cross-sectional comparisons within policy areas where different policy types co-exist side-by-side (e.g., asbestos litigation and workers' compensation); (4) longitudinal comparisons across and within policies at different stages of development (e.g., the politics of creating asbestos litigation versus the creation of SSDI or the politics of creating, expanding, and retrenching vaccine injury compensation); and (5) longitudinal comparisons within a policy where one type of regime replaced another (e.g., the vaccine compensation program and vaccine litigation).
6. U.S. v. Windsor, 570 U.S.____(2013) (Docket No. 12–307).
7. Ibid. (Scalia Dissent), pp. 25–26.
8. Commentators often decry judicial policymaking as inherently undemocratic and "counter-majoritarian," as Scalia did in *Windsor*. Our finding of intentionally shared policymaking powers adds to the long list of reasons for questioning simplistic arguments that judicial policymaking is necessarily less "democratic" than its legislative counterparts (see Barnes 2004; Friedman 2001, 1993; Whittington 2001; Peretti 1999; Feeley and Rubin 1998; Mishler and Sheenan 1993; Klarman 1994; Graber 1993; Rosenberg

1992). At its core, this argument—the so-called counter-majoritarian difficulty (Bickel 1962)—presupposes that the president and Congress are majoritarian and represent the "will of the People" simply by virtue of their elected status. Elections clearly matter in any democracy, but they do not guarantee majoritarian results, given low voter turnout, incumbency advantages, gerrymandering, unregulated campaign financing, and many other staple features of today s elections. Even if we accept that elections produce members of Congress that fairly represent the preferences of a majority of citizens in their districts or states (and effectively resist pressure from well-organized and wealthy groups) —a big "if"—no guarantee exists that a majority of lawmakers will be able to act given the large number of veto points in the American legislative process, including a host of supermajority requirements in the Senate. Conversely, majority rule legislative processes may not produce laws that reflect a clear majority preference of elected officials, much less concerns about public opinion; preferences cycle and votes can be manipulated (Arrow 1963; Shepsle 1992.). Moreover, legislation can reflect a variety of motivations and purposes, some of which are plainly inconsistent with the majoritarian ideal, such as credit claiming, blaming shifting, and providing benefits to groups that can help officials get reelected (Mayhew 1974; Fiorina 1989; Arnold 1990). By the same token, federal judges are not heedless of public opinion simply because they are appointed for life (see, e.g., Mishler and Sheenan 1993; Marshall 1989; Feeley and Rubin 1998; Peretti 1999: 178–180 (collecting authority); Devins 2004). The question then is not whether judicial policymaking is *inherently* anti-democratic or counter-majoritarian; it is how reliance on litigation shapes the ongoing inter-branch colloquy on significant policy matters and whether it advances important democratic activities, such as broad political participation, coalition building among divergent interests, and deliberation within diversely representative branches and levels of government. That is why, in this book, we move beyond simplistic criticisms of judicial policymaking based on the counter-majoritarian difficulty and explore how adversarial legalism shapes the underlying interest group politics that drive inter-branch relations over the making of policy.

9. See Powell (2006: 318), quoting Charles Evans Hughes, *Addresses of Charles Evans Hughes* 185 (1916). As Powell notes, Hughes did not literally believe that the Supreme Court controlled the meaning of the Constitution, and lived to regret the way the quotation was used.

10. We recognize that the term "mechanism" is deeply contested. In a thoughtful review, John Gerring (2010: 1500–1501) finds no less than ten definitions of mechanism in the relevant literature, some of which are contradictory. We have no desire to become bogged down in this debate, nor is it necessary to do so. In using the term "mechanism," we simply mean a pathway or link between an explanatory variable and an outcome, which is analogous to an intervening variable (see Weller and Barnes 2014; Gerring 2004, 2007).

Con Law Expert Gordon Silverstein

Prop 8 Ruling Could Cost the Gay Rights Movement

Alexander C. Hart

With news breaking this afternoon that Prop 8 (an amendment to California's constitution banning gay marriage) has been overturned in a federal court, Citizen Cohn
reached out to Gordon Silverstein, assistant professor of political science at the University
of California-Berkeley, for his take on the ruling. Silverstein is an expert in constitutional law
and American politics and the author of *Law's Allure: How Law Shapes, Constrains, Saves,
and Kills Politics*. While a proponent of the ruling, Silverstein speculates on how it might
play in the Supreme Court and says today's verdict could undermine the policy goals of the
gay-rights movement in the long term:

> Judge Vaughn [R. Walker] is probably right, but by drawing the sharpest possible
> line in the sand, his principled decision might possibly prove to be a moral victory
> but one that could undercut the deeper social policy goals advocates had in mind
> in pushing this forward as a legal and constitutional case.
>
> Walker took the strongest line imaginable—Prop 8, he said, can't even pass
> the lowest, least demanding constitutional test there is for any sorts of rules that
> discriminate: The Rational Basis test. If you can show even the barest rational
> justification for a law, you can survive this test. Prop 8, Walker ruled, fails.
>
> This means, of course, that if you measure it against the far tougher standard that
> is typically applied in cases involving suspect classification (like race, or religion) it
> would, of course, fail miserably.
>
> This ruling, though, leaves the Supreme Court little wiggle room. Yes, they could
> of course agree with Walker, and strike down Prop 8—along the way fundamentally
> raising the barrier to any rules that might adversely affect homosexuals or same-sex
> couples. They could do that—but hard to believe they will.
>
> At the other extreme, Walker's line-in-the-sand invites the Supreme Court to
> make a clear statement, to draw their own line, which would formally and explicitly

Alexander Hart, "Con Law Expert Gordon Silverstein: Prop 8 Ruling Could Cost the Gay Rights Movement,"
New Republic. Copyright © 2010 by New Republic. Reprinted with permission provided by PARS
International Corp.

carve out areas where such discrimination would in fact be constitutional. And by opening the door for such a ruling, those who brought this case to Walker's court in the first place may live to regret that choice.

The alternative, of course, is politics. Change minds. Elect candidates. The original Prop 8 passed in large measure because so many Californians who did not favor Prop 8 failed to participate, failed to vote. A political campaign is the sort of thing that can persuade and change minds—and that is, in the long run, the only way to truly lock in change. Judicial rulings can change behavior, but not minds. At least not by themselves.

An adverse ruling from the Supreme Court would only make it that much harder to effect change through political channels.

Walker might well say that his job is to read the constitution. Period. And he's right, as was his decision, I think. But Walker didn't force gay marriage advocates to bring this case—that was their choice. They will probably savor their moral and constitutional victory in the short term, but may regret it down the road.

This case is a stark reminder of a harsh choice that rights advocates often have to make: Is it right to sacrifice moral and constitutional claims in the short term to achieve long-term policy goals? Or, insist on the moral high ground, regardless of the practical costs?

Could be, though, that Walker has drawn his line so starkly that even the Roberts Court will be persuaded. Could be. But not likely.

Beyond Backlash

Assessing the Impact of Judicial Decisions on LGBT Rights

Thomas M. Keck

This article evaluates the widespread scholarly claim that the courtroom victories of the lesbian, gay, bisexual, and transgender rights movement have invariably provoked a counterproductive political backlash. Those victories have indeed provoked conservative countermobilization, but that has not been their only or even their most prominent effect. Assessing the political reaction to the movement s judicial victories, the policy impact of those victories, and the alternative strategic paths that were available to the movement at the outset, I argue that here, as elsewhere, legal mobilization has sometimes been a promising avenue tor pursuing policy changes whose prospects were otherwise quite limited.

Judicial decisions defending the rights of lesbian, gay, bisexual, and transgender (LGBT) persons have regularly been criticized for going too far, too fast. It is no surprise that opponents of gay rights have denounced these decisions as examples of illegitimate judicial activism, hut some supporters of gay rights have also criticized them as strategically unwise. In doing so, these supporters have echoed a long-standing scholarly argument that rights-based litigation strategies are ineffective at best and counterproductive at worst. In the gay rights context, one version of this argument has been particularly prominent: even when rights advocates win in court, those victories inevitably spark a political backlash, with the voters and their elected representatives reversing the judicial decisions and enacting regressive policies that are worse than the status quo ante.

A closer inspection of the actual sequence of victories and defeats for LGBT rights advocates in the United States, both in court and out, complicates this backlash narrative to a significant degree. Judicial decisions supporting LGBT rights have repeatedly fueled political countermobilization, but that has not been their only 01 even their most prominent effect. To the contrary, litigation has contributed in a variety of ways to expanding the rights of LGBT persons to act on their sexual identities without government interference, to be protected

Thomas Keck, "Beyond Backlash: Assessing the Impact of Judicial Decisions on LGBT Rights," Law & Society Review, vol. 43, no. 1, pp. 151-185. Copyright © 2009 by John Wiley & Sons, Inc. Reprinted with permission.

from invidious discrimination, and to form family relationships that are recognized by the state. If the backlash thesis is misleading even in this context—which its proponents have recently adopted as an illustrative case providing clear confirmation of their preexisting thesis then it may be worth reexamination in other contexts as well.

THE BACKLASH THESIS

One of the leading claims of the scholarly literature on the limits of judicial power is that unpopular judicial decisions provoke political reactions that undercut their effectiveness. This thesis has been developed most fully by Klarman, who has argued for more than a decade that the chief impact of the Supreme Court's landmark decision in *Brown v. Board of Education* (1954) was to exacerbate the racist rhetoric and segregationist policies that characterized Southern politics at the time. On Klarman's account, *Brown* sparked massive resistance, polarizing Southern racial politics and undermining the efforts of white moderates. As a result, when Southern blacks turned to direct action protest in the earl) 1960s, they were met with increasing violence. Because it was Northern revulsion at Bull Connor's fire hoses and police dogs that led to the 1964 Civil Rights Act, Klarman sometimes suggests that the *Brown* litigation ultimately produced progress on civil rights (Klarman 2004:385, 441-2; see also 1994). At other times, however, he emphasizes that racial liberalism was gradually but steadily advancing before the Court clumsily intervened, sparking a resurgence of white supremacy and thus undermining the very cause the justices were hoping to promote (2004:442, 464-5). Toward the end of his 2004 book on civil rights, Klarman identifies same-sex marriage (SSM) litigation as one of several recent examples that fit the counterproductive pattern set by *Brown* (2004:465). Elaborating the claim in a subsequent article, he insists that the Massachusetts high court's landmark 2003 decision legalizing SSM met a fate similar to that which followed every other effort by judges to defend a rights claim that lacked popular support: "The most significant short-term consequence of *Goodridge v. Department of Public Health* 2003], as with *Brown,* may have been the political backlash that it inspired. By outpacing public opinion on issues of social reform, such rulings mobilize opponents, undercut moderates, and retard the cause they purport to advance" (Klarman 2005:482).

Like Klarman, Rosenberg is most well known for his revisionist and pessimistic account of *Brown* but has also advanced a similarly negative assessment of contemporary SSM litigation. Where Klarman has long emphasized the political backlash sparked by *Brown,* Rosenberg has generally characterized the decision as inconsequential rather than counterproductive, emphasizing that judges are usually unwilling and always unable to impose unpopular rights on the nation at large. In the original 1991 edition of *The Hollow Hope: Can Courts Bring About Social Change* Rosenberg noted the backlash phenomenon only in passing, and he even responded to an early version of Klarman's argument by objecting that Klarman had overstated *Browns* negative impact (1991:342, 1994; see also Garrow 1994). In a revised

2008 edition of *The Hollow Hope,* however, Rosenberg has added 80 pages of new material on SSM litigation, extensively documenting the conservative countermobilization that followed the LGBT rights movement's state high court victories in Hawaii, Vermont, and Massachusetts.

According to this backlash narrative, SSM litigators won three big cases from 1993 to 2003, but each of these judicial decisions provoked political setbacks that made things worse. The Hawaii Supreme Court's 1993 decision in *Baehr v. Lew in* reached no final judgment on the state's discriminatory marriage laws but imposed a legal standard for justifying those laws that the state was unlikely to meet. Far from advancing the cause, however, this judicial victory produced a state constitutional amendment reversing the decision, a similar state constitutional amendment reversing a copycat judicial decision in .Alaska, a federal statute declaring that the national government would not recognize SSMs and authorizing state governments to refuse such recognition as well, and statutory bans on SSM in more than 30 states by the end of 1999. At that point, the Vermont Supreme Court revived the movement's hopes by ordering the state to extend all the rights and benefits of marriage (though not the name) to same-sex couples, but this victory in *Baker v. State of Vermont* was followed by six more states banning SSM, including constitutional bans in Nebraska and Nevada. In Vermont itself, the state legislature responded to the court by enacting a Civil Unions Act in 2000, but the legislators paid for this decision at the polls, with an unusually large number of incumbents voted out of office later that year. Finally, 2003 witnessed the U.S. Supreme Court's invalidation of the last remaining criminal sodomy statutes in *Lawrence v. Texas*, followed several months later by the first decision from an American court to actually legalize SSM (*Goodridge v. Department of Public Health* 2003). In a pattern that should now be clear, these landmark victories led to significant electoral setbacks, including President George W. Bush's reelection the following year and the enactment of 23 new state constitutional bans on SSM by 2006. In sum, the litigation campaigns waged by LGBT rights advocates have regularly provoked both electoral and policy setbacks, reversing the gains won in court and producing executives, legislatures, and eventually judiciaries that are less supportive of LGBT rights than they were before.

Despite objections from a number of quarters, the general argument about the limited and unintended consequences of judicial decisions has been widely influential. This account is sometimes presented as a cautionary lesson for judges, urging them to temper principle with prudence (Posner 1997; Rosen 2003, 2006; Sunstein 1996:96-8). In addition to this lesson about judicial humility, the backlash account is often framed as a warning to (or rebuke of) movement activists, whose purportedly unreasonable demands for the courts to guarantee equal marriage rights are blamed for every subsequent political setback. The most recent iteration of this argument has revolved around whether SSM advocates are to blame for President Bush's 2004 reelection, but the wisdom of the SSM lawsuits has been a subject of considerable debate within the LGBT rights movement for a long time. When the Hawaii suit was filed in 1991, most leaders of the movement opposed the effort. The case was initiated by three same-sex couples and their private attorney, and both the Lambda

Legal Defense and Education Fund and the American Civil Liberties Union (AGLI) declined invitations to sign on. Writing two years earlier, the executive director of Lambda Legal had noted that "[a]s far as [he could] tell, no gay organization of any size, local or national, [had] yet declared the right to marry as one of its goals" (Stoddard 1989:1 1-12). t his choice was partly ideological—some gays and lesbians had no interest in joining the patriarchal institution of marriage but it was partly strategic as well, with most advocates concluding that the goal was politically unattainable at the time.

The organized movement is now fully committed to the SSM campaign, but some of its most prominent scholarly supporters have continued to object on strategic grounds. Relying heavily on Rosenberg's account, Rimmerman has emphasized the limited capacity of judicial institutions to effectively construct and implement public policy and has suggested that the 1993 *Baehr* decision did "more for opponents of lesbian and gay marriage than for its proponents" (2002:78). Expressing the point even more sharply, D'Emilio has complained that "[t]he campaign for same-sex marriage has been an unmitigated disaster. Never in the history of organized queerdom have we seen defeats of this magnitude." In fact, "[t]he battle to win marriage equality through the courts has done something that no other campaign or issue in our movement has done: it has created a vast bodv of *new* antigay law" (2006:10, emphasis in original; see also 2007:59). Echoing the conclusions of the Rosenberg Klarman thesis, these internal movement critics have complained that litigation leads either to judicial defeats that achieve nothing or to judicial "victories" that provoke a counterproductive backlash. Either way, litigation campaigns draw resources from alternative strategies that are likely to be more effective.

A number of detailed scholarly accounts of LGBT rights litigation have advanced more optimistic (or at least more nuanced) assessments, but these works have drawn less attention than have the broad critiques of litigation. In a noteworthy comparative study, Smith (2008) has argued that the American LGBT rights movement has been less successful than its Canadian counterpart over the past 15 years, but that much of the success that both movements have had has been the product of litigation. Likewise, Andersen's definitive study of Lambda Legal emphasizes "both the promise and the limits of legal mobilization as a tactic for achieving social reform" and makes clear that "there are at least some circumstances in w hich reformers can be served by turning to the courts" (Andersen 2005:216). Citing Rosenberg, Andersen agrees that 'courts do not have the capacity to produce social change when their decisions diverge too radically from the values and expectations of the other two branches of government," but she insists nonetheless that "litigation [has] produced some favorable shifts in the legal and cultural frames surrounding gay rights" (2005: 216-18). Eskridge likewise acknowledges the "antigay backlash" provoked by *Baehr* but also notes that "the litigation in Hawaii sowed the seeds for [the subsequent litigation in] Vermont" (Eskridge 2002:26, 45). Drawing on interviews with many of the key participants, Eskridge concludes that "*Baehr* opened up lesbian and gay imaginations to the possibility that their relationships might be recognized by the state as civil marriages, and it can hardly be surprising that many of the galvanized ended up as plaintiffs in court" (2002:45). Drawing on a similar set of interviews a few years later, Pinello argues that

> *Goodridge* brought about enormous social change... With nearly all other state and national policy makers at odds with its goal, the Massachusetts [high court] nonetheless achieved singular success in expanding the ambit of who receives the benefits of getting married in America, in inspiring political elites elsewhere in the country to follow suit, and in mobilizing grass-roots supporters to entrench their legal victory politically. (2006:192-3; see also Mezey 2007)

COURTS AND CAUSAL MECHANISMS

These competing assessments are rooted in competing conceptions of judicial power and historical change. If American courts are too weak to do anything helpful, then LGBT rights advocates should stop appealing to them for help. But if litigation sometimes has positive—even if complex—effects, then it may remain a promising avenue for pursuing policy changes whose prospects are otherwise quite limited. The original edition of *The Hollow Hope* (Rosenberg 1991) sparked a vigorous debate in the sociolegal literature, and from the beginning, one of the chief complaints has been that Rosenberg's account of social change conveyed a sense of inevitability that obscured the contingencies of human history (McCann 1992, 1996; Gar row 1994). Rosenberg (1991:169) and Klarman (2004:468; 1994:14) each argue that mid-twentieth-century racial progress would have occurred regardless of the actions of judges and lawyers, and in their recent work, they have each extended this causal narrative to the gay rights context. Klarman emphasizes that "[t]he demographics of public opinion on issues of sexual orientation virtually ensure that one day in the not-too-distant future a substantial majority of Americans will support same-sex marriage" (2005:484-5), and Rosenberg likewise details the increasing public acceptance of gays and lesbians, as evidenced by public opinion polls, legislative change, the policies of leading corporations and professional associations, and the representation of gays and lesbians on television and in movies (2008:407-15). They each argue that discrimination against gays and lesbians has decreased in recent decades, but that "these changes are not primarily the result of litigation. Rather, they are the result of a changing culture" (Rosenberg 2008:415; see also Klarman 2005: 484-5; D'Emilio 2005:12, 2006:10-11).

Treating law and culture as wholly separate independent variables, these accounts fail to adequately explore the causal significance of the litigation campaigns. Rosenberg is surely correct that the television shows *Ellen* and *Will & Grace* have helped make LGBT persons more visible and less hated than before, but it is not clear why he treats this claim as mutually exclusive with the proposition that SSM lawsuits have helped make LGBT persons more visible and less hated than before. Likewise, it is certainly true that controversial court decisions sometimes provoke immediate and hostile political reactions, but even then, their long-term causal implications tend to be complex and multidirectional. Unpacking these causal dynamics can be difficult, but the alternative is to accept an overly simple set of causal attributions. Throughout the Clinton and Bush eras, the legal and political conflicts over LGBT rights have been highly decentralized, with multiple simultaneous battles proceeding in various state judiciaries, 12 federal circuits, and at times the Supreme Court, the White House and the governors' mansions, the halls of Congress and the state legislatures, and in about half the states, the direct democracy process as Miriam Smith has argued at some length, this sort of institutional fragmentation has slowed the pace of LGBT rights progress in the United States, contributing to a constant and complex pattern of starts and stops, advances and retreats, successes and failures (2008:182). Amidst this configuration of causal forces, however, there are a variety of mechanisms by which litigation and court decisions have sometimes produced meaningful change.

Most directly, court orders are sometimes effectively implemented. In at least 20 states, for example, litigation led directly to the decriminalization of consensual sodomy, with a long series of state-court victories from 1990 to 2002, followed by the U.S. Supreme Court's landmark 2003 decision in *Lawrence*. Similarly, while much has been made of the political reaction to judicial decisions expanding partnership rights, state officials have complied with the vast majority of those decisions, including the widely noted cases legalizing SSM or civil unions (CUs) in Vermont, Massachusetts, New Jersey, and California, as well as a number of state court decisions expanding partnership rights in smaller ways.[1]

Even where advocates have relied primarily on legislative strategies, litigation has sometimes been necessary to remove legal barriers to such legislative change. For example, LGBT rights advocates have won statutory protections against employment discrimination in 20 states, along with similar protections in a number of local jurisdictions. Each of these policy changes was the result of legislative action, but in at least one state, such legislative action was constitutionally precluded until the Rehnquist Court's 1996 decision in *Romer v. Evans*. By persuading the High Court to invalidate the Colorado constitutional provision prohibiting such antidiscrimination protections, LGBT rights litigators enabled the state's legislature to adopt these protections a decade later. If not for this decision, moreover, opponents of gay rights would have replicated Colorado's Amendment 2 in other states, and it is likely that the effort to enact antidiscrimination protections via democratic means would have been closed off in a substantial portion of the country.

---

1   The earliest such decision I am aware of is *Braschi v. Stahl Associates Company*. 74 N.Y.2d 201 (NY Ct. of App. 1989), in which the ACLU's Lesbian and Gay Rights Project persuaded New York's high court to construe the term *family member* in New York City's Rent and Eviction regulations to include domestic partners. See also T*anner v. Oregon Health Sciences University*, 971 P.2d 435 (Or. Ct. of App. 1998); S*netsinger v. Montana University System*. 104 P.3d 445 (Sup. Ct. Mon. 2094); *Alaska Civil Liberties Union v. Alaska*, 122 P.3d 781 (Sup. Ct. Alas. 2993); and *Martinez v. County of Monroe*. 850 N.Y.S.2d 749 (App. Div. 4,h Dept. 20981.

Less directly, but no less significantly, successful instances of rights-claiming often heighten expectations that further change is possible, particularly by "altering the expectations of potential activists that already apparent injustices might realistically be challenged at a particular point in time" (McCann 1994:89; see also Garrow 1994). In this regard, as Eskridge has argued, the *Baehr* decision "contributed to the politics of recognition by stirring the aspirations of GLBT people everywhere in the country" (Eskridge 2002:3). Indeed, every judicial decision expanding marriage rights for same-sex couples has inspired more couples to claim such rights. The courtroom victories in Hawaii sparked further litigation in Alaska and, even more important, political organizing followed by further litigation in Vermont (Andersen 2005:183-4, 197-8). In turn, the courtroom victory in Vermont sparked the litigation that led to *Good ridge* (2003), with Mary Bonauto of Gay & Lesbian Advocates & Defenders (GLAD) serving as lead attorney in both New England cases. And the most immediate and widespread reaction to *Goodridge* was not opposition, but mass public action by supporters, with thousands of same-sex couples holding public weddings in almost every region of the country. Drawing on interviews with 50 such couples, Pinello argues that *Goodridge* led to a significant increase in political participation among LGBT persons. Indeed, the decision "had a profound inspirational effect for the marriage movement, among elites and the grass roots. … Time and again, same-sex couples volunteered in interviews across the nation that they never expected marriage to be available to them during their lifetimes. Yet *Goodridge* opened a floodgate of heightened expectations" (2006:190-3).

In addition to heightening expectations among supporters, legal mobilization can some-times transform the agenda of the nation's lawmakers as well. Before the 1993 *Baehr* decision, no state legislature had passed even a limited domestic partnership bill; the vast majority were unwilling even to consider the issue. But the decision had what Eskridge calls an "agenda-seizing" effect (2002:3), fueling the efforts by advocates on both sides and drawing the broader public's attention as well. McGann has demonstrated that "[o]ne key to effective legal mobilization as a movement building strategy [is] the tremendous amount of mainstream media attention generated by dramatic … lawsuits" (McGann 1994:58), and Rosenberg documents an exponential increase in media coverage of SSM from 1980 to 2004 (Rosenberg 2008:382-400). Rosenberg argues that the rise in coverage was driven more by the political reaction to the litigation than by the litigation itself, but even so, the litigants had launched a process that transformed the issue from one that lawmakers everywhere were ignoring to one that was firmly placed on the nation's agenda. Once there, of course. SSM advocates lost many of the legislative battles to come, but they won some battles too, with elected legislators in 12 states voting to expand the legal rights of same-sex couples between 1997 and 2008.

One reason lawmakers became increasingly willing to expand partnership rights after *Baehr* is that the Hawaii decision immediately changed domestic partnership policies from radical, cutting-edge proposals to moderate compromises (Dupuis 2002:92; Andersen 2005:237). In other words, by pushing the policy envelope, ambitious litigation can clear space for legislative progress in its wake. In Hawaii itself, the 1993 *Baehr* decision led to the state's 1997

Time Period	Electoral Setbacks	Electoral victories
Between HI and VT decisions	Antigay initiatives in Cinicinnati, OH; Tampa, FL; Lewiston, ME, and 16 localities in OR (1993); Alachua Cry. FL; Austin. TX; Springfield, MO; and 10 localities in OR (1994); ME (1998) Defeat of antidiscrimination provisions in Lansing, MI (1996); Ft. Collins, CO; Fayetteville, AR; and Ogunquit, ME (1998); Albuquerque, NM: and Greeley, CO (1999) Anti-SSM constitutional amendments in HI and AK (1998) Repeal of DP policy in Northampton. MA (1995)	Defeat of antigay initiatives in ID, OR (1994); ME and West Palm Beach, FL (1995); Ypsilanti, MI (1998); Spokane, WA (1999) Enactment of antidiscrimination provision in South Portland, ME (1998) Enactment of DP policy in San Francisco (1994)
Between VT and MA decisions	Statutory ban on SSM in CA and constitutional bans in NE and NV (200-2002) GOP captures VT House (2000) Antigay inititives in ME and Ferndale, MI (2000) Ban on DP benefits in Houston. TX (2001)	Democrats retain control of VT Senate and governorship (2000) Defeat of antigay initiatives in OR (2000); Traverse City, Kalamazoo, and Huntington Woods, MI (2001); Miami-Dade Cty, FL; Westbrook, ME; Ypsilanti, MI; and Tacoma, WA (2002) Enactment of DP policies in Miami Beach, FL (2001); Cleveland Heights, OH (2003) Enactment of antidiscrimination provisions in Weston, FL (2000); Sarasota, FL (2002);
Between MA and NJ decisions	Constitutional bans on SSM in 16 states (2004–Oct. 2006) Pres. Bush's reelection and GOP Senate victories in KY, SD, OK (2004)	State legislative pickups in MA (2004-2005) Defeat of antigay initiative in ME and repeal of anti-ay initiative in Cincinnati, OH (2005)
Between NJ and CA decisions	Constitutional bans on SSM in 7 states (Nov. 2006) Rejection of DP law in CO (Nov. 2006)	Defeat of SSM ban in AZ (2006) State legislative pickups in MA (2006) Democrats recapture Congress (2006)

Table I Electoral Aftermath of Judicial Victories

Reciprocal Beneficiaries Act, which fell far short of full equality but nonetheless granted gay and lesbian couples more legal rights than anywhere else in the nation at the time. Asking for too much, too soon is sometimes counterproductive, but aggressive demands can also shift the spectrum of compromise in valuable ways. In this sense, every state legislature that has expanded partnership rights has done so in the shadow of the ongoing litigation campaign. The operation of this causal mechanism does not require judges to persuade or enlighten legislators who were once opposed or blinded, though Eskridge (2002) and Pinello (2006) have documented several instances in which that appears to have occurred. The mechanism simply requires judges to provide political cover for legislators to declare their support for a policy that they previously considered too great a political liability. In this regard, it is no coincidence that a steady stream of state legislatures has enacted antidiscrimination laws while the SSM conflict has proceeded in the courts. Opponents of gay rights once fought these policies tooth and nail, but compared to equal marriage rights, the prohibition of employment discrimination now seems significantly less threatening.

Even when they spark substantial opposition, moreover, court decisions can change the policy status quo in ways that are difficult to reverse. As Smith (2008) has argued, LGBT rights have progressed more rapidly in Canada than in the United States in part because of the greater degree of centralized authority in Canada's parliamentary system. But once gay rights advocates have won a policy victory in the United States, the famously gridlocked American lawmaking process begins to work in their favor. Before *Baker* (1999) and *Goodridge* (2003), SSM opponents in Vermont and Massachusetts needed only to block legislative proposals to expand partnership rights, while SSM supporters had to run the gauntlet of legislating in a system of separated powers. After the decisions, those positions were reversed.

In addition to reversing the relevant veto points, these decisions immediately created a group of people with a vested interest in defending the new, legally recognized same-sex partnerships. In the first eight months of SSM in Massachusetts, more than 6,000 gay and lesbian couples married, and many of these 12,000 citizens subsequently expended significant political effort to defend their existing marriages (see Table 4 ahead). Once these marriages were in place, moreover, it became more difficult for opponents to maintain that they would have severely negative social consequences. In a development that SSM advocates predicted, by spring 2005, the vast majority of Massachusetts residents indicated to pollsters that SSM had had no negative impact on the quality of life in the state (Garrow 2004; Adams 2005).

In a variety of ways, then, judicially crafted policies can have significant self-reinforcing effects. By compelling compliance, re-moving barriers to legislative change, heightening expectations, forcing the issue, pushing the policy envelope, providing an excuse for sympathetic or apathetic legislators, reversing the relevant veto points, and creating new constituencies inspired to claim and defend their rights, even unpopular judicial decisions can prove difficult to dislodge. With these causal mechanisms in mind, I turn . now to an examination of the broad patterns of legal and political change affecting LGBT rights from May 1993, when the Hawaii Supreme Court first threatened to legalize SSM, through November 2008. In the course of this examination, I assess the degree to which these patterns are consistent with three principal claims advanced by backlash proponents: (1) that judicial victories have regularly been followed by political defeats, (2) that the end result has been regressive policy change, and (3) that some other strategic choice would have worked better.

	before HI Decision	Between HI and VT	Between VT and MA	Between MA and NJ	Between NJ and GA	After CA Decision
NORG/GSS	12					
CNN/*Time*	23–27	26–31	33	30–32	40	42–47
Newsweek	30–35	29–35	34–35	33		
Pew		27	30–35	29–39		38–40
Gallup	23	27–35	34–39	31–39–42	40–46	
Quinnipiac				31–35	34	36
ABC News			37	36–41		
FOX News		22	26	25–33		
CBS/NYT			28–40	30–34		
Harris		10–11	15–16	26–27		
NBC/WSJ		25–28	32	30–32		
AP		31	34	35		

Table II Public Support for Same-Sex Marriage

THE POLITICAL REACTION

As I have noted, backlash proponents argue that judicial victories are almost always followed by electoral setbacks. This claim is true but partial, as judicial victories are sometimes followed by electoral gains as well. On both counts, the causal relationship between the court decisions and the subsequent developments is complex, but if the judges and litigators are to be blamed for everything bad that follows their decisions, they may deserve some credit for the good things that follow as well.

With respect to the initial round of litigation in Hawaii, Rosenberg's and Klarman's primary emphasis has been the negative legislative response in Congress and the state capitols a policy reaction that I examine below but there were some clear electoral consequences as well. These electoral consequences were mostly, but not entirely, negative. The 1993 *Baehr* decision came clown in the midst of a period of heavy use of ballot initiatives by opponents of gay rights. This strategy had succeeded in Colorado the previous year and was rapidly proliferating nationwide. The chief electoral impact of *Baehr* was to add SSM bans to the list of antigay policies that were regularly included in these initiatives. The fact that the Hawaii and Alaska electorates voted by significant margins to reverse pro-SSM judicial decisions was certainly a setback for the movement, as were the large number of antigay initiatives adopted at the municipal level during this period. Often overlooked are the electoral defeats of antigay initiatives in Idaho, Oregon, and Maine, but the balance is clearly negative 011 the whole, as indicated by the top row of Table 1.

In Vermont, the local legislative reaction to the high court ruling was positive, but backlash proponents have emphasized the subsequent electoral setbacks that occurred (Rosenberg 2008:344-7). On this account, the *Baker* decision (1999) forced Vermont's legislators to take a politically unacceptable position and those legislators paid for it at the polls. As

	Before HI Decision	Between HI and VT	Between VT and MA	Between NA and NJ	Between NJ and CA	After CA Decision
Support for rights of marriage without the name						
Gallup (same rights as ...)	23		40			
Gallup (GUs, some legal rights)			40–49	49–54–**56**		
PSRA (same job benefits)	39	**58–59**	**58**	**60**		
Newsweek (health insurance and other employee benefits)		37				
ABC/*Wash. Post* (same benefits. such as health benefits, etc.)						
ABC (CUs, legal rights in areas such as health insurance, etc.)			40	**45–51**	54	
Pew (legal agreements with many of the same rights)			45	**48**–53–54		51
Quinnipiac (CUs, many of the legal rights)				**40–45**	45	
CNN (CUs, some of the legal rights)			**40–49**	54		
Combined support for SSm and CUs						
Quinnipiac					68	**65**
FOX			**43**	**51–53**	60	
National Exit Poll				60		
LA *Times*				**61–64**	56	
CNN				**47–53**	51	
Newsweek				**47–51**	50	57
CBS/NYT				**53–59**	57	58

Table III Public Support for the Legal Rights of Marriage Without the Name

Eskridge has noted, the fall 2000 statewide elections were "conducted in significant part as a referendum on civil unions" (Eskridge 2002:81), and 16 incumbent legislators who supported the civil union bill were unseated (Eskridge 2002:80-2; Pinello 2006:33; Robinson 2001). This electoral backlash was real, but its severity should not be overstated. The state house switched hands from Democratic to Republican, and from pro-civil union to anti-, but the senate and governor's mansion remained in the hands of civil union supporters. The Democratic governor who signed the civil union bill was reelected handily, as was the

Democratic lieutenant governor, who supported full marriage equality. Democrats who supported the civil union bill were elected secretary of state and state auditor as well. The only statewide race won by the GOP was for the U.S. Senate, where incumbent Senator Jim Jeffords bucked his party to support the civil union bill, was reelected in a landslide, and then quit the Republican Party a few months later.

The local electoral reaction to the 2003 *Goodridge* decision was even more striking. As Massachusetts legislators considered their options, there was much discussion about the electoral costs that their colleagues had suffered in Vermont just three years earlier. But this time around, SSM advocates successfully fended off all seven primary challenges faced by their legislative supporters in 2004, while unseating two incumbents who opposed SSM and picking up three open seats as well. SSM supporters picked up three additional seats in special elections held in early 2005, and in 2006, they captured the governor's mansion as well, with SSM supporter Deval Patrick elected to succeed SSM opponent Governor Mitt Romney (Bonauto 2005; Pinello 2006:45-72). In sum, once *Goodridge*'s dust had settled, the state's elected institutions were significantly more supportive of SSM than they had been at the outset. These electoral gains enabled SSM advocates to defeat multiple constitutional amendments designed to reverse the *Goodridge* decision, culminating in a June 2007 vote in which SSM opponents were unable to persuade even one-quarter of the state legislators to keep their proposed amendment alive. Contemporaneous accounts attributed this final victory for *Goodridge* to heavy lobbying by the national gay rights groups and the state Democratic leadership, as well as influential pressure from the legislators' married gay constituents (Belluck 2007; Phillips & Estes 2007; Wangsness & Estes 2007).

The nationwide electoral impact of *Goodridge* was more complex, but it was far from uniformly negative. The most direct result was that voters in 16 states enacted anti-SSM constitutional amendments in 2004, 2005, and the first half of 2006. These amendments represented significant policy setbacks for SSM advocates, and they may have had broader electoral consequences as well, Klarman emphasizes that they were approved by such large margins—the median vote share for these 16 proposals was 73.9 percent—that they represented a stinging popular rebuke of the Massachusetts judges, and Klarman and Rosenberg each argue that the presence of these amendments on state ballots in November 2004 contributed to President Bush's reelection and the OOP's pickup of four additional seats in the U.S. Senate. Since President Bush and the Republican Senate subsequently named then-Judges John Roberts and Samuel Alito to the Supreme Court, Klarman suggests that SSM litigators may bear responsibility for entrenching a conservative judicial majority as well (2005:468).

In drawing out these electoral implications, Rosenberg and Klarman each rely more heavily on the post-election spin advanced by SSM opponents than on the leading accounts of the election by professional political scientists. They each note that Republican political adviser Karl Rove "appeared to stifle a grin" when asked whether he was "indebted" to the Massachusetts high court; they each quote Robert Knight's observation that "President Bush should send a bouquet of flowers" to Massachusetts Chief Justice Margaret Marshall;

	HI	CA	VT	MA	NJ	ME	CT	WA	Annual Total	Total to Date
1997	293								293	293
1998	148								148	441
1999	62								62	503
2000	46	4,894	1,709						6,649	7,152
2001	70	3,980	1,876						5,926	13,078
2002	117	8,187	1,707						10,011	23,089
2003	117	6,596	1,398						8,111	31,200
2004	136	5,615	712	6,121	2,832	373			15,789	46,989
2005	141	6,202	452	2,060	1,068	205	619		10,777	57,766
2006	158	6,038	429	1,442	943	163	681		9,854	67,620
2007	160	5,406	333	545	2,437	184	214	3,169	12,448	80,068
Total	1,448	46,918	8,616	10,168	7,280	925	1,544	3,169		80,068

Table IV Number of Same-Sex Marriages, Civil Unions, and Domestic Partnerships by State

and they each emphasize the widely noted exit poll in which 22 percent of voters indicated that "moral values" was the most important issue facing the nation (Klarman 2005:467, 482; Rosenberg 2008:370, 376). One of the leading scholars of American elections and public opinion has argued that the widespread attribution of President Bush's reelection to *Goodridge* is substantially misleading, but neither Rosenberg nor Klarman addresses his arguments (Fiorina et al. 2006:145-57; see also Hillygus & Shields 2005; Egan & Sheirill 2006). Nonetheless, the backlash proponents are certainly correct that the *Goodridge* decision was polarizing and unpopular and that the national Republican Party stoked this unpopularity with some success in November 2004. Rove and his fellow Republican operatives helped place anti-SSM amendments on the ballot in key swing states, and those initiatives may have aided Republican candidates up and down the ballot. Taken together, Rosenberg and Klarman make a strong case that the Massachusetts decision contributed to President Bush's victories in Ohio and Iowa and to GOP Senate victories in Kentucky, Oklahoma, and South Dakota (Klarman 2005:467-70; Rosenberg 2008:369-82).

But while the *Goodridge* decision clearly mobilized opponents of SSM, it seems to have mobilized supporters as well. In February 2004, San Francisco Mayor Gavin Newsom responded to President Bush's recent denunciation of the "activist judges" of the Massachusetts court by announcing that city officials would begin issuing marriage licenses to same-sex couples. Within weeks, 4,000 such couples had married in the streets of San Francisco, drawing nationwide front-page coverage and inspiring a variety of copycat efforts, with 3,000 marriages performed by public officials in Portland, Oregon, and similar but smaller actions in Asbury Park, New Jersey; Sandoval County, New Mexico; and New Paltz, New York (Andersen 2005:235-6; Mezey 2007:109-13). In short, the *Goodridge* decision sparked a wave of mass action to claim the rights that the Massachusetts court had promised. Rosenberg and Klarman emphasize that Mayor Newsom's actions provoked yet more backlash, but again,

Time Period	Legislative Setbacks	Legislative Victories
Between HI and VT Decisions	Constitutional ban on SSM in AK (1998) Constitutional aurhorization of legislative ban on SSm in HI (1998) Statutory restrictions on SSM in UT (1993); HI (1994); UT (1995); AK, AZ, DE, GA, ID, IL, KS, MI, MO, NC, OK, PA, SC, SD, TN (1996); AR, FL, IN, ME, MN, MS, MT, ND,TX, VA (1997); AL, IA, KY, WA (1998); La (1999)	Sodomy decriminalization in NV (1993); RI (1998) Hate crimes regulation in ME, NV (1995); MA (1996); AZ, DE, LA, NF, (1997); CA, KY, RI (1998); MO, VT (1999) Antidiscrimination laws in RI (1995); NH (1997); CA, NV (1999) Partnership rights in HI (1997); CA (1999)
Between VT and MA Decisions	Constitutional bans on SSM in NE (2000): NV (2002) Statutory restrictions on SSM in CA, CO, CT, SD, WV, TX (2000) MO (2001); TX (2003)	Sodomy decriminalization in NY (2000); AZ (2001) Hate crimes regulations in CT, KY, NY, TN (2000); HI, RI, TX, (2001); NJ, PA (2002); HI, NM (2003) Antidiscrimination laws in MD, RI (2001); NY (2002); CA, NM (2003) Partnership rights in VT (2000); CA (2001); CA, CT, DC, (2002); CA, DC, NV (2003)
Between MA and NJ Decisions	Constitutional bans on SSM in AR, GA, KY, LA, MI, MO, MS, MT, ND, OH, OK, OR, UT (2004); KN, TX (2005); AL (June 2006) Statutory restrictions on SSM in NH. OH (2004)	Hate crimes regulation in CT (2004); CO, MD (2005) Antidiscrimination laws in ME (2005); DC, IL, WA (2006) Partnership rights in ME, NJ, NY (2004); CT (2005); CA, NY, DC (2006)
Between NJ and CA Decisions	Constitutional bans on SSM in CO, ID, SC, SD, TN, VA,WI (Nov. 2006)	Hate crimes regulation in OR (2007); NJ (2008) Antidiscrimination laws in CO, IA, NJ,OR, VT (2007) Partnership rights in NH, NJ, OR, WA (2007)

Table V State-Level Legislative Change After Judicial Victories

those actions seem to have inspired supporters as well as opponents. In particular, they encouraged more same-sex couples to claim their rights and more public officials to support those claims. In addition to the copycat actions by local executive officials, the controversy led to a nationwide wave of new SSM lawsuits, with the leading national LGBT rights organizations filing state constitutional challenges in Connecticut. Florida, Maryland, New York,

Number of States ...	May 1993	November 2008
... with statutory prohibitions on SSM	3	45
... with constititional prohibitions on SSM	0	27
... with constititional prohibitions on SSM that do or may prohibit recognition of CUs, DPs, and the like	0	17
... with criminal prohibitions on consensual sodomy	23	0
... with hate crimes statutes that cover sexual orientation	11	32
... with hate crimes statutes that cover gender identity	1	12
... with antidiscrimation statutes that cover sexual orientation	8	20
... with antidiscrimation statutes that cover gender identity	1	12
... that offer domestic partership benefits to public employees	0	15
... that grant some legal right to non-employee same-sex couples	0	11
... that grant substantial legal equality to same-sex couples	0	7
... that issue marriage licenses to same-sex couples	0	2

Table VI State-Level LGBT Rights Policies, 1993-2008

Oregon, and Washington during the spring and summer of 2004. Mayor Newsom's actions also drew the litigators into such a challenge in California, and Lambda Legal continued to pursue the state constitutional challenge it had hied in New Jersey in 2002. Most of these lawsuits eventually ended in defeat—although even these, as I note below, often sparked legislative progress—but three of them resulted in landmark victories. In New Jersey, California, and Connecticut, the state legislature voluntarily expanded partnership rights while the legal challenges were pending, but in each case, the state high court held that the existing policies did not go far enough. In October 2006, the New Jersey Supreme Court ordered the state to provide same-sex couples with all the legal rights and benefits of marriage: a year and a half later, the California Supreme Court ordered the state to provide same-sex couples with access to marriage itself; and five months after that, the Connecticut Supreme Court followed California's lead (*Lewis v. Harris 2006; In re Marriage Cases 2008; Kerrigan v. Commissioner of Public Health 2008*).

The New Jersey and Connecticut victories are particularly notable for causing no discernible electoral backlash. *Lewis v. Harris (2006)* came down two weeks before the nation's congressional elections, including a close Senate race in New Jersey, but it had no apparent electoral spillover, either locally or nationally. Civil union supporter Robert Menendez won the Senate race, helping the Democratic Party to capture both houses of Congress for the first time in 12 years, and unlike 2004, the national exit polls revealed little evidence that SSM was a key issue, despite the presence of anti-SSM initiatives on the ballot in eight states (Egan & Sherrill 2006). In a landmark development, one of these initiatives was defeated, receiving support from just 48.2 percent of Arizona voters, and in contrast to 2004, only two of the eight received more than 70 percent support. The Connecticut decision likewise came down shortly before a national election, and likewise seemed to have little effect. Some SSM opponents in the state urged the public to support an already-existing ballot measure calling for a convention to propose amendments to the state constitution, but 59 percent of the state's voters rejected the proposal, and the high court's decision took effect shortly after the election.

In contrast, the California Supreme Court's May 2008 marriage decision was reversed at the polls, with 52 percent of the state's voters supporting an anti-SSM constitutional amendment on November 4, 2008. This vote represented a major setback for the LGBT rights movement, a setback compounded by the voters' enactment of anti-SSM amendments in Arizona and Florida on the same day, as well as a ballot measure banning unmarried couples from fostering or adopting children in Arkansas. Notably, however, the California vote does not appear to have ended the long-running campaign lor SSM in the state. To the contrary, SSM supporters have responded with dozens of protests throughout the state, a novel and probably long-shot legal challenge to the amendment, and plans for an initiative campaign to re-amend the state constitution, perhaps as early as 2010 (Garrison 2008). Given the increasing public support for SSM in the state—voter opposition to the state's two anti-SSM initiatives increased from 38.6 percent in 2000 to 47.8 percent in 2008, and according to the 2008 exit polls, it reached as high as 61 percent among 18- to 29-year-old voters—it seems likely that the final word has not yet been heard.

The available polling data indicate a similar pattern of increasing public support for SSM nationwide. As indicated in Table 2, national polls conducted since *Goodridge* almost always find at least 30 percent support for SSM and on several occasions have found support exceeding 40 percent, marking an unambiguous increase over pre-*Baehr* levels. Public support for extending the legal rights of marriage without the name has increased even more dramatically. Finding a pre-*Baehr* baseline for comparison on this point is difficult—polling on "civil unions'* did not occur until the concept was invented in Vermont in 2000—but Rosenberg has identified some early polls that provide close approximations. As indicated in Table 3, when a 1989 Gallup poll asked whether "homosexual couples [should] have the same legal rights as married couples" only 23 percent of respondents said yes. In the wake of the Vermont decision, Gallup found 40 percent support for the proposition that "gay partners who make a legal commitment to each other should ... be entitled to the same rights and benefits as couples in traditional marriages," and after *Goodridge*, Gallup found support as high as 56 percent for "allowing] homosexual couples to legally form civil unions, giving them some of the legal rights of married couples." Rosenberg also cites a 1991 poll conducted by Princeton Survey Research Associates (PSRA) in which 39 percent of respondents indicated that homosexual couples should "be able to get the same job benefits as a married couple" (Rosenberg 2008:405). After *Goodridge, Newsweek* found 60 percent support for "health insurance and other employee benefits for gay spouses," and other polls with different question wording have found support ranging from 40 to 54 percent.

The breadth of public support for granting same-sex couples the legal rights of marriage is most clearly indicated by polls providing respondents with the full range of policy options: that is, asking whether they support SSM, civil unions, or no legal recognition for same-sex couples. As indicated in the bottom half of Table 3, aggregating the public support for SSM and civil unions in these polls makes clear that a position that "would have been considered a Utopian gay fantasy" at the outset of the litigation campaign—that same-sex couples should have access to all the legal rights and benefits of marriage—now receives consistent support from popular majorities (Hirsch 2005: ix; see also Egan & Sherrill 2005b; Persily et al. 2006:43-4). Evan Wolfson, Mary Bonauto, and their fellow LGBT rights litigators probably deserve some credit for this increased support. At the very least, they should not be blamed for increasing public opposition to gay rights, because no such increase has occurred.

THE POLICY IMPACT

Even if the general public has not turned against gay rights, the courtroom victories may have provoked regressive policy change—that is, legislative actions that left LGBT rights advocates worse off than they were at the beginning. In support of this claim, backlash proponents repeatedly emphasize that 45 states have banned the recognition of SSM, with 27 of those states enshrining the ban in their state constitutions.[2] The Utah legislature was the first to act, clarifying its own rules for marriage eligibility just months after the *Baehr* decision in 1993 and prohibiting the recognition of out-of-state SSMs two years later. As a number of states considered similar measures. Congress declared in the 1996 Defense of Marriage Act (DOMA) that the federal government would not recognize SSMs and that each state was free to refuse recognition as well. "Long after the current homophobic panic is over," D'Emilio notes, "these DOMA statutes and state constitutional amendments will survive as a residue that slows the forward movement of the gay community toward equality" (2007:61; see also Klarman 2005:466; Rosenberg 2008:416).

This claim implies a greater degree of policy retrogression than has actually occurred. No state recognized SSM prior to the onset of litigation, so the statutory bans effected no actual change of policy. The constitutional bans have made it more difficult for SSM advocates to achieve their desired policy change, but in the vast majority of these 27 states, the odds that either the legislature or the courts would have legalized SSM were pretty low from the beginning. If and when SSM comes to states such as Alabama, Mississippi, Oklahoma, and Texas, it is likely to be the result of a federal judicial order, and state constitutional prohibitions will not stand as a bar to such federal legal action.[3]

---

2   Note that the latter number does not include Hawaii. Hawaii's voters adopted an anti-SSM amendment in 1998, but unlike the other 27 state constitutional amendments on the topic, this one merely authorized the legislature to limit marriage to opposite-sex couples As such, Hawaii remains free to legalize SSM by simple legislative action.

3   Judging by their legal treatment of LGBT persons more generally, California and Wisconsin are the only states in which an anti-SSM constitutional amendment foreclosed an effort to achieve legal recognition tor same-sex couples that had any reasonable chance of success in the near term (Pinello 2006:176).

In 17 of these 27 states, the policy setback was somewhat worse, as the language of the constitutional ban either clearly or potentially prohibits state recognition of civil unions and domestic partnerships as well as SSM. Many of these 17 states were unlikely to recognize such statuses anyway, but in at least eight of them, the constitutional ban has rendered some existing policies legally vulnerable. Prior to the recent amendments, at least one local jurisdiction or state agency (such as a public college) in Georgia, Kentucky, Louisiana, Michigan, Ohio, Texas, Utah, and Wisconsin provided domestic partnership benefits to its employees, in tour of these states, at least one local jurisdiction maintained a domestic partnership registry for local residents as well.[4] The full legal effect of the anti-SSM amendments on these policies is not yet clear, but the Michigan Supreme Court has already held that public employers in the state can no longer offer domestic partnership benefits, and it is likely that LGBT residents of the other seven states will face similar threats to their existing rights and benefits.[5] The scope of these existing rights is quite narrow—none of these states had anything approaching a statewide marriage law but for the affected couples, the deprivation (or potential deprivation) may well have significant adverse consequences.

These concrete policy setbacks, however, should be weighed against the concrete policy advances that have occurred during the same period. Most directly, tens of thousands of same-sex couples have won access to legal rights and economic benefits that they did not have before. Beginning with Hawaii, every state in which a court has ruled in favor of expanded partnership rights for same-sex couples has indeed subsequently seen an expansion of such rights. None of these expansions represent full victories for SSM advocates, but in every state, there has been progress rather than retrogression. Several additional states have expanded partnership rights in the absence of a court order, and most if not all of these policy changes are at least partly attributable to the ongoing litigation campaign.

All told, since the Hawaii suit was filed, 10 states and the District of Columbia have created a legal status, similar to marriage, which same-sex couples may choose to enter.[6] The specific rights and benefits attached to these alternative legal statuses vary from state to state, but even the narrowest policies provide certain crucially important rights that legal spouses take for granted, such as the right to own property jointly, to make medical decisions

---

4   In the other nine states that adopted constitutional bans that may apply to civil unions and domestic partnerships: Alabama. Arkansas. Idaho, Nebraska, North Dakota, Oklahoma, South Carolina, South Dakota, and Virginia. I have been unable to find any record of such policies on the books prior to the enactment of the constitutional amendment, though some isolated policies may have escaped notice.

5   *National Pride at Work v. Governor of Michigan 748 N W. 2d 524 (Mich. 2008). See also Brinkman v. Miami University 2007 Ohio 4372 (Ohio Ct. of App.. 2007).*

6   In addition. New York has extended a narrow set of rights to unmarried couples, regardless of gender, who meet a statutorily defined set of criteria (as opposed to affirmatively registering with the state), and Nevada has authorized adults to make written designations of other, unrelated adults for purposes of hospital visitation and funeral arrangements.

for one another, and to inherit property and receive life insurance benefits in the event of a partner's death. Seven states provide same-sex couples with all or virtually all of the state law rights and benefits of marriage, including parental rights. Given the importance of such rights and benefits, it is no surprise that more than 80,000 couples have chosen to take advantage of them, as indicated in Table 4. An even greater number of same-sex couples have benefited from the rapid proliferation of employer-provided domestic partnership policies that has coincided with the SSM litigation campaign. When the *Baehr* decision came down in 1993, only a handful of private employers offered such policies; by 2008, more than 8,000 did so. Among Fortune 500 corporations, the number providing such benefits rose from 10 in 1993 to 270 in 2008.[7] In the public sector, no states provided domestic partnership benefits to their own employees until 1994; by 2008, 15 states (and the Distric t of Columbia) did so (ibid.).

Many of these policy changes resulted directly or indirectly from litigation. In California, Massachusetts, New Jersey, and Vermont, state lawmaking institutions complied with judicial decisions ordering expanded partnership rights. In Hawaii, the legislature helped reverse such a decision, but simultaneously granted some of the rights that the litigants had sought. In California, Connecticut, New Jersey, and New York, lawmakers expanded partnership rights while an SSM lawsuit was pending in the state's courts. In each of these states, elected legislators were relatively supportive of LGBT rights before the SSM suit was filed, but they were unwilling to expand partnership rights until they had the political cover provided by the legal challenge. In Oregon and Washington, legislators ducked the issue while litigation was pending—perhaps hoping the courts would take the hot potato off their hands but stepped in once the judges refused to do it for them. In other words, they responded to recently concluded lawsuits by voluntarily extending some of the legal rights that same-sex partners had unsuccessfully sought in court. Only in Maine and New Hampshire have legislators significantly expanded partnership rights in the absence of local litigation, and even there, they surely did so at least in part because the prior, litigation-prompted policy changes in neighboring states had raised the expectations of local gays and lesbians.

The expansion of workplace domestic partnership benefits has generally been less directly tied to litigation, but here too, legal mobilization has played a role. Alaska, Montana, and Oregon have each extended domestic partnership benefits to public employees as a result of court orders, and even those employers who have adopted such policies in response to other forms of pressure have surely been influenced by the pervasive litigation on this issue since *Baehr*. After all, it was the SSM lawsuits that first drew public attention to the difficulties faced by gay and lesbian couples in accessing health insurance and other spousal benefits,

---

7   These numbers are drawn from the Human Rights Campaign›s database of employee benefit policies, available at http://www.hrc.org/issues/workplace/search_employers.htm. See also the Human Rights Campaign Foundation Report, "The State of the Workplace tor Gay, Lesbian. Bisexual, and Transgender Americans. 2006-2007,' available at http://www.hrc.org/documentsState_of_the_Workplace.pdf.

and it was the lawsuits that transformed workplace domestic partnership policies from a cutting-edge proposal in the early 1990s to the moderate compromise they represent today.

SSM advocates have repeatedly supported such compromise policies as important steps toward their goal of full marriage equality. Most SSM advocates endorsed the civil union proposal during the pivotal Vermont legislative debates of 2000, and as Eskridge has argued at some length, this sort of incremental policy change has often been followed by subsequent expansion (Eskridge 2002; see also Andersen 2005:184-8; Robinson 2001). In California, Massachusetts, New Jersey, New York, Vermont, Washington, and the District of Columbia, SSM advocates succeeded in enacting some limited statewide recognition of same-sex relationships and subsequently expanding the range of legal rights and benefits offered to such couples. As I have noted, moreover, all this legislative progress has occurred in the shadow of the ongoing litigation campaign.

Examining partnership rights as part of a broader continuum of LGBT rights issues, Eskridge (2000) paints an even clearer picture of incremental policy change over time. Beginning in the 1970s, states have tended to reform their regulations of gays and lesbians in the following sequence: decriminalizing consensual sodomy, establishing protections against hate crimes, prohibiting discrimination in the workplace (and sometimes in public accommodations), establishing some minimal legal recognition for same-sex partnerships (particularly at the municipal level), and then expanding the scope of that recognition in a series of steps toward full marriage equality. Backlash proponents often claim that premature litigation efforts have the effect of derailing a movement's more cautious campaigns through democratic institutions, but this incremental pattern of state-level policy change has continued without significant interruption—and may even have accelerated—during the period of active SSM litigation.

Consider the state-level policy changes on four leading LGBT rights issues in the wake of the courtroom victories in Hawaii, Vermont, Massachusetts, and New Jersey, as summarized in Table 5. In the six years following the *Baehr* decision, only two state legislatures repealed their criminal sodomy laws, but this progress was no slower than it had been in the years leading up to *Baehr*. Twenty state legislatures had repealed their sodomy laws in the 1970s and early 1980s—generally as part of a wholesale adoption of the Model Penal Code—but this wave of legislative reform had run its course by 1983 (Andersen 2005:60-72). Likewise, the willingness of state courts to invalidate criminal sodomy laws appears to have been unaffected by the Hawaii decision. If anything, they became more willing after the decision than before, with courts in Michigan and Kentucky doing so in the early 1990s and courts in Tennessee, Montana, Georgia, and Maryland doing so in the late 1990s. On the issue of hate crimes regulation, there had been somewhat more legislative progress prior to *Baehr*, but this progress continued after the decision. From May 1993 through the end of 1999, 12 states expanded their hate crimes protections for LGBT persons. Only Hawaii and California extended formal legal recognition to same-sex partnerships during this period, but since no states had done so prior to *Baehr,* this level of activity represented a positive change. On only one key legislative priority of LGBT rights advocates did the Hawaii decision appear to stall forward progress. In the two years preceding *Baehr*, six states had amended their antidiscrimination laws to expand protections for LGBT persons; in the six years following it, only Rhode Island, New Hampshire, California, and Nevada did so.

The pattern of legislative change in the wake of *Baker v. State of Vermont* (1999) was similar. The legislatures of Arizona and New York repealed their states' criminal sodomy statutes (as did courts in Arkansas, Massachusetts, and Minnesota), and 10 states enacted or expanded laws covering hate crimes against LGBT persons. The hate crimes laws represented a nationwide legislative response to the October 1998 murder of Matthew Sheppard in Wyoming, but the December 1999 marriage decision from the Vermont Supreme Court does not appear to have slowed this response. In addition, California, Maryland, New Mexico, New York, and Rhode Island extended their antidiscrimination laws to cover sexual orientation and/or gender identity; the District of Columbia joined Vermont in extending formal legal recognition to same-sex couples; Connecticut extended some minimal legal rights to unmarried couples and commissioned a study to assess options for providing further such rights; and California repeatedly expanded the range of legal rights provided to domestic partners, culminating with a 2003 statute extending all state law rights and responsibilities of marriage. Again, none of this progress came quickly, but it was no slower than it had been prior to the onset of SSM litigation.

In the wake of *Goodridge* (2003), the pace of antigay legislation picked up considerably, but the pace of pro-gay policy change picked up as well. Just prior to *Goodridge*, the *Lawrence* decision (2003) had decriminalized sodomy in the 13 states that had not yet done so, thus removing this issue from the LGBT legislative agenda. Most states had already made at least some legislative response to antigay violence by this point as well, but three states extended their hate crimes laws during this period, and three states and the District of Columbia extended their antidiscrimination laws. Anecdotal evidence indicates that the post-*Goodridge* backlash made some state legislators more reluctant to enact gay rights policies, but these barriers have not proven insuperable. In Illinois, for example, early reports blamed the Massachusetts decision for sinking a then-pending antidiscrimination bill, but the legislature enacted an even stronger bill three years later (Brown 2003). During this same period, the elected institutions in five states and the District of Columbia expanded the range of partnership rights provided to same-sex couples.

Following the 2006 decision in *Lewis v. Harris*, LGBT rights advocates witnessed the most remarkable year of legislative success in the entire history of the movement. In 2007 alone, Oregon extended its existing hate crimes law to cover gender identity, and Colorado, Iowa, New Jersey, Oregon, and Vermont extended their antidiscrimination laws, marking a significant acceleration of legislative progress on this issue. In addition. New Hampshire. New jersey, and Oregon extended the full range of spousal rights and benefits to same-sex couples, and Washington extended a substantial list of such rights as well. It is too soon to assess the full policy impact of the California marriage decision. The state's voters reversed the decision in November 2008, but the legal status of the approximately 18,000 SSMs that were performed prior to Election Day remains unclear. Elsewhere, SSM advocates continued their legislative progress from the year before. Washington expanded the list of legal rights extended to domestic partners, as did the District of Columbia. New York Governor David Paterson directed all state agencies to recognize lawful SSMs from other jurisdictions, and Massachusetts repealed the residency requirement that had prevented most out-of-state same-sex couples from marrying there. Massachusetts also extended Medicaid benefits, at state expense, to same-sex spouses who were ineligible for federally funded benefits, and Missouri authorized same-sex partners to designate one another to make decisions regarding the disposition of remains in the event of one of their deaths. None of these policy changes received as much national media attention as the anti-SSM initiatives enacted in November, but they are not insignificant.

Table 6 summarizes the overall pattern of state-level policy change from May 1993, when the *Baehr* decision came down, November 2008. At the outset. 23 states still criminalized consensual sodomy, as did the District of Columbia and Puerto Rico; no state does so today. Only 11 states had laws addressing hate crimes on the basis of sexual orientation or gender identity; 32 states have such laws today. Only eight states prohibited private employers from firing a worker on the basis of his or her sexual orientation, and only one did so on the basis of gender identity; today, those numbers are 20 and 12, respectively. No state provided any legal recognition or economic benefits to same-sex partnerships, and only a small number of local jurisdictions did so. Today, 15 states provide health care benefits to the same-sex partners of their own employees, with 11 of them extending some broader set of legal rights to same-sex couples as well.

COMPARED TO WHAT?

Despite these policy victories, backlash proponents repeatedly charge that SSM advocates have been lured by the "myth of rights" to adopt a suboptimal strategy. In a concluding section of his 2008 chapters on SSM, titled "When Will They Ever Learn?" Rosenberg complains that if SSM advocates had read his book, they "could have foreseen the negative reaction to the Hawaii litigation" and they would have avoided "succumbing to the 'lure of litigation'" (Rosenberg 2008:419). Instead, as with so many other left-liberal movements since the mid-twentieth century,

> the liberal agenda was hijacked by a group of elite, well-educated and comparatively wealthy lawyers who uncritically believed that rights trump politics and that successfully arguing before judges is equivalent to building and sustaining political movements. ... Political organizing, political mobilization and voter registration may not be glamorous, or pay six-figure salaries, but they are the best if not the only hope to produce change. (2008:430-1)

Rosenberg provides no direct evidence that LGBT rights litigators have been so taken in by a civics-book understanding of American courts as to repeatedly ignore what would have been preferable strategies. (Even less does he provide any evidence that the movement litigators are blinded by their own desires for wealth and glamour.) Legal mobilization scholars have long observed that it is difficult to find any actual litigators who have succumbed to the myth that legal rights are magic recipes for instant change, and as Andersen makes clear, the observation holds for LGBT rights advocates. She concludes her study of Lambda Legal by noting that "every litigator" she interviewed was "well aware that the struggle lor legal reform does not begin and end in the courtroom" (2005:214-15; see also McCann 1992:728-9, 1994).

Leaving aside the question of the advocates' motivations, the backlash argument amounts to a series of post hoc judgments that particular instances of litigation were strategically unwise because they provoked more political opposition than some other available strategy would have provoked. In Rosenberg's judgment, strategies that emphasized legislation rather than litigation and incremental rather than radical change would have provoked less opposition and hence been more successful (2008:383, 417). Klarman has likewise emphasized that when gay rights litigators began pushing for SSM in the early 1990s, there was strong public support for the decriminalization of sodomy, the prohibition of employment discrimination, and the extension of limited domestic partnership benefits, but not for SSM. By forcing SSM to the fore, courts (and litigators) undermined the cause (2005:475-7).

In claiming that SSM advocates in the early 1990s should have pursued their goals both more cautiously and more democratically, backlash proponents tend to mis-specify the actual strategic dilemma that these advocates faced. The modern wave of SSM lawsuits was not initiated by the national LGBT rights organizations and could not have been stopped by them. It was initiated by gay and lesbian couples in Hawaii (and elsewhere) seeking health insurance, parental rights, and other legal and financial protections for their families (Andersen 2005:239; Chauncey 2004:87-136; Egan & Sherrill 2005a; Gar row 2004). The actual choice faced by movement leaders was whether to join and help shape these efforts or to watch them continue as uncoordinated actions of individual plaintiffs and their private counsel. Since the latter choice would have left the advocacy organizations with no influence over important tactical decisions regarding when and where to file, what to argue, and whether to appeal -and since it might also appear as a significant rebuke of their own members and supporters—all the national LGBT rights organizations eventually signed on. But they did so only when it became clear that the Hawaii case was headed to the state high court with or without them, at which point they concluded that it was unwise to let the courts rule on the issue without having heard from the nation's most knowledgeable and experienced LGBT rights advocates (Andersen 2005:1 78; Eskridge 2002:16-8; Garrow 2004; Pinello 2006:23-30). From this angle, in a world of constant litigation by friend and foe, the choice faced by movement leaders is not whether the courts should be involved but whether they should hear your claims before deciding your fate.

Once having joined the fray, moreover, the LGBT rights advocates did not decide to litigate and do nothing else. Like their opponents, these advocates have relied on both judicial politics and nolitics, making a series of tactical decisions in individual circumstances. Drawing on their earlier experience litigating against criminal sodomy laws and the military ban on service by gays and lesbians, they were well aware of the cautious, incremental, and deferential tendencies of judicial institutions, and they knew full well that their efforts had to proceed on multiple, simultaneous fronts. As such, when the leaders of the LGBT public interest bar signed onto the SSM campaign, they collectively agreed to litigate only where the odds seemed most in their favor and, in the meantime, to devote significant resources to a broader campaign of public education, media relations, and legislative lobbying (Andersen 2005:178-83). These advocates selected Vermont as the site of their first test case, but they held off on launching the suit until four years after the initial Hawaii decision; only then did they conclude that their political organizing had progressed far enough to make a judicial victory sustainable (Johnson 2000; Eskridge 2002:45-8).

Their landmark victory in *Baker* (1999) seemed to confirm the viability of the test-case strategy, and they moved quickly to identify their next targets. As with Vermont, they sought out states whose courts had been relatively supportive of gay rights (indicating that their legal arguments would get a fair hearing) and whose political cultures were relatively supportive as well (indicating that the strength of any backlash would be relatively contained) (Anderson 2005:219-20; (arrow 2004). These factors led them to file suit in Massachusetts in 2001 and New Jersey in 2002, with the litigators in each case building on years of local political organizing on behalf of increased partnership rights (Bonauto 2005; Pinello 2006:34-41). Unlike the Hawaii suit, then, the legal battles in Vermont, Massachusetts, and New Jersey were intentionally chosen by the LGBT rights organizations. Each of these lawsuits led to a landmark legal victory, and each of these victories survived the resulting political backlash.

SSM advocates filed a number of other suits that turned out less well, but even there, it is not clear that the strategic decision to file them was wrong. After *Baehr* (1993), SSM was on the nation's legal and political agendas whether LGBT rights advocates liked it or not. Thus, they no longer had the option of taking the status quo for granted and focusing on something else. The SSM campaign had been launched by same-sex couples acting independently; once launched, the issue was kept on the table by conservative opponents. In Massachusetts, for example, SSM opponents were pursuing a state constitutional amendment well before *Goodridge* was filed. In this context, LGBT rights advocates could either play defense or open some new fronts of their own. Their opponents were pursuing every available avenue—attacking SSM at the polls, in state and federal legislatures, and in state and federal courts—and it is not clear how a unilateral decision to steer clear of one of these avenues would have helped their cause.

That said, SSM advocates often decided to discourage litigation when the time was not right. Prior to the Hawaii case, movement litigators repeatedly rejected requests to bring SSM lawsuits, and while that litigation was pending, the leading advocates discouraged gay and lesbian couples from filing or continuing SSM lawsuits in Alaska, Arizona, Florida, and New

York. After the *Baker* decision in Vermont, the leading national LGBT rights organizations jointly issued a pamphlet that discouraged precipitous litigation by same-sex couples, and after *Lawrence* and *Goodridge*, they discouraged further unplanned litigation in Arizona and Florida. In 2006, the national LGBT rights groups urged the Ninth Circuit to dismiss a constitutional challenge to DOMA and in 2008, they issued yet another pamphlet discouraging litigation.[8]

The fact that LGBT rights advocates have often decided not to litigate a particular claim at a particular time and place suggests that when they have decided to litigate, it is because they have concluded that such a tactic is more promising than (or complementary to) the available alternatives. As Zackin (2008) has noted in another context, social movements often turn to judicial politics only after democratic politics proves unavailing. In this light, it is noteworthy that prior to the litigation campaign, SSM advocates had made very little progress in state or federal legislative institutions. Several local gay rights organizations were lobbying for statewide domestic partnership policies in the 1990s, but these policies were quite limited in scope, and their advocates were having very little success. The D.C. City Council voted to create a domestic partnership registry in 1992, but Congress blocked the bill from taking effect for another 10 years. The California legislature voted to do so in 1994, but Governor Pete Wilson vetoed the bill. The first such policy to become law was Hawaii's Reciprocal Beneficiaries Act, but that act was the direct result of litigation. Prior to the onset of that litigation, no state legislature was willing to extend even limited partnership rights to same-sex couples.

This legislative unresponsiveness has extended even to issues where the public is broadly supportive of LGBT rights. For at least 30 years—since the Gallup Poll began asking the question in 1977 a majority of the public has agreed that "homosexuals should ... have equal rights in terms of job opportunities." For the past 15 years, the level of support has exceeded 80 percent (see http:www.gallup.com/poll/1651/Homosexual-Relations.aspx). Despite repeated efforts, however, Congress has failed to enact the Employment Non-Discrimination Act. More than 80 percent of the public now thinks that gays and lesbians should be allowed to serve in the military as well, but again, Congress has failed to respond (Egan & Sherrill 2005b; Mezey 2007:179-80, 221-2). As noted above, LGBT rights advocates have had more success in banning employment discrimination at the state level, but most of this progress has come in the midst of the SSM litigation campaign. Likewise with sodomy decriminalization, at the time *Baehr* was filed, the substantial public support for reform was not producing legislative change (Andersen 2005:60-72).

In addition to overstating the degree of legislative progress that had occurred prior to the litigation campaign, backlash proponents generally fail to acknowledge that when LGBT rights advocates did win legislative victories, these victories frequently provoked political

---

8 Most of the events referenced in this paragraph are documented in the monthly publication *Lesbian Gay Love Notes,* available at http:www.qrd.org. See also Andersen (2005:187). (Dupuis 2002:62-3). Garrow (2004). The 2008 pamphlet is entitled "Make Change, Not Lawsuits."

backlash. As Lemieux has argued, the backlash thesis rests on a (sometimes implicit) claim that controversial judicial decisions tend to provoke a more severe negative reaction than otherwise similar legislative decisions. Lemieux finds little evidence to support this claim in the abortion context, noting that *Roe v. Wade* sparked substantial opposition but that the pro-choice movement's earlier attempts at abortion reform via state legislative action had provoked a similar reaction (2004:218-9). The story of conservative countermobilization in response to legislative protections of gay rights is similar, with citizen lawmaking procedures repeatedly used to repeal gay rights policies that have been enacted by elected officials (Andersen 2005:149; Mezey 2007:31-2).

Some episodes of this story are so well-known that it is hard to justify the lack of attention given to them by backlash proponents. As early as 1977, Anita Bryant made national head-lines with her campaign to repeal the antidiscrimination ordinance that had been enacted by the Dade County Metropolitan Commission in Florida. The popular singer and advertising icon spearheaded a populist backlash that produced not only a local referendum repealing the ordinance but also a state statute imposing a blanket prohibition on adoptions by "homo-sexuals." Signed by the governor just one day after the Dade County referendum, this statute represented a significant retrogression in parental rights for gays and lesbians in Florida (Riminerman 2002:127-9). The Bryant campaign sparked several similar efforts in the late 1970s, and once gay rights advocates started winning legislative victories more often, their conservative opponents repeatedly responded with this sort of electoral countermobilization.

The most well-known story took place in Colorado, where a series of state and local lawmakers either enacted or considered proposals to ban discrimination against gays and lesbians in the late 1980s and early 1990s, prompting local leaders of the religious right to launch a campaign to amend the state constitution to prohibit any governmental unit in the state from adopting or enforcing such policies. The state's voters enacted this proposal in November 1992, a result that immediately prompted copycat efforts around the country. Over the next three years, similar bans on antidiscrimination protections reached statewide ballots in Idaho, Maine, and Oregon, and local ballots in more than 30 jurisdictions in Florida, Ohio, and Oregon. Each of the statewide initiatives was narrowly defeated at the polls, but most of the local measures were successful. The LGBT rights movement responded with multiple state and federal legal challenges, raising both procedural and substantive objections to these antigay initiatives. After several preliminary victories in state courts, this litigation campaign culminated in *Romer v. Evans*, the 1996 Supreme Court decision invalidating Colorado's Amendment 2 (Andersen 2005:151-2, 253-4, note 13). *Romer v. Evans* was a landmark legal victory lor the LGBT rights movement, but its precise scope remained some-what unclear. Opponents exploited this ambiguity by continuing to advance antigay initiatives that were distinguishable from Amendment 2, either because they merely repealed existing antidiscrimination protections (rather than banning their future enactment) or because they applied to a single local jurisdiction (rather than statewide). In a series of initiatives and referenda in Maine, for example, the voters repealed the state's antidiscrimination protec-tions for gays and lesbians in 1998, blocked the reenactment of those protections in 2000, and nearly repealed them again after their legislative reenactment in 2005. At the local level, the frequency of antigay initiatives slowed somewhat alter *Romer,* but opponents of gay rights continued to respond to the legislative enactment (or consideration) of antidiscrimination protections with ballot campaigns designed to repeal (or forestall) those protections. Such measures have reached the ballot in at least eight local jurisdictions since 1996, including Miami-Dade County, in an unsuccessful 2002 rerun of the Anita Bryant campaign.[9]

In similar fashion, the legislative expansion of partnership rights for same-sex couples has repeatedly sparked countermobilization. In at least 28 local jurisdictions since 1993, the actual or prospective expansion of partnership rights by elected officials has provoked either a ballot campaign seeking to repeal the policy or a lawsuit seeking to invalidate it. In nine of these jurisdictions, this countermobilization has been successful.[10] When local elected officials around the country began issuing marriage licenses to same-sex couples in spring 2004, SSM opponents responded with lawsuits in San Francisco and in New Paltz, New York, each of which was successful in halting the local efforts.[11] State lawmakers that have expanded partnership rights have often sparked similar reactions. Hawaii's Reciprocal Beneficiaries Act, Vermont's Civil Unions Act, and California's series of domestic partnership laws have each provoked legal challenges as well as electoral backlashes, and when the Oregon legislature enacted both domestic partner-ship and antidiscrimination statutes in 2007, opponents responded with petition drives against both statutes and, once the state ruled they had collected insufficient signatures, a federal constitutional challenge to the state's signature verification process.[12]

In short, all victories by LGBT rights advocates have sparked legal and political coun-termobilization, regardless of whether the victories occurred through legislative, executive, or judicial channels. Each such victory has been a defeat for opponents of LGBT rights,

---

9   The jurisdictions include Fort Collins, CO (1998); Ypsilanti, MI (1998, and again in 2002); Traverse City, MI (2001); Kalamazoo. MI (2001); Huntington Woods. MI (2001); Miami-Dade County, FL (2002); Westbrook, MF (2002); and Tacoma. VVA (2002).

10   From 1994 to 2001, initiative or referendum campaigns led to the repeal of existing domestic partnership policies in Austin, Texas; Columbus. Ohio; Northampton, Massachusetts: and Santa Clara County, California; a ballot initiative banned the enactment of such a policy then under consideration in Houston; and state high courts invalidated such policies in Atlanta, Boston, Minneapolis, and Arlington County, Virginia. In addition, the cities of San Francisco and Santa Barbara, California; Denver, Colorado; Chicago, Illinois; New Orleans, Louisiana; Portland, Maine; Cambridge, Massachusetts; Albany and New York. New York; Chapel Hill, North Carolina; Philadelphia, Pennsylvania; and Vancouver, Washington have all faced legal challenges to one or more of their domestic partnership policies, as have public school districts in Illinois and Wisconsin and counties in Arizona, Florida, and Maryland.

11   *Lockyer v. San Francisco*, 95 P.3d 459 (2004); *Hebel v. West*, 25 A.D.3d 172 (Sup. Ct. NY. App. l)Div., 3rd Dept. 2005).

12   *Lemons v. Bradbury*, No. 08-35209 (9th Cir., August 14, 2008).

and here, as in the abortion context, "defeats in the legislature, just as surely as defeats in the courts, are likely to generate opposition when issues remain contested" (Lemieux 2004:244). In this light, the strategy of avoiding political backlash by steering clear of the courts seems unlikely to work.

HOW WEAK IS THE WEAKEST BRANCH?

Given the complex pattern of decentralized policymaking on LGBT rights issues, it is difficult to reach a definitive evaluation of the movement's overall success. But whether or not the policy victories summarized in Tables 5 and 6 outweigh the defeats, it does not seem reasonable to treat this record as evidence supporting a sweeping indictment of the movement's leaders. LGBT rights advocates have surely made some strategic errors along the way, but since their efforts have produced widespread legal and policy gains, the sharply negative conclusions (and the hectoring tone) of the backlash accounts seem unwarranted. Put another way, the backlash narrative captures several important features of the recent history of LGBT rights litigation, but it does not support the sweeping and one-sided conclusions that have often been drawn from it. Rosenberg and Klarman are right that courts usually will not act until some progress has been made in the culture at large, but as Frymer (2003) has recently emphasized, they may still act before any other lawmaking institution is willing to do so. Likewise, Rosenberg and Klarman are right that "litigation on behalf of the relatively disadvantaged, if successful, is likely to be met with powerful political resistance," and that "[lrrigation is unlikely to help those most desperately in need" (Rosenberg 2008:417; Klarman 2004:463). But all political strategies employed by or on behalf of the relatively disadvantaged are likely to be met with powerful political resistance, and all such strategies are unlikely to help those most desperately in need. The fact in need of explanation is why some such strategies overcome these odds in a particular context. What was it about the combination of litigation, lobbying, direct action, and all the rest that produced dramatic progress on civil rights in the 1950s and 1960s and dramatic progress on gay rights 40 years later?

I lie lesson of these historical episodes is that the effectiveness of legal mobilization is quite variable, depending on a variety of contextual factors, including political and legal opportunity structures and the political and legal resources available to advocates. As McCann has argued at some length, "[c]ourt decisions and legal norms are not self-generating forces of defiant action. Rather, they constitute only potential resources that may or may not be mobilized in practical action. Moreover, the effectiveness of legal mobilization is likely to vary widely with differing groups, issues, and circumstances" (1994:91; see also Andersen 2005). In seeking to impose a single narrative on the role of courts in American politics, purveyors of the backlash thesis flatten this complex reality.

For outsider groups facing public and private violence, the criminalization of their family relationships, and systematic discrimination in all sectors of civil society, constitutional litigation may look like a fool's errand. But it may nonetheless be the best available tool. So long as this country's courts remain open to groups whose interests are inadequately represented in our elected institutions, those groups will turn to the courts, in conjunction with other protest strategies, in an effort to eke out what victories they can. Conventional scholarly wisdom has it that the story of all such efforts since *Brown* is a story of failure. That wisdom may not be so wise.

REFERENCES

Adams, William Lee (2005) "Gay to Wed;' *NEWSWEEK* (May 23) 12.

Andersen, Ellen Ann (2005) *Out of the Closets and Into the Courts: Legal Opportunity Structure and Gay Rights Litigation*. Ann Arbor: Univ. of Michigan Press.

Belluck, Pam (2007) "Massachusetts Gay Marriage Referendum Is Rejected," *THE NEW YORK TIMES*, 15 June, p. A16.

Bonauto. Mary L. (2005) "Goodridge in Context," 40 *Harvard Civil Rights-Civil Liberties Law Rev.* 1-69.

Brown, Mark (2003) "Meet Gays' New Enemy in Springfield: Democrats," *CHICAGO SUN-TIMES,* 20 Nov., p. 2.

Chauncey, George (2004) *Why Marriage? The History Shaping Today's Debate over Gay Equality*. New York: Basic Books.

D'Emilio, John (2005) "Some Lessons from *LAWRENCE*," in H. N. Hirsch, ed., *THE FUTURE OF GAY RIGHTS IN AMERICA*. New York: Routledge.

"The Marriage Fight Is Setting Us Back," *GAY & LESBIAN REVIEW WORLDWIDE,* (Nov.-Dec.): 10-11.

"Will the Courts Set Us Free? Reflections on the Campaign for Same-Sex Marriage," in C. A. Rimmerman & C. Wilcox, eds.. *THE POLITICS OF SAME-SEX MARRIAGE*. Chicago: Univ. of Chicago Press

Dupuis, Martin (2002) *Same-Sex Marriage, Legal Mobilization, and the Politics of Rights*. New- York: Peter Lang Publishing.

Egan. Patrick J., & Kenneth Sherrill (2005a) "Marriage and the Shifting Priorities of a New Generation of Lesbians and Gays," 38 *PS: POLITICAL SCIENCE AND POLITICS* 229-32.

(2005b) "Neither an In-Law Nor an Outlaw Be: Trends in Americans' Attitudes Toward Gay People," Public Opinion Pros (February), http://www.publicopinionpros.com/features/2005/feb/sherrill_egan.html.

(2006) "Same-Sex Marriage Initiatives and Lesbian, Gay and Bisexual Voters in the 2006 Elections," Research report, National Gay and Lesbian Task Force, http:// wwwthetaskforce.org/downloads/reports/arriageAndLGBVoters2006.pdf.

Eskridge, William N. Jr. (1999) *GAY LAW: CHALLENGING THE APARTHEID OF THE CLOSET*. Cambridge, MA: Harvard Univ. Press.

(2000) "Comparative Law and the Same-Sex Marriage Debate: A Step-by-Step Approach Toward State Recognition," 31 MCGEORGE LAW REV. 641-72.

(2002) Equality Practice: Civil Unions and the Future of Gay Rights. New York: Routledge.

Fiorina, Morris P, Samuel J. Abrams, & Jeremy C. Pope (2006) CULTURE WAR? THE MYTH OF A POLARIZED AMERICA, 2d ed. New York: Pearson Longman.

Frymer, Paul (2003) Acting When Elected Officials Won t: Federal Courts and Cavil Rights Enforcement in L .S. Labor Unions, 1935-85," 97 AMERICAN POLITICAL SCIENCE REV. 483-99.

Garrison, Jessica (2008) "Prop. 8 Foes, Backers Still in Thick of It," Los ANGELES TIMES, 22 Nov.! p. Bl.

Garrow, David J. (1994) "Hopelessly Hollow History : Revisionist Devaluing OF BROWN V. BOARD OF EDUCATION," 80 VIRGINIA LAW REV. 151-60.

(2004) "Toward a More Perfect Union," THE NEW YORK TIMES, 9 May, sec. 6, p. 52.

Flillygus, D. Sunshine, & Todd G. Shields (2005) "Moral Issues and Voter Decision Making in the 2004 Elections," 38 PS: POLITICAL SCIENCE AND POLITICS 201-9.

Hirsch, H. N. (2005) "Introduction," in H. N. Hirsch. ed.. THE FUTURE OF GAY RIGHTS IN AMERICA. New York: Routledge.

Johnson. Greg (2000) "Vermont Cavil Unions: The New Language of Marriage," 25 VERMONT LAW REV. 15-59.

Klarman, Michael J. (1994) "BROWN, Racial Change, and the Cavil Rights Movement," 80 VIRGINIA LAW REV. 7—150.

— (2004) From Jim Crow to Civil Rights: The Supreme Court and the Struggle for Racial Equality. New York: Oxford Univ. Press.

(2005) "Brown and Lawrence (and Coodridge)," 104 Michigan Law Rev. 431-89.

Lemieux, Scott (2004) "Constitutional Politics and the Political Impact of Abortion Litigation: Judicial Power and Judicial Independence in (Comparative Perspective." Ph.D. diss. University of Washington.

McCann, Michael (1992) "Reform Litigation on Trial." 17 Law and Social Inquiry 715-43.

(1994) Rights at Work: Pay Equity Reform and the Politics of Legal Mobilization. Chicago: Univ. of Chicago Press.

— (1996) "Causal versus Constitutive Explanations (or. On the Difficulty of Being so Positive ...)," 21 LAW AND SOCIAL INQUIRY 457-82.

Mezey, Susan Gluck (2007) QUEERS IN COURT: GAY RIGHTS LAW AND PUBLIC POLICY. Lanham, MD: Rowman & Littlefield.

Persily, Nate, et al. (2006) "Gay Marriage, Public Opinion and the Courts." University of Pennsylvania Law School, Public Law and Legal Theory Research Paper Series, Research Paper No. 06-17, http: papers.ssrn.com abstract = 900208.

Phillips, Frank, &: Andrea Estes (2007) "Right of Gays to Many Set for Years to Come." BOSTON GLOBE, 15 June, p. A1

Pinello, Daniel (2006) AMERICA'S STRUGGLE FOR SAME-SEX MARRIAGE. New York: (Cambridge Univ. Press.

Posner, Richard A. (1997) "Should There Be Homosexual Marriage? And If So. Who Should Decide?," 95 MICHIGAN LAW REV. 1578-87.

Rimmerman, Craig A. (2002) *From Identity to Politics: The Lesbian and Gay Movements in the United States.* Philadelphia: Temple Univ. Press.

Robinson, Beth (2001) "The Road to Inclusion for Same-Sex Couple*: Lessons From Vermont," 11 SETON HALL CONSTITUTIONAL LAW J. 237-57.

Rosen, Jeffrey (2003) "How to Reignite the Culture Wars," THE SEW YORK TIMES. 7 Sept., sec. (), p. 48.

(2000) *The Most Democratic Branch: How the Courts Serve America.* New York: Oxford Lniv. Press.

Rosenberg, Gerald N. (1991) THE HOLLOW HOPE: CAN COURTS BRING ABOUT SOCIAL CHANGE? Chicago: Univ. of Chicago Press.

(1994) "*BROWN* Is Dead! Long Live *BIOWN!* The Endless Attempt to Canonize a Case," 80 VIRGINIA LAW REV. 161-71.

(2008) THE HOLLOW HOPE: CAN COURTS BRING ABOUT SOCIAL CHANGE? rev. ed. Chicago: Univ. of Chicago Press.

Smith, Miriam (2008) *Political Institutions and Lesbian and Gay Rights in the United States and Canada.* New York: Routledge.

Stoddard, Thomas (1989) "Why Gay People Should Seek the Right to Marry," 2 OUT LOOK 9-13.

Sunstein, (Cass R. (1996) "Foreword: Leaving Things Undecided," 110 HARVARD LAW REV. 4-101.

Wangsness, Lisa, & Andrea Estes (2097) "Personal Stories (Changed Minds," BOSTON GLOBE, 15 June, p. A1

Zackin, Emily (2008) "Popular Constitutionalism's Hard When You're Not Very Popular: Why the ACLU Turned to Courts," 42 LAW & SOCIETY REV. 367-95.

CASES CITED

Alaska Civil Liberties Union v. Alaska, *122 P3d 781 (Sup. (Ct. Alas. 2005).*

Baehr v. lewin, 852 P.2d 44 (Haw. 1993).

Baker v. State of Vermont, 744 A.2d 864 (Yt. 1999).

Brascki v. Stahl Associate Company,* 74 N.Y.2d 201 (NY Ct. of App. 1989).

Brinkman v. Miami University, 2007 Ohio 4372 (Ohio Cr. of App. 2007).

Brown v. Board of Education, 347 U.S. 483 (1954).

Goodridge v. Dtp. of Public Health, 798 NT.2d 941 (Mass. 2003).

Hebel v. West, 25 A.D.3d 172 (Sup. Ct. NY, App. Div., 3rd Dept. 2005).

In Re Marriage Cases, 43 Cal. 4th 757 (Calif. Sup. Ct. 2008).

Kerrigan v. Cianmissiotur of Public Health, *289 Conn. 135 (Conn. Sup.* Ct. *2008).*

Ijiwrence v. Texas, 539 U.S. 558 (2003).

Lemons v. Bradbury, No. 08-35209 (9th Cir., August 14, 2008).

Lewis v. Harris, 908 A. 2d 196 (N.J. 2006).

Lockyer v. San Francisco, 95 P. 3d 459 (2004).

Martinez v. County of Monroe, 850 N.Y.S.2d 740 (App. Div. 4th Dept. 2008).

National Pride at Work v. Governor of Michigan, 748 N.W.2d 524 (Mich. 2008).

Romer v. Evans, 517 U.S. 620 (1996).

Snetsinger v. Montana University System, 104 P.3d 445 (Sup. Ct. Moil. 2004).

Tanner v. Oregon Health Sciences University, 971 P.2d 435 (Or. Ct. of App. 1998).

STATUTES CITED

Civil Unions Act. 15 Y.S.A. § 1201 et seq. (2008 [originally enacted 2000]).

Defense of Marriage Act, 1 U.S.C. § 7 and 28 U.S.C. §1738C1996.

Reciprocal Beneficiaries Act of 1997, H.R.S. § 572C-3 et seep (2008).

Thomas M. Keck is Associate Professor of Political Science at Syracuse University's Maxwell School of Citizenship and Public Affairs. He is the author of *The Most Activist Supreme Court in History: The Road to Modern Judicial Conservatism* (University of Chicago Press, 2004).

Under the Gaydar

How gays won the right to raise children without conservatives even noticing.

By Alison Gash

No one knows for sure how the Supreme Court will rule on the two high-profile gay marriage cases it is now considering. The betting, however, is that, regardless of the outcome, progress towards marriage equality will persist. A majority of the public now believes gays and lesbians should have the right to wed. Nine states and the District of Columbia have laws on the books conferring such rights. A stampede of Democratic elected officials has announced support for same-sex marriage, and in its recent "autopsy" report the Republican National Committee hinted its members should do the same.

Alison Gash, "Under the Gaydar," Washington Monthly. Copyright © 2013 by Washington Monthly. Reprinted with permission.

Although progress has been unusually swift, this story of same-sex marriage rights has followed a familiar path, one blazed by women and African Americans in their struggles for equality. Members of an out-group, advocating for their rights, demand a fundamental change in the legal interpretation of the constitution, which causes a series of high-profile court cases, state and federal laws and counter-laws, and all of it accompanied by a broadly-held national conversation that leads to a change in public attitudes, laws and legal interpretations.

But this isn't the only way that civil rights advance. A few decades ago, openly gay and lesbian Americans did not have the legal right to raise their own biological children, much less adopt. Today, more than 25 states recognize the same legal benefits and responsibilities of parenthood regardless of sexual orientation. It is now routine for gays and lesbians to jointly adopt, to be recognized as co-parents, and to collect child support or demand custody or visitation rights—even without a biological connection to the child in question. All this has happened without the hallmarks of a traditional rights campaign. There were very few high-profile court cases, few legislative battles, and little public debate. In sharp contrast to marriage equality—where between 1993 and 2003 two pro-marriage rulings incited over 35 state bans—parenting litigation has provoked minimal public backlash.

At first blush, this would seem unlikely. Gay marriage, after all, is between consenting adults, whereas gay adoption involves children, so one would think society would be at least as skittish about the latter. Even countries that pioneered marriage equality, such at Denmark, have been slower to extend full parenting rights to same sex couples. And yet, paradoxically, in the United States, the opposite is the case: we've had a contentious, two-decade-long national debate about same sex marriage, one that has repeatedly featured in battles for the presidency, but have allowed same-sex couples to quietly begin legally adopting and co-parenting with hardly any national discussion at all. Why the difference?

The answer is that same-sex parenting rights have successfully advanced precisely because the legal wrangling over them has remained largely below the radar—a fact highlighted by Justice Scalia's confusion about whether California even permits same-sex adoption during Supreme Court hearings on that state's Proposition 8. Where marriage equality advocates had little choice but to engage in open political battles and bring high profile constitutional court cases on behalf of their fundamental rights, the fight for same-sex parental rights has mostly played out in obscure family courts, with few reporters present, and with advocates consciously delaying or avoiding high court review. This below-the-radar strategy created a foundation of "facts on the ground"—tens of thousands of intact gay and lesbian-headed families with children-well before most conservative activists were even aware the phenomenon existed, making their subsequent efforts to block same-sex parenting an uphill fight.

The legal struggle over same-sex parenting began in the 1950 and 1960s. As divorce laws loosened, a growing number of closeted gays and lesbians came out to their heterosexual spouses, leading to legal disputes over custody and visitation rights over the couples' children. These cases were handled in local family courts, where records tend to be sealed. Few were ever covered in the newspapers. Fewer still resulted in victories for the gay spouses. Judges typically ruled that simply being homosexual made a parent unfit.

In one such case, in 1967, a lesbian woman named Ellen Doreen Nadler lost custody of her daughter to the child's heterosexual father. Nadler petitioned the California appellate court, which found that the previous court was wrong to base its decision solely on Nadler's homosexuality. Instead, the court wrote that the "primary consideration must be given to the welfare of the child." In a retrial, Nadler still didn't regain custody of her daughter, but the case set a key precedent: in custody cases, "the best interests of the child," a legal doctrine dating back to the mid-1800s, and not the sexual orientation of the parent, should be the deciding factor.

That precedent proved decisive in 1973, when an Oregon court ruled in favor of a gay father when the mother—who had not seen her children in over ten years—challenged custody because of the father's sexual orientation. The court determined that it was not necessarily in the "best interests of the child" to alter the custody arrangement, despite the father's homosexuality. Similarly, in two companion cases in 1978, the Washington Supreme Court ruled that withdrawing custody from two lesbian mothers who were raising children together from both of their previous marriages, would not serve the children's best interests. Although the court expressed some trepidation about the mothers' relationship, it determined that a change in custody would be more harmful.

While groundbreaking in many ways, these unorthodox rulings attracted little public interest, largely because they were focused on the particulars of the cases and not framed in terms of broader homosexual rights. This was in sharp contrast to the budding gay rights movement, which at that time was starting to push for statutory changes in the law. In 1977, for instance, gay rights activists convinced Miami-Dade County to amend its anti-discrimination ordinance to include gays and lesbians. In response, an anti-gay rights coalition, "Save Our Children," was formed, with country singer and Florida orange juice spokeswoman Anita Bryant as its leader. "As a mother, I know that homosexuals cannot biologically reproduce children," she proclaimed, "therefore, they must recruit our children." Yet despite her rhetoric and the group's name, Bryant and her allies didn't focus on gay parenting. Instead they went after higher-profile anti-discrimination ordinances that included sexual orientation and, in some instances, tried to remove gay and lesbian teachers from public schools. The Florida legislature did subsequently pass a law barring single gays and lesbians, as well as same-sex couples, from adopting children, but only one other state, New Hampshire, followed suit.

In the 1980s, the same-sex parenting movement continued to move quietly forward. Family courts began to see cases where gay and lesbian couples with children were petitioning for parental rights for the non-biological partner. Because these "other" parents were essentially legal strangers to the children they were raising, they were often barred from engaging in the most routine—and important—parenting functions: picking up their kids at school, visiting them in the hospital, or listing them as dependents on health or life insurance policies. That decade, family or lower courts in Oregon, Alaska, California, and Washington granted co-parent adoptions to same sex couples, with relatively little reaction from gay rights opponents.

Again, the secret to this progress was that gay parents and couples—who were by now aided by newly-formed gay rights advocacy groups—fought these cases in family court, where judges had wide discretion and public scrutiny was minimal Aware of the perils of drawing public attention to these cases, advocates from national gay rights groups worked hard to camouflage their efforts. They removed their names from briefs, provided behind-the-scenes support, and avoided appealing losses to appellate courts, out of fear that higher-level court approval would awaken the sleeping giant of public opposition.

Some even developed strategies to educate judges who were likely to hear same sex parenting cases through seminars and bench books. They quietly met with judges to reassure them that their rulings would not be politicized. Says one advocate:

> "You have to take steps to keep it under the radar. I make sure to tell these judges that this is not a test case. We are not going to put you on the spot. I appreciate that you are an elected judge and I am not going to do something that will hurt you."

Eventually, same-sex parenting cases did make their way to higher courts in two states —ironically in the same year, 1993, that gay marriage hit the supreme court docket in Hawaii (the case that launched a nationwide debate). But rather than rally opposition to both issues, conservatives chose to focus their attention only on same sex marriage. Why?

For one, the co-parenting cases received relatively little attention from the mainstream press—again, because they were not being argued as matters of "gay rights." Also, many pro-family activists also assumed, or at least hoped, that anti-marriage efforts would limit both marriage and parenting progress. They theorized that same-sex marriage bans would, like anti-sodomy statutes, impose a chilling effect on judges. So while conservatives were busy getting the 1996 Defense of Marriage Act through Congress and initiating state level bans on same-sex marriage, gay parents and their advocates continued to quietly amass significant court victories in Delaware, the District of Columbia , Illinois, Indiana, Maryland, Massachusetts, New Jersey, New York, Pennsylvania , and Vermont.

Meanwhile, by the end of 2004, anti-gay rights forces had won measures banning gay marriage in 40 states. Hoping to leverage these gains, pro-family advocates finally turned their attention to parenting. Between 2004 and 2006 the pro-family movement initiated over 35 attempts to limit same-sex parenting. In 2006, alone, 16 states were poised to initiate bans on same sex parenting legislatively or through the ballot process.

But—happily, for gay rights advocates—the anti-gay forces were too late. Despite dire predictions, very few of these anti-same-sex parenting measures went anywhere. Legislation died in committee and proposed initiatives never made it to the ballot. All the while—on the strength of decades of precedents and "facts on the ground"—family, appellate, and state supreme courts continued to grant adoptions to and recognize the parental rights of gay and lesbian parents.

Why did the backlash against same-sex parenting fail? It certainly wasn't public opinion. The handful of polls from 2006 that questioned participants about both same sex marriage and adoption rights show that average Americans were no more comfortable with gay parent-hood than with gay marriage. In fact, they opposed both by well over fifty percent. And if we take their arguments seriously, it is precisely concern about gay parenthood that drives opposition efforts against marriage equality.

Rather, the main problem for conservatives was that they were trying to roll back gay parenting rights that had, in effect, already been granted. This proved a tough sell. The media didn't much cover the conservative anti-same-sex parenting campaign, and what few stories did run typically featured heartwarming narratives of gay and lesbian couples raising well-adjusted kids. Such families existed in the thousands precisely because the under-the-radar strategy had allowed them to flourish over the previous twenty years. Whereas gay marriage was still an abstraction that opponents could rally the public to prevent, gay families were a reality that the public would have to tear asunder to stop.

Also, by the mid-2000s, social scientists had conducted studies on same-sex families. In general, this research demonstrated that children of same sex couples were not appreciably different from kids raised by straight couples—including their propensity to identify as gay or lesbian. These studies were widely quoted in the media and used to foster support among child welfare experts.

All this made it a tough fight for anti-gay advocates. As an official at Focus on Family, a conservative Christian advocacy group, concedes, the issue was low on the "radar for pro-family conservatives" because of the "confusing rhetoric of same-sex adoption, the media bombarding the public with images of happy gay couples taking in disadvantaged kids" and the argument that "this kind of family is better than no family." Adds another opponent, "trying to take the kids away... it's a ridiculous battle to fight."

That doesn't mean the fight is completely over. Taking a page from the playbook of parenting advocates, opponents of gay parenting have begun engaging at the level of family courts as well. They are now advocating on behalf of gay biological parents who are in custody battles with their estranged gay partners who are not the children's biological parents. Still, apart from such skirmishes, the right of same sex parents to raise their kids seems well on its way to being secured.

Same-sex parenting advocates weren't the first to use an under-the-radar strategy to advance their cause, and probably won't be the last. The Kennedy administration employed low-visibility tactics to both attract black voters during his campaign and encourage voter registration after he was elected. Some disability advocates, in their attempt to secure group housing for their disabled clients, circumvent public notification procedures when looking for appropriate housing and instead procure the property, move the clients in and wait to be discovered. And groups like the Nature Conservancy long ago figured out that instead of engaging in contentious public campaigns to get elected officials to do protect environmentally sensitive parcels of land it is often easier to raise money and quietly buy the land themselves.

History books suggest that our society has made its greatest leaps on the shoulders of high profile campaigns. But change can also be the result of quiet battles that play out in courtrooms, boardrooms and bedrooms all across the country. And it is often these hidden battles that most effectively propel our society forward.

Alison Gash is an assistant professor of political science at University of Oregon. She is completing a manuscript entitled "Below the Radar: How Silence Can Save Civil Rights," which will be published in 2014.

Discussion Questions

1. What are the alleged political risks associated with using litigation to make policy?

2. What is "crowd out?"

3. What is "path dependence?"

4. What is "backlash?"

5. What is "individualization?"

6. How should we assess these risks?

Notes

_____

_____

_____

_____

_____

_____

_____

_____

_____

_____

_____

_____

_____

_____

CPSIA information can be obtained
at www.ICGtesting.com
Printed in the USA
LVHW102126291118
598683LV00001B/1/P